KEYS TO SUCCESS

KEYS TO SUCCESS

Building Analytical, Creative, and Practical Skills

SEVENTH EDITION

ANALYTICAL CREATIVE PRACTICAL

Carol Carter

Joyce Bishop

Sarah Lyman Kravits

Boston • Columbus • Indianapolis • New York • San Francisco • Upper Saddle River
Amsterdam • Cape Town • Dubai • London • Madrid • Milan • Munich • Paris • Montreal • Toronto
Delhi • Mexico City • Sao Paulo • Sydney • Hong Kong • Seoul • Singapore • Taipei • Tokyo

Editor-in-Chief: Jodi McPherson
Development Editor: Charlotte Morrissey
Editorial Assistant: Clara Ciminelli
Executive Marketing Manager: Amy Judd
Director of Production: Elaine Ober
Production Editor: Gregory Erb
Editorial Production Service: Omegatype Typography, Inc.
Manufacturing Buyer: Megan Cochran
Electronic Composition: Omegatype Typography, Inc.
Interior Design: Carol Somberg
Photo Researcher: Sarah Lyman Kravits
Cover Administrator: Linda Knowles
Cover Designer: John Wincek

Credits and acknowledgments borrowed from other sources and reproduced, with permission, in this textbook appear on appropriate page within text or on page 377.

Library of Congress Cataloging-in-Publication Data

Carter, Carol.
   Keys to success building analytical, creative, and practical skills / Carol Carter, Joyce Bishop, Sarah Lyman Kravits.—7th ed.
         p.   cm.
   Includes bibliographical references and index.
   ISBN-13: 978-0-13-707360-3 (paperbound)
   ISBN-10: 0-13-707360-7 (paperbound)
  1. College student orientation—United States—Handbooks, manuals, etc.   2. Study skills—Handbooks, manuals, etc.   3. Career development—United States—Handbooks, manuals, etc.   I. Bishop, Joyce (Joyce L.) II. Kravits, Sarah Lyman.   III. Title.
   LB2343.32.C37 2012
   378.1'98—dc22

                                             2010033674

10 9 8 7 6 5 4 3 2   CKV   15 14 13 12 11

www.pearsonhighered.com

ISBN-10: 0-13-707360-7
ISBN-13: 978-0-13-707360-3

BRIEF CONTENTS

CONTENTS

PREFACE

> "It's not just what you know;
> it's what you know <u>how</u> to do."

Since its publication, *Keys to Success* has set the standard for helping students understand *how* to be successful in **College, Career, and Life.** This Seventh Edition presents *Keys'* tried-and-true system, revised for even greater efficacy, for building students' ability to think analytically, creatively, and practically. These three thinking skills increase students' power to choose and to act as they progress through college and the world of work.

■ **Text-wide Theme of Successful Intelligence Focuses on Analytical, Creative, and Practical Thinking Skills:** Based on Robert Sternberg's concept of using successful intelligence to maximize learning and life success, the way to achieve College, Career, and Life success is through building analytical, creative, and practical thinking skills. Here's what you'll see:

1. *Get Analytical, Get Creative,* and *Get Practical* **exercises** are geared toward building the specific skill.
2. *SI Wrap-Up* summarizes how students have built their thinking skills in the context of the chapter topics and exercises.
3. *Steps to Success: Boost Your Brain Power* **exercises** build all thinking skills at three levels of challenge, starting with recall and moving to application and analysis, making it easy to accommodate students' abilities.
4. **The theme, introduced in Chapter 1,** has been retained and strengthened with the latest research and a stronger link to motivation, mindset, and future success.
5. **Pre- and Post-course assessments, found in Chapters 1 and 12,** help students assess their progress in building these thinking skills and their motivation to persist in achieving goals.

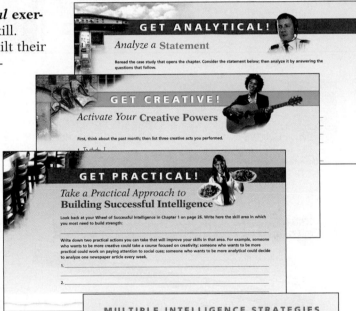

■ **Emphasis on How Students Learn:** This text gives the tools to find out how students think and learn best and what to do to apply that information usefully. Chapter 3's Self-Assessments help explore learning strengths and weaknesses. Then, in Chapters 5–12, Multiple Intelligence Strategies grids help find ways to relate the chapter topic to learning preferences. In-chapter material (especially the Communication and Careers chapters) shows how to apply how you learn to specific situations.

■ **Success Skills That Transfer to Today's Global Workplace . . . and to Life:** *Keys* skills transfer to success in today's global marketplace. The Partnership for 21st Century Skills, an organization founded by top educators and business leaders, developed a framework to identify the core knowledge and skills people need to learn to be effective in a global workplace. In every chapter, *Keys'* coverage builds the skills covered in that framework.

What's <u>New</u> in this edition?

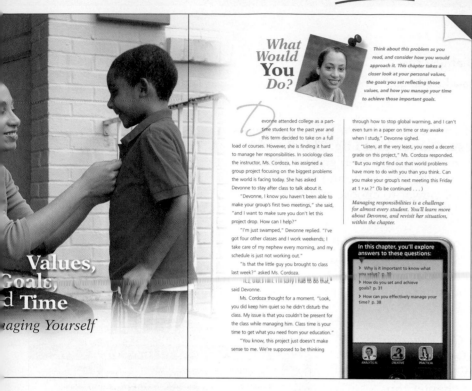

Annotated Instructor's Edition offers quick access to icebreakers, extra activities, "fast facts," resource links to instructor materials such as PowerPoints and MyStudentSuccessLab, coaching tips, use of social networking, and real-world benefits.

Compelling case stories and activities open and are revisited throughout each chapter. Through others' experiences, students learn to question, spot issues, solve problems, evaluate their own choices, and plan for similar situations in the future. Mid-chapter and end-of-chapter case activities (Change the Conversation and Case Wrap-up) encourage critical, creative, and practical thinking about personal, local, and global issues.

Real-World Benefits to Jump-Starting Career and Life Success: In addition to fully integrated coverage of college–career–life connections in each chapter, here's how *Keys* helps students connect.

1. Social Networking and Media is integrated in the text, in an appendix and as a segment of the *Career Portfolio* activity, where students use social media to build a profile on an effective career and internship networking site step-by-step.

2. 21st Century Skills, findings from a partnership of educators and business people who have discovered skills that recent graduates lack but employers require and reward, are covered. *Keys* develops these skills—including teamwork, communication, innovation, and personal accountability.

3. Student Profiles connect the skill in the chapter to the world of work.

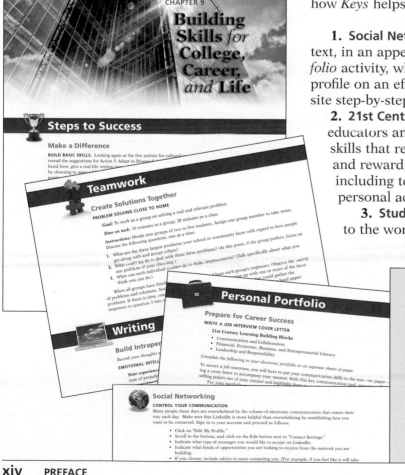

What else has **changed in this edition?**

Stronger Study and Life Skills Organization: To reflect current educational best practices and better address student concerns, these five chapters were reorganized.

Revised! **Chapter 5, Reading and Information Literacy:** This chapter now focuses on reading, text annotating and notes, and information literacy. Studying, formerly a section in Chapter 5, is updated, expanded, and relocated in Chapter 7.

Revised! **Chapter 6, Listening and Note Taking:** This is now a more streamlined chapter that focuses on the listening process and taking notes in class. Memory has been moved to Chapter 7.

New! **Chapter 7, Memory and Studying:** A brand-new chapter that includes the latest information on brain-based learning, how to lock information into memory, and how to study effectively.

Revised! **Chapter 11, Managing Money:** An entire chapter is now devoted to financial literacy, a key issue for students living in today's economy. Includes new information. It includes new credit and student loan regulations.

Revised! **Chapter 12, Careers and More:** Now a full chapter of coverage is provided on this crucial topic.

Updated and Expanded Coverage: All chapters have been updated, but these topics deserve special mention: chapter opening self-assessments (all chapters), motivation (Chapter 1), emotional intelligence (Chapter 1 and in every chapter's end-of-chapter "emotional intelligence" journal activity), information literacy (Chapter 5), and brain-based learning (Chapter 7).

MyStudentSuccessLab (www.mystudentsuccesslab .com): An online solution designed to help students acquire the basic skills needed to succeed in college and beyond. It is organized to support these goals:

1. **Connect:** Promote higher engagement & retention through real student video interviews on key issues.
2. **Practice:** Facilitate skill-building with three exercises per topic that provide interactive experience and practice.
3. **Personalize:** Students apply what is learned and create personally relevant projects; Instructors assess skill mastery.

Many of our best suggestions come from you. Please contact your Pearson representative with questions or requests for resources or materials. Send suggestions for ways to improve *Keys to Success* to Carol Carter at **caroljcarter@lifebound .com**. We look forward to hearing from you!

ACKNOWLEDGMENTS

With the help of many, this stellar Seventh Edition has taken yet another leap forward. We thank:

Seventh Edition Reviewers

Mary Adams, Northern Kentucky University
Shawn Bixler, The University of Akron
Julia Brown, South Plains College
Frederick Charles, Indiana University
Carrie Cokely, Curry College
Donna Dahlgren, Indiana University Southeast
Ann French, New Mexico State University
Lewis Grey, Middle Tennessese State University
Valerie Jefferson, Rock Valley College
Gary G. John, Richland College
Elvira Johnson, Central Piedmont Community College
Natalie McLellan, Holmes Community College
Kimberly O'Connor, Community College of Baltimore City
Tom Peterson, Grand View University
Jack E. Sallie, Jr., Montgomery College
Tia Short, Boise State University
Julie Stein, California State University
Rose Stewart-Fram, McLennan Community College
Karla Thompson, New Mexico State University
Susannah Waldrop, University of South Carolina, Upstate
Jill Wilks, Southern Utah University
Kim Winford, Blinn College

Reviewers for Previous Editions

Peg Adams, Northern Kentucky University
Raishell Adams, Palm Beach Community College—Palm Beach Gardens
Veronica Allen, Texas Southern University
Fred Amador, Phoenix College
Angela A. Anderson, Texas Southern University
Robert Anderson, The College of New Jersey
Manual Aroz, Arizona State University
Dirk Baron, California State University–Bakersfield
Glenda Belote, Florida International University
Todd Benatovich, University of Texas at Arlington
John Bennett, Jr., University of Connecticut
Lynn Berkow, University of Alaska
Susan Bierster, Palm Beach Community College–Lake Worth
Ann Bingham-Newman, California State University–LA
Mary Bixby, University of Missouri–Columbia
Barbara Blandford, Education Enhancement Center at Lawrenceville, NJ
Jerry Bouchie, St. Cloud State University
D'Yonne Browder, Texas Southern University
Mary Carstens, Wayne State College
Mona Casady, SW Missouri State University
Christy Cheney, Valencia Community College–East Campus
Leslie Chilton, Arizona State University
Kobitta Chopra, Broward Community College
Jim Coleman, Baltimore City Community College
Sara Connolly, Florida State University
Kara Craig, University of Southern Mississippi
Jacqueline Crossen-Sills, Massasoit Community College
Janet Cutshall, Sussex County Community College

Carolyn Darin, California State University–Northridge
Deryl Davis-Fulmer, Milwaukee Area Technical College
Valerie DeAngelis, Miami-Dade Community College
Joyce Annette Deaton, Jackson State Community College
Rita Delude, NH Community Technical College
Marianne Edwards, Georgia College and State University
Judy Elsley, Weber State University in Utah
Ray Emett, Salt Lake Community College
Jacqueline Fleming, Texas Southern University
Patsy Frenchman, Santa Fe Community College
Rodolfo Frias, Santiago Canyon College
Ralph Gallo, Texas Southern University
Jean Gammon, Chattanooga State Technical Community College
Skye Gentile, California State University, Hayward
Bob Gibson, University of Nebraska–Omaha
Jennifer Guyer-Wood, Minnesota State University
Sue Halter, Delgado Community College
Suzy Hampton, University of Montana
Karen Hardin, Mesa Community College
Patricia Hart, California State University, Fresno
Maureen Hurley, University of Missouri–Kansas City
Karen Iversen, Heald Colleges
Valerie Jefferson, Rock Valley College
Cynthia Johnson, Palm Beach Community College–Lake Worth
S. Renee Jones, Florida Community College at Jacksonville–North Campus
Georgia Kariotis, Oakton Community College
Laura Kauffman, Indian River Community College
Kathryn K. Kelly, St. Cloud State University
Cathy Keyler, Palm Beach Community College–Palm Beach Gardens
Quentin Kidd, Christopher Newport University
Nancy Kosmicke, Mesa State College
Patsy Krech, University of Memphis
Dana Kuehn, Florida Community College at Jacksonville–Deerwood Center
Noreen Lace, California State University–Northridge
Charlene Latimer, Daytona Beach Community College–Deland
Paul Lede, Texas Southern University
Lanita Legan, Texas State University
Linda Lemkau, North Idaho College
Kristina Leonard, Daytona Beach Community College–Flagler/Palm Coast
Christine A. Lottman, University of Cincinnati
Frank T. Lyman, Jr., University of Maryland
Judith Lynch, Kansas State University
Patricia A. Malinowski, Finger Lakes Community College
Marvin Marshak, University of Minnesota
Kathy Masters, Arkansas State University
Howard Masuda, California State University–Los Angeles
Antoinette McConnell, Northeastern Illinois University
Caron Mellblom-Nishioka, California State University–Dominguez Hills
Jenny Middleton, Seminole Community College
Barnette Miller Moore, Indian River Community College
Gladys Montalvo, Palm Beach Community College
Rebecca Munro, Gonzaga University
Nanci C. Nielsen, University of New Mexico–Valencia Campus
Sue Palmer, Brevard Community College
Alan Pappas, Santa Fe Community College
Bobbie Parker, Alabama State University
Carolyn Patterson, Texas State Technical College–West Texas
Curtis Peters, Indiana University Southeast
Virginia Phares, DeVry of Atlanta
Brenda Prinzavalli, Beloit College
Margaret Quinn, University of Memphis

Corliss A. Rabb, Texas Southern University
Terry Rafter-Carles, Valencia Community College–Orlando
Jacqueline Robinson, Milwaukee Area Technical College
Eleanor Rosenfield, Rochester Institute of Technology
Robert Roth, California State University–Fullerton
Manuel Salgado, Elgin Community College
Rebecca Samberg, Housatonic Community College
Karyn L. Schulz, Community College of Baltimore County–Dundalk
Pamela Shaw, Broward Community County–South Campus
Jacqueline Simon, Education Enhancement Center at Lawrenceville, NJ
Carolyn Smith, University of Southern Indiana
Cheryl Spector, California State University–Northridge
Rose Stewart-Fram, McLennan Community College
Joan Stottlemyer, Carroll College
Jill R. Strand, University of Minnesota–Duluth
Tracy Stuck, Lake Sumter Community College–Leesburg Campus
Toni M. Stroud, Texas Southern University
Cheri Tillman, Valdosta State University
Ione Turpin, Broward Community College
Thomas Tyson, SUNY Stony Brook
Joy Vaughan-Brown, Broward Community College
Arturo Vazquez, Elgin Community College
Eve Walden, Valencia Community College
Marsha Walden, Valdosta State University
Debbie Warfield, Seminole Community College
Rose Wassman, DeAnza College
Ronald Weisberger, Bristol Community College
Angela Williams, The Citadel
Don Williams, Grand Valley State University
William Wilson, St. Cloud State University
Tania Wittgenfeld, Rock Valley College
Michelle G. Wolf, Florida Southern College

• Robert J. Sternberg, Dean of the School of Arts and Sciences at Tufts University, for his groundbreaking work on successful intelligence and for his gracious permission to use and adapt that work for this text.

• Those who generously contributed personal stories, exhibiting courage in being open and honest about their life experiences: Charlotte Buckley, Hinds Community College; Androuw Carrasco, University of Arizona; Kelly Carson, Project Bridge; Louise Gaile Edrozo; Jad El-Adaimi, California Polytechnic State University; Norton Ewart; Aneela Gonzales, Golden West College; Andrew Hillman, Queens College; Kevin Ix, Bergen Community College; Tomohito Kondo, De Anza College; Joe A. Martin, Jr., Creator of Real World University website; Gary Montrose; Zack Moore, University of Rhode Island; Kelly Thompson, Colorado State University; Ming-Lun Wu, National Chengchi University, Taipei, Taiwan; Brad Zak, Boston College; Alexis Zendejas, Brigham Young University.

• Our Executive Editor Sande Johnson, Editorial Assistant Clara Ciminelli, and Development Editor Charlotte Morrissey for their dedication, vision, and efforts.

• Our production team for their patience, flexibility, and attention to detail, especially Production Editor Greg Erb; Director of Production Elaine Ober; interior book designer Carol Somberg; cover designer Linda Knowles; and Diana Neatrour and the rest of the team at Omegatype.

• Mary Gumlia for her contribution to the instructor's manual; Cynthia Johnson for her work on the PowerPoint presentation; John Kowalczyk for his work on the Test Item File; Martha Martin for creating the clicker questions; and Cheri Tillman for her work on the MyStudentSuccessLab Study Plan Quizzes and Enrichment activities.

- Our marketing gurus, especially Amy Judd, Executive Marketing Manager; Margaret Waples, Vice President, Director of Marketing; and our Sales Director Team: Connie James, Director of Sales Programs; Deb Wilson, Senior Sales Director; and Sean Wittmann, Missy Bittner, Lynda Sax, Chris Cardona, and Hector Amaya, Sales Directors.

- Editor-in-Chief of Student Success and Career Development Jodi McPherson; President of Pearson Teacher Education and Student Success Nancy Forsyth; CEO of Teacher Education & Development Susan Badger; and Prentice Hall President Tim Bozik, for their interest in the *Keys* series.

- The Pearson representatives and the management team led by Brian Kibby, Senior Vice President Sales/Marketing.

- The staff at LifeBound for their hard work and dedication: Heather Brown, Kelly Carson, and Cynthia Nordberg.

- Our families and friends, who have encouraged us and put up with our commitments.

- Special thanks to Judy Block, who contributed research and writing to this book.

Finally, for their ideas, opinions, and stories, we would like to thank all of the students and professors with whom we work. Joyce, in particular, would like to thank the thousands of students who have allowed her, as their professor, the privilege of sharing part of their journey through college. We appreciate that, through reading this book, you give us the opportunity to learn and discover with you—in your classroom, in your home, on the bus, and wherever else learning takes place.

Chelsey Emmelhainz, Student Developmental Manager, began her work with Carol Carter's company, LifeBound, as a college junior. As a developmental editing intern, she was involved in a variety of projects including LifeBound books *Leadership for Teenagers,* and the revision of *Majoring in the Rest of Your Life.* Based on these contributions, Chelsey was hired as an editorial assistant to work on this revision of *Keys to Success.*

Initially responsible for contributing ideas to make the book student-centered, she also researched and contributed ideas to update chapter revisions, culled information from other students, conducted and coordinated interviews, and made recommendations for visuals and photo research. Chelsey also assisted the authors with the instructor's materials and servicing program. In the final months of production, Chelsey researched photos and worked on *Keys'* sister publications, *Quick* and *Keys to College Studying.*

For Students!

Why is this course important?

This course will help you transition to college, introduce you to campus resources, and prepare you for success in all aspects of college, career, and life. You will:
- Develop Skills to Excel in Other Classes
- Apply Concepts from College to Your Career and Life
- Learn to Use Media Resources

How can you get the most out of the book and online resources required in this class?

Purchase your book and online resources before the First Day of Class. Register and log in to the online resources using your access code.

Develop Skills to Excel in Other Classes
- Helps you with your homework
- Prepares you for exams

Apply Concepts from College to Your Career and Life
- Provides learning techniques
- Helps you achieve your goals

Learn to Use Media Resources
- **www.mystudentsuccesslab.com** helps you build skills you need to succeed through peer-led videos, interactive exercises and projects, journaling and goal setting activities.
- Connect with real students, practice skill development, and personalize what is learned.

Want to get involved with Pearson like other students have?

Join www.PearsonStudents.com
It is a place where our student customers can incorporate their views and ideas into their learning experience. They come to find out about our programs such as the **Pearson Student Advisory Board**, **Pearson Campus Ambassador**, and the **Pearson Prize** (student scholarship!).

Here's how you can get involved:

- Tell your instructors, friends, and family members about **PearsonStudents**.
- To get daily updates on how students can boost their resumes, study tips, get involved with Pearson, and earn rewards:

  Become a fan of **Pearson Students on Facebook**

  Follow **@Pearson_Student on Twitter**

- Explore **Pearson Free Agent**. It allows you get involved in the publishing process, by giving student feedback.

See you on **PearsonStudents** where our student customers live. When students succeed, we succeed!

PEARSON
mystudentsuccesslab™

Succeed in college and beyond!
Connect, practice, and personalize with MyStudentSuccessLab.

www.mystudentsuccesslab.com

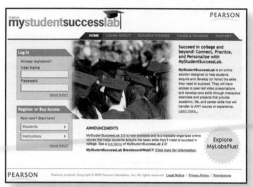

MyStudentSuccessLab is an online solution designed to help students acquire the skills they need to succeed. They will have access to peer-led video presentations and develop core skills through interactive exercises and projects that provide academic, life, and career skills that will transfer to ANY course.

It can accompany any Student Success text, or be sold as a stand-alone course offering. To become successful learners, students must consistently apply techniques to daily activities.

How will MyStudentSuccessLab make a difference?

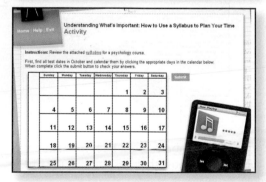

Is motivation a challenge, and if so, how do you deal with it?
Video Presentation — Experience peer led video 'by students, for students' of all ages and stages.

How would better class preparation improve the learning experience?
Practice activities — Practice skills for each topic — beginning, intermediate, and advanced — leveled by Bloom's taxonomy.

What could you gain by building critical thinking and problem-solving skills in this class? **Apply (final project)** — Complete a final project using these skills to create 'personally relevant' resources.

MyStudentSuccessLab Feature set:

Topic Overview: Module objectives.

Video Presentation – Connect: Real student video interviews on key issues.

Practice: Three skill–building exercises per topic provide interactive experience and practice.

Apply – Personalize: Apply what is learned by creating a personally relevant project and journal.

Resources: Plagiarism Guide, Dictionary, Calculators, and Assessments (Career, Learning Styles, and Personality Styles).

Additional Assignments: Extra suggested activities to use with each topic.

Text–Specific Study Plan (available with select books): Chapter Objectives, Practice Tests, Enrichment activities, and Flashcards.

MyStudentSuccessLab Topic List –

1. Time Management/Planning
2. Values/Goal Setting
3. Learning How You Learn
4. Listening and Taking Class Notes
5. Reading and Annotating
6. Memory and Studying
7. Critical Thinking
8. Problem-Solving
9. Information Literacy
10. Communication
11. Test Prep and Test Taking
12. Stress Management
13. Financial Literacy
14. Majors and Careers

MyStudentSuccessLab Support:

• **Demos, Registration, Log-in** – www.mystudentsuccesslab.com under "Tours and Training" and "Support."

• **Email support** – Send an inquiry to MyStudentSuccessLab@pearson.com

• **Online Training** – Join one of our weekly WebEx training sessions.

• **Peer Training** – Faculty Advocate connection for qualified adoptions.

• **Technical support** – 24 hours a day, seven days a week, at http://247pearsoned.custhelp.com

Quick Start to College, with coverage of some basic information you need at the beginning of your coursework, is designed to help you feel more in control as you start this important journey toward the achievement of a college education. As you read, consult your college handbook and/or website to learn about the specific resources, policies, and procedures of your college.

Start by learning what your college expects of you—and what you have a right to expect in return as a consumer of education. Continue on to explore the people and resources that can assist you while you are enrolled. Finally, consider the financial aid possibilities that can help you pay for it all.

What Your College Expects of You

If you clarify what it means to be a college student right at the start, you will minimize surprises that may be obstacles later on. What is expected of you may be different from anything you encountered in high school or in other educational settings. Because expectations differ from college to college, use the material that follows as general guidelines.

Follow procedures and fulfill requirements

Understanding and following college procedures will smooth your path to success.

Registration

Registration may take place through your school's computer network, via an automated phone system, or in the school gym or student union. Scan the college catalog and website and consider key factors as you make your selections.

- ▶ Core/general requirements for graduation
- ▶ Your major or minor or courses in departments you are considering
- ▶ Electives that sound interesting, even if they are out of your field

Once you choose courses, but before you register, create a schedule that shows daily class times to see if the schedule will work out. Meet with your advisor for comments and approval.

Graduation and curriculum requirements

Every college has degree requirements stated in the catalog and website. Make sure you understand those that apply to you, such as the following:

- ▶ Number of credits needed to graduate, including credits in major and minor fields
- ▶ Curriculum requirements, including specific course requirements
- ▶ Departmental major requirements

School procedures

Your college has rules and regulations, found in the college handbook and on the website, for all students to follow, such as the following common procedures:

Letter grade	A	A–	B+	B	B–	C+	C	C–	D+	D	F
Numerical grade	4.0	3.7	3.3	3.0	2.7	2.3	2.0	1.7	1.3	1.0	0.0

▶ *Adding or dropping a class.* If you find that a course is not right for you or that there are better choices, adding or dropping courses should be done within the first few days of the term. Withdrawals after a predetermined date, except those approved for special cases, usually receive a failing grade.

▶ *Taking an incomplete.* If you can't finish your work due to circumstances beyond your control—an illness or injury, for example—many colleges allow you to take a grade of Incomplete. The school will require approval from your instructor and you will have to make up the work later.

▶ *Transferring schools.* Research the degree requirements of other schools and submit transfer applications. If you are a student at a community college and intend to transfer to a 4-year school, take the courses required for admission to that school. In addition, be sure all your credits are transferable, which means they will be counted toward your degree at the 4-year school.

Understand your school's grading system

When you receive grades, remember that they reflect your work, not your self-worth. Most schools use grading systems with numerical grades or equivalent letter grades (see Key QS.1 above). Generally, the highest course grade is an A, or 4.0, and the lowest is an F, or 0.0.

In every course, you earn a certain number of college credits, called *hours.* For example, Accounting 101 may be worth three hours. These numbers generally refer to the number of hours the course meets per week. When you multiply each numerical course grade by the number of hours the course is worth, take the sum of all these numbers, and divide by the total number of credit hours you are taking, you obtain your **grade point average,** or GPA.

Learn the minimum GPA needed to remain in good standing and to be accepted and continue in your major. Key QS.2 shows you how to calculate your GPA. You can also use Web resources such as www.back2college.com/gpa.htm to calculate your GPA electronically.

GRADE POINT AVERAGE (GPA)

A measure of academic achievement computed by dividing the total number of grade points received by the total number of credits or hours of coursework taken.

Make the most of your school's computer system

A large part of college communication and work involves the computer. In a given day you might access a syllabus online, e-mail a student, use the Internet to tap into a library database, write a draft of an assignment on a computer, and send a paper draft to an instructor electronically. Most dorm rooms are wired for computers, and an increasing number of campuses have wireless networks. Some schools are even moving to a "paperless" system where all student notifications are sent via e-mail, requiring every student to activate an e-mail account and check it regularly. Here are some suggestions for using your computer effectively:

▶ *Get started right away.* Register for an e-mail account and connect to the college network. In addition, register your cell phone number with the school so you can get emergency alerts, if your school offers this service.

AN EXAMPLE SHOWS HOW TO
CALCULATE YOUR GPA

COURSE	SEMESTER HOURS	GRADE	POINTS EARNED FOR THIS COURSE
Chemistry I	4	C (2.0 points)	4 credits × 2.0 points = 8
Freshman Writing	3	B+ (3.3 points)	3 credits × 3.3 points = 9.9
Spanish I	3	B– (2.7 points)	3 credits × 2.7 points = 8.1
Introduction to Statistics	3	C+ (2.3 points)	3 credits × 2.3 points = 6.9
Social Justice	2	A– (3.7 points)	2 credits × 3.7 points = 7.4
Total semester hours **Total grade points for semester**	**15**		**40.3**

GPA for semester (total grade points divided by semester hours): 40.3 divided by 15 = 2.69

Letter equivalent grade: C+/B–

▶ *Use the system.* Communicate with instructors and fellow students using e-mail. Browse the college website. Search databases at the college library. If you don't know how, find someone to show you.

▶ *Save and protect your work.* Save electronic work periodically onto a primary or backup hard drive, CD, or flash drive. Use antivirus software if your system needs it.

▶ *Stay on task.* During study time, try to limit Internet surfing, instant messaging, visiting MySpace and Facebook, and playing computer games.

One of the most important directives for college students communicating via computer is to *follow guidelines* when contacting instructors via e-mail. When you submit assignments, take exams, or ask questions electronically, follow the rules of etiquette promoting civility and respect. Try these suggestions the next time you e-mail an instructor:

▶ *Use your university account.* Instructors are likely to delete unfamiliar e-mails from their overloaded e-mail inboxes. Helen_Miller@yourschool.edu will get read—but disastergirl@yahoo.com may not.

▶ *Don't ask for information you can find on your own or bother your instructor with minor problems.* Flooding your instructor with unnecessary e-mails may work against you when you really need help.

▶ *Write a clear subject line.* State exactly what the e-mail is about.

▶ *Address the instructor by name and title.* "Hello Professor Smith" or "Hi Dr. Reynolds" is better than "Hey."

▶ *Be clear and comprehensive.* First, state your question or problem and what you want to achieve. For example, "In my essay, I believe I covered the key points. I would like to meet to discuss your critique." Next, if necessary, support your position, using bullet points if you have a number of support statements. Finally, end by thanking the instructor and signing your full name.

> ▶ *Avoid abbreviations and acronyms.* Write as though you were crafting a business letter, not a social e-mail to a friend.
>
> ▶ *Use complete sentences, correct punctuation, and capitalization.* Be sure to reread your e-mail before sending, so that you have a chance to correct any mistakes.
>
> ▶ *Give the instructor time to respond.* Don't expect a reply within 2 hours. If you hear nothing after a couple of days, send a follow-up note that contains the full text of your first message. A note that simply says "Did you get my last e-mail?" won't be helpful if for any reason your instructor didn't receive or read the first one.

Read and use your syllabi

SYLLABUS
A comprehensive outline of course topics and assignments.

You will receive a ⟨**syllabus**⟩ for each of your courses, either online or in person at the first class meeting (or both). Each syllabus is a super-resource for that course, providing the following information:

▶ Focus and goals of the course
▶ Required and optional reading, with a schedule of when that reading is covered
▶ Dates of quizzes and exams and due dates for assignments
▶ The instructor's grading system and components of your final grade
▶ Your instructor's policy regarding latecomers and missed class meetings
▶ How and when to connect with your instructor in person, by phone, or online
▶ Important college-wide policies such as the academic integrity policy

You might consider each syllabus as a "contract" between you and your instructor, outlining what your instructor expects of you (readings, assignments, class participation) as well as what you can expect from your instructor (availability, schedule of topics, clarification of grading system).

Put this super-resource to use by reading syllabi thoroughly and referring to them throughout the term. When you have a question, look for an answer in your syllabus first before contacting your instructor. Marking up your syllabus will remind you of responsibilities, as will "backdating"—noting in your written or electronic planner the interim goals to achieve by particular dates in order to complete assignments. For example, if you have a fifteen-page paper due on October 12, you would enter dates in September and October for goals such as topic chosen, first draft, and final draft. Key QS.3 shows a portion of an actual syllabus with important items noted.

Get involved

Extracurricular activities give you a chance to meet people who share your interests and to develop teamwork and leadership skills as well as other skills that may be important in your career. In addition, being connected to friends and a supportive network of people is one of the main reasons people stay in school.

Some freshmen take on so many activities that they become overwhelmed. Pace yourself the first year. You can always add activities later. As you seek the right balance, consider this: Studies have shown that students who join organizations tend to persist in their educational goals more than those who don't branch out.[1]

Books
and
materials
to get
ASAP

How to
connect
with the
instructor

Course
coverage,
expectations,
responsibilities

How
grades are
determined
for this
course

Reflects
school's
academic
integrity
policy

Topic of
that day's
class
meeting

Notice of
due date
for paper
draft

Notice of
reading
assignments
to complete

Notice of
quiz

Notice of
final due
date for
paper

ENG 122 Spring 2007

Instructor: Jennifer Gessner
Office Hours: Tue & Thur 12:30–1:30 (or by appointment) in DC 305
Phone: 303-555-2222
E-mail: jg@abc.xyz

Required Texts: *Good Reasons with Contemporary Arguments,* Faigley and Selzer
A Writer's Reference, 5th ed., Diana Hacker

Required Materials:

- a notebook with lots of paper
- a folder for keeping everything from this class
- an active imagination and critical thinking

Course Description: This course focuses on argumentative writing and the researched paper. Students will practice the rhetorical art of argumentation and will gain experience in finding and incorporating researched materials into an extended paper.

Writer's Notebook: All students will keep, and bring to class, a notebook with blank paper. Throughout the semester, you will be given writing assignments to complete in this book. You must bring to class and be prepared to share any notebook assignment. Notebook assignments will be collected frequently, though sometimes randomly, and graded only for their completeness, not for spelling, etc.

Grading:

- Major Writing Assignments worth 100 points each.
- Final Research Project worth 300 points.
- Additional exercises and assignments range from 10 to 50 points each.
- Class participation: Based on the degree to which you complete the homework and present this in a thoughtful, meaningful manner in class.
- Attendance: Attendance is taken daily and students may miss up to three days of class without penalty, but will lose 5 points for each day missed thereafter.
- Late work: All work will lose 10% of earned points per class day late. No work will be accepted after five class days or the last class meeting.

Final Grade: The average of the total points possible (points earned divided by the total possible points). 100–90% = A; 89–80% = B; 79–70% = C (any grade below 70% is not passing for this class).

Academic Integrity: Students must credit any material used in their papers that is not their own (including direct quotes, paraphrases, figures, etc.). Failure to do so constitutes plagiarism, which is illegal, unethical, <u>always recognizable</u>, and a guaranteed way to fail a paper. The definition of plagiarism is "to steal and use (the writings or ideas of another) as one's own."

Week 4

2/1 <u>The Concise Opinion.</u>
HW: Complete paper #1 Rough Draft (5–7 pages double-spaced)

2/3 How Professionals Argue
HW: <u>Read Jenkins Essay (p 501 of *Good Reasons) and* Rafferty Essay (p 525)</u>; compare argumentative style, assess and explain efficacy of arguments.

Week 5

2/15 Developing an Argument
Essay Quiz on Jenkins and Rafferty Essays
HW: Chap 5 of *Good Reasons;* based on components of a definition of argument, write a brief explanation of how your argument might fit into this type.

2/17 Library Workday: Meet in Room 292
PAPER #1 DUE

Source: Jennifer Gessner, Community College of Denver.

Connect with **People and Resources**

During your first weeks of school, as you navigate through what may seem like a maze of classes and business offices, it is important to know that instructors, administrators, advisors, and a range of support staff are available to help. Groups and organizations also provide support and opportunities to broaden your experience. Tap into the various resources at your school.

Instructors and teaching assistants

The people who teach your courses—instructors and teaching assistants—are your most available human resources at college. You see them from one to five times per week and interact with them more directly than with any other authority on campus. They see your work and, if your class size is small, they hear your ideas and consequently may get to know you quite well. Instructors are potential resources and necessary allies in your education.

What kind of help might you seek from an instructor or teaching assistant?

- ▶ Clarification on material presented in class
- ▶ Help on homework
- ▶ Information about how to prepare for a test
- ▶ Consultation on a paper you are working on
- ▶ Details about why you received a particular grade on a test or assignment
- ▶ Advice about the department—courses, majoring—or related career areas

When you want to speak personally with an instructor for longer than a minute or two, choose your time carefully. Before or after class is usually not the best time for anything more than a quick question. When you need your instructor's full attention, there are three ways to get it: make an appointment during office hours, send e-mail, or leave voice-mail messages.

- ▶ *Office hours.* Instructors keep regular office hours, generally appearing on your syllabus or posted on instructors' office doors and on instructors' or departmental Web pages. Always make an appointment for a meeting. Face-to-face conferences are ideal for working through ideas and problems (for example, deciding on a term paper topic) or asking for advice (for example, looking for guidance on choosing courses in the department).
- ▶ *E-mail.* Use e-mail to clarify assignments and assignment deadlines, to ask questions about lectures or readings, or to clarify what will be covered on a test. Using the e-mailing guidelines presented earlier in Quick Start will increase the likelihood of receiving a positive response. Instructors' e-mail addresses are generally posted on the first day of class and may also appear in your handbook or syllabus.
- ▶ *Voice mail.* If something comes up at the last minute, you can leave a message in

your instructor's voice mailbox. Make your message short but specific ("This is Rick Jones from your 10 o'clock Intro to Psychology class. I'm supposed to present my project today, but have a fever of 102 degrees"). Avoid calling instructors at home unless they give specific permission to do so.

If you are taking a large lecture course, you may have a primary instructor plus a *teaching assistant* (TA) who meets with a small group of students on a regular basis and grades your papers and exams. You may want to approach your TA with course-related questions and problems before approaching the instructor. Because TAs deal with fewer students, they may have more time to devote to specific issues.

Academic advisors

In most colleges, every student is assigned an advisor who is the student's personal liaison with the college. (At some schools, students receive help at an advising center.) Your advisor will help you choose courses every term, plan your overall academic program, and help you understand college regulations, including graduation requirements. He or she will point out possible consequences of your decisions ("If you put off taking biology now, you're facing two lab courses next term"), help you shape your educational goals, and monitor your academic progress.

Although you are responsible for fully understanding graduation requirements—including credit requirements—and choosing the courses you need, your advisor is there to help you with these critical decisions. You will most likely be required to meet with your advisor once each term; however, you can schedule additional meetings if and when you need them.

Mentors

You may find a (mentor) during college who can give you a private audience for questions and problems and advice tailored to your needs, as well as support, guidance, and trust. In return, you owe it to a mentor to respectfully take advice into consideration. A mentor might be your advisor, an instructor in your major or minor field, or a resident assistant (RA). Some schools have faculty or peer mentoring programs to match students with people who can help them.

→ MENTOR
A trusted counselor or guide who takes a special interest in helping you reach your goals.

Tutors and academic centers

Tutors can give you valuable and detailed help on specific academic subjects. Most campuses have private tutoring available, and many schools offer free peer tutoring. If you feel you could benefit from the kind of one-on-one work tutoring can give, ask your instructor or your academic advisor to recommend a tutor. If your school has one or more academic centers, you may be able to find one there. *Academic centers,* including reading, writing, math, and study skills centers, offer consultations and tutoring to help students improve skills at all levels.

Administrators

Every college needs an administrative staff to operate smoothly and efficiently. One of the most important administrative offices for students is the office of the dean of student affairs, which, in many colleges, is the center for student services. Staff members there can answer your questions

or direct you to others who can help. You will also encounter administrataive offices involved with tuition payments, financial aid, and registration.

▶ The *bursar's office* (also called the *office of finance* or *accounting office*) issues bills for tuition and room and board and collects payments from students and financial aid sources.

▶ The *financial aid office* helps students apply for financial aid and understand the eligibility requirements of different federal, state, and private programs (see Chapter 11 for more details on financial aid).

▶ The *registrar's office* handles course registration, sends grade reports, and compiles your official *transcript* (a comprehensive record of your courses and grades). Graduate school admissions offices require a copy of your transcript, as do many prospective employers.

Student-centered services

Colleges provide a host of services that help students succeed in college and deal with problems that arise.

▶ *Academic computer center.* Most schools have computer facilities that are open daily, usually staffed by technicians who can assist you. Many facilities also offer training workshops.

▶ *Student housing or commuter affairs office.* Residential colleges provide on-campus housing for undergraduate students. The housing office handles room and roommate placement and deals with special needs (for example, an allergic student's need for a room air conditioner) and problems. Schools with commuting students may have transportation and parking programs.

▶ *Health services.* Generally including sick care, prescriptions, routine diagnostic tests, vaccinations, and first aid, college clinics are affiliated with nearby hospitals for emergency care. In addition, psychological counseling is sometimes offered through health services or at a separate facility. Many colleges require proof of health insurance at the time of registration.

▶ *Career services.* Helping students find part-time and full-time jobs, as well as summer jobs and internships, career offices have reference files on careers and employers. They also help students learn to write resumés and cover letters and search job sites on the Internet. These offices sponsor career fairs and provide space for employers to interview students on campus.

▶ *Services for disabled students.* For students with documented disabilities, federal law requires that assistance be provided in the form of accommodations ranging from interpreters for the hearing impaired to ramps for students in wheelchairs. If you have a disability, visit this office to learn what is offered, and remember that this office is your advocate if you encounter problems.

▶ *Veterans' affairs.* The veterans' office provides services including academic and personal counseling and current benefit status, which may affect tuition waivers.

Resources for minority students

The term *minority* includes students of color; gay, lesbian, and bisexual students; and students from underrepresented cultures or religious backgrounds. Along with activities that appeal to the general student population, most colleges have organizations and services that support minority groups, including specialized student associations, cultural centers, arts groups with a minority focus, minority fraternities and sororities, and political action groups.

Many minority students seek a balance, getting involved with members of their group as well as with the college mainstream. For example, a student may join the Latino Students Association as well as clubs for all students, such as the campus newspaper or an athletic team.

You are beginning the journey of your college education and lifelong learning. The work you do in this course will help you achieve your goals in your studies, your personal life, and your career. Psychologist Robert J. Sternberg, the originator of the successful intelligence concept that is the theme of *Keys to Success,* has said that those who achieve success "create their own opportunities rather than let their opportunities be limited by the circumstances in which they happen to find themselves."[2] Let this book and this course help you create new and fulfilling opportunities on your path to success.

KEYS TO SUCCESS

chapter 1

Welcome to College

Growing Toward Success

What Would You Do?

Think about this problem as you read, and consider how you would approach it. This chapter jump-starts your entry into the college experience, with information on how to make the transition and gather the ingredients for success.

Jo Luck runs a group called Heifer International, which aims to combat poverty and hunger through training, livestock donation, and other services. In the late 1980s, Ms. Luck encouraged a group of women in a Zimbabwe village to follow their dreams.

One of the women, a cattle herder named Tererai Trent, wrote down four goals on a scrap of paper: to study abroad, earn a B.A. degree, then a master's, and finally a doctorate. She put the paper in a tin and buried it under a rock in the pasture. Having endured abuse from her husband and years of hard work raising the five children born since her marriage at age 11, she hoped education would change her life. To prepare for college, she took correspondence courses paid for with money she made working for Heifer and other organizations. Eventually she applied to and was accepted by Oklahoma State University, moving with her family to the United States with support from Heifer and the fundraising efforts of family and friends.

Despite satisfying her first goal, Trent faced more struggle ahead. Her family lived in a trailer and often went hungry. She continued to endure beatings and was nearly expelled for missing tuition payments. With support from OSU she pressed on to earn her B.A., but her husband fell ill with AIDS and required her care around the clock as she began work toward her master's degree. (To be continued . . .)[1]

Throughout this book, you will meet people like Tererai who have worked through issues to achieve academic, career, and life goals. Whether you have something in common with these people or not, they will expand your perspective and inspire you to move ahead on your own path. You'll learn more about Tererai, and revisit her situation, within the chapter.

In this chapter, you'll explore answers to these questions:

> Where are you now—and where can college take you? p. 2

> How can successful intelligence help you achieve your goals? p. 7

> How can a "growth mindset" motivate you to persist? p. 11

> Why do you need emotional intelligence? p. 15

> How can this book prepare you to succeed? p. 17

 ANALYTICAL

 CREATIVE

 PRACTICAL

STATUS *Check*

▶ *How prepared are you for college?*

> "Successfully intelligent people . . . have a can-do attitude. They realize that the limits to what they can accomplish are often in what they tell themselves they cannot do, rather than in what they really cannot do."
>
> —Robert Sternberg

Where are you now—and where can college take you?

Think about how you got here. Are you going to college straight from high school or its equivalent? Or are you returning after working one or more jobs or completing a tour of duty in the armed forces? Do you have life skills from experience as a partner or parent? No matter what your background or motivation, you have enrolled, found a way to pay for tuition, signed up for courses, and shown up for class. You have earned this opportunity to be a college student.

If you are wondering how this or any other college course will make a difference for you, know that your experience in this course and during this term has the potential to:

▶ Allow you to discover more about how you learn and what you want
▶ Build academic skills as well as transferable life skills
▶ Help you set and reach your most important goals
▶ Increase your ability to relate effectively to others and work together

Now that you *have* the opportunity, you need to *use it*. This book, and your course, offer tools that will help you grow and achieve your goals, perhaps

student profile

Zack Moore
University of Rhode Island, Kingston

About me:

I major in communications, have added a business minor, and play wide receiver on the URI (University of Rhode Island) football team. Although I have some great mentors in several fields, I am not sure what my career choice will be. I hope to play football for as long as possible, but when I am done on the field, I might like to become a motivational speaker, open a warehouse-style gym, or help my grandfather run Horseless Carriage Carriers, his automobile transportation business.

What I focus on:

Ever since I was a toddler, my parents encouraged me to interact with as many people as possible. My life experiences have brought me in contact with people of many backgrounds, ages, races, and beliefs. I've developed an ability to carry on a conversation with practically anyone about practically anything. I like to think that I make as great an impact on people I meet as they often do on me.

Two years into my college career, I find it interesting to look back at how far I have come since arriving at summer football camp before my freshman year. Not only have I learned a lot in the classroom, but daily interactions with classmates, professors, teammates, coaches, roommates, and others in the college community have shaped me in ways that I would never have anticipated.

To me, college is a place where I am exploring who I am, gaining a better understanding of what makes others tick, and figuring out who I will be when I enter the professional world.

What will help me in the workplace:

While I don't know exactly what I will do with my life, I believe that the communication, social, and emotional skills I am developing each day will help me succeed in whatever career I choose.

beyond what you've ever imagined. You will be able to make the most of them—if you start by believing that you can grow.

When a high jumper or pole vaulter gets over a bar of a certain height, someone raises the bar so that the athlete can work toward a new goal. The college experience will "raise the bar" for you with tougher instructors, demanding coursework, and fellow students whose sights are set high. Others' goals and expectations are only part of the picture, though. College is a place where *you* can raise the bar to reach your personal aspirations, whatever they might be. As amazing as Tererai Trent's story is, know that you don't have to live in poverty halfway across the world to want to make changes for the better. Think about how you want to improve *your* life. This book and course will challenge you to set the bar to the height that's right for you.

First, however, begin your transition to college by looking at the present— the culture of college, what you can expect, and what college expects of you.

Then, consider the future—what a college education means for you in the workplace and life.

The culture of college

Whatever your age or stage of life, knowing what to expect in college will help you to transition more successfully. You are likely to experience most or all of the following aspects of college culture (spend some time with your college's student handbook to get informed about details specific to your school).

■ *Independent learning.* College offers you the chance to learn with a great deal of freedom and independence. In exchange, though, instructors expect you to function without much guidance. This culture requires strong self-management skills. You are expected to make the following—and more—happen on your own:

> ▶ Use syllabi to create, and follow, a schedule for the term (see Quick Start to College)
> ▶ Navigate course materials electronically (if your school uses an online course management system such as BlackBoard)
> ▶ Get to class on time with the materials you need
> ▶ Complete text and other reading with little to no in-class review of the reading
> ▶ Set up and attend study group meetings
> ▶ Turn in projects and coursework on time and be prepared for exams
> ▶ Get help when you need it

■ *Fast pace and increased workload.* The pace of each course is typically twice as fast as high school courses and requires more papers, homework, reading, and projects. Although demanding, learning at this speed can also energize and motivate you, especially if you did not feel inspired by high school assignments. The heavy, fast-paced workload demands more study time. For each hour spent in class, plan two to three hours of study and work time outside of class. For example, if you are in class for nine hours a week, you need to spend at least twice that number each week studying and working outside of class time.

■ *Challenging work.* Although challenging, college-level work offers an enormous opportunity to learn and grow. College texts often have more words per page, higher-level terminology, and more abstract ideas compared to high school texts. In addition to difficult reading, college often involves complex assignments, challenging research papers, group projects, lab work, and tests.

■ *More out-of-class time to manage.* The freedom of your schedule requires strong time management skills. On days when your classes end early, start late, or don't meet at all, you will need to use the open blocks of time effectively as you juggle other responsibilities, including perhaps a job and family.

■ *Diverse culture.* Typically, you will encounter different ideas and diverse people in college. Your fellow students may differ from you in age, life experience, ethnicity, political mindset, family obligations, values, and much more. Also, if you commute to school or attend class with others who do, you may find it challenging to connect with others.

■ *Higher-level thinking.* You'll be asked to move far beyond recall in college. Instead of just summarizing and taking the ideas of others at face value, you will interpret, evaluate, generate new ideas, and apply what you know to new situations (more on thinking skills later in this chapter).

You are not alone as you adjust. Look for support resources, including instructors, academic advisors, mentors, other students, or tutors; technology such as the Internet, library search engines, and electronic planning aids; and this book (see Quick Start to College for more information on resources). Seek help from campus officials, as when Tererai asked Oklahoma State University personnel to help her with housing and finances. And to give meaning to your efforts in college, consider how your efforts will serve you in the workplace.

Your place in the world of work

Although this is likely to be one of your first courses, it can lay the foundation for career exploration and workplace skill development. You will learn to distinguish yourself in a global marketplace, in which North American workers often compete with workers from other countries. Thomas Friedman, author of *The World Is Flat*, explains how the digital revolution has transformed the working environment you will enter after college:

Getting through the day-to-day activities of college demands basic computer know-how as well as an understanding of the school's research and communication technology.
© iStockPhoto

> It is now possible for more people than ever to collaborate and compete in real time with more other people on more different kinds of work from more different corners of the planet and on a more equal footing than in any previous time in the history of the world—using computers, e-mail, networks, teleconferencing, and dynamic new software.[2]

DIGITAL REVOLUTION
The change in how people communicate brought on by developments in computer systems.

These developments in communication, combined with an enormous increase in knowledge work such as Internet technology and decrease in labor-based work such as factory jobs, mean that you may compete for information-based jobs with highly trained and motivated people from around the globe. The working world, too, has raised the bar.

KNOWLEDGE WORK
Work that is primarily concerned with information rather than manual labor.

What can help you achieve career goals in this new "flat" world?

■ *College degree.* Statistics show that getting a degree increases your chances of finding and keeping a highly skilled, well-paying job. College graduates earn, on average, around $20,000 more per year than those with a high school diploma (see Key 1.1). Furthermore, the unemployment rate for college graduates is less than half that of high school graduates (see Key 1.2).

■ *21st century skills.* Taking a careful look at what the current workplace demands of workers and what it rewards, education and business leaders have founded an organization called the Partnership for 21st Century Skills. Together these leaders developed the Framework for 21st Century Learning shown in Key 1.3, delineating the categories of knowledge and skills that successful workers need to acquire.

Looking at this framework, you will see that success in today's workplace requires more than just knowing skills specific to an academic area or job. Author Daniel Pink argues that the ability to create, interact interpersonally, generate ideas, and lead diverse teams—skills all found in the Framework for 21st Century Learning—will be more and more important in the workplace. Because coursework traditionally focuses more on logical and analytical skills, building your interpersonal and creative skill set will require personal initiative from you. Often, these skills can be developed through in-class collaboration and teamwork as well as volunteer work, internships, and jobs.[3]

MORE EDUCATION
IS LIKELY TO MEAN **MORE INCOME**

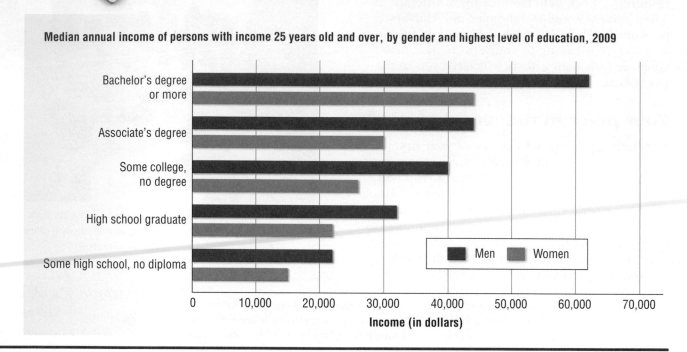

Median annual income of persons with income 25 years old and over, by gender and highest level of education, 2009

Bachelor's degree or more
Associate's degree
Some college, no degree
High school graduate
Some high school, no diploma

■ Men   ■ Women

0   10,000   20,000   30,000   40,000   50,000   60,000   70,000
Income (in dollars)

Source: U.S. Census Bureau, "Income, Poverty, and Health Insurance Coverage in the United States, 2009," *Current Population Reports,* Series P60-238, September 2010.

MORE EDUCATION
IS LIKELY TO MEAN **MORE CONSISTENT EMPLOYMENT**

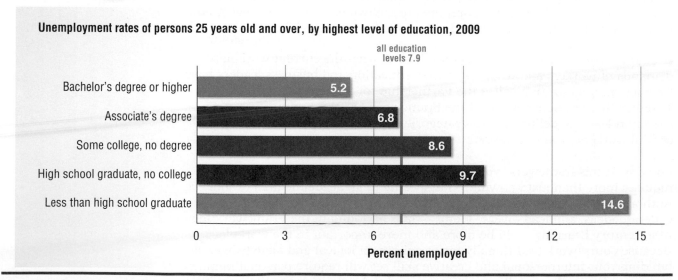

Unemployment rates of persons 25 years old and over, by highest level of education, 2009

all education levels 7.9

Bachelor's degree or higher — 5.2
Associate's degree — 6.8
Some college, no degree — 8.6
High school graduate, no college — 9.7
Less than high school graduate — 14.6

0   3   6   9   12   15
Percent unemployed

Source: U.S. Department of Labor, Bureau of Labor Statistics, Office of Employment and Unemployment Statistics, "Current Population Survey," May 2010.

THE **FRAMEWORK FOR 21ST CENTURY LEARNING** SHOWS WHAT YOU NEED TO SUCCEED

Key 1.3

CORE SUBJECTS AND 21ST CENTURY THEMES	LEARNING AND INNOVATION SKILLS
• Global Awareness • Financial, Economic, Business, and Entrepreneurial Literacy • Civic Literacy—Community Service • Health Literacy	• Creativity and Innovation • Critical Thinking and Problem Solving • Communication and Collaboration

INFORMATION, MEDIA, AND TECHNOLOGY SKILLS	LIFE AND CAREER SKILLS
• Information Literacy • Media Literacy • ICT (Information, Communications, and Technology) Literacy	• Flexibility and Adaptability • Initiative and Self-Direction • Social and Cross-Cultural Skills • Productivity and Accountability • Leadership and Responsibility

Source: Adapted from Partnership for 21st Century Skills Framework. www.p21.org/index.php?option=com_content&task=view&id=254&Itemid=120.

As you read the content and do the exercises in *Keys to Success*, you will grow in every area of this framework. There are links between these 21st century skills and what you will be reading and doing in the weeks to come, and the Personal Portfolio activity at the end of each chapter indicates which 21st century skills it builds. In fact, the three thinking skills that take focus in this text—analytical, creative, and practical—are all included within the framework. These three thinking skills will help you achieve your most important goals because they are critical to delivering what the world needs workers to do.

How can successful intelligence **help you achieve your goals?**

How do you define *intelligence?* Is an intelligent person someone who excels in high-level analytical courses? A successful professional in science or law? Or a person who scores well on standardized tests such as IQ (intelligence quotient) tests? The idea of using an IQ test to gauge intelligence and predict success is based on the belief that each person is born with a fixed amount of intelligence that can be measured. However, cutting-edge researchers such as Robert Sternberg and Carol Dweck have challenged these ideas.[4]

When test anxiety caused Sternberg (a psychologist and dean of students at Tufts University) to score poorly on IQ and other standardized tests during elementary school, he delivered what was expected of him—very little. However, his fourth-grade teacher turned his life around when she expected more. Sternberg has conducted extensive research supporting his sense that traditional intelligence measurements lock people into poor performance and often do not reflect their potential.[5]

Stanford psychologist Carol Dweck also had a life-changing experience when, as a young researcher, she conducted an experiment to see how elementary school children coped with failure. She gave students a set of puzzles that grew increasingly difficult. To her surprise, certain students welcomed the tough puzzles and saw failure as an opportunity. "They knew that human qualities, such as intellectual skills, could be cultivated through effort. And that's what they were doing—getting smarter. Not only weren't they discouraged by failure, they didn't even think they were failing. They thought they were learning."[6] Dweck's research since then has focused on the potential for increasing intelligence and the attitude that fosters that potential (more on that attitude later in the chapter).

The research of Sternberg, Dweck, and others suggests that intelligence is *not* fixed; people have the capacity to increase intelligence as they learn. In other words, *you can grow what you are born with.* Studies in neuroscience support this perspective, showing that the brain can develop throughout life if you continue to learn. Recent brain research shows that when you are learning, your brain and nerve cells (neurons) are forming new connections (synapses) from cell to cell by growing new branches (dendrites).[7] These increased connections then enable the brain to do and learn more.

The three thinking skills

How can you unlock your potential and achieve your important goals in college, work, and life? According to Sternberg, it takes three types of thinking: analytical (critical), creative, and practical. He calls this combination *successful intelligence,*[8] and he illustrates it with a story.

> Two boys are walking in a forest. They are quite different. The first boy's teachers think he is smart, his parents think he is smart, and as a result, he thinks he is smart. He has good test scores, good grades, and other good paper credentials that will get him far in his scholastic life.
>
> Few people consider the second boy smart. His test scores are nothing great, his grades aren't so good, and his other paper credentials are, in general, marginal. At best, people would call him shrewd or street smart.
>
> As the two boys walk along in the forest, they encounter a problem— a huge, furious, hungry-looking grizzly bear, charging straight at them. The first boy, calculating that the grizzly bear will overtake them in 17.3 seconds, panics. In this state, he looks at the second boy, who is calmly taking off his hiking boots and putting on his jogging shoes.
>
> The first boy says to the second boy, "You must be crazy. There is no way you are going to outrun that grizzly bear!"
>
> The second boy replies, "That's true. But all I have to do is outrun you!"[9]

This story shows that successful goal achievement and problem solving require more than book smarts. When confronted with a problem, using *only* analytical thinking put the first boy at a disadvantage. On the other hand, the second boy *analyzed* the situation, *created* options, and took practical *action.* He knew his goal—to live to tell the tale—and he achieved it.

How thinking skills move you toward your goals

Sternberg explains that although those who score well on tests display strong recall and analytical skills, they are not necessarily able to put their knowledge to work.[10] No matter how high you score on a library science test, for example, as a librarian you will also need to be able to devise useful keyword searches (creative thinking) and communicate effectively with patrons and other librarians (practical thinking). Of course, having *only* practical "street smarts" isn't enough either. Neither boy in the bear story, if rushed to the hospital with injuries sustained in a showdown with the bear, would want to be treated by someone lacking in analytical skills.

What do each of the three thinking skills contribute to goal achievement?

■ *Analytical thinking.* Commonly known as *critical thinking*, analytical thinking starts by engaging with information through asking questions and then proceeds to analyzing and evaluating information, often to work through a problem or decision. It often involves comparing, contrasting, and cause-and-effect thinking.

■ *Creative thinking.* Creative thinking concerns generating new and different ideas and approaches to problems, and, often, viewing the world in ways that disregard convention. It often involves imagining and considering different perspectives. Creative thinking also means taking information that you already know and thinking about it in a new way.

■ *Practical thinking.* Practical thinking refers to putting what you've learned into action to solve a problem or make a decision. Practical thinking often means learning from experience and emotional intelligence (explained later in the chapter), enabling you to work effectively with others and to accomplish goals despite obstacles.

Together, these abilities move you toward a goal, as Sternberg explains:

> Analytical thinking is required to solve problems and to judge the quality of ideas. Creative intelligence is required to formulate good problems and ideas in the first place. Practical intelligence is needed to use the ideas and their analysis in an effective way in one's everyday life.[11]

The following example illustrates how this works.

The goal-achieving thinking skills of Tererai Trent

▶ She *analyzed* her experience and abilities to determine what she was capable of accomplishing. She analyzed her circumstances to determine a course of action she could manage.
▶ She *created* a dream plan—to live in the United States and pursue a B.A., master's, and PhD.
▶ She took *practical action* to gain admittance to college, pay for her family to move to the United States, and care for her family while attending classes.

Why is developing successful intelligence so important to your success?

1. *It improves understanding and achievement, increasing your value in school and on the job.* People with critical, creative, and practical thinking skills are in demand because they can apply what they know to new situations, innovate, and accomplish their goals.

2. *It boosts your motivation.* Because it helps you understand how learning propels you toward goals and gives you ways to move toward those goals, it increases your willingness to work.

3. *It shows you where you can grow.* Students who have trouble with tests and other analytical skills can see the role that creative and practical thinking play. Students who test well but have trouble innovating or taking action can improve their creative and practical skills.

Chapter 4—the chapter on thinking—goes into more detail about all three skills.

Although thinking skills provide tools with which you can achieve college and life goals, you need **motivation** to put them to work and grow from your efforts. Explore a mindset that will motivate you to vault over that bar (and then set a higher one).

MOTIVATION
A goal-directed force that moves a person to action.

GET ANALYTICAL!

Define Your "College Self"

Making the most of the opportunities that college offers starts with knowing, as much as you can, about who you are and what you want. Analyze your "college self" using questions like the following to think through your personal profile. Write and save your description to revisit later in the course.

What is your student status—traditional or returning, full- or part-time?

_____

_____

How long are you planning to be in your current college? Is it likely that you will transfer?

_____

_____

What goal, or goals, do you aim to achieve by going to college?

_____

_____

_____

_____

What family and work obligations do you have?

_____

_____

What is your culture, ethnicity, gender, age, lifestyle?

_____

_____

What is your current living situation?

_____

_____

What do you feel are your biggest challenges in college?

_____

_____

_____

What do you like to study, and why does it interest you?

_____

_____

_____

_____

How can a "growth mindset" motivate you to persist?

Different people have different forces or *motivators*—grades, love of a subject, the drive to earn a degree—that encourage them to keep pushing ahead. Motivators can change with time and situations. Your motivation can have either an external or internal *locus of control*—meaning that you are motivated either by external factors (your parents, circumstances, luck, grades, instructors' feedback, and so on) or internal factors (values and attitudes).

Often, you will be motivated by some combination of external and internal factors, but internal motivation may have a greater influence on success. Why? Although you cannot control what happens around you, you *can* control your attitude, or *mindset*, and the actions that come from that mindset. Based on years of research, Carol Dweck has determined that the perception that talent and intelligence can develop with effort—what she calls a *growth mindset*—promotes success. "This view creates a love of learning and resilience that is essential for great accomplishment," reports Dweck. People with a growth mindset "understand that no one has ever accomplished great things—not Mozart, Darwin, or Michael Jordan—without years of passionate practice and learning."[12]

By contrast, people with a *fixed mindset* believe that they have a set level of talent and intelligence. They think their ability to succeed matches what they've been born with, and they tend to resist effort. "In one world [that of the fixed mindset], effort is a bad thing. It . . . means you're not smart or talented. If you were, you wouldn't need effort. In the other world [growth mindset], effort is what *makes* you smart or talented."[13]

For example, two students do poorly on an anatomy midterm. One blames the time of day of the test and her dislike of the subject, whereas the other feels that she didn't study enough. The first student couldn't change the subject or meeting time, of course, and didn't change her approach to the material (no extra effort). As you may expect, she did poorly on the final. The second student put in more study time after the midterm (increased, focused effort) and improved her grade on the final as a result. This student knows that "smart is as smart does."

You don't have to be born with a growth mindset. *You can build one.* "You have a choice," says Dweck. "Mindsets are just beliefs. They're powerful beliefs, but they're just something in your mind, and you can change your mind."[14] One way to change your mind is through specific actions that demonstrate your beliefs. Such actions include being responsible, practicing academic integrity, facing your fears, and approaching failure as an opportunity to learn and improve.

Build self-esteem with responsible actions

You may think that you need to have a strong sense of (self-esteem) to take action toward your goals. In fact, the reverse is true. Taking responsible action builds strong self-esteem because it gives you something to be proud of. Your actions change your thinking. Basketball coach Rick Pitino explains: "If you have established a great work ethic and have begun the discipline that is inherent with that, you will automatically begin to feel better about yourself."[15]

A growth mindset helps you build self-esteem because it encourages you to put forth effort. If you know you have the potential to do better, you will be more likely to try. A research study of employees taking a course in computer training supports this idea. Half the group, told their success depended on innate ability, lost confidence by the end of the course. By contrast, the other half, told their skills could be developed through practice, reported a good deal *more* confidence after they had completed the same course and made, in many cases, the same mistakes.[16]

> → SELF-ESTEEM
> Belief in your value as a person that builds as you achieve your goals.

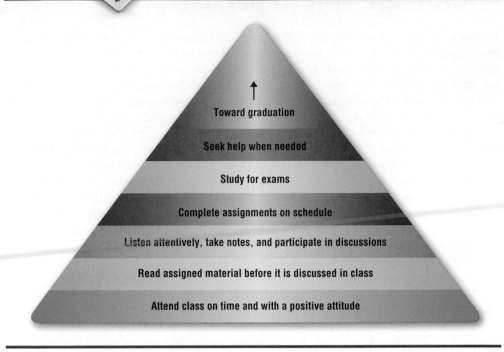

↑
Toward graduation

Seek help when needed

Study for exams

Complete assignments on schedule

Listen attentively, take notes, and participate in discussions

Read assigned material before it is discussed in class

Attend class on time and with a positive attitude

Even simple responsible actions can build the foundation for powerful self-esteem. What actions will you take to build your confidence? Consider using Key 1.4 as a starting point for ideas. Taking daily responsible actions such as these will help you to succeed in any course. Your efforts will enable you to grow no matter what your starting point.

Practice academic integrity

Having **academic integrity** means valuing learning and ensures an education based on *ethics* (your sense of what is right to do) and hard work. Find your school's code of honor or academic integrity policy in your student handbook, school website, or in your syllabus. Read it thoroughly so you know exactly what it asks of you. When you enrolled, you agreed to abide by it.

The Center for Academic Integrity, part of the Kenan Institute for Ethics at Duke University, defines *academic integrity* as a commitment to five fundamental values:[17]

ACADEMIC INTEGRITY
Following a code of moral values in all aspects of academic life—classes, assignments, tests, papers, projects, and relationships with students and faculty.

▶ *Honesty.* Honesty defines the pursuit of knowledge and implies a search for truth in your classwork, papers and lab reports, and teamwork with other students.

▶ *Trust.* Trust means being true to your word. Mutual trust—between instructor and student, as well as among students—makes the exchange of ideas possible.

▶ *Fairness.* Instructors must create a fair academic environment where students are judged against clear standards and in which procedures are well defined.

▶ *Respect.* In a respectful academic environment, both students and instructors accept and honor a wide range of opinions, even if the opinions are contrary to core beliefs.

▶ *Responsibility.* You are responsible for making choices that will provide you with the best education—choices that reflect fairness and honesty.

Violations of academic integrity include turning in previously submitted work, using unauthorized devices during an exam, providing unethical aid to another student, and downloading passages or whole papers from the Internet. When violations are found (often by computer programs designed for this purpose), consequences vary from school to school and include academic integrity seminars, grade reduction or course failure, suspension, and expulsion.

What does academic integrity have to do with a growth mindset? Well, first of all, being fair, honest, and responsible takes effort and choice. Second, and more important, academic integrity comes naturally to students who aim to grow and see struggle and failure as opportunities to learn. If you want to learn something, you know that cheating is likely to keep you from reaching your goal. In this sense, maintaining a growth mindset actually promotes academic integrity and makes the reasons for its worth that much more obvious (see Key 1.5).

Face your fears

Anything unknown—starting college, meeting new people—can be frightening. Facing fear with a growth mindset will allow you to proceed with courage as you reignite your motivation and learn. Following a step-by-step process can help you deal with otherwise overwhelming feelings.

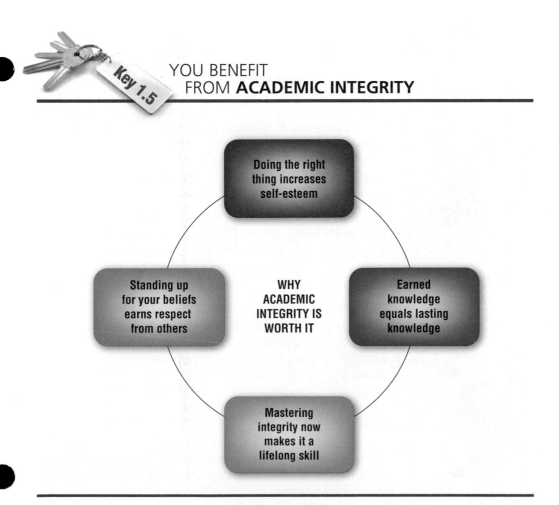

Key 1.5 YOU BENEFIT FROM **ACADEMIC INTEGRITY**

- Doing the right thing increases self-esteem
- WHY ACADEMIC INTEGRITY IS WORTH IT
- Standing up for your beliefs earns respect from others
- Earned knowledge equals lasting knowledge
- Mastering integrity now makes it a lifelong skill

1. *Acknowledge fears.* Naming your fear can begin to release its hold on you. "I'm worried about understanding a Shakespeare play I have to read."

2. *Examine fears.* Determine what exactly is causing your fear. Sometimes deeper fears emerge. "I feel that if I don't understand the play, I won't do well on the test and it will affect my GPA. That could cause trouble with my financial aid or my major."

3. *Develop and implement a plan.* Come up with ways to manage your fear, choose how to move forward, and put the plan into action. "I will rent a film of the play and watch it after I read. I will talk to my instructor about my concerns."

When you've put your plan into action, you've done what a growth mindset gives you the power to do—take action and learn from the experience. Then perhaps next time you face a similar situation, your fear may not be as strong.

Learn from failure

Failure approached with a growth mindset can spark motivation, showing you what you can do better and driving you to improve. Increased effort in the face of failure is a hallmark of successful people—witness the fact that Michael Jordan got cut from his high school basketball team as a sophomore (and clearly took that as a cue to work harder).

However, for people with a fixed mindset, failure is evidence of low intelligence and ability and means that you should give up and try something else. "This mindset gives you no good recipe for overcoming it," says Dweck. "If failure means you lack competence or potential—that you are a failure—where do you go from there?"[18]

Approach failure as a "problem to be faced, dealt with, and learned from."[19] Employ analytical, creative, and practical thinking as you take action.

■ *Analyze what happened.* Look carefully at what caused the situation. For example, imagine that after a long night of studying for a chemistry test, you forgot to complete a U.S. history paper due the next day. You realize that your focus on the test caused you to neglect everything else. Now you may face a lower grade on your paper if you turn it in late, or you may be inclined to rush it and turn in a product that isn't as good as it could be.

■ *Come up with creative ways to improve the situation and change for the future.* In the present, you can request an appointment with the instructor to discuss the paper. For the future, you can make a commitment to set alarms in your planner and to check due dates more often.

■ *Put your plan into action now—and what you've learned into action in the future.* Talk with the instructor and see if you can hand in your paper late. If you decide you have learned to pay more attention to deadlines, in the future you might work backward from your paper due date, setting dates for individual tasks related to the paper and planning to have it done two days before it is due to have time for last-minute corrections.

People who can manage the emotions produced by failure learn from the experience. They also demonstrate the last of this chapter's ingredients in the recipe for success—emotional intelligence.

Change the
CONVERSATION

Challenge yourself and your friends to ask—and answer—tough questions. Use the following to inspire discussion in pairs or groups.

▶ Describe a dream you have that you feel is out of reach. Why does it feel impossible? Why do you still dream it? How might a growth mindset help you achieve it?

▶ How do you tend to respond to challenges—do they inspire you to take action, or do they make you want to give up and set your sights lower?

▶ **CONSIDER THE CASE:** If you had traveled with Jo Luck to Zimbabwe, would you have thought that Tererai Trent had any hope of achieving her dream? Tererai's first step was to raise money to travel to the United States. What would your first step be toward your dream?

GET CREATIVE!

Consider How to Connect

Making connections with people and groups in your school early can benefit you later on. Brainstorm how you would like to spend whatever time you have available outside of your obligations (class time, work, family). On paper or on your computer, list your ideas. Try one or more of the following questions as a starting point:

If you had no fear, what horizon-broadening experience would you sign up for?

_____

_____

When you were in elementary school, what were your favorite activities? Which ones might translate into current interests and pursuits?

_____

_____

What kinds of organizations, activities, groups, experiences, or people make you think, "Wow, I want to do that"?

_____

_____

Think about the people that you feel bring out the best in you. What do you like to do with them? What kinds of activities are they involved with?

_____

_____

Why do you need emotional intelligence?

Success in a diverse world depends on relationships, and effective relationships demand emotional intelligence. Psychologists John Mayer, Peter Salovey, and David Caruso define *emotional intelligence* (EI) as the ability to understand "one's own and others' emotions and the ability to use this information as a guide to thinking and behavior."[20] Reading this definition carefully shows it isn't enough to just *understand* what you and others feel. An emotionally intelligent person uses that understanding to make choices about how to *think* and how to *act*.

In the past, and perhaps for some even today, the "head" (thought) was thought of as separate from, and perhaps more valuable than, the "heart" (emotion). However, modern science connects thought and emotion, and values both. "Emotions influence both what we think about and how we think," says Caruso. "We cannot check our emotions at the door because emotions and thought are linked—they cannot, and should not, be separated."[21]

Emotions also connect you to other people, as recent research has demonstrated. When a friend of yours is happy, sad, or fearful, you may experience similar feelings out of concern or friendship. Your brain and nervous system

The more able you are to work and communicate with others, the more you will learn as well as develop teamwork skills.
© Mary Kate Denny/PhotoEdit

have cells called *mirror neurons* that mimic an observed emotion, allowing you to "participate" in the feeling even though it comes from somewhere else. An MRI brain scan would show that the same area of your friend's brain that lit up during this emotional experience lit up in your brain as well.[22]

How emotional intelligence promotes success

Two short stories illustrate the power of emotional intelligence.

■ *Two applicants are competing for a job at your office.* The first has every skill the job requires, but doesn't respond well to your cues when you interview him. He answers questions indirectly and keeps going back to what he wants to say instead. The second isn't as skilled, but you feel during the interview as though you are talking with a friend. He listens carefully, picks up on your emotional cues, and indicates that he intends to make up for any lack of skill with a willingness to learn on the job. Whom would you hire?

■ *Two students are part of a group you are working with on a project.* One always gets her share of the job done but has no patience for anyone who misses a deadline. She is quick to criticize group members. The other is sometimes prepared, sometimes not, but always has a sense of what is going on with the group and responds to it. She works to make up for it when she hasn't gotten everything done, and when she is on top of her tasks she helps others. Which person would you want to work with again?

To be clear: Skills are crucial. The most emotionally tuned-in person in the world, for example, can't perform surgery without medical training. However, the role of emotional intelligence in communication and relationships makes it a strong predictor of success in work and life, as indicated by the following conclusions of research using an assessment measuring EI (MSCEIT).[23]

▶ Emotionally intelligent people are more competent in social situations and have higher quality relationships.
▶ Managers in the workplace with high EI have more productive working relationships and greater personal integrity.
▶ Employees scoring high in EI were more likely to receive positive ratings from peers and salary raises.
▶ Lower levels of EI are connected to higher amounts of drug, alcohol, and tobacco use, as well as aggression and conflict in teens.

The bottom line: More emotional intelligence means stronger relationships and more goal achievement.

The abilities of emotional intelligence

Emotional intelligence is a set of skills, or abilities, that can be described as *reasoning with emotion* (an idea illustrating how thought and emotion work together). Key 1.6 shows how you move through these skills when you reason with emotion.

TAKE AN **EMOTIONALLY INTELLIGENT** APPROACH

PERCEIVING EMOTIONS	**UNDERSTANDING EMOTIONS**	**MANAGING EMOTIONS**
Recognizing how you and others feel	Determining what the emotions involved in a situation tell you, seeing how they affect your thinking and mindset, and considering how you can adjust mindset or direct thinking in a productive way	Using what you learn from your emotions and those of others to choose behavior and actions that move you toward positive outcomes

Source: Adapted from John D. Mayer, Peter Salovey, and David R. Caruso, "Emotional Intelligence: New Ability or Eclectic Traits?" September 2008, *American Psychologist,* 63(6), pp. 505–507.

These skills allow you to create the best possible outcomes from your interactions. Given that you will interact with others in almost every aspect of school, work, and life, EI is a pretty important tool. You will see references to emotional intelligence throughout the text.

How might emotional intelligence fit into the rest of the skills discussed in this chapter? Think of it as *thinking skills applied to relationships.* Putting emotional intelligence to work means taking in and analyzing how you and others feel, shifting your thinking based on those feelings, and taking action in response—all with the purpose of achieving a goal.

How can this book prepare you to succeed?

Keys to Success is designed to help you build what you need for success in school and beyond, including thinking skills, attitudes, and emotional abilities that you can use to reach your goals.

Chapter content

Each chapter has several standard features:

> ▶ A chapter case showing how to think through and solve problems. Some cases are fact; some are fiction. All provoke thought and perhaps even conversation.
> ▶ An opening self-assessment so you can gauge your prior knowledge about chapter topics.
> ▶ In-chapter content and student profiles that illustrate growth mindset and thoughtful, emotionally intelligent choices.
> ▶ **Change the Conversation** questions that encourage you to revisit the case and investigate your thinking and emotions.
> ▶ A **Successful Intelligence Wrap-Up** that summarizes, in a visual format, the analytical, creative, and practical skills you have explored.

In-chapter activities

Within each chapter, three activities focus on building your thinking skills:

> ▶ **Get Analytical** gives you an opportunity to analyze a chapter topic.

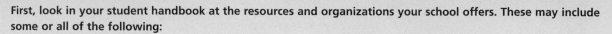

Use Emotional Intelligence to Get Involved

First, look in your student handbook at the resources and organizations your school offers. These may include some or all of the following:

Academic centers (reading, writing, etc.)	On-campus work opportunities
Academic organizations	Religious organizations
Adult education center	School publications
Arts clubs (music, drama, dance, etc.)	School TV/radio stations
Disabled student groups	Sports clubs
Fraternities/sororities	Student associations
International student groups	Student government
Minority student groups	Volunteer groups

As you read the list of possibilities, tune into your emotional intelligence and take note of how different organizations or activities make you feel. What do you want to try right away . . . what makes you turn the page . . . what scares you . . . and why? And is a positive outcome possible from trying something that scares you at first?

Taking this emotional intelligence feedback—as well as your analysis of yourself (Get Analytical, p. 10) and your creative ideas (Get Creative, p. 15)—into consideration, use the left-hand column on the grid that follows to list the three offices or organizations you plan to check out this term. Then use your school publications or online resources to fill in the next four columns of the grid. The last column requires action—fill it in when you have made contact with each office or organization. Finally, if you wish to become more involved after your initial contact, go for it.

OFFICE OR ORGANIZATION	LOCATION	HOURS, OR TIMES OF MEETINGS	WHAT IT OFFERS	PHONE NUMBER OR E-MAIL	INITIAL CONTACT— DATE AND WHAT HAPPENED

- ▶ **Get Creative** prompts you to think creatively about chapter material.
- ▶ **Get Practical** provides a chance to consider a practical application of a chapter idea.

End-of-chapter exercises

Here you apply what you have learned to important tasks:

- ▶ **Steps to Success** has you apply chapter skills at three levels of challenge, each building on the last.
- ▶ **Teamwork: Create Solutions Together** encourages you to apply different thinking abilities in a group setting.
- ▶ **Writing: Build Intrapersonal and Communication Skills** provides an "Emotional Intelligence Journal" question to respond to as well as a "Real-Life Writing" assignment that builds practical writing and communication skills.
- ▶ **Personal Portfolio: Prepare for Career Success** gets you ready for the workplace by helping you to build a portfolio of information useful in your academic and working life. As you complete portfolio items, you will also build a variety of 21st century skills.

Learning for life

The signs in Key 1.7 point to the need to be a *lifelong learner,* continuing to build knowledge and skills as your career and life demand. This book will help you fulfill that need.

A **CHANGING WORLD** MEANS LEARNING IS FOR LIFE

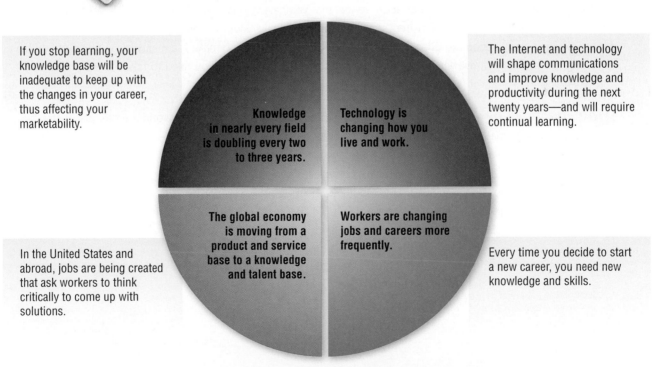

If you stop learning, your knowledge base will be inadequate to keep up with the changes in your career, thus affecting your marketability.

Knowledge in nearly every field is doubling every two to three years.

Technology is changing how you live and work.

The Internet and technology will shape communications and improve knowledge and productivity during the next twenty years—and will require continual learning.

In the United States and abroad, jobs are being created that ask workers to think critically to come up with solutions.

The global economy is moving from a product and service base to a knowledge and talent base.

Workers are changing jobs and careers more frequently.

Every time you decide to start a new career, you need new knowledge and skills.

This text gives you tools with which you can learn for life, meeting the changing demands of the modern world. Imagine: You are sitting in class with your *growth mindset,* open to learning. You are ready to use *analytical* and *creative* skills to examine the knowledge you take in and come up with new ideas. You are motivated to use your *practical* skills to move toward your goals. Your *emotional intelligence* has prepared you to adjust to and work with all kinds of people. The bar has been raised. **Get ready to use *Keys to Success* to fly over it and find out just how much you can grow.**

Case
Wrap-up

What happened to Tererai? Feeling the pull of family obligation despite what she had been through, Trent worked to support her family while caring for her husband. Though her progress toward her master's degree slowed to part-time, she still completed it. After her husband's death, she began doctoral work on AIDS prevention in Africa. Tererai checked off the last of her goals on the worn piece of paper when she received her PhD. Now she has new goals, which include bringing others the opportunity to pursue their dreams. She works for Heifer as a program evaluator. She continues her quest to "work for the causes of women and girls in poverty" (as she wrote on the piece of paper that contained her original four goals).

What does this mean for you? You don't need to begin your life in poverty in another country, have five children by your early twenties, or suffer abuse to feel that you have a long road ahead to achieve your highest goals and most far-flung dreams. Let Tererai Trent's story inspire you to take your own dreams seriously. Think about the dream you have described in the Change the Conversation exercise. Start to make it a reality by mapping out a plan to achieve it—over a year, five years, or even ten years or more. List the steps you need to take toward your dream and when you think you can achieve each step.

What effects go beyond your world? Every dream realized can make the world a better place, step by step. Perhaps a goal that is meaningful to you can make a difference for someone else—or you can be inspired to create a new goal for yourself by learning about an area of need in the world. Go to www.heifer.org and click on "Our Work" and then on "Our Initiatives." There you will see seven areas in which Heifer International intends to make a difference. Choose one that you find important and read about what Heifer is doing. Then explore what you can do—either through Heifer (the "Get Involved" button) or through another organization or path. *Set one small goal that can make a difference for someone in the world.*

Successful Intelligence *Wrap-up*

HERE'S HOW YOU HAVE
BUILT SKILLS IN **CHAPTER 1** :

ANALYTICAL THINKING	CREATIVE THINKING	PRACTICAL THINKING
❯ In the Get Analytical exercise, you examined who you are as a college student and what you want out of college.	❯ Thinking about the three thinking skills may have provided a new view of your skills and potential as a student.	❯ You examined actions that can help you build a growth mindset and increase your potential.
❯ In learning about Sternberg's research, you considered how thinking skills can enable you to reach important goals.	❯ In the Get Creative exercise, you brainstormed ideas about how you want to spend out-of-class time.	❯ By investigating emotional intelligence, you explored highly practical skills that allow you to work effectively with others.
❯ You explored how learning—in college and throughout life—can promote success.	❯ You examined how to use creativity to face fears and learn from failure.	❯ In the Get Practical exercise, you made plans to pursue specific extracurricular activities.

Word*for*Thought

Literally translated, the **Hungarian** phrase *egyszer volt budán kutyavásár* (edge-zehr volt bu-darn ku-tcho-vah-shahr) reads, "There was a dog-market in Buda only once."[24] In other words, it refers to a favorable opportunity that comes along one time only. College is that opportunity—make the most of it now.

Look at the motivation blocker on your page. Under it, write one practical idea about how to overcome it. When everyone is finished, pass your page to the person on the left. Then, on your new page, write an idea about the new blocker below any other ideas already listed. If you can't think of anything, pass the page as is. Continue this way until your page comes back to you. Then discuss the ideas as a group, analyzing which might work better than others. Add other ideas if you think of them.

Finally, on your own but keeping in mind the group discussion, list three specific actions that you can take to keep motivation high when the going gets rough.

1. _____

2. _____

3. _____

Writing

Build Intrapersonal and Communication Skills

Record your thoughts on a separate piece of paper, in a journal, or electronically.

EMOTIONAL INTELLIGENCE JOURNAL

How you are feeling now. First, describe what you are feeling right now about college. Then discuss what those feelings tell you about how ready you are for the experience. Last, brainstorm some actions that will help you be as prepared as possible to benefit from the experience of college. (For example, if shyness prevents you from feeling ready to meet new people on campus, one action might be to join an organization or study group that will help you get to know people more easily.)

REAL-LIFE WRITING

Skills you have now. No matter what professional goals you ultimately pursue, the skills that the 21st century workplace demands will be useful in any career area. Look back at Key 1.3 to remind yourself of the four skill areas—and the individual skills within each category—defined as 21st century essentials for success. Identify three skills you have already built and can demonstrate. If you would like to read further, go to www.21stcenturyskills.org/route21 and click on any of the four areas to see details about specific skills.

For each skill, write a short paragraph that contains the following elements:

- A description of your abilities in this skill area
- Specific examples, from school or work, demonstrating these abilities
- Jobs or coursework in which you have built this skill

Keep this information on hand for building your resumé—or if you already have a resumé, use it to update your information and add detail that will keep your resumé current.

Personal Portfolio

Prepare for Career Success

ASSESS YOUR SUCCESSFUL INTELLIGENCE

This is the first of twelve portfolio assignments you will complete, one for each chapter. By the end of the term, you will have compiled a portfolio of documents that can help you achieve career exploration and planning goals.

Type your work and save the documents electronically in one file folder. Use loose paper for assignments that ask you to draw or make collages, and make copies of assignments that ask you to write in the book. For safekeeping, scan and save loose or text pages to include in your portfolio file.

21st Century Learning Building Blocks
- Initiative and Self-Direction
- Critical Thinking and Problem Solving

As you begin this course, use this exercise to get a big picture look at how you perceive yourself as an analytical, creative, and practical thinker. For the statements in each of the three self-assessments, circle the number that best describes how it applies to you.

ASSESS YOUR ANALYTICAL THINKING SKILLS

For each statement, circle the number that feels right to you, from 1 for "not at all true for me" to 5 for "very true for me."

1. I recognize and define problems effectively.   1 2 3 4 5

2. I see myself as a "thinker," "analytical," "studious."   1 2 3 4 5

3. When working on a problem in a group setting, I like to break down the problem
    into its components and evaluate them.   1 2 3 4 5

4. I need to see convincing evidence before accepting information as fact.   1 2 3 4 5

5. I weigh the pros and cons of plans and ideas before taking action.   1 2 3 4 5

6. I tend to make connections among bits of information by categorizing them.   1 2 3 4 5

7. Impulsive, spontaneous decision making worries me.   1 2 3 4 5

8. I like to analyze causes and effects when making a decision.   1 2 3 4 5

9. I monitor my progress toward goals.   1 2 3 4 5

10. Once I reach a goal, I evaluate the process to see how effective it was.   1 2 3 4 5

Total your answers here: _____

ASSESS YOUR CREATIVE THINKING SKILLS

For each statement, circle the number that feels right to you, from 1 for "not at all true for me" to 5 for "very true for me."

1. I tend to question rules and regulations.   1 2 3 4 5

2. I see myself as "unique," "full of ideas," "innovative."   1 2 3 4 5

3. When working on a problem in a group setting, I generate a lot of ideas.   1 2 3 4 5

4. I am energized when I have a brand-new experience.   1 2 3 4 5

5. If you say something is too risky, I'm ready to give it a shot.   1 2 3 4 5

6. I often wonder if there is a different way to do or see something.   1 2 3 4 5

7. Too much routine in my work or schedule drains my energy.   1 2 3 4 5

8. I tend to see connections among ideas that others do not.   1 2 3 4 5

9. I feel comfortable allowing myself to make mistakes as I test out ideas.   1 2 3 4 5

10. I'm willing to champion an idea even when others disagree with me.   1 2 3 4 5

Total your answers here: _____

ASSESS YOUR PRACTICAL THINKING SKILLS

For each statement, circle the number that feels right to you, from 1 for "not at all true for me" to 5 for "very true for me."

1. I can find a way around any obstacle.   1 2 3 4 5

2. I see myself as a "doer," the "go-to" person; I "make things happen."   1 2 3 4 5

3. When working on a problem in a group setting, I like to figure out who will do what and when it should be done.   1 2 3 4 5

4. I apply what I learn from experience to improve my response to similar situations.   1 2 3 4 5

5. I finish what I start and don't leave loose ends hanging.   1 2 3 4 5

6. I note my emotions about academic and social situations and use what they tell me to move toward a goal.   1 2 3 4 5

7. I can sense how people feel and can use that knowledge to interact with others effectively.   1 2 3 4 5

8. I manage my time effectively.   1 2 3 4 5

9. I adjust to the teaching styles of my instructors and the communication styles of my peers.   1 2 3 4 5

10. When involved in a problem-solving process, I can shift gears as needed.   1 2 3 4 5

Total your answers here: _____

With your scores in hand, use the Wheel of Successful Intelligence to look at all the skills at once. In each of the three areas of the wheel, draw a curved line approximately at the level of your number score and fill in the wedge below that line. Look at what the wheel shows about the level of balance you perceive in your three aspects of successful intelligence. If it were a real wheel, would it roll?

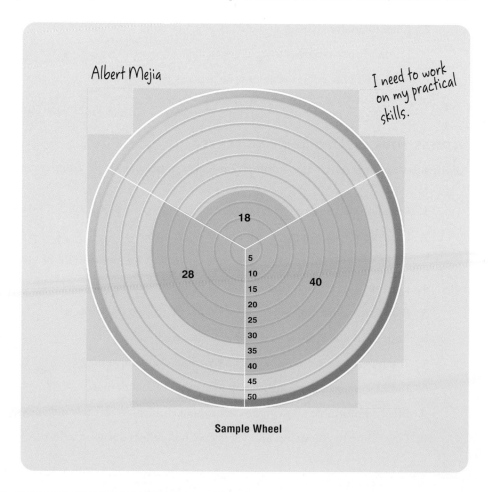

Albert Mejia

I need to work on my practical skills.

18

5
10
15
20
25
30
35
40
45
50

28

40

Sample Wheel

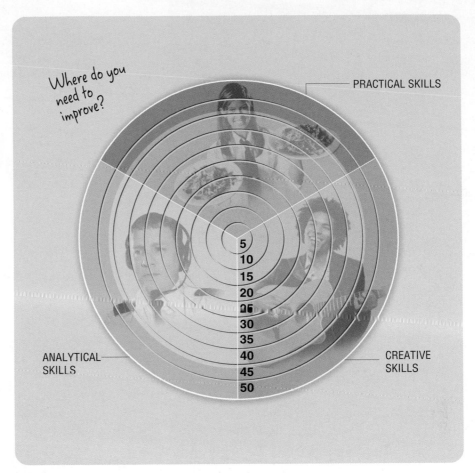

Where do you need to improve?

PRACTICAL SKILLS

ANALYTICAL SKILLS

CREATIVE SKILLS

5
10
15
20
25
30
35
40
45
50

Source: Based on "The Wheel of Life" model developed by the Coaches Training Institute. © Co-Active Space 2000.

Based on the appearance of the wheel, in which skill do you most need to build strength? Keep this goal in mind as you proceed through the text. In each chapter, pay special attention to the exercise that builds this thinking skill.

Social Networking

CONNECT TO THE WORKING WORLD

One of the most productive uses of online social networking is to help people market themselves and develop networks of professional contacts in the work world. At the end of each Personal Portfolio exercise, this segment will help you build a profile on one of the most widely used tools for this purpose—LinkedIn. The mission of LinkedIn is to help you connect to people you know and trust, and access wider networks of people through them, to become a more successful professional in the career of your choice.

Set up your account on LinkedIn to get started. Do the following:

- Go to www.linkedin.com and click on "What is LinkedIn?" to get an overview.
- Click on "Join Today" and follow the instructions to establish your account name and password.
- Be sure to read the User Agreement and Privacy Policy.

If you already have a LinkedIn account, sign on and make sure your basic information is up to date.

Values, Goals, and Time

Managing Yourself

What Would You Do?

Think about this problem as you read, and consider how you would approach it. This chapter takes a closer look at your personal values, the goals you set reflecting those values, and how you manage your time to achieve those important goals.

Devonne Henley attended college as a part-time student for the past year and this term decided to take on a full load of courses. However, she is finding it hard to manage her responsibilities. In sociology class the instructor, Ms. Cordoza, has assigned a group project focusing on the biggest problems the world is facing today. She has asked Devonne to stay after class to talk about it.

"Devonne, I know you haven't been able to make your group's first two meetings," she said, "and I want to make sure you don't let this project drop. How can I help?"

"I'm just swamped," Devonne replied. "I've got four other classes and I work weekends; I take care of my nephew every morning, and my schedule is just not working out."

"Is that the little guy you brought to class last week?" asked Ms. Cordoza.

"Yes, that's him. I'm sorry I had to do that," said Devonne.

Ms. Cordoza thought for a moment. "Look, you did keep him quiet so he didn't disturb the class. My issue is that you couldn't be present for the class while managing him. Class time is your time to get what you need from your education."

"You know, this project just doesn't make sense to me. We're supposed to be thinking through how to stop global warming, and I can't even turn in a paper on time or stay awake when I study," Devonne sighed.

"Listen, at the very least, you need a decent grade on this project," Ms. Cordoza responded. "But you might find out that world problems have more to do with you than you think. Can you make your group's next meeting this Friday at 1 P.M.?" (To be continued . . .)

Managing responsibilities is a challenge for almost every student. You'll learn more about Devonne, and revisit her situation, within the chapter.

In this chapter, you'll explore answers to these questions:

> Why is it important to know what you value? p. 30

> How do you set and achieve goals? p. 31

> How can you effectively manage your time? p. 38

ANALYTICAL

CREATIVE

PRACTICAL

For each statement, circle the number that feels right to you, from 1 for "not at all true for me" to 5 for "very true for me."

▶ I am aware of my values and beliefs.	1 2 3 4 5
▶ I have a system for reminding myself of what my goals are.	1 2 3 4 5
▶ I find ways to motivate myself when I am working toward a goal.	1 2 3 4 5
▶ When I set a long-term goal, I break it down into a series of short-term goals.	1 2 3 4 5
▶ I am aware of my time-related needs and preferences.	1 2 3 4 5
▶ I understand my time traps and have ways to avoid them.	1 2 3 4 5
▶ I know how to use the SMART approach to plan achievable goals.	1 2 3 4 5
▶ When I procrastinate, I know how to get back on track.	1 2 3 4 5
▶ I record tasks, events, and responsibilities in a planner of some kind and refer to it regularly.	1 2 3 4 5
▶ I understand how managing my time can help reduce my level of stress.	1 2 3 4 5

Each of the topics in these statements is covered in this chapter. Note those statements for which you circled a 3 or lower. Skim the chapter to see where those topics appear, and pay special attention to them as you read, learn, and apply new strategies.

REMEMBER: *No matter how effectively you set goals and manage time, you can improve with effort and practice.*

"Successfully intelligent people are well aware of the penalties for procrastination. They schedule their time so that the important things get done—and done well."

—Robert Sternberg

VALUES
Principles or qualities that you consider important.

Why is it important to know what you value?

You make life choices—what to do, what to believe, what to buy, how to act—based on your personal **values.** The choice to pursue a degree, for example, may reflect how a person values the personal and professional growth that come from a college education. If you like to be on time for classes, you may value punctuality. If you pay bills regularly and on time, you may value financial stability.

Values play a key role in your drive to achieve important goals and use your time wisely, helping you do the following:

▶ *Understand what you want out of life.* Your most meaningful goals will reflect what you value most.
▶ *Choose how to use your valuable time.* When your day-to-day activities align with what you think is most important, you gain greater fulfillment from them.
▶ *Build "rules for life."* Your values form the foundation for your decisions and behavior throughout your life. You will return repeatedly to these rules for guidance, especially in unfamiliar territory.
▶ *Find people who inspire you.* Spending time with people who share similar values will help you clarify how you want to live while finding support for your goals.

How values develop and change

Your value system is complex, built piece by piece over time, and coming from many sources—such as family, friends, culture, media, school, work, neighborhood, religious beliefs, and world events. These powerful external influences can so effectively instill values that you don't think about why you believe what you believe. However, you have a *choice* whether or not to adopt any value. Taking advantage of the power to choose requires evaluating values with questions like the following:

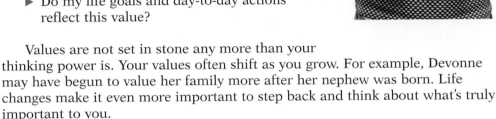

▶ Where did the value come from?
▶ Is this value something from my family or culture that I have accepted without questioning, or have I truly made it my own?
▶ What other different values could I consider?
▶ What might happen as a result of adopting this value?
▶ Have I made a personal commitment to this choice? Have I told others about it?
▶ Do my life goals and day-to-day actions reflect this value?

Values are not set in stone any more than your thinking power is. Your values often shift as you grow. For example, Devonne may have begun to value her family more after her nephew was born. Life changes make it even more important to step back and think about what's truly important to you.

How values affect your life experience

Because what you value often determines the choices you make, it also shapes your life experiences. For example, the fact that you value education may have led you to college, a practical choice that will help you build skills and persistence, choose a major and career direction, find meaningful friends and activities, and achieve learning goals.

Another example is found on today's college campus in the growing diversity of the student body, a diversity also increasingly seen in the working population. If you value human differences, you have taken an important step on the way to working successfully with people of various cultures, stages of life, and value systems both in college and beyond.

Values become goals when you've transformed your beliefs into something tangible and long-lasting. Not every value becomes a goal, but every goal stems from your values.

How do you set and achieve goals?

GOAL
An end toward which you direct your efforts.

When you set a (**goal,**) you focus on what you want to achieve and create a path that can get you there. Setting goals involves defining your aims in both long-term and short-term time frames. *Long-term* goals are broader objectives you

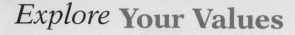

GET ANALYTICAL!

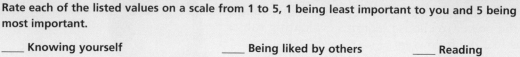

Explore Your Values

Rate each of the listed values on a scale from 1 to 5, 1 being least important to you and 5 being most important.

____ Knowing yourself	____ Being liked by others	____ Reading
____ Self-improvement	____ Taking risks	____ Time to yourself
____ Improving physical/mental health	____ Time for fun/relaxation	____ Lifelong learning
____ Leadership and teamwork skills	____ Staying fit through exercise	____ Competing and winning
____ Pursuing an education	____ Spiritual/religious life	____ Making a lot of money
____ Good relationships with family	____ Community involvement	____ Creative/artistic pursuits
____ Helping others	____ Keeping up with the news	____ Getting a good job
____ Being organized	____ Financial stability	____ Other _____

List your top three values:

1. _____

2. _____

3. _____

Now connect your values to educational goals. Choose one top value that is a factor in an educational choice you have made. Explain the choice and how the value is involved. Example: A student who values helping others chooses to study nursing.

_____

_____

want to achieve over a long period of time, perhaps a year or more. *Short-term* goals move you toward a long-term goal in manageable and achievable steps (see Key 2.1).

Establish your personal mission

Start with the biggest big picture: Defining your *personal mission* can help you anchor your values and goals in a comprehensive view of what you want out of life. Think of a personal mission as your longest-term goal, within which all other long-term and short-term goals should fit.

Dr. Stephen Covey, author of *The Seven Habits of Highly Effective People*, defines a *mission statement* as a philosophy outlining what you want to be (character), what you want to do (contributions and achievements), and the principles by which you live (your values).[1] Defining your personal mission involves creating a mission statement. The following mission statement was written by Carol Carter, one of the authors of *Keys to Success*.

My mission is to use my talents and abilities to help people of all ages, stages, backgrounds, and economic levels achieve their human potential through fully developing their minds and their talents. I aim to create opportunities for others through work, service, and family. I also aim to balance work with people in my life, understanding that my family and friends are a priority above all else.

How can you start formulating a mission statement? Try using Covey's three aspects of personal mission as a guide. Think through the following:

▶ *Character.* What aspects of character do you think are most valuable? When you consider the people you admire most, which of their qualities stand out?
▶ *Contributions and achievements.* What do you want to accomplish in your life? Where do you want to make a difference?
▶ *Values.* How do your values inform your life goals? What in your mission could help you live according to what you value most highly?

Because what you want out of life changes as you do, your personal mission should remain flexible and open to revision. Your mission can be the road map for your personal journey, giving meaning to your daily activities, promoting responsibility, and inspiring action. You will have a chance to craft a personal mission at the end of this chapter.

Goals take effort and planning to reach. This music producer spends days, and even weeks, adjusting equipment and recording tracks on the way to the production of just one song.
©UpperCut Images/Getty Images

GOALS REINFORCE ONE ANOTHER

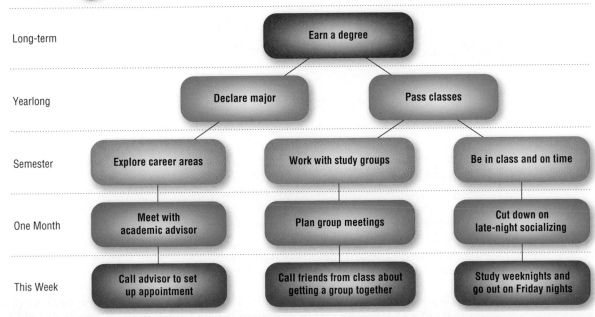

Long-term		Earn a degree	
Yearlong	Declare major		Pass classes
Semester	Explore career areas	Work with study groups	Be in class and on time
One Month	Meet with academic advisor	Plan group meetings	Cut down on late-night socializing
This Week	Call advisor to set up appointment	Call friends from class about getting a group together	Study weeknights and go out on Friday nights

student profile

Ming-Lun Wu
National Chengchi University, Taipei, Taiwan (graduate)
University of Denver, Denver, Colorado

About me:

I grew up in Taiwan. After completing high school and my undergraduate degree in Taiwan, I traveled to Boston, Massachusetts, for a summer ESL program and, later, Denver, Colorado, for graduate school. I'm currently attending the University of Denver and am working on my master's degree in marketing.

What I focus on:

Growing up in Taiwan, I had a dream of experiencing education in the United States. To me, American schools seemed more open-minded than the schools I attended in Taiwan. That dream became my goal and I quickly started to pay attention to any information related to studying abroad. When I received a chance to make that dream a reality, I jumped at it. However, even though I had my chance, I knew that I was going to need to improve my English immensely if I wanted to succeed.

Upon arriving in Boston for a study-abroad experience, I began looking for opportunities to work on my language skills. I joined a Toastmasters club as well as an English training club, which focused on leadership and public speaking. In the summer, I went to a Boston-based language school. Besides improving my language skills, experiences like applying for my visa, finding a host family, and scheduling trips around Boston helped me gain independence and confidence in a strange place. I had to test both my language skills and my independence to achieve my goal and succeed in the United States.

What will help me in the workplace:

Even though knowing the big picture is essential, understanding every baby step needed in order to accomplish a vision and having the hands-on plan moving towards the vision little by little can be more important.

Set long-term goals

What do you want your life to look like in 5 or 10 years? What degree do you want to earn, what job do you want, where do you want to live? How do you want to live your values and activate your personal mission? Answers to questions like these help identify long-term goals.

Long-term goals are objectives that sit out on the horizon, at least 6 months to a year away. They're goals that you can imagine and maybe even visualize, reflecting who you are and what is important to you, but they're too far out for you to touch. The more you know about yourself, the better able you are to set and work toward meaningful long-term goals. One way to make long-term goals real is to put them in writing, as in the following example.

My goal is to build a business in which I, as a family doctor, create opportunities to expose young people in my community to the medical field.

A student 2 years away from college graduation who is pursuing this long-term goal might establish the following supporting set of 1-year long-term goals:

Design courses for the year to make sure I am on track for pre-med course completion. Find medical practices in the area that could serve as a model for my business. Research medical schools.

To determine your long-term goals, think about the values that anchor your personal mission. For someone who values health and fitness, for example, possible long-term goals might involve working for an organic food company or training as a physical therapist. Basing your long-term goals on values increases your motivation to succeed. The stronger the link between your values and your long-term goals, the happier, more motivated, and more successful you are likely to be in setting and achieving those goals.

Set short-term goals

Lasting from an hour or less to as long as several months, *short-term goals* narrow your focus and encourage progress toward long-term goals. If you have a long-term goal of graduating with a degree in nursing, for example, you may set these short-term goals for the next 6 months:

▶ I will learn the name, location, and function of every human bone and muscle.
▶ I will work with a study group to understand the muscular-skeletal system.

These goals can be broken down into even smaller parts, such as the following 1-month goals:

▶ I will work with on-screen tutorials of the muscular-skeletal system until I understand and memorize the material.
▶ I will spend 3 hours a week with my study partners.

In addition to monthly goals, you may have short-term goals that extend for a week, a day, or even a couple of hours. To support your goal of regularly meeting with your study partners, you may set the following short-term goals:

▶ *By the end of today.* Text or e-mail study partners to ask them when they might be able to meet
▶ *1 week from now.* Schedule each of our weekly meetings this month
▶ *2 weeks from now.* Have our first meeting
▶ *3 weeks from now.* Type and distribute notes from first meeting; have second meeting

Set up a SMART goal-achievement plan

At any given time, you are working toward goals of varying importance. First, decide which goals matter most to you and are most deserving of your focus. Then draw

GET CREATIVE!

Find Ways to Get Unstuck

To start, think of a problem on which you tend to get stuck. It could be scheduling homework around extracurricular activities, finding time to hang out with friends, coming up with interesting career paths, or simply figuring out the theme of a literary work.

_____

_____

_____

Now come up with three reasonable ways to get unstuck. For example, if your issue is scheduling homework, one way to get unstuck might be to start your day earlier with a 1-hour work session.

1. _____

2. _____

3. _____

Now that you've determined the most logical solutions, use a visual organizer to think outside of the problem-solving box. First, write your problem in the center bubble. Then, begin filling in the surrounding bubbles with as many ideas as you can think of. Don't question their validity or whether or not they'll work; just keep writing until you've filled in every bubble with a possible solution.

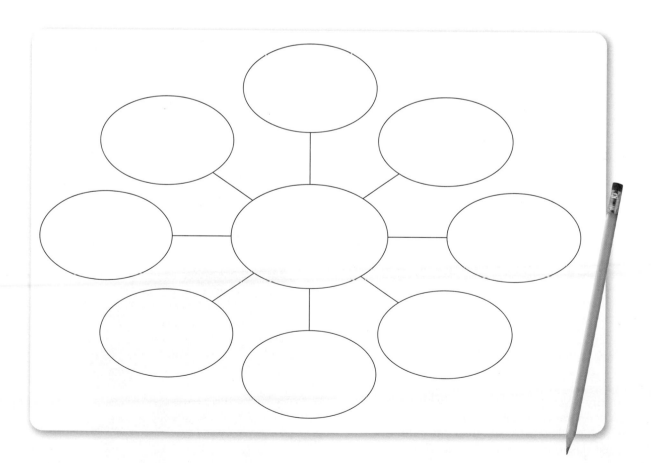

When you're finished, read through all of your creative solutions. Do any of them stick out to you? Find your two favorites and briefly describe how you might be able to use them next time you are faced with a similar situation.

_____

_____

_____

_____

_____

_____

_____

_____

_____

You just got yourself unstuck. Consider using this method when faced with a tough problem. Thinking creatively can be an extremely productive (not to mention fun) way to solve any problem you may encounter.

up a plan to achieve those goals, using the SMART system to make your goals Specific, Measurable, Achievable, Realistic, and linked to a Time Frame.

▶ *Step 1.* Define an Achievable, Realistic goal. *What do you want?* Is it **achievable**—do you have the skill, ability, and drive to get there? Is it **realistic**—will the external factors (time available, weather, money, other people, and so on) help or hinder you? To develop an achievable, realistic goal, consider your hopes, interests, and abilities. Then, reflect on how realistic it is, given your resources and circumstances. Write out a clear description of your goal.

▶ *Step 2.* Define a Specific path. *How will you get there?* Brainstorm different paths. Choose one; then map out its **specific** steps. Focus on behaviors and events that are under your control.

▶ *Step 3.* Link to a Time Frame. *When do you want to accomplish your goal?* Schedule steps within a realistic **time frame.** Create specific deadlines for each step you defined in Step 1. Charting your progress will help you stay on track.

▶ *Step 4.* Measure your progress. *What safeguards will keep you on track?* Will you record your progress in a weekly journal? Report to a friend? Use an alarm system on your smartphone to remind you to do something? Create a system to **measure** how well you are moving along.

▶ *Step 5.* Get unstuck: *What will you do if you hit a roadblock?* The path to a goal is often rocky and stressful. Anticipate problems and define **specific** ways to alter your plans if you run into trouble (stress management strategies are presented later in the chapter). Reach out to friends, family, and college personnel who can help you. Remind yourself of the benefits of your goal. Be ready to brainstorm other ideas if your plans don't work. The Get Creative activity will help you think your way past roadblocks.

▶ *Step 6.* Action time. Follow the steps in your plan until you achieve your goal.

GOAL: To decide on a major.

SMART KEY	MEANING	EXAMPLE
Specific	Name exactly how you will achieve your goal.	I will read the list of available majors, meet with my academic advisor, talk with instructors, and choose a major by the deadline.
Measurable	Find ways to measure your progress over time.	I will set alarms on my smartphone to remind me of when I should have accomplished steps. I will ask my mom to check in to make sure I'm getting somewhere.
Achievable	Set a goal that your abilities and drive can handle.	I'm driven to declare a major because I want to earn my degree, graduate, and gain work-ready skills.
Realistic	Define a goal that is workable given the resources (time and money) and other circumstances.	Because I'm starting early and already know how the process works, I should have time to think through this carefully.
Time Frame	Set up a time frame for achieving your goal and the steps toward it.	I have a year until the deadline. I will read the catalog in the next month; I will meet with my advisor by the end of the term; I will talk with instructors at the beginning of next term; I will declare a major by the end of next term.

MAJOR or
CONCENTRATION
An academic subject area
chosen as a field of
specialization, requiring a
specific course of study.

See Key 2.2 for a way to apply this goal-setting plan to an important objective that nearly every college student will need to achieve—declaring a **major** or **concentration** (for the sake of simplicity, the term *major* will appear throughout the rest of the text).

Through the process of working toward your most important goals, you will often be thinking about how well you are using your time. In fact, being able to achieve any significant goal is directly linked to effective time management.

How can you effectively **manage your time?**

No matter how well you define the steps to your goals, you need to set those steps within a time frame to achieve them. Although the idea of "managing time" may seem impossible, time management can also be thought of as *behavioral management*—adjusting what you do so that you can meet your needs in the time you have available.

Everyone has only 24 hours in a day, and 8 or so of those hours involve sleeping (or should, if you want to remain healthy and alert enough to achieve your goals). You can't manage how time passes, but you *can* manage how you use it. Only by making active choices about your time can you hope to avoid that feeling of being swept along in time's swift tide that Devonne is experiencing. The first step in time management is to figure out your time profile and your preferences.

Identify your time profile and preferences

People have unique body rhythms and habits that affect how they deal with time. Some people are night owls who have lots of energy late at night. Others are early birds who do their best work early in the day. Some people are chronically late, whereas others get everything done with time to spare.

The more you're aware of your own time-related behaviors, the better able you'll be to create a schedule that maximizes your strengths and reduces stress. The following steps can help you get in touch with your own inner time clock:

■ **Create a personal time "profile."** Ask yourself these questions: At what time of day do I have the most energy? The least energy? Do I tend to be early, on time, or late? Do I focus well for long stretches or need regular breaks? Your answers will help you determine your profile.

■ **Evaluate the effects of your profile.** Which of your time-related habits and preferences will have a positive impact on your success at school? Which are likely to cause problems? Which can you make adjustments for, and which will just require you to cope?

■ **Establish schedule preferences.** Based on the time profile you have developed, list your preferences—or even map out an ideal schedule as a way of illustrating them. For example, one student's preference list might read, "Classes bunched together on Mondays, Wednesdays, and Fridays. Tuesdays and Thursdays free for studying and research. Study time primarily during the day."

Next, build a schedule that takes your profile and preferences into account wherever possible. You will have more control over some things than others. For example, a student who functions best late at night may have more luck scheduling study time than class meeting times (unless he attends one of several colleges that have begun to schedule late-night classes to handle an overload of students).

Build a schedule

Schedules help you gain control of your life in two ways: They provide segments of time for goal-related tasks and they remind you of tasks, events, due dates, responsibilities, and deadlines.

Use a planner

A planner is a tool for managing your time. Use it to keep track of events and commitments, schedule goal-related tasks, and rank tasks according to priority. Time management expert Paul Timm says that "rule number one in a thoughtful planning process is: Use some form of a planner where you can write things down."[2]

There are two major types of planners. One is a book or notebook, showing either a day or a week at a glance, in which to note commitments. Some planners contain sections for monthly and yearly goals. The other option is an electronic planner or smartphone such as an iPhone or iPod Touch, BlackBerry, or Sidekick. Basic functions allow you to schedule days and weeks, note due dates, make to-do lists, perform mathematical calculations, and create and store an address book. You can also transfer information to and from a computer.

Though electronic planners are handy and have a large data capacity, they cost more than the paper versions, and they can fail due to software or battery

Managing time effectively often means taking advantage of opportunities whenever they arise. This student, also a mother, fits schoolwork in during naptime.
© Michael Newman/PhotoEdit

Monday, March 14

Time	Tasks		Priority
6:00 A.M.			
7:00			
8:00	Up at 8am — finish homewo		
9:00			
10:00	Business Administration		
11:00	Renew driver's license @ DM		
12:00 P.M.			
1:00	Lunch		
2:00	Writing Seminar (peer editin		
3:00	↓		
4:00	check on Ms.Schwartz's off		
5:00	5:30 work out		
6:00	↳6:30		
7:00	Dinner		
8:00	Read two chapters for		
9:00	Business Admin.		
10:00			
11:00			
12:00			

Monday, March 28

8		Call: Mike Blair	1
9	BIO 212	Financial Aid Office	2
10			3
11	CHEM 203	EMS 262 *Paramedic	4
12		role-play*	5
Evening	6pm yoga class		

Tuesday, March 29

8	Finish reading assignment!	Work @ library	1
9			2
10	ENG 112	(study for quiz)	3
11	↓		4
12		↓	5
Evening		until 7pm	

Wednesday, March 30

8		Meet w/advisor	1
9	BIO 212		2
10		EMS 262	3
11	CHEM 203 *Quiz		4
12		Pick up photos	5
Evening	6pm Dinner w/study group		

problems. Analyze your preferences and options, and decide which tool you are most likely to use every day. A blank notebook, used conscientiously, may work as well for some people as a top-of-the-line smartphone. You might also consider online calendars, such as Google Calendar, which can "communicate" with your phone or other electronic planning device.

Keep track of events and commitments

Your planner is designed to help you schedule and remember events and commitments. A quick look at your notations will remind you when items are approaching. Your class syllabus is a crucial tool for keeping track of reading and homework assignments and test dates (see Key 2.3).

When you get your syllabi for the term, enter all relevant dates in your planner right away so you can prepare for crunch times. For example, if you see that you have three tests and a presentation coming up all in one week, you may have to rearrange your schedule during the preceding week to create extra study time.

Among the events and commitments worth noting in your planner are the following:

- ▶ Test and quiz dates; due dates for papers, projects, and presentations
- ▶ Details of your academic schedule, including term and holiday breaks
- ▶ Club and organizational meetings
- ▶ Personal items—medical appointments, due dates for bills, birthdays, social events
- ▶ Milestones toward a goal, such as due dates for sections of a project

It's important to include class prep time—reading and studying, writing, and working on assignments and projects—in the planner. As you read in Chapter 1, you should schedule at least 2 hours of preparation for every hour of class—that is, if you take twelve credits, you'll spend 24 hours or more a week on course-related activities in and out of class. It's tough to get that much studying in, especially if you are an athlete, a working student, or a parent. Situations like these demand creative time management and attention to your schedule.

Schedule tasks and activities that support your values and goals

Linking day-to-day events in your planner to your values and broader goals will give meaning to your efforts, bring order to your schedule, and keep you motivated. Planning study time for an economics test, for example, will mean more to you if you link the hours you spend to your goal of being accepted into business school and your value of meaningful employment. Here is how a student might translate his goal of entering business school into action steps over a year's time:

- ▶ *This year.* Complete enough courses to meet curriculum requirements for business school and maintain class standing
- ▶ *This term.* Complete my economics class with a B average or higher
- ▶ *This month.* Set up economics study group schedule to coincide with quizzes and tests
- ▶ *This week.* Meet with study group; go over material for Friday's test
- ▶ *Today.* Go over Chapter 3 in econ text

The student can then arrange his time to move him in the direction of his goal. He schedules activities that support his short-term goal of doing well on the test and writes them in his planner. Achieving his overarching long-term goal of doing well in a course he needs for business school is the source of his motivation.

Before each week begins, remind yourself of your long-term goals and what you can accomplish over the next 7 days to move you closer to them. Additionally, every once in a while, take a hard look at your schedule to see whether you are spending time on what you most value. Key 2.3 shows parts of a daily schedule and a weekly schedule.

Make to-do lists and prioritize

Many people find it useful to create a daily or weekly *to-do list* and check off the items as they are completed. A to-do list can be useful on an especially busy day, during exam week, or at any other time that you anticipate being overloaded.

Making a list, however, is more than doing a "brain dump" of everything you have to do. You need to (**prioritize**) your list—code it, or organize it, according to how important each item is. Some people use numbers, some use letters (A, B, C), and some use different-colored pens or, for electronic planners, highlighting and font color tools. Prioritizing helps you focus the bulk of your energy and time on the most important tasks. Because many top-priority items (classes, work) occur at designated times, prioritizing helps you lock in these activities and schedule less urgent items around them.

Prioritizing isn't just for time management. You should also prioritize your long-term and short-term goals and the steps leading up to each. Keep these priorities alongside your daily lists so you can see how they influence one another. For instance, arriving at school a half hour early so you can meet with an advisor influences your long-term goal of deciding on a major.

Whether it's a task or goal you're scheduling, set basic priority levels according to the following guidelines.

- **Priority 1.** The most crucial items—you must do them. They may include attending class, working at a job, picking up a child from day care, and paying bills. Enter Priority 1 items in your planner first, before scheduling anything else.

- **Priority 2.** Important items but with flexibility in scheduling. Examples include library study time and working out. Schedule these around the Priority 1 items.

- **Priority 3.** Least important items—the "nice to do" activities. Examples include phoning a friend or upgrading software for your iPod.

Plan and track

As you work on the tasks in your to-do lists and planner, follow these guidelines to stay focused on your goals:

▶ *Plan regularly.* Set aside a regular time each day to plan your schedule (right before bed, with your morning coffee, on your commute to or from school, or whatever time and situation works best for you). This reduces stress and saves the hassle of forgetting something important.

▶ *Actively manage your schedule.* The most detailed planner won't do you a bit of good unless you look at it. Check your schedule at regular intervals throughout the day or week.

▶ *Use monthly and yearly calendars at home.* A standard monthly or yearly wall calendar is a great place to keep track of your major commitments. A wall calendar like the monthly calendar in Key 2.4 gives you the "big picture" overview you need.

▶ *Work to stay motivated.* If you can get a task done ahead of time, get it done; it will help you avoid pressure later. Focus on your growth mindset, reminding yourself that achievement requires persistent effort.

▶ *Avoid time traps.* Stay away from situations that eat up time. Learn to say no when you just can't fit in an extra responsibility. Reduce time spent with anything that distracts you, such as your cell phone, social networking sites, or Twitter account.

▶ *Schedule downtime.* It's easy to get so caught up in completing tasks that you forget to relax and breathe. Even a half hour of downtime a day will refresh you and improve your productivity when you get back on task.

PRIORITIZE
To arrange or deal with in order of importance.

MARCH

SUNDAY	MONDAY	TUESDAY	WEDNESDAY	THURSDAY	FRIDAY	SATURDAY
	1 WORK	2 Turn in English paper topic	3 Dentist 2 pm	4 WORK	5	6
7 Frank's birthday	8 Psych Test 9 am WORK	9	10 6:30 pm Meeting @ Acad Ctr	11 WORK	12	13 Dinner @ Ryan's
14	15 English paper due WORK	16 Western Civ paper	17	18 Library 6 pm WORK	19 Western Civ makeup class	20
21	22	23 2 pm meeting, psych group	24 Start running: 2 miles	25 WORK	26 Run 2 miles	27
28 Run 3 miles	29 WORK	30 Western Civ paper due	31 Run 2 miles			

Confront procrastination

It's human, and common for busy students, to leave difficult or undesirable tasks until later. If taken to the extreme, however, procrastination can develop into a habit that causes serious problems. For example, procrastinators who don't get things done in the workplace may prevent others from doing their work, possibly losing a promotion or even a job because of it.

This excerpt from the Study Skills Library at California Polytechnic State University at San Luis Obispo illustrates how procrastination can quickly turn into a destructive pattern.

> The procrastinator is often remarkably optimistic about his ability to complete a task on a tight deadline. . . . For example, he may estimate that a paper will take only five days to write; he has fifteen days; there is plenty of time, no need to start. Lulled by a false sense of security, time passes. At some point, he crosses over an imaginary starting time and suddenly realizes, "Oh no! I am not in control! There isn't enough time!"
>
> At this point, considerable effort is directed toward completing the task, and work progresses. This sudden spurt of energy is the source of the erroneous feeling that "I work well only under pressure." Actually, at this point you are making progress only because you haven't any choice. . . . Progress is being made, but you have lost your freedom.

PROCRASTINATION
The act of putting off a task until another time.

Conquer Your Time Traps

Different people get bogged down by different time traps. What are yours? They could be productive activities, like working out, or less productive activities, like checking your e-mail. Think of two common time traps that you encounter. For each, come up with two ways to say no graciously—to someone else, or even to yourself, as in the following example.

Time Trap: Text Messaging

Response 1: "I'll call you in an hour. I need to finish this paper."

Response 2: "I will respond to my text messages after I've read five pages."

Your turn:

Time Trap: _____

Response 1: _____

_____

Response 2: _____

_____

Time Trap:

Response 1: _____

_____

Response 2: _____

_____

Choose one of the situations you just named and use one or both of your responses the next time the trap threatens your time. Afterward, answer these questions:

How did the response affect your ability to take control of the situation? Did it help? Hurt? How?

_____

_____

_____

What did the response teach you about your personal time traps? Do you find yourself needing to be stricter with your time? Why?

_____

_____

_____

_____

Barely completed in time, the paper may actually earn a fairly good grade; whereupon the student experiences mixed feelings: pride of accomplishment (sort of), scorn for the professor who cannot recognize substandard work, and guilt for getting an undeserved grade. But the net result is *reinforcement:* The procrastinator is rewarded positively for his poor behavior ("Look what a decent grade I got after all!"). As a result, the counterproductive behavior is repeated time and time again.[3]

People procrastinate for various reasons.

■ ***Perfectionism.*** According to Jane B. Burka and Lenora M. Yuen, authors of *Procrastination: Why You Do It and What to Do About It,* habitual procrastinators often gauge their self-worth solely by their ability to achieve. In other words, "an outstanding performance means an outstanding person; a mediocre performance means a mediocre person."[4] To the perfectionist procrastinator, not trying at all is better than an attempt that falls short of perfection.

■ ***Fear of limitations.*** Some people procrastinate in order to avoid the truth about what they can achieve. "As long as you procrastinate, you never have to confront the real limits of your ability, whatever those limits are," say Burka and Yuen.[5] A fixed mindset naturally leads to procrastination. "I can't do it," the person with the fixed mindset thinks, "so what's the point of trying?"

■ ***Being unsure of the next step.*** If you get stuck and don't know what to do, sometimes it seems easier to procrastinate than to make the leap to the next level of your goal.

■ ***Facing an overwhelming task.*** Some big projects create fear, as Devonne feels about her group project. If a person facing such a task fears failure, she may procrastinate in order to avoid confronting the fear. Get into your growth mindset and use the strategies from Chapter 1 to work through this or any other kind of fear, taking steps forward and knowing that you stand to learn something valuable.

Although it can bring relief in the short term, avoiding tasks almost always causes problems, such as a buildup of responsibilities and less time to complete them, work that is not up to par, the disappointment of others who depend on your work, and stress brought on by unfinished tasks. Particular strategies can help you avoid procrastination and its associated problems.

▶ *Analyze the effects.* What may happen if you continue to put off a task? Chances are you will benefit more in the long term facing the task head-on.

▶ *Set reasonable goals.* Unreasonable goals intimidate and immobilize you. If you concentrate on achieving one small step at a time, the task becomes less burdensome.

▶ *Get started whether you "feel like it" or not.* Take the first step. Once you start, you may find it easier to continue.

▶ *Ask for help.* Once you identify what's holding you up, find someone to help you face the task. Another person may come up with an innovative method to get you moving again.

- *Don't expect perfection*. People learn by starting at the beginning, making mistakes, and learning from them. If you avoid mistakes, you deprive yourself of learning and growth.
- *Reward yourself*. Boost your confidence when you accomplish a task. Celebrate progress with a reward—a break, a movie, whatever feels like a treat to you.

Take a look at Key 2.5 to explore five major reasons that people waste time and procrastinate—and how to take control of each.

Be flexible

Change is a part of life. No matter how well you think ahead and plan your time, sudden changes—ranging from a room change for a class to a medical emergency—can upend your plans. However, you have some control over how you handle circumstances. Your ability to evaluate situations, come up with creative options, and put practical plans to work will help you manage changes.

Small changes—the need to work an hour overtime at your after-school job, a meeting that runs late—can result in priority shifts that jumble your schedule. For changes that occur frequently, think through a backup plan ahead of time. For surprises, the best you can do is to keep an open mind about possibilities and rely on your internal and external resources.

TAKE CONTROL OF TIME WASTERS

1. **Television**   It's easy to just keep flipping the channels when you know you've got something due. *Take Control:* Record favorite shows using a digital video recorder (DVR) or watch a movie instead. When your program of choice is over, turn the TV off.

2. **Commute**   Though not often something you can control, the time spent commuting from one place to another can be staggering. *Take Control:* Use your time on a bus or train to do homework, study, read assignments, or work on your monthly budget.

3. **Internet Browsing**   Currently, Internet misuse in the American workplace costs companies more than $178 billion per year in lost productivity. *Take Control:* If you use the Internet for research, consider subscribing to RSS feeds that can alert you when relevant information becomes available. When using the Internet for social or personal reasons, stick to a time limit.

4. **Fatigue**   Being tired can lead to below-quality work that may have to be redone and can make you feel ready to quit altogether. *Take Control:* Determine a stop time for yourself. When your stop time comes, put down the book, turn off the computer, and *go to bed.* During the day when you can, take naps to recharge your battery.

5. **Confusion**   When you don't fully understand an assignment or problem, you may spend unintended time trying to figure it out. *Take Control:* The number one way to fight confusion is to *ask.* As the saying goes, ask early and ask often. Students who seek help show that they want to learn.

When change involves serious problems—your car breaks down and you have no way to get to school, or you fail a class and have to consider summer school—use problem-solving skills to help you through (see Chapter 4). Resources available at your college can help you throughout this process. Your academic advisor, counselor, dean, financial aid advisor, and instructors may have ideas and assistance.

Manage stress by managing time

If you are feeling more (stress) in your everyday life as a student, you are not alone. Stress levels among college students have increased dramatically.[6] Stress factors for college students include adjusting to a new environment with increased work and difficult decisions as well as juggling school, work, and personal responsibilities.

> STRESS
> Physical or mental strain or tension produced in reaction to pressure.

Dealing with the stress of college life is, and will continue to be, one of your biggest challenges. But here's some good news: *Every time management strategy in this chapter contributes to your ability to cope with stress.* Remember that stress refers to how you react to pressure. When you create and follow a schedule that gets you places on time and helps you take care of tasks and responsibilities, you reduce pressure. Less pressure, less stress.

Analyze, and adjust if necessary, the relationship between stress and your time management habits. For example, if you're a night person with early classes and are consistently stressed about waking up in time, use strategies such as going to bed earlier a few nights a week, napping in the afternoon, exercising briefly before class to boost energy, or exploring how to schedule later classes next term. Reduce anxiety by thinking before you act.

The following practical strategies can help you cope with stress through time management. You will find more detail on stress in Chapter 9.

■ *Be realistic about time commitments.* For example, many students attempting to combine work and school find that they have to trim one or the other to reduce stress and promote success. Overloaded students often fall behind and experience high stress levels that can lead to dropping out. Determine what is reasonable for you; you may find that taking longer to graduate is a viable option if you need to work while in school.

■ *Put sleep into your schedule.* Sleep-deprived bodies and minds have a hard time functioning, and research reports that one-quarter of all college students are chronically sleep deprived.[7] Figure out how much sleep you need and do your best to get it. When you pull an all-nighter, make sure you play catch-up over the days that follow. With time for relaxation, your mind is better able to manage stress, and your schoolwork improves.

■ *Actively manage your schedule.* The most detailed datebook page can't help you unless you look at it. Get in the habit of checking at regular intervals throughout the day. Also, try not to put off tasks. If you can get it done ahead of time, get it done.

■ *Focus on one assignment at a time.* Stress is at its worst when you have five pressing assignments in five different classes all due in the next week. Focus on one at a time, completing it to the best of your ability as quickly as you can before moving to the next and the next until you're through.

■ *Check things off.* Each time you complete a task, check it off your to-do list, delete it from your electronic scheduler, or crumple up the sticky note. This physical action promotes the feeling of confidence that comes from getting something done.

Sometimes stress freezes you in place and blocks you from finding answers. At those times, remember that taking even a small step is a stress management strategy because it begins to move you ahead.

Case *Wrap-up*

What happened to Devonne? After agreeing to give the problems-of-the-world assignment a try, Devonne made it to the next meeting and listened to what her group had researched so far about the problem of worldwide water shortages. She realized that though her own problems felt overwhelming, the effects of the lack of water—food shortages, people in need who tap the resources of others, widespread pollution—could touch her life as well. She felt a little more committed to the project and to attending meetings. As a bonus, Devonne connected with a group member living nearby with her young son who also is home most mornings. She and Devonne discussed coming up with a schedule to trade off caring for the boys.

What does this mean for you? What is your take on the world's problems? Are you interested, or do you just pass right by that section of the news, perhaps because there is too much else on your mind? Explore the information about five large-scale issues at World's Biggest Problems (www.arlingtoninstitute.org/wbp/portal/home). Choose the one that interests you most and read the site's in-depth information about it. Write about your reaction: How do you think this problem touches—or could touch—your life directly? What can you do on a day-to-day scale that is manageable for you and might make a difference?

What effects go beyond your world? Project yourself 10 years into the future. You are using some of your best talents and passions working in a field that is somehow involved in improving this same world problem. What is your job, and what are you doing? What does this imaginary self and job tell you about the academic and personal goals you are pursuing now?

Successful Intelligence *Wrap-up*

HERE'S HOW YOU HAVE BUILT SKILLS IN **CHAPTER 2** :

ANALYTICAL THINKING	CREATIVE THINKING	PRACTICAL THINKING
› As you read the section on goals, you broke down the goal-setting process into parts.	› You considered how to create a personal time profile.	› You explored the practical action of pursuing goals step by step.
› In the Get Analytical exercise, you explored your values and connected them to your educational goals.	› In the Get Creative exercise, you thought of innovative ideas to move past your toughest obstacles.	› In the Get Practical exercise, you identified your time traps and then thought of ways to say "no" in different situations.
› You thought about how who you are as a time manager affects your scheduling and procrastination habits.	› Exploring flexibility in time management showed you the role of creativity in the face of change.	› At the end of the chapter, you gathered practical techniques for managing stress.

Word*for*Thought

The **Spanish** word *paseo* (pah-say'-oh) refers to a relaxed late afternoon walk outdoors.[8] The relaxed pace of traditional life in many European countries holds a lesson for the overscheduled, harried student. Relaxation is crucial for stress management. Define your version of the paseo and make it a part of your life.

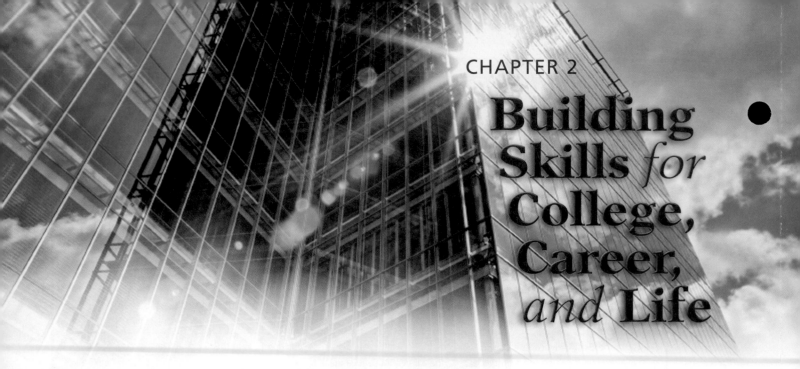

Building Skills *for* College, Career, *and* Life

Steps to Success

Discover How You Spend Your Time

BUILD BASIC SKILLS. Everyone has exactly 168 hours in a week. How do you spend yours? Start by making a guess, or estimate, about three particular activities. In a week, how much time do you spend on the following?

_____ hours   Studying

_____ hours   Sleeping

_____ hours   Interacting with media and technology (computer, online services, cell phone, texting, video games, television) for nonstudy purposes

Now, to find out the real story, record how you spend your time for 7 days. The chart on the next pages has blocks showing half hour increments. As you go through the week, write down what you do each hour, indicating starting and stopping times. Include sleep and leisure time. Record your *actual* activities instead of the activities you think you should be doing. There are no wrong answers.

After a week, add up how many hours you spent on each activity (round off to half hours—that is, mark 15 to 44 minutes of activity as a half hour and 45 to 75 minutes as one hour). Log the hours in the boxes of the table on page 53 using tally marks, with a full mark representing one hour and a half-size mark representing a half hour. In the third column, total the hours for each activity, and then add the totals in that column to make sure that your grand total is approximately 168 hours (if it isn't, go back and check your grid and calculations and fix any errors you find). Leave the "Ideal Time in Hours" column blank for now.

TAKE IT TO THE NEXT LEVEL. Take a look at your results, paying special attention to how your estimates of sleep, study, and technology time compare to your actual logged activity hours for the week. Use a separate sheet of paper or electronic file to answer the following questions:

- What surprises you about how you spend your time?
- Do you spend the most time on the activities representing your most important values—or not?
- Where do you waste the most time? What do you think that is costing you?
- On which activities do you think you should spend *more* time? On which should you spend *less* time?

TIME	MONDAY activity	TUESDAY activity	WEDNESDAY activity	THURSDAY activity
6:00 A.M.				
6:30 A.M.				
7:00 A.M.				
7:30 A.M.				
8:00 A.M.				
8:30 A.M.				
9:00 A.M.				
9:30 A.M.				
10:00 A.M.				
10:30 A.M.				
11:00 A.M.				
11:30 A.M.				
12:00 P.M.				
12:30 P.M.				
1:00 P.M.				
1:30 P.M.				
2:00 P.M.				
2:30 P.M.				
3:00 P.M.				
3:30 P.M.				
4:00 P.M.				
4:30 P.M.				
5:00 P.M.				
5:30 P.M.				
6:00 P.M.				
6:30 P.M.				
7:00 P.M.				
7:30 P.M.				
8:00 P.M.				
8:30 P.M.				
9:00 P.M.				
9:30 P.M.				
10:00 P.M.				
10:30 P.M.				
11:00 P.M.				
11:30 P.M.				
12:00 A.M.				
12:30 A.M.				
1:00 A.M.				
1:30 A.M.				
2:00 A.M.				

TIME	FRIDAY activity	SATURDAY activity	SUNDAY activity
6:00 A.M.			
6:30 A.M.			
7:00 A.M.			
7:30 A.M.			
8:00 A.M.			
8:30 A.M.			
9:00 A.M.			
9:30 A.M.			
10:00 A.M.			
10:30 A.M.			
11:00 A.M.			
11:30 A.M.			
12:00 P.M.			
12:30 P.M.			
1:00 P.M.			
1:30 P.M.			
2:00 P.M.			
2:30 P.M.			
3:00 P.M.			
3:30 P.M.			
4:00 P.M.			
4:30 P.M.			
5:00 P.M.			
5:30 P.M.			
6:00 P.M.			
6:30 P.M.			
7:00 P.M.			
7:30 P.M.			
8:00 P.M.			
8:30 P.M.			
9:00 P.M.			
9:30 P.M.			
10:00 P.M.			
10:30 P.M.			
11:00 P.M.			
11:30 P.M.			
12:00 A.M.			
12:30 A.M.			
1:00 A.M.			
1:30 A.M.			
2:00 A.M.			

Activity	Time Tallied Over One-Week Period	Total Time in Hours	Ideal Time in Hours
Example: Class	ꞱꞱꞱꞱ ꞱꞱꞱꞱ ꞱꞱꞱꞱ ꞱꞱ	16.5	
Class			
Work			
Studying			
Sleeping			
Eating			
Family time/child care			
Commuting/traveling			
Chores and personal business			
Friends and important relationships			
Telephone time			
Leisure/entertainment			
Spiritual life			
Other			

MOVE TOWARD MASTERY. Go back to the chart above and fill in the "Ideal Time in Hours" column. Consider the difference between actual hours and ideal hours. What changes are you willing to make to get closer to how you want to be spending your time? Write a short paragraph describing, in detail, two time management changes you plan to make this term so that you are focusing your time more effectively on your most important goals and values.

Teamwork

Create Solutions Together

SET A SMART GOAL

Goal: To utilize the SMART goal-setting system as a group.

Time on task: 20 minutes

Instructions: As a group, brainstorm important academic goals that can be accomplished within one year at school. Write your ideas on a piece of paper. From that list, pick out one goal to explore together.

Each group member takes 2 minutes alone to think about this goal in terms of the second goal achievement step on page 37—defining a *specific* strategy. In other words, answer the question: "How would I do it?" Each person writes down all of the paths they can think of.

The group then gathers for everyone to share strategies. The group evaluates strategies and chooses one that seems *achievable* and *realistic*. Finally, as a group, brainstorm the rest of the goal achievement process, based on the chosen strategy or path:

- *Set a timetable.* When do you plan to reach your goal? Discuss different *time frames* and how each might change the path.
- *Be accountable.* What safeguards will keep you on track? Talk about different ways to *measure* your progress.
- *Get unstuck.* What will you do if you hit a roadblock? Brainstorm the roadblocks that could get in the way of this particular goal. For each, come up with ways to overcome the obstacle.

At the end of the process, you should have a wealth of ideas for how to approach one particular academic goal—and an appreciation for how many paths you could take in order to get there.

Writing

Build Intrapersonal and Communication Skills

Record your thoughts on a separate piece of paper, in a journal, or electronically.

EMOTIONAL INTELLIGENCE JOURNAL

How you feel about your time management. Paying attention to your feelings about how you spend time can be a key step toward making time management choices that are more in line with your values. Think, and then write, about how your most time-demanding activities make you feel. What makes you happiest, most fulfilled, or most satisfied? What makes you most anxious, frustrated, or drained? What do these feelings tell you about your day-to-day choices? Describe how you could adjust your mindset, or make different choices, to feel better about how you spend your time.

REAL-LIFE WRITING

Examine two areas of academic specialty. Use your course catalog to identify two academic areas that look interesting. Write a short report comparing and contrasting the majors or concentrations in these areas, being sure to note GPA requirements, number of courses, relevance to career areas, campus locations, "feel" of the department offices, other requirements, and any other relevant characteristics. Conclude your report with observations about how this comparison and evaluation process has refined your thinking.

Personal Portfolio

Prepare for Career Success

EXPLORE CAREER GOALS THROUGH PERSONAL MISSION

21st Century Learning Building Blocks

- Initiative and Self-Direction
- Creativity and Innovation
- Productivity and Accountability

Complete the following in your electronic portfolio or separately on paper.

No matter what employment goals you ultimately pursue, a successful career will be grounded in your personal mission in one or more ways.

First, write a draft of your personal mission. Refer to the list on page 33 to remind yourself of the elements of a personal mission statement. Use these questions to get you thinking:

1. You are at your retirement dinner. You have had an esteemed career in your chosen field. Your best friend stands up and talks about the five aspects of your character that have taken you to the top. What do you think they are?
2. You are preparing for a late-in-life job change. Updating your resumé, you need to list your contributions and achievements. What would you like them to be?
3. You have been told that you have 1 year to live. With family or close friends, you talk about the values that mean the most to you. Based on that discussion, how do you want to spend your time in this last year? Which choices will reflect what is most important to you?

After you have a personal mission statement to provide vision and motivation, take some time to think more specifically about your working life. Spend 15 minutes brainstorming everything that you wish you could be, do, have, or experience in your career 10 years from now—the skills you want to have, money you want to earn, benefits, experiences, travel, anything you can think of. List your wishes, draw them, depict them using cutouts from magazines, or combine ideas—whatever you like best.

Now, group your wishes in order of priority. On paper or computer pages labeled Priority 1, Priority 2, and Priority 3, write each wish where it fits, with Priority 1 being the most important, Priority 2 the second most important, and Priority 3 the third.

Look at your priority lists. What do they tell you about what is most important to you? What fits into your personal mission, and what doesn't? Circle or highlight three high-priority wishes that mesh with your personal mission. For each, write down one action step you may have to take soon to make it come true.

You may want to look back at these materials at the end of the term to see what changes may have taken place in your priorities.

Social Networking

IDENTIFY YOURSELF

Sign in to your LinkedIn account and begin to build your profile. Click on "Edit My Profile" and then click on the Edit mark next to your name. Then fill in or edit this basic information:

- First and last name
- Display name (how you want it to appear to others viewing your profile)
- Professional "Headline"—how you identify yourself now (If you are not currently working, you may choose to identify yourself as a student and perhaps include your area of study.)
- Country and zip code
- Industry (if you are working)

chapter 3

Learning How You Learn

Making the Most of Your Abilities

What Would You Do?

Think about this problem as you read, and consider how you would approach it. This chapter focuses on self-assessments to help you explore your learning strengths and challenges and how you interact with people. With this information you can make practical decisions about work and study.

As a college student, author Joyce Bishop was confused by her spotty record—doing well in some classes but feeling totally lost in others, especially those that were lecture based. She couldn't make sense of what she was hearing when she wasn't familiar with the information. If she read the material ahead of time, she could make visual pictures in her mind and look up concepts. This helped, but there wasn't often time for it.

Joyce also had trouble in small classes, because she heard voices around her as much as she heard the instructor. She would borrow classmates' notes in exchange for typing their term papers. The notes and the typing helped her to retain information. Ultimately, finding that science classes were somewhat less difficult than others, she majored in biology and managed to graduate.

Twelve years later, pursuing a master's in public health, Joyce was having trouble reading and her eye doctor was concerned about the stress it put on her eyes. He sent her to a center that usually tests small children for learning disabilities. The therapist who tested her determined that Joyce processed language on a fourth-grade level, a condition that had not changed in her adult life. Guessing that she had not made it past the tenth grade, the therapist was shocked to hear that she was completing her master's degree. Joyce was beginning to understand what was behind so many years of mediocre grades and an intense struggle to learn. (To be continued . . .)

You don't have to have a learning disability to face learning challenges. For Joyce, doing adventure sports like riding ATVs is a way to grow from taking a risk, just as she did when working through her disability. You'll learn more about Joyce, and revisit her situation, within the chapter.

In this chapter, you'll explore answers to these questions:

ANALYTICAL

CREATIVE

PRACTICAL

For each statement, circle the number that feels right to you,
from 1 for "not at all true for me" to 5 for "very true for me."

▶ I believe I can develop my skills and abilities through self-knowledge and hard work.	1 2 3 4 5
▶ I have a pretty clear idea of my strengths and abilities.	1 2 3 4 5
▶ I understand which subjects and situations make it more difficult for me to succeed.	1 2 3 4 5
▶ In my work in the classroom and out, I try to maximize what I do well.	1 2 3 4 5
▶ I recognize that being comfortable with the subject matter isn't necessarily enough to succeed in a course.	1 2 3 4 5
▶ I assess an instructor's teaching style and make adjustments so that I can learn effectively.	1 2 3 4 5
▶ I choose study techniques that tap into how I learn best.	1 2 3 4 5
▶ I try to use technology that works well with how I learn.	1 2 3 4 5
▶ I've taken a skills and/or interests inventory to help find a major or career area that suits me.	1 2 3 4 5
▶ I understand what a learning disability is and am aware of several different types of disabilities.	1 2 3 4 5

Each of the topics in these statements is covered in this chapter. Note those statements for which you circled a 3 or lower. Skim the chapter to see where those topics appear, and pay special attention to them as you read, learn, and apply new strategies.

REMEMBER: *No matter how well know yourself as a learner, you can improve with effort and practice.*

"Successfully intelligent people figure out their strengths and their weaknesses, and then find ways to capitalize on their strengths—make the most of what they do well—and to correct for or remedy their weaknesses—find ways around what they don't do well, or make themselves good enough to get by."

—Robert Sternberg

LEARNING STYLE
A particular way in which the mind receives and processes information.

Why explore who **you are as a learner?**

Have you thought about how you learn? Now, as you begin college, is the perfect time for thinking about how you learn, think, and function in the world. Thinking about thinking is known as *metacognition* (something you are building with each chapter-opening self-assessment). Building metacognition and self-knowledge will help you become a better student and decision maker because the more you know about yourself, the more effectively you can analyze courses, study environments, and study partners; self-knowledge can also help you come up with ideas as well as make practical choices about what, how, and where to study.

Use assessments to learn about yourself

Every person is born with a unique **learning style** and particular levels of ability and potential in different areas. This combines with effort and environment to create a "recipe" for what you can achieve. Part of that recipe is the way you perceive your strengths and challenges, which comes from many different sources and starts in childhood. Maybe your mother thinks you are "the funny one" or "the quiet one." A grade school teacher may have called you a "thinker" or "slacker," "go-getter" or "shy." These labels—from yourself and others—influence your ability to set and achieve goals.

The danger in accepting a label as truth, as Sternberg did as a child (see Chapter 1), is that it can put you in a fixed mindset and limit your potential. You are not simply stuck with what you've been given. As you read in the first chapter, brain studies show that humans of any age are able to build new neuropathways and thereby learn new ideas and skills, supporting theories that intelligence can grow over time if you work to keep learning.

Picture a bag of rubber bands of different sizes. Some are thick, and some are thin; some are long, and some are short—*but all of them can stretch*. A small rubber band, stretched out, can reach the length of a larger one that lies unstretched. In other words, with effort and focus, you can grow whatever raw material you have at the start, perhaps beyond the natural gifts of someone not making any effort. Joyce's story illustrates just how far effort can stretch a person's natural abilities.

Ask yourself: Who am I right now? Where could I be, and where would I like to be, in 5 years? Assessments focused on how you learn and interact with others can help you start to answer these big questions. Assessments have a different goal than tests. Whereas a test seeks to identify a level of performance, an assessment, as professor and psychologist Howard Gardner puts it, is "the obtaining of information about a person's skills and **potentials**. . . providing useful feedback to the person."[1] You can think of an assessment as an exploration that, if honest, will reliably produce interesting and helpful information.

→ POTENTIALS
Abilities that may be developed.

The assessments you will take in this chapter provide the questions that get you thinking actively about your strengths and challenges. (Learning disabilities—diagnosed, specific issues different from the learning challenges that all students face—are discussed at the end of the chapter.) As you search for answers, you will be gathering important information about yourself. With this information, you will be able to define your rubber band and get ready to stretch it to its limit.

Use assessments to make choices and to grow

There is much about yourself, your surroundings, and your experiences that you cannot control. However, self-knowledge gives you tools to choose how you respond to circumstances. Although you cannot control the courses you are required to take or how your instructors teach, for example, you can manage how you respond in each situation.

The two assessments in this chapter—Multiple Pathways to Learning and the Personality Spectrum—will give you greater insight into your strengths and weaknesses. The material after the assessments will help you think practically about how to maximize what you do well and compensate for challenging areas by making specific choices about what you do in class, during study time, and in the workplace.

Understanding yourself as a learner will also help you choose how to respond to others in a group situation. In a study group, classroom, or workplace, each person takes in material in a unique way. You can use what you know about how others learn to improve communication and teamwork.

Remember: An assessment is simply a snapshot of where you are at a given moment. There are no "right" answers, no "best" scores. And because many educators are aware of research that shows the benefit from learning in a variety of ways—kind of like cross-training for the brain—they will often challenge you to learn in ways that aren't as comfortable for you.

As you complete this chapter's assessments, compare the experience to trying on new glasses to correct blurred vision. The glasses will not create new paths and possibilities, but they will enable you to see more clearly the ones in front of you. Furthermore, as you gain experience, build skills, and learn more, your learning patterns are apt to change over time. You may want to take the assessments again in the future to see whether your results are different.

What tools can help you assess how you learn and interact with others?

Many different tools can help you become more aware of how you think, process information, and relate to others. Some focus on learning preferences, some on areas of potential, and some on personality type. This chapter examines two assessments in depth. The first—Multiple Pathways to Learning—is a learning preferences assessment focusing on eight areas of potential, based on Howard Gardner's multiple intelligences (or MI) theory. The second—the Personality Spectrum—is a personality-type assessment based on the Myers-Briggs Type Indicator and helps you evaluate how you react to people and situations.

Following each assessment is information about the typical traits of each (intelligence) or personality spectrum dimension. As you will see from your scores, you have abilities in all areas, though some are more developed than others.

INTELLIGENCE
As defined by H. Gardner, an ability to solve problems or create products that are of value in a culture.

Assess your multiple intelligences with Pathways to Learning

In 1983, Howard Gardner changed the way people perceive intelligence and learning with his theory of multiple intelligences. Like Robert Sternberg, Gardner had developed the belief that the traditional view of intelligence—based on mathematical, logical, and verbal measurements comprising an intelligence quotient, or IQ—did not comprehensively reflect the spectrum of human ability. Whereas Sternberg focused on the spectrum of actions that help people achieve important goals, Gardner honed in on the idea that humans possess a number of different areas of natural ability and potential.

The theory of multiple intelligences

Gardner's research led him to believe that there are eight unique "intelligences," or areas of ability. These include the aptitudes traditionally associated with the term *intelligence*—logic and verbal skills—but go beyond, to encompass a wide range of potentials of the human brain.[2] These intelligences almost never function in isolation. You will almost always use several at a time for any significant role or task.[3]

Look at Key 3.1 for a description of each intelligence along with examples of people who have unusually high levels of ability in each intelligence. Although few people will have the verbal-linguistic intelligence of William Shakespeare

Students drawn to the sciences may find that they have strengths in logical-mathematical or naturalistic thinking.
© iStockPhoto

EACH INTELLIGENCE IS LINKED TO
SPECIFIC ABILITIES

INTELLIGENCE		DESCRIPTION	HIGH-ACHIEVING EXAMPLES
Verbal-Linguistic		Ability to communicate through language; listening, reading, writing, speaking	• Author J. K. Rowling • Orator and President Barack Obama
Logical-Mathematical		Ability to understand logical reasoning and problem solving; math, science, patterns, sequences	• Physicist Stephen Hawking • Mathematician Svetlana Jitomirskaya
Bodily-Kinesthetic		Ability to use the physical body skillfully and to take in knowledge through bodily sensation; coordination, working with hands	• Gymnast Nastia Liukin • Survivalist Bear Grylls
Visual-Spatial		Ability to understand spatial relationships and to perceive and create images; visual art, graphic design, charts and maps	• Artist Walt Disney • Designer Stella McCartney
Interpersonal		Ability to relate to others, noticing their moods, motivations, and feelings; social activity, cooperative learning, teamwork	• Media personality Ellen DeGeneres • Former Secretary of State Colin Powell
Intrapersonal		Ability to understand one's own behavior and feelings; self-awareness, independence, time spent alone	• Animal researcher Jane Goodall • Philosopher Friedrich Nietszche
Musical		Ability to comprehend and create meaningful sound; sensitivity to music and musical patterns	• Singer and musician Alicia Keys • Composer Andrew Lloyd Webber
Naturalist		Ability to identify, distinguish, categorize, and classify species or items, often incorporating high interest in elements of the natural environment	• Social activist Wangari Maathai • Bird cataloger John James Audubon

or the interpersonal intelligence of Oprah Winfrey, everyone has some level of ability in each intelligence. Your goal is to identify what your levels are and to work your strongest intelligences to your advantage.

Different cultures value different abilities and therefore place a premium on different intelligences. In Tibet, mountain dwellers prize the bodily-kinesthetic ability of a top-notch Himalayan guide. In Detroit, auto makers appreciate the visual-spatial talents of a master car designer.

Your own eight intelligences

Gardner believes that all people possess some capacity in each of the eight intelligences and that every person has developed some intelligences more fully than others. When you find a task or subject easy, you are probably using a more fully developed intelligence. When you have trouble, you may be using a less developed intelligence.[4]

Furthermore, Gardner believes your levels of development in the eight intelligences can grow or recede throughout your life, depending on your efforts and experiences. Although you will not become a world-class pianist if you have limited musical ability, for example, you still can grow what you have with focus and work. Conversely, even a highly talented musician will lose ability without practice. This reflects how the brain grows with learning and becomes sluggish without it.

A related self-assessment that you may have heard of, or have already taken, is the VAK or VARK questionnaire. VAK/VARK assesses learning preferences in three (or four) areas: visual, auditory, (read/write), and kinesthetic. The multiple intelligences (MI) assessment is this book's choice because it incorporates and expands on the elements of VAK/VARK, giving you a more comprehensive picture of your abilities. For further information about VAK/VARK, go to www.vark-learn.com or search online using the keywords "VAK assessment."

A note about auditory learners who learn and remember best through listening: Auditory learning is part of two MI dimensions: *verbal intelligence* (hearing words) and *musical intelligence* (associating information with sounds and rhythms). If you tend to absorb information better through listening, try study suggestions for these two intelligences. Podcasts are especially helpful to auditory learners, and an increasing number of instructors are converting their lectures into digital format for downloading.

Use the Multiple Pathways to Learning assessment to determine where you are right now in the eight intelligence areas. Then look at Key 3.2 immediately following the assessment to identify specific skills associated with each area. Finally, the Multiple Intelligence Strategies grids in Chapters 5 through 11 will help you apply your learning styles knowledge to key college success skills and to specific areas of study.

Assess your style of interaction with the Personality Spectrum

Personality assessments help you understand how you respond to the world around you, including people, work, and school. They also can help guide you as you explore majors and careers.

The concept of dividing human beings into four basic personality types, as in the Personality Spectrum, goes as far back as Aristotle

MULTIPLE PATHWAYS TO LEARNING

Each intelligence has a set of numbered statements. Consider each statement on its own. Then, on a scale from 1 (lowest) to 4 (highest), rate how closely it matches who you are right now and write that number on the line next to the statement. Finally, total each set of six questions. Enter your scores in the grid on page 64.

1. rarely   2. sometimes   3. usually   4. always

1. ____ I enjoy physical activities.
2. ____ I am uncomfortable sitting still.
3. ____ I prefer to learn through doing.
4. ____ When sitting I move my legs or hands.
5. ____ I enjoy working with my hands.
6. ____ I like to pace when I'm thinking or studying.

____ **TOTAL for BODILY-KINESTHETIC**

1. ____ I enjoy telling stories.
2. ____ I like to write.
3. ____ I like to read.
4. ____ I express myself clearly.
5. ____ I am good at negotiating.
6. ____ I like to discuss topics that interest me.

____ **TOTAL for VERBAL-LINGUISTIC**

1. ____ I use maps easily.
2. ____ I draw pictures/diagrams when explaining ideas.
3. ____ I can assemble items easily from diagrams.
4. ____ I enjoy drawing or photography.
5. ____ I do not like to read long paragraphs.
6. ____ I prefer a drawn map over written directions.

____ **TOTAL for VISUAL-SPATIAL**

1. ____ I like math in school.
2. ____ I like science.
3. ____ I problem-solve well.
4. ____ I question how things work.
5. ____ I enjoy planning or designing something new.
6. ____ I am able to fix things.

____ **TOTAL for LOGICAL–MATHEMATICAL**

1. ____ I listen to music.
2. ____ I move my fingers or feet when I hear music.
3. ____ I have good rhythm.
4. ____ I like to sing along with music.
5. ____ People have said I have musical talent.
6. ____ I like to express my ideas through music.

____ **TOTAL for MUSICAL**

1. ____ I need quiet time to think.
2. ____ I think about issues before I want to talk.
3. ____ I am interested in self-improvement.
4. ____ I understand my thoughts and feelings.
5. ____ I know what I want out of life.
6. ____ I prefer to work on projects alone.

____ **TOTAL for INTRAPERSONAL**

1. ____ I like doing a project with other people.
2. ____ People come to me to help settle conflicts.
3. ____ I like to spend time with friends.
4. ____ I am good at understanding people.
5. ____ I am good at making people feel comfortable.
6. ____ I enjoy helping others.

____ **TOTAL for INTERPERSONAL**

1. ____ I like to think about how things, ideas, or people fit into categories.
2. ____ I enjoy studying plants, animals, or oceans.
3. ____ I tend to see how things relate to, or are distinct from, one another.
4. ____ I think about having a career in the natural sciences.
5. ____ As a child I often played with bugs and leaves.
6. ____ I like to investigate the natural world around me.

____ **TOTAL for NATURALISTIC**

Source: Developed by Joyce Bishop, PhD, Golden West College, Huntington Beach, CA. Based on Howard Gardner, *Frames of Mind: The Theory of Multiple Intelligences,* New York: Harper Collins, 1993.

SCORING GRID FOR MULTIPLE PATHWAYS TO LEARNING

For each intelligence, shade the box in the row that corresponds with the range where your score falls. For example, if you scored 17 in bodily-kinesthetic intelligence, you would shade the middle box in that row; if you scored a 13 in visual-spatial, you would shade the last box in that row. When you have shaded one box for each row, you will see a "map" of your range of development at a glance.

A score of 20–24 indicates a high level of development in that particular type of intelligence, 14–19 a moderate level, and below 14 an underdeveloped intelligence.

	20–24 (HIGHLY DEVELOPED)	14–19 (MODERATELY DEVELOPED)	BELOW 14 (UNDERDEVELOPED)
Bodily-Kinesthetic			
Visual-Spatial			
Verbal-Linguistic			
Logical-Mathematical			
Musical			
Interpersonal			
Intrapersonal			
Naturalistic			

and Hippocrates, ancient Greek philosophers. Modern psychologist Carl Jung focused on personality **typology,** defining the following parameters:[5]

TYPOLOGY
A systematic classification or study of types.

▶ *An individual's preferred "world."* Jung said that *extroverts* tend to prefer the outside world of people and activities, whereas *introverts* tend to prefer the inner world of thoughts, feelings, and fantasies.

▶ *Different ways of dealing with the world, or "functions."* Jung defined four distinct interaction dimensions, which are used to different degrees: *sensing* (learning through what your senses take in), *thinking* (evaluating information rationally), *intuiting* (learning through an instinct that comes from many integrated sources of information), and *feeling* (evaluating information through emotional response).

Katharine Briggs and her daughter, Isabel Briggs Myers, developed an assessment based on Jung's typology, called the Myers-Briggs Type Inventory or MBTI (www.myersbriggs.org). One of the most widely used personality inventories in the world, it creates sixteen possible types. David Keirsey and Marilyn Bates later condensed the MBTI types into four temperaments, creating the Keirsey Sorter (found at www.keirsey.com).

When author Joyce Bishop developed the Personality Spectrum assessment in this chapter, she adapted and simplified the Keirsey Sorter and MBTI material into four personality types—Thinker, Organizer, Giver, and Adventurer. Like the assessments on which it is based, the Personality Spectrum helps you identify the kinds of interactions that are most, and least, comfortable for you. As with the multiple intelligences, these results may change over time as you experience new things, change, and continue to learn. Key 3.3, on page 68, shows skills characteristic of each personality type.

Activity (individual): After students take the Personality Spectrum Assessment, have them identify one weakness and one strength. Then ask how this action can help them achieve academic, career, and life success. *(Time: about 7–10 minutes)*

Social Media: Have students post results from both assessments on their Facebook profiles. With a classmate whose strength is one of their weaknesses, have them brainstorm how to improve the weakness.

Resource Link: Read the vignette under "Convince Yourself" in Ch. 3 of the Instructor's Manual and discuss it with the class.

PARTICULAR **ABILITIES AND SKILLS** ARE ASSOCIATED WITH EACH INTELLIGENCE

Verbal-Linguistic		• Remembering terms easily • Mastering a foreign language • Using writing or speech to convince someone to do or believe something
Musical		• Sensing tonal qualities • Being sensitive to sounds and rhythms in music and in spoken language • Using an understanding of musical patterns to hear music
Logical-Mathematical		• Recognizing abstract patterns • Using facts to support an idea and generating ideas based on evidence • Reasoning scientifically (formulating and testing a hypothesis)
Visual-Spatial		• Recognizing relationships between objects • Representing something graphically • Manipulating images
Bodily-Kinesthetic		• Strong mind–body connection • Controlling and coordinating body movement • Using the body to create products or express emotion
Intrapersonal		• Accessing one's internal emotions • Understanding feelings and using them to guide behavior • Understanding self in relation to others
Interpersonal		• Seeing things from others' perspectives • Noticing moods, intentions, and temperaments of others • Gauging the most effective way to work with individual group members
Naturalistic		• Ability to categorize something as a member of a group or species • Understanding of relationships among natural organisms • Deep comfort with, and respect for, the natural world

PERSONALITY SPECTRUM

STEP 1 Rank-order all four responses to each question from most like you (4) to least like you (1) so that for each question you use the numbers 1, 2, 3, and 4 one time each. Place numbers in the boxes next to the responses.

4. most like me   **3. more like me**   **2. less like me**   **1. least like me**

1. I like instructors who

   a. ____ tell me exactly what is expected of me.

   b. ____ make learning active and exciting.

   c. ____ maintain a safe and supportive classroom.

   d. ____ challenge me to think at higher levels.

2. I learn best when the material is

   a. ____ well organized.

   b. ____ something I can do hands-on.

   c. ____ about understanding and improving the human condition.

   d. ____ intellectually challenging.

3. A high priority in my life is to

   a. ____ keep my commitments.

   b. ____ experience as much of life as possible.

   c. ____ make a difference in the lives of others.

   d. ____ understand how things work.

4. Other people think of me as

   a. ____ dependable and loyal.

   b. ____ dynamic and creative.

   c. ____ caring and honest.

   d. ____ intelligent and inventive.

5. When I experience stress I would most likely

   a. ____ do something to help me feel more in control of my life.

   b. ____ do something physical and daring.

   c. ____ talk with a friend.

   d. ____ go off by myself and think about my situation.

6. I would probably not be close friends with someone who is

   a. ____ irresponsible.

   b. ____ unwilling to try new things.

   c. ____ selfish and unkind to others.

   d. ____ an illogical thinker.

7. My vacations could be described as

   a. ____ traditional.

   b. ____ adventuresome.

   c. ____ pleasing to others.

   d. ____ a new learning experience.

8. One word that best describes me is

   a. ____ sensible.

   b. ____ spontaneous.

   c. ____ giving.

   d. ____ analytical.

STEP 2 Add up the total points for each letter.

TOTAL FOR   a. ____ Organizer   b. ____ Adventurer   c. ____ Giver   d. ____ Thinker

STEP 3 Plot these numbers on the brain diagram on page 67.

SCORING DIAGRAM FOR PERSONALITY SPECTRUM

Write your scores from page 66 in the four squares just outside the brain diagram—Thinker score at top left, Giver score at top right, Organizer score at bottom left, and Adventurer score at bottom right.

Each square has a line of numbers that go from the square to the center of the diagram. For each of your four scores, place a dot on the appropriate number in the line near that square. For example, if you scored 15 in the Giver spectrum, you would place a dot between the 14 and 16 in the upper right-hand line of numbers. If you scored a 26 in the Organizer spectrum, you would place a dot on the 26 in the lower left-hand line of numbers.

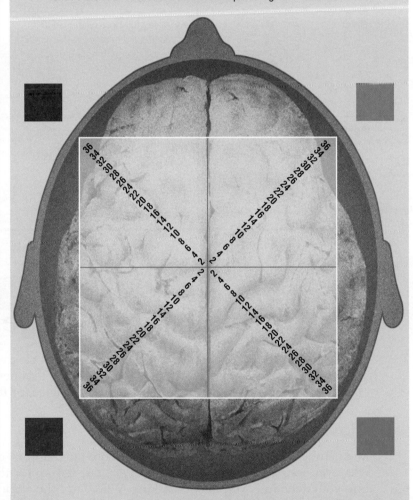

Connect the four dots to make a four-sided shape. If you like, shade the four sections inside the shape using four different colors.

THINKER

Technical
Scientific
Mathematical
Dispassionate
Rational
Analytical
Logical
Problem Solving
Theoretical
Intellectual
Objective
Quantitative
Explicit
Realistic
Literal
Precise
Formal

ORGANIZER

Tactical
Planning
Detailed
Practical
Confident
Predictable
Controlled
Dependable
Systematic
Sequential
Structured
Administrative
Procedural
Organized
Conservative
Safekeeping
Disciplined

GIVER

Interpersonal
Emotional
Caring
Sociable
Giving
Spiritual
Musical
Romantic
Feeling
Peacemaker
Trusting
Adaptable
Passionate
Harmonious
Idealistic
Talkative
Honest

ADVENTURER

Active
Visual
Risking
Original
Artistic
Spatial
Skillful
Impulsive
Metaphoric
Experimental
Divergent
Fast-paced
Simultaneous
Competitive
Imaginative
Open-minded
Adventuresome

For the Personality Spectrum,
26–36 indicates a strong tendency in that dimension,
14–25 a moderate tendency,
and below 14 a minimal tendency.

Source for brain diagram: Understanding Psychology, 3rd ed., by Charles G. Morris, © 1996. Reproduced by permission of Pearson Education, Inc./Prentice Hall, Inc.

PARTICULAR ABILITIES AND SKILLS ARE ASSOCIATED WITH EACH **PERSONALITY SPECTRUM** DIMENSION

Thinker

- Solving problems
- Developing models and systems
- Analytical and abstract thinking

Organizer

- Responsibility, reliability
- Neatness, organization, attention to detail
- Comprehensive follow-through on tasks

Giver

- Successful, close relationships
- Making a difference in the world
- Negotiation; promoting peace

Adventurer

- Courage and daring
- Hands-on problem solving
- Active and spontaneous style

How can you use your self-knowledge?

In completing the assessments, you have developed a clearer picture of who you are and how you interact with others. Now, use this new picture to choose effective strategies for class, study time, the workplace, or technology.

Classroom choices

Most students have to complete a set of "core curriculum" courses, as well as whatever courses their majors require. As you sign up for the sections that fit into your schedule, you may be asking, Where are the choices in this situation?

The opportunity for choice lies in how you interact with your instructor and function in the classroom. It is impossible for instructors to tailor classroom presentation to 15, 40, or 300 unique learners. As a result, you may find yourself in a great situation with one teacher and in a mismatch with another. Sometimes, the way the class is structured can have more of an effect on your success than the subject matter.

After several class meetings, you should be able to assess each instructor's dominant teaching styles (see Key 3.4) and figure out how to maximize your

INSTRUCTORS OFTEN PREFER
ONE OR MORE **TEACHING STYLES**

TEACHING STYLE	WHAT TO EXPECT IN CLASS
Lecture, verbal focus	Instructor speaks to the class for the entire period, with little class interaction. Lesson is taught primarily through words, either spoken or written on the board, on PowerPoints, handouts, or text.
Lecture with group discussion	Instructor presents material but encourages class discussion.
Small groups	Instructor presents material and then breaks class into small groups for discussion or project work.
Visual focus	Instructor uses visual elements such as PowerPoint slides, diagrams, photographs, drawings, transparencies, and videos.
Logical presentation	Instructor organizes material in a logical sequence, such as by steps, time, or importance.
Random presentation	Instructor tackles topics in no particular order and may jump around a lot or digress.
Conceptual presentation	Instructor spends the majority of time on the big picture, focusing on abstract concepts and umbrella ideas.
Detailed presentation	Instructor spends the majority of time, after introducing ideas, on the details and facts that underlie them.
Hands-on presentation	Instructor uses demonstrations, experiments, props, and class activities to show key points.

learning. As with learning styles, most instructors will demonstrate some combination of styles.

Although styles vary and instructors may combine styles, the word-focused lecture is still most common. For this reason, the traditional college classroom is generally a happy home for the verbal or logical learner and the Thinker and the Organizer. However, many students need to experience other modes in order to learn effectively. What can you do when your preferences don't match up with how your instructor teaches? Here are three suggestions:

▶ *Play to your strengths.* For example, a musical learner whose instructor delivers material in a random way might record lecture highlights digitally and listen to them on an MP3 player (be sure to see whether your instructor and school permit recording). Likewise, if you are a Giver with an instructor who delivers straight lectures, you should consider setting up a study group to go over details and fill in factual gaps.

▶ *Work to strengthen weaker areas.* A visual learner reviewing notes from a structured lecture could use logical-mathematical strategies such as

Add a new dimension to your experience of a course, and your learning, by talking to your instructor outside of class time.
© ThinkStock

Androuw Carrasco

University of Arizona, Tucson

About me:

I went to college right out of a high school from Tucson, Arizona. I lived at home for my first year of college while working two jobs and making the 11-mile, round-trip commute to and from school by bicycle. I am the youngest of three, have worked since I was 16, and was raised by my single mother who had no college education. After 4 years at the UA (University of Arizona), I've graduated and have received three medical school acceptance offers.

What I focus on:

I believe that what sets a 4.0 student apart from a 2.0 student is what the student does immediately before, during, and soon after class. In college, you'll have access to lecture slides online and a syllabus with the associated textbook readings for each lecture. There are several things I do to maximize my learning in the classroom.

I print the class syllabus and have ready access to this in my folder. I also practice a technique that requires you to be consistent. Other students may look at you funny for doing it—but just smile and keep doing it. It goes something like this:

1. Preview lecture notes and textbook (~15 min before class): Familiarize yourself with headings, bold text, and figures. Summarize what you already know. Write down a list of preliminary questions and set them aside.
2. During the lecture: Listen for the answers of your preliminary questions, look for lecture patterns (general to specific, etc.), and predict the content of lecture.
3. After the lecture: study the material from lecture the SAME day, focus on what was emphasized, make an "important concepts" summary for your notes. Then organize, condense, and understand the implications. The next time you study this lecture, you can address all the things to be memorized.

What will help me in the workplace:

When I realized that my preparation could help my class lecture time become the *second* time I see that material, my studying became much more proficient and effective. In school, work, or life, this approach gives me room for other, more important, parts of my life like people, hospital internships, research work, volunteering, and church. You can be a serious student without taking yourself too seriously. Stay diligent and be ready to make small or big sacrifices!

outlining notes or thinking about cause-and-effect relationships within the material. An Organizer, studying for a test from notes delivered by an instructor with a random presentation, could organize material using tables and timelines.

▶ *Ask your instructor for help.* If you are having trouble with coursework, communicate with your instructor or teaching assistant through e-mail or during office hours. This is especially important in large lectures where you are anonymous unless you speak up. A visual learner, for example, might ask the instructor to recommend graphs, figures, or videos that illustrate the lecture.

Maximize Your Classroom Experience

Using what you know about yourself as a learner and about your instructors' teaching styles this term, decide which classroom situation is the most challenging for you. Use this exercise to think analytically, creatively, and practically about the situation.

Course: _____ Instructor style: _____

Your analysis of the problem: _____

_____

Next, brainstorm at least three ideas about actions you can take to improve the situation:

1. _____

2. _____

3. _____

Finally, choose one action and put it to practical use. Briefly note what happened: Were there improvements as a result? _____

_____

No instructor of a diverse group of learners can provide exactly what each one needs. However, adjusting to instructors' teaching styles builds flexibility that you need for career and life success. Just as you can't hand-pick your instructors, you will rarely, if ever, be able to choose your work colleagues or their ways of working or interacting with others.

A final point: Some students try to find out more about an instructor by asking students who have already taken the course or looking up comments online. Be careful with investigations like this. You may not know or be able to trust an anonymous poster. Even if you hear a review from a friend you do trust, every student–instructor relationship is unique, and an instructor your friend loved may turn out to be a bad match for you. Prioritize the courses that you need, and know that you will find a way to make the most of what your instructors offer, no matter who they are.

Study choices

Start now to use what you have learned about yourself to choose the best study techniques. For example, if you tend to learn successfully from a linear, logical presentation, you can look for order (for example, a *chronology*—information organized sequentially according to event dates—or a problem–solution structure) as you review notes. If you are strong in interpersonal intelligence, you can try to work in study groups whenever possible.

When faced with a task that challenges your weaknesses, use strategies that boost your ability. For example, if you are an Adventurer who does *not* respond well to linear information, you can apply your strengths to the material—for example, through a hands-on approach. Or you can focus on developing your area of weakness—try skills that work well for Thinker-dominant learners.

Verbal-Linguistic		• Read text; highlight selectively • Use a computer to retype and summarize notes • Outline chapters • Recite information or write scripts/debates
Musical		• Create rhythms out of words • Beat out rhythms with your hand or a stick while reciting concepts • Write songs/raps that help you learn concepts • Write out study material to fit into a wordless tune you have on a CD or MP3 player; chant or sing the material along with the tune as you listen
Logical-Mathematical		• Organize material logically; if it suits the topic, use a spreadsheet program • Explain material sequentially to someone • Develop systems and find patterns • Analyze and evaluate information
Visual-Spatial		• Develop graphic organizers for new material • Draw mind maps/think links • Use a computer to develop charts and tables • Use color in notes to organize
Bodily-Kinesthetic		• Move while you learn; pace and recite • Rewrite or retype notes to engage "muscle memory" • Design and play games to learn material • Act out scripts of material
Intrapersonal		• Reflect on personal meaning of information • Keep a journal • Study in quiet areas • Imagine essays or experiments before beginning
Interpersonal		• Study in a group • As you study, discuss information over the phone or send instant messages • Teach someone else the material • Make time to discuss assignments and tests with your instructor
Naturalistic		• Break down information into categories • Look for ways in which items fit or don't fit together • Look for relationships among ideas, events, and facts • Study in a natural setting if it helps you to focus

When you study with others, you and the entire group will be more successful if you understand the different learning styles in the group, as in the following examples.

- ▶ An Interpersonal learner could take the lead in teaching material to others.
- ▶ An Organizer could coordinate the group schedule.
- ▶ A Naturalistic learner might organize facts into categories that solidify concepts.

Look at Keys 3.5 and 3.6 for study strategies that suit each intelligence and Personality Spectrum dimension. Because you have some level of ability in each area and because there will be times that you need to boost your ability in a weaker area, you may find useful suggestions under any of the headings. Try different techniques. Pay close attention to what works best for you—you may be surprised at what is useful, as Joyce was about how typing helped her retain information.

Technology choices

Technology is everywhere these days. You see it in social settings as people communicate using e-mail, text messaging, and social networking sites on the

CHOOSE STUDY TECHNIQUES TO MAXIMIZE EACH PERSONALITY SPECTRUM DIMENSION

Key 3.6

Thinker		<ul><li>Convert material into logical charts, flow diagrams, and outlines</li><li>Reflect independently on new information</li><li>Learn through problem solving</li><li>Design new ways of approaching material or problems</li></ul>
Organizer		<ul><li>Define tasks in concrete terms</li><li>Use a planner to schedule tasks and dates</li><li>Organize material by rewriting and summarizing class or text notes</li><li>Create, or look for, a well-structured study environment</li></ul>
Giver		<ul><li>Study with others in person, on the phone, or using instant messages</li><li>Teach material to others</li><li>Seek out tasks, groups, and subjects that involve helping people</li><li>Connect with instructors, advisors, and tutors</li></ul>
Adventurer		<ul><li>Look for environments or courses that encourage nontraditional approaches</li><li>Find hands-on ways to learn</li><li>Use or develop games or puzzles to help memorize terms</li><li>Fight boredom by asking to do something extra or perform a task in a more active way</li></ul>

Internet. It also plays a significant role in academic settings, where you may encounter any of the following:

▶ Instructors who require students to communicate via e-mail
▶ Courses that have their own websites where you can access the syllabus and connect with resources and classmates
▶ Textbooks with corresponding websites that you can, or are required to, use to complete assignments that you e-mail to your instructor

For some with extensive know-how, technology comes easily. For everyone else, knowing their strengths and challenges as learners can help them make decisions about how to approach technology. Are you strong in the logical-mathematical intelligence or Thinker dimension? Working with an online tutorial may be a good choice. Are you an interpersonal learner? Find a tech-savvy classmate to help you get the hang of it. An Adventurer may want to just dive in and try out the features of a book or course website in a random way. Know yourself and make choices that can best help you demystify technology and get you up to speed.

Workplace choices

Knowing how you learn and interact with others will help you work more effectively and make better career planning choices. How can an employee or job candidate benefit from self-awareness?

Better performance and teamwork

When you understand your strengths, you can find ways to use them on the job more readily. For tasks that take you out of your areas of strength, you will be more able to compensate and get help. In addition, you will be better able to work with others effectively. For example, a Giver might help new hires adjust to the people and environment. Or a team leader might offer an intrapersonal team member the chance to take material home to think about before a meeting.

Better career planning

Exploring ways to use your strengths in school will help you make better choices about what jobs or careers will suit you. For most college students, internships and majors are more immediate steps on the road to a career. A strength in one or more intelligences might lead you to particular internships and majors that may make sense for you.

Key 3.7 links majors and internships to the eight intelligences. This list is by no means complete; rather, it represents only a fraction of the available opportunities. Use what you see here to inspire thought and spur investigation. If something from this list or elsewhere interests you, consider looking for an opportunity to "shadow" someone (follow them for a day to see what they do) to see if the more significant commitments of internships and majoring will make sense for you. See Key 12.1, in the section on careers in Chapter 12, for ideas about how intelligences may link to particular careers.

Although all students have areas of strength and weakness, challenges diagnosed as learning disabilities are more significant. These merit specific

Change the
CONVERSATION

Challenge yourself and your friends to ask—and answer—tough questions. Use the following to inspire discussion in pairs or groups.

▶ When you have trouble doing something, what is your first reaction—to try again or to give up? Do you say, "I'm going to have to find a different approach" or "I'm no good at this"?

▶ Do people perceive their own strengths accurately, or do you often see strengths in others that they don't believe they have?

▶ **CONSIDER THE CASE:** Not knowing about Joyce Bishop's learning disability, what would you have assumed as her instructor in college? What might an instructor assume about you that someone who knows you well—or even you yourself—may suspect is not accurate?

INTERNSHIPS
Temporary work programs in which a student can gain supervised practical experience in a job and career area.

MULTIPLE INTELLIGENCES MAY OPEN DOORS TO **MAJORS AND INTERNSHIPS**

MULTIPLE INTELLIGENCE	CONSIDER MAJORING IN	THINK ABOUT AN INTERNSHIP AT A
Bodily-Kinesthetic	• Massage or physical therapy • Kinesiology • Construction engineering • Sports medicine • Dance or theater	• Sports physician's office • Physical or massage therapy center • Construction company • Dance studio or theater company • Athletic club
Intrapersonal	• Psychology • Finance • Computer science • Biology • Philosophy	• Accounting firm • Biology lab • Pharmaceutical company • Publishing house • Computer or Internet company
Interpersonal	• Education • Public relations • Nursing • Business • Hotel/restaurant management	• Hotel or restaurant • Social service agency • Public relations firm • Human resources department • Charter school
Naturalistic	• Geology • Zoology • Atmospheric sciences • Agriculture • Environmental law	• Museum • National park • Environmental law firm • Zoo • Geological research firm
Musical	• Music • Music theory • Voice • Composition • Performing arts	• Performance hall • Radio station • Record label or recording studio • Children's music camp • Orchestra or opera company
Logical-Mathematical	• Math • Physics • Economics • Banking/finance • Computer science	• Law firm • Consulting firm • Bank • Information technology company • Research lab
Verbal-Linguistic	• Communications • Marketing • English/literature • Journalism • Foreign languages	• Newspaper or magazine • PR/marketing firm • Ad agency • Publishing house • Network TV affiliate
Visual-Spatial	• Architecture • Visual arts • Multimedia designs • Photography • Art history	• Photo or art studio • Multimedia design firm • Architecture firm • Interior design firm • Art gallery

attention. Focused assistance can help students with learning disabilities manage their conditions and excel in school.

How can you identify and manage learning disabilities?

Some learning disabilities create reading problems, some produce difficulties in math, some cause issues that arise when working with others, and some make it difficult for students to process the language they hear. The following will help you understand learning disabilities as well as the tools people use to manage them.

Identifying a learning disability

The National Center for Learning Disabilities (NCLD) defines *learning disabilities* as neurological disorders that interfere with one's ability to store, process, and produce information.[6] They do *not* include mental retardation, autism, behavioral disorders, impaired vision, hearing loss, or other physical disabilities. Nor do they include attention-deficit disorder and attention deficit hyperactivity disorder, although these problems may accompany learning disabilities.[7] Often running in families, learning disabilities are lifelong conditions; however, specific strategies can help people with learning disabilities manage and even overcome areas of weakness.

How can you determine whether you should be evaluated for a learning disability? According to the NCLD, persistent problems in any of the following areas may indicate a problem:[8]

▶ Reading or reading comprehension
▶ Math calculations or understanding language and concepts
▶ Social skills or interpreting social cues
▶ Following a schedule, being on time, meeting deadlines
▶ Reading or following maps
▶ Balancing a checkbook
▶ Following directions, especially on multistep tasks
▶ Understanding spoken or heard language
▶ Writing, sentence structure, spelling, and organizing written work

Details on specific learning disabilities appear in Key 3.8. For an evaluation, contact your school's learning center or student health center for a referral to a licensed professional. Note that a professional diagnosis is required in order for a person with learning disabilities to receive federally funded aid.

Managing a learning disability

If you are diagnosed with a learning disability, valuable information is available—information that it took Joyce until graduate school to obtain. Maximize your ability to learn by managing your disability.

▶ *Find information about your disability.* Search the library and the Internet—try NCLD at www.ncld.org or LD Online at www.ldonline.org—or call NCLD at 1-888-575-7373. If you have an individualized education

WHAT ARE **LEARNING DISABILITIES** AND HOW DO YOU RECOGNIZE THEM?

DISABILITY OR CONDITION	WHAT ARE THE SIGNS?
Dyslexia and related reading disorders	Problems with reading (spelling, word sequencing, comprehension) and processing (translating written language to thought or the reverse)
Dyscalculia (developmental arithmetic disorders)	Difficulties in recognizing numbers and symbols, memorizing facts, understanding abstract math concepts, and applying math to life skills (time management, handling money)
Developmental writing disorders	Difficulties in composing sentences, organizing a writing assignment, or translating thoughts coherently to the page
Handwriting disorders (dysgraphia)	Disorder characterized by writing disabilities, including distorted or incorrect language, inappropriately sized and spaced letters, or wrong or misspelled words
Speech and language disorders	Problems with producing speech sounds, using spoken language to communicate, and/or understanding what others say
LD-related social issues	Problems in recognizing facial or vocal cues from others, controlling verbal and physical impulsivity, and respecting others' personal space
LD-related organizational issues	Difficulties in scheduling and in organizing personal, academic, and work-related materials

Source: LD Online: LD Basics, www.ncld.org/content/view/445/389/, © 2009.

program (IEP)—a document describing your disability and recommended strategies—read it and make sure you understand what it says.

▶ *Seek assistance from your school.* Speak with your advisor about getting a referral to the counselor who can help you get specific accommodations in your classes. The following services are mandated by law for students who are learning disabled:

- Extended time on tests
- Note-taking assistance (for example, having a fellow student take notes for you)
- Assistive technology devices (MP3 players, tape recorders, laptop computers)
- Modified assignments
- Alternative assessments and test formats

Other services that may be offered include tutoring, study skills assistance, and counseling.

▶ *Be a dedicated student.* Show up on time and pay attention in class. Read assignments before class. Sit where you can focus. Review notes soon after class. Spend extra time on assignments. Ask for help.

▶ *Build a positive attitude.* See your accomplishments in light of how far you have come. Rely on support from others, knowing that it will give you the best possible chance to succeed.

What happened to Joyce? Bishop now understands how her learning disability, *auditory processing disorder,* causes problems with understanding words she hears. Seeing how her strengths in visual-spatial, logical-mathematical, and bodily-kinesthetic intelligence served her well in science studies, she chose study strategies for those strengths and over time earned her master's and PhD degrees. Now a tenured psychology professor at Golden West College in California, Dr. Bishop has won Teacher of the Year twice at her school. She teaches both in-person and online courses and trains other teachers in online teaching strategies. She manages the challenges of her learning disability while pursuing her intention to learn throughout her life.

Case Wrap-up

What does this mean for you? Getting perspective on strengths and weaknesses isn't just for those with diagnosed learning disabilities. Dr. Bishop got her wake-up call from an eye doctor and a therapist. Who can provide an outside perspective for you? Find someone who knows you well enough to have an opinion about you and who you believe will be honest and constructive. Tell this person ahead of time that you are looking for perspectives about what you do well and what challenges you. Prepare by making a short list of your three strongest and three weakest qualities. After receiving the outside perspective, compare it to your list. What matches up? What surprises you?

What effects go beyond your world? Broaden your knowledge of learning disabilities so you avoid inaccurate assumptions about people and learn how to support them in reaching their potential. Go to www.ldonline.org and read the article entitled "LD Basics." Then browse the articles at www.ldonline.org/indepth/adults to focus more closely on how adults with learning disabilities navigate school, work, and life. Finally, think about an assumption you may have made regarding someone with whom you live, work, or go to school. Address your possibly false idea by approaching that person with an open mind from this point forward, looking for strengths as well as working reasonably with challenges (and maybe even helping the person to combat them). With every person who develops a more positive attitude and understanding perspective about those with learning disabilities or other challenges, the world becomes that much more of a supportive and productive place.

Successful Intelligence *Wrap-up*

HERE'S HOW YOU HAVE
BUILT SKILLS IN **CHAPTER 3** :

ANALYTICAL THINKING	CREATIVE THINKING	PRACTICAL THINKING
❯ You analyzed your levels of ability in the multiple intelligences.	❯ Reading about the assessments may have inspired new ideas about your abilities and talents.	❯ In the in-text exercise, you took action to improve a classroom experience.
❯ You examined how you relate to people and the world around you.	❯ In the in-text exercise, you brainstormed ideas about how to improve a situation with an instructor.	❯ Reading Keys 3.5 and 3.6 gave you practical study strategies relating to each intelligence and Personality Spectrum dimension.
❯ In the in-text exercise, you examined how an instructor's teaching style affects how you learn.	❯ Seeing in Key 3.7 how intelligences relate to majors and internships may have inspired thoughts about major and job plans.	❯ Reading the material on learning disabilities offered practical ways to investigate and address any learning disability you may have.

Word *for* Thought

In the language of the **Yoruba,** an ethnic group living primarily in West Africa, *oruko lonro ni* (oh-roo'-ko lon'-ro ni) translates as "names affect behavior."[9] Think of this as you work to break through the confines of the names and labels that you give yourself or that others give you. Put learning styles information to work as a tool to learn more, not a box into which to fit yourself.

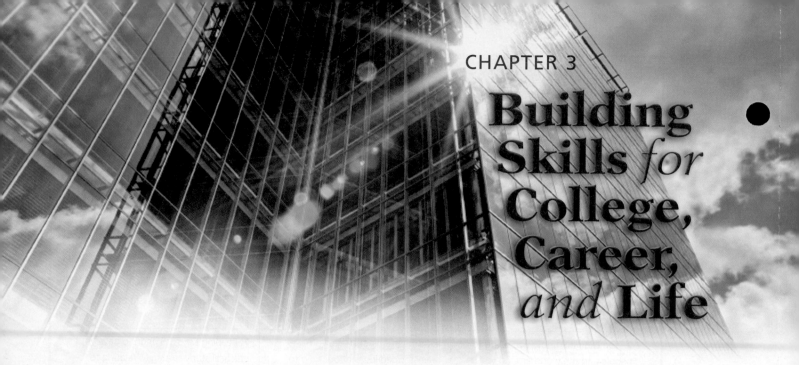

Building Skills *for* College, Career, *and* Life

Steps to Success

Link How You Learn to Coursework and Major

Apply what you know about yourself to some future academic planning.

BUILD BASIC SKILLS. On paper or on a computer, summarize yourself as a learner in a paragraph or two. Focus on what you have learned about yourself from the chapter assessments.

Done? Check here. _____

TAKE IT TO THE NEXT LEVEL. Schedule a meeting with your academic advisor.

Name of advisor: _____

Office location/contact information: _____

Time/date of meeting: _____

Give the advisor an overview of your learning strengths and challenges, based on your summary. Ask for advice about courses that might interest you and majors that might suit you. Take notes. Based on your discussion, name two courses to consider in the next year:

1. _____

2. _____

MOVE TOWARD MASTERY. In your mind, project both of those courses ahead in time. What majors might each of them lead you toward? Based on those courses, name two majors to investigate:

1. _____

2. _____

Finally, create a separate to-do list of how you plan to explore one course offering and one major. Set a deadline for each task. And keep in mind that if you are having trouble choosing a major because of uncertainty about a career direction, see an advisor in the career center for guidance.

Teamwork

Create Solutions Together

IDEAS ABOUT PERSONALITY TYPES

Goal: To learn more about personality types—your own and others'.

Time on task: 25 minutes: 5 minutes to settle into groups, 10 minutes for group work, 10 minutes to share

Instructions: Divide into groups according to the four types of the Personality Spectrum—Thinkers in one group, Organizers in another, Givers in a third, and Adventurers in the fourth. Students whose scores point to more than one type can join whichever group is smaller. With your group, brainstorm about the following aspects of your type:

1. The strengths of this type
2. The struggles, or stressful aspects, of this type
3. Career areas that tend to suit this type
4. Career areas that are a challenge for this type
5. Challenges for this type in relating to the other three Personality Spectrum types

If there is time, each group can present this information to the entire class to boost understanding and acceptance of diverse ways of relating to information and people.

Writing

Build Intrapersonal and Communication Skills

Record your thoughts on a separate piece of paper, in a journal, or electronically.

EMOTIONAL INTELLIGENCE JOURNAL

Your interactions with others. With your Personality Spectrum profile in mind, think about how you generally relate to people. Describe the type(s) of people that you tend to get along well with. How do you feel around these people? Then describe the types that tend to irk you. How do those people make you feel? Use your emotional intelligence to discuss what those feelings tell you and how you can adjust your mindset or take action to create the best possible outcome in interactions with people with whom you just don't get along.

REAL-LIFE WRITING

Ask an instructor for support. Reach out to an instructor for a course that clashes with your learning style—in terms of the material itself, the style in which it is presented, or the way the classroom is run. Draft a friendly and respectful e-mail requesting help that describes how you perceive yourself as a learner and details the issue you are having with the material or coverage. Include any ideas you have about how the instructor might be able to help you.

When you are done, make something happen: Send it and follow through on the response you receive.

Personal Portfolio

Prepare for Career Success

SELF-PORTRAIT

21st Century Learning Building Blocks

- Creativity and Innovation
- Initiative and Self-Direction

Complete the following on separate sheets of paper or electronically (if you can use a graphics program).

Because self-knowledge helps you to make the best choices about your future, a self-portrait can be an important tool in your career exploration. Use this exercise to synthesize everything you have been exploring about yourself into one comprehensive "self-portrait." Design your portrait in think link (mind map) style, using words and visual shapes to describe your dominant multiple intelligences, Personality Spectrum dimensions, values, abilities and interests, personal characteristics, and anything else that you have discovered through self-exploration.

A think link is a visual construction of related ideas, similar to a map or web, representing your thought process. Ideas are written inside geometric shapes, often boxes or circles, and related ideas and facts are attached to those ideas by lines that connect the shapes (see the note-taking section in Chapter 6 for more about think links).

If you want to use the style shown in Key 3.9, create a "wheel" of ideas coming off your central shape. Then, spreading out from each of those ideas (interests, values, and so forth), draw lines connecting the thoughts that go along with that idea. Connected to "Interests," for example, might be "singing," "stock market," and "history."

You don't have to use the wheel image, however. You might instead want to design a treelike think link, a line of boxes with connecting thoughts, or anything else you like. Let your design reflect who you are, just as your writing does. You may want to look back at it at the end of the term to see how you have changed and grown from the self-image you have today.

Social Networking

HELP OTHERS GET TO KNOW YOU

As you are building your self-knowledge, help viewers of your LinkedIn profile get to know you as well. Sign in to your LinkedIn account and click on "Edit My Profile." Look for "Summary" and click on the Edit mark next to it. Then, fill in the two areas there:

- Professional Experience & Goals (If you don't have any professional experience, you can fill in Goals only. Remember, too, that you can include experience from internships, work study, apprenticeships, etc.)
- Specialties (In conjunction with talking about what you do well, you may want to consider including information related to learning styles—that you are highly visual, for example, or a strong organizer.)

In addition, scroll down to the "Personal Information" section and fill in any of the following that you choose to have visible on your profile:

- Phone
- Address
- IM
- Birthday
- Marital status

Finally, you may choose to post a photo. Only use a respectable-looking one. Click on "Edit My Profile," then on "Add Photo" underneath the photo icon. It will then direct you to upload a photo.

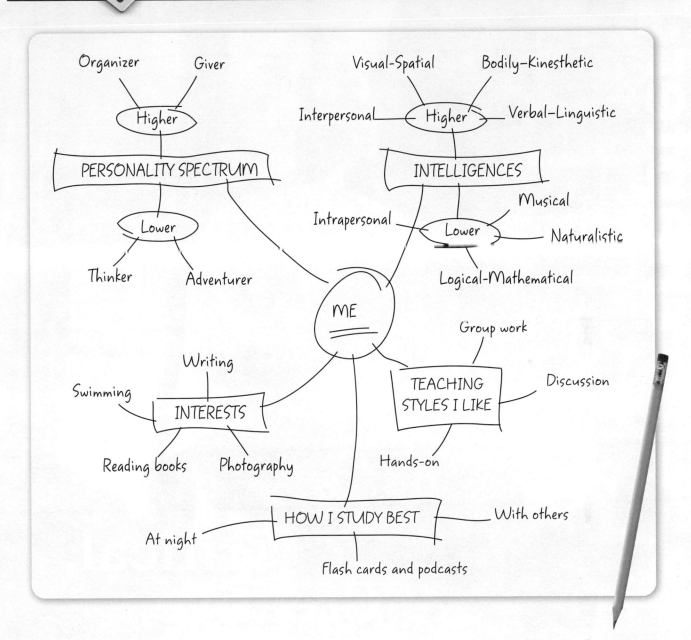

chapter 4

Critical, Creative, and Practical Thinking

*Solving Problems
and Making Decisions*

What Would You Do?

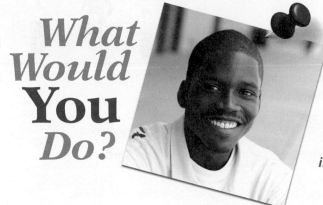

Think about this problem as you read, and consider how you would approach it. This chapter builds problem-solving and decision-making skills that will help you face challenges in college and beyond.

Ethan Gamal is carrying a twelve-credit load this term toward his major in computer programming. He has been working part-time at a local electronics store for his entire college career. It's hard to keep up with both work and school, but he can't afford the tuition without the income.

However, the chain that has employed him for the last 3 years is going into bankruptcy, and the consequences have hit home. He was notified that the store is closing in 2 weeks and all employees have been terminated. Trying to keep cash coming in, Ethan applied for local jobs and sent some resumés electronically to job websites, but hasn't yet gotten any bites.

Ethan's friend and co-worker Adam talked it over with him as they sat in the back room on a break. "Look at it this way: We'll both have more time to get schoolwork done. You know you've complained for weeks about being overloaded."

"What good is time to study if I can't pay tuition?" asked Ethan. "I was looking on the Bureau of Labor website for ideas, and it said demand for computer programmers is going to drop a lot in the next decade. Great. Why bother to stick with my degree if I won't even be able to find a job in a few years?"

"We're in the same boat," said Adam. "All of us need new jobs, and I've got to pay my own tuition just like you."

Ethan replied, "But you're headed toward an education major, and you're going to have job prospects. I don't know what to do, because there's nothing else I'm interested in. The truth is, I'm ready to quit." (To be continued . . .)

Problems can come up suddenly and throw you off balance. You'll learn more about Ethan, and revisit his situation, within the chapter.

In this chapter, you'll explore answers to these questions:

> Why is it important to ask and answer questions? p. 86

> How can you improve your analytical thinking skills? p. 87

> How can you improve your creative thinking skills? p. 93

> How can you improve your practical thinking skills? p. 97

> How can you solve problems and make decisions effectively? p. 101

ANALYTICAL

CREATIVE

PRACTICAL

STATUS *Check*

▶ *How developed are your thinking skills?*

For each statement, circle the number that feels right to you, from 1 for "not at all true for me" to 5 for "very true for me."

▶ I discover information, make decisions, and solve problems by asking and answering questions.	1 2 3 4 5
▶ I don't take everything I read or hear as fact; I question how useful, truthful, and logical it is before I decide whether I can use it.	1 2 3 4 5
▶ I look for biased perspectives when I read or listen because I am aware of how they can lead me in the wrong direction.	1 2 3 4 5
▶ Even if it seems like there is only one way to solve a problem, I brainstorm to think of other options.	1 2 3 4 5
▶ I try not to let the idea that things have *always* been done a certain way stop me from trying different approaches.	1 2 3 4 5
▶ When I work in a group, I try to manage my emotions and to notice how I affect others.	1 2 3 4 5
▶ I think about different solutions before I choose one and take action.	1 2 3 4 5
▶ I spend time researching different possibilities before making a decision.	1 2 3 4 5
▶ I avoid making decisions on the spur of the moment.	1 2 3 4 5
▶ When I make a decision, I consider how my choice will affect others.	1 2 3 4 5

Each of the topics in these statements is covered in this chapter. Note those statements for which you circled a 3 or lower. Skim the chapter to see where those topics appear, and pay special attention to them as you read, learn, and apply new strategies.

REMEMBER: *No matter how developed your thinking skills are, you can improve with effort and practice.*

"Successfully intelligent people define problems correctly and thereby solve those problems that really confront them, rather than extraneous ones. . . . [They] carefully formulate strategies for problem solving. In particular, they focus on long-range planning rather than rushing in and then later having to rethink their strategies."

—Robert Sternberg

Why is it important to ask and answer questions?

What is thinking? According to experts, it is what happens when you ask questions and move toward the answers.[1] "To think through or rethink anything," says Dr. Richard Paul, director of research at the Center for Critical Thinking and Moral Critique, "one must ask questions that stimulate our thought. Questions define tasks, express problems and delineate issues. . . . [O]nly students who have questions are really thinking and learning."[2]

As you answer questions, you turn information into material that you can use to achieve goals. A *Wall Street Journal* article entitled "The Best Innovations Are Those That Come from Smart Questions" relays the story of a cell biology student, William Hunter, whose professor told him that "the difference between good science and great science is the quality of the questions posed." Now a physician, Dr. Hunter asks questions about new ways to use drugs. His questions have helped his company reach the goal of developing a revolutionary product—a drug-coated mesh used to strengthen diseased blood vessels.[3]

How can you question effectively?

■ *Know why you question.* To ask useful questions, you need to know why you are questioning. Start by defining your purpose: What am I trying to accomplish, and why? For example, if Ethan's purpose for questioning were to find another part-time job, that would generate an entirely different set of questions than if his purpose were to find another major. As you continue your thought process, you will find more specific purposes that help you generate questions along the way.

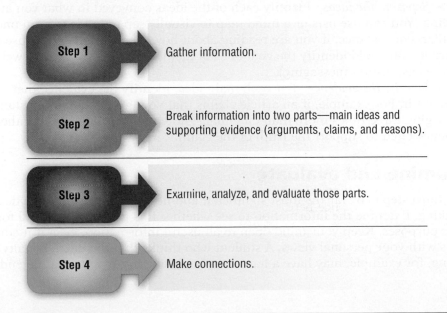

■ *Want to question.* Knowing why you are questioning also helps you *want* to think. "Critical-thinking skills are different from critical-thinking dispositions, or a willingness to deploy these skills," says cognitive psychologist D. Alan Bensley of Frostburg State University in Maryland. In other words, having the skills isn't enough—you also need the desire to use them.[4] Having a clear understanding of your goal can help you be more willing to work to achieve it.

■ *Question in different ways.*

▶ Analyze (How bad is my money situation?)
▶ Come up with creative ideas (How can I earn more money?)
▶ Apply practical solutions (Who do I talk to about getting a job on campus?)

When you need to solve a problem or make a decision, combining all three thinking skills gives you the greatest chance of achieving your goal.[5] This chapter will explore analytical, creative, and practical thinking first individually and then will show how they work together to help you to solve problems and make decisions effectively. Asking questions opens the door to each thinking skill, and in each section you will find examples of the kinds of questions that drive that skill. Begin by exploring analytical thinking.

How can you improve your analytical thinking skills?

Analytical thinking is the process of gathering information, breaking it into parts, examining and evaluating those parts, and making connections for the purposes of gaining understanding, solving a problem, or making a decision.

Step 1	Gather information.
Step 2	Break information into two parts—main ideas and supporting evidence (arguments, claims, and reasons).
Step 3	Examine, analyze, and evaluate those parts.
Step 4	Make connections.

Through the analytical process, you look for how pieces of information relate to one another, setting aside any pieces that are unclear, unrelated, unimportant, or biased. You may also form new questions that change your direction. Be open to them and to where they may lead you.

Gather information

Information is the raw material for thinking, so to start the thinking process you must first gather your raw materials. This requires analyzing how much information you need, how much time to spend gathering it, and whether it is relevant. Say, for instance, that you have to write a paper on one aspect of the media (TV, radio, Internet) and its influence on a particular group. Here's how analyzing can help you gather information for that paper:

Many types of work, such as the elevation drawings this engineering student is working on, involve analytical thinking.
© Shutterstock

▶ Reviewing the assignment terms, you note two important items: The paper should be approximately ten pages and describe at least three significant points of influence.
▶ At the library and online, you find thousands of articles in this topic area. Analyzing your reaction to them and how many articles concentrate on certain aspects of the topic, you decide to focus your paper on how the Internet influences young teens (ages 13–15).
▶ Examining the summaries of six comprehensive articles leads you to three in-depth sources.

In this way you achieve a subgoal—a selection of useful materials—on the way to your larger goal of writing a well-crafted paper.

Break information into parts

The next step is to search for the two most relevant parts of the information: the main idea or ideas (also called the **argument** or *viewpoint*) and the supporting evidence (also called *reasons* or *supporting details*).

ARGUMENT
A set of connected ideas, supported by examples, made by a writer to prove or disprove a point.

▶ *Separate the ideas.* Identify each of the ideas conveyed in what you are reading. You can use lists or a mind map to visually separate ideas from one another. For instance, if you are reading about how teens ages 13 to 15 use the Internet, you could identify the goal of each method of access they use (websites, blogs, instant messaging).

▶ *Identify the evidence.* For each main idea, identify the evidence that supports it. For example, if an article claims that young teens rely on instant messaging three times more than on e-mails, note the facts, studies, or other evidence cited to support the truth of the claim.

Examine and evaluate

The third step is by far the most significant and lies at the heart of analytical thinking. Examine the information to see whether it is going to be useful for your purposes. Keep your mind open to all useful information, even if it conflicts with your personal views. A student who thinks that the death penalty is wrong, for example, may have a hard time analyzing arguments that defend it or may focus his research on materials that support his perspective. Set aside personal prejudices when you analyze information.

The following four questions will help you examine and evaluate effectively.

Do examples support ideas?

When you encounter an idea or claim, examine how it is supported with examples or *evidence*—facts, expert opinion, research findings, personal experience, and so on (see Key 4.1 for an illustration). How useful an idea is to your work may depend on whether, or how well, it is backed up with solid evidence or made concrete with examples. Be critical of the information you gather; don't take it as truth without examining it.

For example, a blog written by a 12-year-old may make statements about what kids do on the Internet. The word of one person, who may or may not be telling the truth, is not adequate support. However, a study of youth technology use by the Department of Commerce under the provisions of the Children's Internet Protection Act may be more reliable.

Is the information factual and accurate, or is it opinion?

A *statement of fact* is information presented as objectively real and verifiable ("The Internet is a research tool"). In contrast, a *statement of opinion* is a belief, conclusion, or judgment that is inherently difficult, and sometimes impossible, to verify ("The Internet is always the best and most reliable research tool"). When you critically evaluate materials, one test of the evidence is whether it is fact or opinion. Key 4.2 defines important characteristics of fact and opinion.

Do causes and effects link logically?

Look at the reasons given for a situation or occurrence (causes) and the explanation of its consequences (effects, both positive and negative). For example, an article might detail what causes young teens to use the Internet after school and

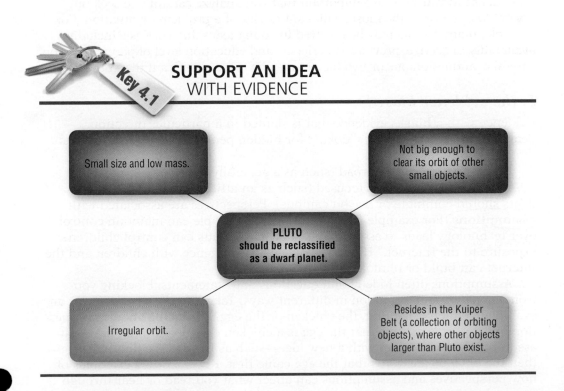

Key 4.1

SUPPORT AN IDEA
WITH EVIDENCE

Small size and low mass.

Not big enough to clear its orbit of other small objects.

PLUTO should be reclassified as a dwarf planet.

Irregular orbit.

Resides in the Kuiper Belt (a collection of orbiting objects), where other objects larger than Pluto exist.

FACTS INCLUDE STATEMENTS THAT . . .	OPINIONS INCLUDE STATEMENTS THAT . . .
. . . **deal with actual people, places, objects, or events.** Example: "In 2002, the European Union introduced the physical coins and banknotes of a new currency—the euro—that was designed to be used by its member nations."	. . . **show evaluation.** Any statement of value indicates an opinion. Words such as *bad, good, pointless,* and *beneficial* indicate value judgments. Example: "The use of the euro has been beneficial to all the states of the European Union."
. . . **use concrete words or measurable statistics.** Example: "The charity event raised $50,862."	. . . **use abstract words.** Complicated words like *misery* or *success* usually indicate a personal opinion. Example: "The charity event was a smashing success."
. . . **describe current events in exact terms.** Example: "Mr. Barrett's course has 378 students enrolled this semester."	. . . **predict future events.** Statements about future occurrences are often opinions. Example: "Mr. Barrett's course is going to set a new enrollment record this year."
. . . **avoid emotional words and focus on the verifiable.** Example: "Citing dissatisfaction with the instruction, seven out of the twenty-five students in that class withdrew in September."	. . . **use emotional words.** Emotions are unverifiable. Words such as *delightful* or *miserable* express an opinion. Example: "That class is a miserable experience."
. . . **avoid absolutes.** Example: "Some students need to have a job while in school."	. . . **use absolutes.** Absolute qualifiers, such as *all, none, never,* and *always,* often express an opinion. Example: "All students need to have a job while in school."

Source: Adapted from Ben E. Johnson, *Stirring Up Thinking.* New York: Houghton Mifflin, 1998, pp. 268–270.

the effects that this has on their family life. The cause-and-effect chain should make sense to you. It is also important that you analyze carefully to seek out *key* or *"root" causes*—the most significant causes of a problem or situation. For example, many factors may be involved in young teens' Internet use, including availability of service, previous experience, and education level of parents, but on careful examination one or two factors may be more significant than others.

Is the evidence biased?

BIAS
A preference or inclination, especially one that prevents even-handed judgment.

Evidence with a **bias** is evidence that is slanted in a particular direction. Searching for a bias involves looking for hidden perspectives or assumptions that lie within the material.

A **perspective** can be broad (such as a generally optimistic or pessimistic view of life) or more focused (such as an attitude about whether students should commute or live on campus). Perspectives are associated with **assumptions.** For example, the perspective that people can maintain control over technology leads to assumptions such as "Parents can control children's exposure to the Internet." Having a particular experience with children and the Internet can build or reinforce such a perspective.

PERSPECTIVE
A characteristic way of thinking about people, situations, events, and ideas.

ASSUMPTION
A judgment, generalization, or bias influenced by experience and values.

Assumptions often hide within questions and statements, blocking you from considering information in different ways. Take this classic puzzler as an example: "Which came first, the chicken or the egg?" Thinking about this question, most people assume that the egg is a chicken egg. If you think past that assumption and come up with a new idea—such as the egg is a dinosaur egg—then the obvious answer is that the egg came first. Key 4.3 offers examples of how perspectives and assumptions can affect what you read or hear through the media.

DIFFERENT ARTICLES MAY PRESENT **DIFFERENT PERSPECTIVES** ON THE SAME TOPIC

Key 4.3

Topic: *How teens' grades are affected by Internet use*

STATEMENT BY A TEACHING ORGANIZATION	STATEMENT BY A PR AGENT FOR AN INTERNET SEARCH ENGINE	STATEMENT BY A PROFESSOR SPECIALIZING IN NEW MEDIA AND EDUCATION
"Too much Internet use equals failing grades and stolen papers."	"The Internet use allows students access to a plethora of information, which results in better grades."	"The effects of the Internet on young students are undeniable and impossible to overlook."

Examining perspectives and assumptions helps you judge whether material is *reliable*. The less bias you can identify, the more reliable the information.

After the questions: What information is most useful to you?

You've examined your information, looking at its evidence, validity, perspective, and any underlying assumptions. Now, based on that examination, you evaluate whether an idea or piece of information is important or unimportant, relevant or not, strong or weak, and why. You then set aside what is not useful and use the rest to form an opinion, possible solution, or decision.

In preparing your paper on young teens and the Internet, for example, you've analyzed a selection of information and materials to see how they apply to the goal of your paper. You then selected what you believe will be most useful in preparation for drafting.

Make connections

The last part of analytical thinking, after you have broken information apart, is to find new and logical ways to connect pieces together. This step is crucial for research papers and essays because it is where your original ideas are born—and it is also where your creative skills get involved (more on that in the next section). When you begin to write, you focus on your new ideas, supporting them effectively with information you've learned from your analysis. Use the following techniques to make connections.

■ *Compare and contrast.* Look at how ideas are similar to, or different from, each other. You might explore how different young teen subgroups (boys versus girls, for example) have different purposes for setting up pages on sites such as Facebook or MySpace.

When you think through something with others in a group, the variety of ideas gives you a better chance of finding a workable solution to a problem.
© iStockPhoto

■ *Look for themes, patterns, and categories.* Note connections that form as you look at how bits of information relate to one another. For example, you might see patterns of Internet use that link young teens from particular cultures or areas of the country together into categories.

Come to new information ready to hear and read new ideas, think about them, and make informed decisions about what you believe. The process will educate you, sharpen your thinking skills, and give you more information to work with as you encounter life's problems. See Key 4.4 for some questions you can ask to build and use analytical thinking skills.

ASK QUESTIONS LIKE THESE TO **ANALYZE**

To gather information, ask:
- What kinds of information do I need to meet my goal?
- What information is available? Where and when can I get to it?
- Of the sources I found, which ones will best help me achieve my goal?

To analyze, ask:
- What are the parts of this information?
- What is similar to this information? What is different?
- What are the reasons for this? Why did this happen?
- What ideas, themes, or conclusions emerge from this material?
- How would you categorize this information?

To see whether evidence or examples support an idea, ask:
- Does the evidence make sense?
- How do the examples support the idea/claim?
- Are there examples that might disprove the idea/claim?

To distinguish fact from opinion, ask:
- Do the words in this information signal fact or opinion?
- What is the source of this information? Is the source reliable?
- If this is an opinion, is it supported by facts?

To examine perspectives and assumptions, ask:
- What perspectives might the author have, and what may be emphasized or deemphasized as a result?
- What assumptions might lie behind this statement or material?
- How could I prove—or disprove—an assumption?
- How might my perspective affect the way I see this material?

To evaluate, ask:
- What information will support what I'm trying to prove or accomplish?
- Is this information true or false, and why?
- How important is this information?

Source: Adapted from www-ed.fnal.gov/trc/tutorial/taxonomy.html (Richard Paul, *Critical Thinking: How to Prepare Students for a Rapidly Changing World,* 1993) and from www.kcmetro.edu/longview/ctac/blooms.htm (Barbara Fowler, Longview Community College "Bloom's Taxonomy and Critical Thinking").

Pursuing your goals, in school and in the workplace, requires not just analyzing information but also thinking creatively about how to use what you've learned from your analysis.

How can you improve your creative thinking skills?

What is creativity?

▶ Some researchers define creativity as combining existing elements in an innovative way to create a new purpose or result (after doctors noticed that patients taking aspirin had fewer heart attacks, the drug was reinvented as a preventer of coronary disease).

▶ Others see creativity as the ability to generate new ideas from looking at how things are related (noting what ladybugs eat inspired organic farmers to bring them in to consume crop destroying aphids).[6]

▶ Still others, including Sternberg, define it as the ability to make unusual connections—to view information in quirky ways that bring about unique results (using a weak adhesive to mark pages in a book, a 3M scientist created Post-it notes).

To think creatively is to generate new ideas that may bring change. Even though some people seem to have more or better ideas than others, creative thinking is a skill that can be developed. Creativity expert Roger von Oech highlights mental flexibility. "Like race-car drivers who shift in and out of different gears depending on where they are on the course," he says, you can enhance creativity by learning to "shift in and out of different types of thinking depending on the needs of the situation at hand."[7]

The following tips will help you make those shifts and build your ability to generate and capture the ideas that pop up. Get in the habit of writing them down as you think of them. Keep a pen and paper by your bed, your smartphone in your pocket, a notepad in your car, or a recorder in your backpack so that you can grab ideas before they fade.

Brainstorm

Brainstorming is also referred to as *divergent thinking:* You start with a question and then let your mind diverge—go in many different directions—in search of solutions. Brainstorming is *deliberate* creative thinking. When you brainstorm, you generate ideas without thinking about how useful they are, and evaluate their quality later. Brainstorming works well in groups because group members can become inspired by, and make creative use of, one another's ideas.[8]

One way to inspire ideas when brainstorming is to think of similar situations—in other words, to make *analogies* (comparisons based on a resemblance of things otherwise unlike). For example, Velcro is a product of analogy: After examining how burrs stuck to his dog's fur after a walk in the woods, the inventor imagined how a similar system of hooks and loops could make two pieces of fabric stick to each other.

When you are brainstorming ideas, don't get hooked on finding one right answer. Questions may have many "right answers"—answers that have degrees of usefulness. The more possibilities you generate, the better your chance of

> BRAINSTORMING
> Letting your mind wander to come up with different ideas or answers.

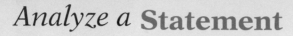

GET ANALYTICAL!

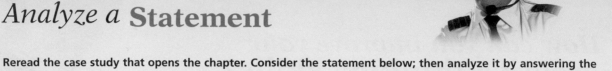

Analyze a Statement

Reread the case study that opens the chapter. Consider the statement below; then analyze it by answering the questions that follow.

There's no point in pursuing a career area that you love
if it isn't going to earn you a living.

Is this statement fact or opinion? Why?

_____

_____

_____

_____

What examples can you think of that support or negate this statement?

_____

_____

_____

_____

What perspective(s) are guiding this statement?

_____

_____

_____

_____

What assumption(s) underlie the statement? What negative effects might result from accepting these assumptions without investigation?

_____

_____

_____

_____

As a result of your critical thinking, what is your evaluation of this statement?

_____

_____

_____

_____

finding the best one. Ethan might brainstorm things he likes to do and people he admires, for example, and from those lists he may come up with ideas of other majors that he wants to investigate.

Finally, don't stop the process when you think you have the best answer—keep going until you are out of steam. You never know what may come up in those last gasps of creative energy.[9]

Take a new and different look

If no one ever questioned established opinion, people would still think the sun revolved around the earth. Here are some ways to change how you look at a situation or problem:

■ **Challenge assumptions.** In the late 1960s, conventional wisdom said that school provided education and television provided entertainment. Jim Henson, a pioneer in children's television, asked, Why can't we use TV to educate young children? From that question, the characters of *Sesame Street*, and eventually many other educational programs, were born. Ethan might try to challenge his assumptions about what people with a computer programming major do in the workplace.

■ **Shift your perspective.** Try on new perspectives by asking others for their views, reading about new ways to approach situations, or deliberately going with the opposite of your first instinct.[10] Then use those perspectives to inspire creativity. For a political science course, for example, you might craft a position paper for a senatorial candidate that goes against your view of that particular issue. For a fun example of how looking at something in a new way can unearth a totally different idea, look at the perception puzzles in Key 4.5.

USE **PERCEPTION PUZZLES** TO EXPERIENCE
A SHIFT IN PERSPECTIVE

There are two possibilities for each image. What do you see? (See page 113 for answers.)

Source of middle puzzle: "Sara Nadar" illustration from *Mind Sights* by Roger Shepard. Copyright © 1990 by Roger Shepard. Reprinted by permission of Henry Holt and Company, LLC.

GET CREATIVE!

Activate Your Creative Powers

First, think about the past month; then list three creative acts you performed.

1. To study, I _____

2. In my personal life, I _____

3. At work or in the classroom, I _____

Now think of a problem or situation that is on your mind. Brainstorm one new idea for how to deal with it.

_____

Write down a second idea—but focus on the risk-taking aspect of creativity. What would be a risky way to handle the situation? How do you hope it would pay off?

_____

_____

Finally, sit with the question—write down one more idea *only* after you have been away from this page for at least 24 hours.

_____

Keep these in mind. You may want to use one soon!

■ *Ask "what if" questions.* Set up imaginary environments in which new ideas can grow, such as, What if I had unlimited money or time? For example, the founders of Seeds of Peace, faced with long-term conflict in the Middle East, asked, What if Israeli and Palestinian teens met at a summer camp in Maine so that the next generation has greater understanding and respect? And what if follow-up programs and reunions strengthen friendships so that relationships change the politics of the Middle East? Based on the ideas that came up, they created an organization that helps teenagers from the Middle East develop leadership and communication skills.

Set the stage for creativity

Use these strategies to generate creative ideas.

■ *Choose, or create, environments that free your mind.* Find places that energize you. Play music that moves you. Seek out people who inspire you.[11]

■ *Be curious.* Try something new and different: Take a course outside of your major, listen to a new genre of music, read a book on an unfamiliar topic. Try something you don't think you will like to see if you have misjudged your reaction. Seeking out new experiences will broaden your knowledge, giving you more raw materials with which to build creative ideas.[12]

■ *Give yourself time to "sit" with a question.*
American society values speed, so much so that we
equate being "quick" with being smart.[13] In fact, creative ideas often come when you give your brain permission to "leave the job" for a while.[14] Take breaks
when figuring out a problem—get some exercise, nap,
talk with a friend, work on something else, do something fun. Even though he may not have the luxury of
too much time, Ethan may benefit from sitting with
the question of his major for as long as he can.

Take risks

Creative breakthroughs can come from sensible risk
taking.

■ *Go against established ideas.* The founders of
Etsy.com went against the idea that the American
consumer prefers cheap, conventional, mass-pro-
duced items. In 2005 they created an online company
that allows artisans to offer one-of-a-kind, handmade
products to the consumer. The site has also created a
community of artists and connects each artist personally to his or her customers.

■ *Let mistakes be okay.* Open yourself to the learning that comes from not
being afraid to mess up. When a pharmaceutical company failed to develop a
particular treatment for multiple sclerosis, the CEO said, "You have to celebrate the failures. If you send the message that the only road to career success
is experiments that work, people won't ask risky questions, or get any dramatically new answers."[15] If majoring in computer programming turns out not to
be the best choice for Ethan, for example, he may find that what he considers a
mistake was also a crucial voyage of self-discovery.

As with analytical thinking, asking questions powers creative thinking. See
Key 4.6 for examples of the kinds of questions you can ask to get your creative
juices flowing.

Creativity connects analytical and practical thinking. When you
generate ideas, solutions, or choices, you need to think analytically
to evaluate their quality. Then, you need to think practically about
how to make the best solution or choice happen.

How can you improve
your practical
thinking skills?

You've analyzed a situation. You've brainstormed ideas. Now,
with your practical skill, you make things happen.

Practical thinking—also called "common sense" or "street
smarts"—refers to how you adapt to your environment (both
people and circumstances), or shape or change your environment to adapt to you, to pursue important goals. Think again
about the successfully intelligent boy in the story in Chapter 1:

To brainstorm, ask:	• What do I want to accomplish? • What are the craziest ideas I can think of? • What are ten ways that I can reach my goal? • What ideas have worked before and how can I apply them?
To shift your perspective, ask:	• How has this always been done—and what would be a different way? • How can I approach this task or situation from a new angle? • How would someone else do this or view this? • What if . . . ?
To set the stage for creativity, ask:	• Where, and with whom, do I feel relaxed and inspired? • What music helps me think out of the box? • When in the day or night am I most likely to experience a flow of creative ideas? • What do I think would be new and interesting to try, to see, to read?
To take risks, ask:	• What is the conventional way of doing this? What would be a totally different way? • What would be a risky approach to this problem or question? • What is the worst that can happen if I take this risk? What is the best? • What have I learned from this mistake?

He quickly sized up his environment (bear and slower boy) and adapted (got ready to run) to pursue his goal (to escape becoming the bear's dinner).

Another example: Your goal is to pass freshman composition. You learn most successfully through visual presentations. To achieve your goal, you can use the instructor's PowerPoints or other visual media to enhance your learning (adapt to your environment) or enroll in a heavily visual Internet course (change your environment to adapt to you)—or both.

Why practical thinking is important

Real-world problems and decisions require you to add understanding of experiences and social interactions to your analytical abilities. Your success in a sociology class, for example, may depend almost as much on getting along with

your instructor as on your academic work. Similarly, the way you solve a personal money problem may have more impact on your life than how you work through a problem in an accounting course.

Keep in mind, too, that in the workplace you need to use practical skills to apply academic knowledge to problems and decisions. For example, although students majoring in elementary education may successfully quote child development facts on an exam, their career success depends on the ability to evaluate and address real children's needs in the classroom. Successfully solving real-world problems demands a practical approach.

Through experience, you build emotional intelligence

You gain much of your ability to think practically from personal experience, rather than from formal training.[16] What you learn from experience answers "how" questions—how to talk, how to behave, how to proceed.[17] For example, after completing several papers for a course, you may learn what your instructor expects—or, after a few arguments with a friend or partner, you may learn how to avoid topics that cause conflict. See Key 4.7 for ways in which this kind of knowledge can be shown in "if-then" statements.

As you learned in Chapter 1, emotional intelligence gives you steps you can take to promote success. For example, when Ethan was let go from his job, he was angry about it. With effort, his response involved these practical and emotionally and socially intelligent actions:

▶ After he received the letter, *recognizing* his feelings
▶ Working to *understand* what his feelings and mindset told him about what he wanted and how he perceived the situation
▶ *Adjusting* his thinking in order to gain something out of a bad situation

Key 4.7 HERE IS ONE WAY TO MAP OUT WHAT YOU **LEARN FROM EXPERIENCE**

Goal: You want to talk to the soccer coach about your status on the team.

IF the team has had a good practice and IF you've played well during the scrimmage and IF the coach isn't rushing off somewhere, THEN grab a moment with him right after practice ends.

IF the team is having a tough time and IF you've been sidelined and IF the coach is in a rush and stressed, THEN drop in during his office hours tomorrow.

▶ *Managing* his emotions by scheduling a meeting when he had calmed down, making his points at the meeting, keeping a productive goal in mind, and listening to what his supervisor said in response

▶ Politely requesting something related to his goal (such as a positive recommendation)

These emotionally intelligent actions make it more likely that Ethan's supervisor will be receptive and helpful and that there will be a positive outcome from the interaction.

If you know that social interactions are difficult for you, enlist someone to give you some informal coaching. Ask a friend to role-play the meeting with your instructor (your friend will act as if he is the instructor) and give you feedback on your words, tone, and body language. Or bring a friend with you to the actual meeting and talk later about how things went.

Practical thinking means action

Action is the logical result of practical thinking. Basic student success strategies that promote action—staying motivated, making the most of your strengths, learning from failure, managing time, seeking help from instructors and advisors, and believing in yourself—will keep you moving toward your goals.[18]

The key to making practical knowledge work is to use what you discover, assuring that you will not have to learn the same lessons over and over again. As Sternberg says, "What matters most is not how much experience you have had but rather how much you have profited from it—in other words, how well you apply what you have learned."[19]

See Key 4.8 for some questions you can ask in order to apply practical thinking to your problems and decisions.

ASK QUESTIONS LIKE THESE
TO ACTIVATE **PRACTICAL THINKING**

To learn from experience, ask:

• What worked well, or not so well, about my approach? My timing? My tone? My wording?
• What did others like or not like about what I did?
• What did I learn from that experience, conversation, event?
• How would I change things if I had to do it over again?
• What do I know I would do again?

To apply what you learn, ask

• What have I learned that would work here?
• What have I seen others do, or heard about from them, that would be helpful here?
• What does this situation have in common with past situations I've been involved in?
• What has worked in similar situations in the past?

To boost your ability to take action, ask:

• How can I get motivated and remove limitations?
• How can I, in this situation, make the most of what I do well?
• If I fail, what can I learn from it?
• What steps will get me to my goal, and what trade-offs are involved?
• How can I manage my time more effectively?

Take a Practical Approach to
Building Successful Intelligence

Look back at your Wheel of Successful Intelligence in Chapter 1 on page 26. Write here the skill area in which you most need to build strength:

_____

Write down two practical actions you can take that will improve your skills in that area. For example, someone who wants to be more creative could take a course focused on creativity; someone who wants to be more practical could work on paying attention to social cues; someone who wants to be more analytical could decide to analyze one newspaper article every week.

1. _____

   _____

2. _____

   _____

How can you solve problems and make decisions **effectively?**

The best problem solvers and decision makers put their analytical, creative, and practical thinking skills together to solve problems and make decisions. Problem solving and decision making follow similar paths, both requiring you to identify and analyze a situation, generate possibilities, choose one, follow through on it, and evaluate its success. Key 4.9 gives an overview indicating the process at each step. Keys 4.11 and 4.12 show examples of how to map out problems and decisions effectively.

Understanding the differences between problem solving and decision making will help you know how to proceed. See Key 4.10 for more information. Remember, too, that whereas all problem solving involves decision making, not all decision making requires you to solve a problem.

Solve a problem

The following strategies will help you move through the problem-solving process outlined in Key 4.9.

■ *Use probing questions to define problems.* Ask, What is the problem? And what is causing the problem? Engage your emotional intelligence. If you determine that you are not motivated to do your work for a class, for example, you could ask questions like these:

▶ Do my feelings stem from how I interact with my instructor or classmates?
▶ Is the subject matter difficult? Uninteresting?

Chances are that how you answer one or more of these questions may help you define the problem—and ultimately solve it.

■ *Analyze carefully.* Gather information that will help you examine the problem. Consider how the problem is similar to, or different from, other problems. Clarify facts. Note your own perspective and look for others. Make sure your assumptions are not getting in the way.

■ *Generate possible solutions based on causes, not effects.* Addressing a cause provides a lasting solution, whereas "putting a Band-Aid on" an effect cannot. Say, for example, that your shoulder hurts when you type. Getting a massage is a helpful but temporary solution, because the pain returns whenever you go back to work. Changing your keyboard height is a lasting solution to the problem, because it eliminates the cause of your pain.

■ *Consider how possible solutions affect you and others.* What would suit you best? What takes other people's needs into consideration?

SOLVE PROBLEMS AND MAKE DECISIONS
USING SUCCESSFUL INTELLIGENCE

PROBLEM SOLVING	THINKING SKILL	DECISION MAKING
Define the problem—recognize that something needs to change, identify what's happening, look for true causes.	**STEP 1 DEFINE**	**Define the decision**—identify your goal (your need) and then construct a decision that will help you get it.
Analyze the problem—gather information, break it down into pieces, verify facts, look at perspectives and assumptions, evaluate information.	**STEP 2 ANALYZE**	**Examine needs and motives**—consider the layers of needs carefully, and be honest about what you really want.
Generate possible solutions—use creative strategies to think of ways you could address the causes of this problem.	**STEP 3 CREATE**	**Name and/or generate different options**—use creative questions to come up with choices that would fulfill your needs.
Evaluate solutions—look carefully at potential pros and cons of each, and choose what seems best.	**STEP 4 ANALYZE (EVALUATE)**	**Evaluate options**—look carefully at potential pros and cons of each, and choose what seems best.
Put the solution to work—persevere, focus on results, and believe in yourself as you go for your goal.	**STEP 5 TAKE PRACTICAL ACTION**	**Act on your decision**—go down the path and use practical strategies to stay on target.
Evaluate how well the solution worked—look at the effects of what you did.	**STEP 6 ANALYZE (REEVALUATE)**	**Evaluate the success of your decision**—look at whether it accomplished what you had hoped.
In the future, apply what you've learned—use this solution, or a better one, when a similar situation comes up again.	**STEP 7 TAKE PRACTICAL ACTION**	**In the future, apply what you've learned**—make this choice, or a better one, when a similar decision comes up again.

EXAMINE HOW **PROBLEMS AND DECISIONS** DIFFER

SITUATION	YOU HAVE A PROBLEM IF . . .	YOU NEED TO MAKE A DECISION IF . . .
Planning summer activities	Your low GPA means you need to attend summer school—and you've already accepted a summer job.	You've been accepted into two summer abroad internship programs.
Declaring a major	It's time to declare, but you don't have all the prerequisites for the major you want.	There are three majors that appeal to you and you qualify for them all.
Handling communications with instructors	You are having trouble following the lecture style of a particular instructor.	Your psychology survey course has seven sections taught by different instructors; you have to choose one.

■ *Evaluate your solution and act on it in the future.* Once you choose a solution and put it into action, ask yourself, What worked that you would do again? What didn't work that you would avoid or change in the future?

What happens if you don't work through a problem comprehensively? Take, for example, a student having an issue with an instructor. He may get into an argument with the instructor, stop showing up to class, or take a quick-and-dirty approach to assignments. Any of these choices may have negative consequences. Now look at how the student might work through this problem using analytical, creative, and practical thinking skills. Key 4.11 shows how his effort can pay off.

Make a decision

As you use the steps in Key 4.9 to make a decision, remember these strategies.

■ *Look at the given options—then try to think of more.* Some decisions have a given set of options. For example, your school may allow you to major, double major, or major and minor. However, you may be able to brainstorm with an advisor to come up with more options such as an interdisciplinary major. Consider similar situations you've been in or heard about, what decisions were made, and what resulted from those decisions.

■ *Think about how your decision affects others.* What you choose might have an impact on friends, family, and others around you.

■ *Gather perspectives.* Talk with others who have made similar decisions. If you listen carefully, you may hear ideas you haven't thought about.

■ *Look at the long-term effects.* As with problem solving, it's key to examine what happens after you put the decision into action. For important decisions, do a short-term evaluation and another evaluation after a period of time. Consider whether your decision sent you in the right direction or whether you should rethink your choice.

WORK THROUGH A PROBLEM
RELATING TO AN INSTRUCTOR

DEFINE PROBLEM HERE:	ANALYZE THE PROBLEM
I don't like my Sociology instructor	We have different styles and personality types—I am not comfortable working in groups and being vocal. I'm not interested in being there, and my grades are suffering from my lack of motivation.

Use boxes below to list possible solutions:

POTENTIAL POSITIVE EFFECTS	SOLUTION #1	POTENTIAL NEGATIVE EFFECTS
List for each solution: Don't have to deal with that instructor Less stress	Drop the course	List for each solution: Grade gets entered on my transcript I'll have to take the course eventually; it's required for my major
Getting credit for the course Feeling like I've honored a commitment	**SOLUTION #2** Put up with it until the end of the semester	Stress every time I'm there Lowered motivation Probably not such a good final grade
A chance to express myself Could get good advice An opportunity to ask direct questions of the instructor	**SOLUTION #3** Schedule meetings with advisor and instructor	Have to face instructor one-on-one Might just make things worse

Now choose the solution you think is best—circle it and make it happen.

ACTUAL POSITIVE EFFECTS	PRACTICAL ACTION	ACTUAL NEGATIVE EFFECTS
List for chosen solution: Got some helpful advice from advisor Talking in person with the instructor actually promoted a fairly honest discussion I won't have to take the course again	I scheduled and attended meetings with both advisor and instructor and opted to stick with the course.	List for chosen solution: Still have to put up with some group work I still don't know how much learning I'll retain from this course

FINAL EVALUATION: Was it a good or bad solution?

The solution has improved things. I'll finish the course, and I got the chance to fulfill some class responsibilities on my own or with one partner. I feel more understood and more willing to put my time into the course.

student profile

Brad Zak
Boston College, Chestnut Hill, Massachusetts

About me:

Always a sports enthusiast, I played basketball and football throughout high school in northern New Jersey, but decided not to pursue a sports career in college. I now attend BC's (Boston College's) Carroll School of Management.

What I focus on:

Early on, I developed a quiet, analytical way of weighing pros and cons before committing to a decision. Knowing I want a strong business background, I picked a major in finance even though I am not terribly interested in becoming an invest-

ment banker. When I arrived on campus, I decided it was crucial that I explore career options and build my resumé. I also realized that I missed being involved in sports, so I made my way over to the school newspaper and became a sports reporter.

Pretty quickly, I concluded that I want to pursue a career combining sports with business . . . but BC does not offer a sports management major. I needed some creative thinking to solve this problem! I declared communications as a second major and looked for more opportunities to develop skills in that field. In addition to writing for the BC newspaper, I've announced games on radio, written for ESPN Boston, worked as a campus rep for CBS College Sports,

competed in intramural sports . . . and became a Division I athlete. Well, not exactly—but I am a practice player for the women's basketball team.

What will help me in the workplace:

I believe I've used my problem-solving and decision-making skills to create the finance major's resumé for landing a job in the sports world. I certainly have some great experiences to talk about on job interviews!

Business world success is all about problem solving and decision making. My experiences will help me navigate the challenges ahead.

What happens when you make important decisions too quickly? Consider a student trying to decide whether to transfer schools. If she makes her decision based on a reason that ultimately is not the most important one for her (for example, close friends go to the other school), she may regret her choice.

Now look at how this student might make an effective decision. Key 4.12 shows how she worked through the analytical, creative, and practical parts of the process.

Keep your balance

No one has equal strengths in analytical, creative, and practical thinking. However, you think and work toward goals most effectively when you combine all three. Staying as balanced as possible requires that you analyze your levels

MAKE A DECISION ABOUT
WHETHER TO TRANSFER SCHOOLS

DEFINE PROBLEM HERE:	EXAMINE NEEDS AND MOTIVES
Whether or not to transfer schools	My father has changed jobs and can no longer afford my tuition. My goal is to become a physical therapist, so I need a school with a full physical therapy program. My family needs to cut costs. I need to transfer credits.

Use boxes below to list possible solutions:

POTENTIAL POSITIVE EFFECTS	SOLUTION #1	POTENTIAL NEGATIVE EFFECTS
List for each solution: No need to adjust to a new place or new people Ability to continue course work as planned	Continue at the current college	List for each solution: Need to finance most of my tuition and costs on my own Difficult to find time for a job Might not qualify for aid
Many physical therapy courses available School is close so I could live at home and save room costs Reasonable tuition; credits will transfer	SOLUTION #2 Transfer to the community college	No personal contacts there that I know of Less independence if I live at home No bachelor's degree available
Opportunity to earn tuition money Could live at home Status should be intact	SOLUTION #3 Stop out for a year	Could forget so much that it's hard to go back Could lose motivation A year might turn into more

Now choose the solution you think is best—circle it and make it happen.

ACTUAL POSITIVE EFFECTS	PRACTICAL ACTION	ACTUAL NEGATIVE EFFECTS
List for chosen solution: Money saved Opportunity to spend time on studies rather than on working to earn tuition money Availability of classes I need	Go to community college for two years; then transfer to a four-year school to get a B.A. and complete physical therapy course work.	List for chosen solution: Loss of some independence Less contact with friends

FINAL EVALUATION: Was it a good or bad solution?
I'm satisfied with the decision. It can be hard being at home at times, but my parents are adjusting to my independence and I'm trying to respect their concerns. With fewer social distractions, I'm really getting my work done. Plus the financial aspect of the decision is ideal.

of ability in the three thinking areas, come up with creative ideas about how to build areas where you need to develop, and put them to use with practical action. Above all, believe in your skills as a thinker.

"Successfully intelligent people," says Sternberg, "defy negative expectations, even when these expectations arise from low scores on IQ or similar tests. They do not let other people's assessments stop them from achieving their goals. They find their path and then pursue it, realizing that there will be obstacles along the way and that surmounting these obstacles is part of the challenge."[20] Let the obstacles come, as they will for everyone, in all aspects of life. You can face and overcome them with the power of your successfully intelligent thinking.

Case Wrap-up

What happened to Ethan? First of all, a savvy friend got him to look carefully at his short-term money situation. He realized that with his severance pay, even though it will only last a month, he can cover tuition expenses through the rest of the term. That will buy him time to think more carefully about what to do next. He also went back to the Bureau of Labor website to look at the thirty occupations anticipated to grow the most in the next 5 years. He noted that although programming is estimated to shrink, other related areas such as network systems and software engineering are looking good. He also reminded himself that a projection isn't necessarily going to come true. His mood began to turn more positive as he opened his mind up to other possibilities for how to use what he does well and has chosen to study.

What does this mean for you? Think about the areas of study that interest you at this point. Examine information at www.bls.gov to see if your interest(s) relate to any career areas projected to grow or recede in the next 10 years. Look up any other articles you can find on career projections. Then write about where you stand. How does what you've read change, or reinforce, your educational and career goals?

What effects go beyond your world? The volatile job market is affecting workers from the bottom of the ladder to the top. Imagine you are the president of your college, speaking at graduation. What would you say to your graduating students to prepare them to successfully enter—and thrive in—today's workplace?

Successful Intelligence *Wrap-up*

HERE'S HOW YOU HAVE
BUILT SKILLS IN **CHAPTER 4** :

ANALYTICAL THINKING	CREATIVE THINKING	PRACTICAL THINKING
❯ You explored the steps and parts of analytical thinking in the section on analytical thinking skills.	❯ You developed a detailed understanding of creative thinking as you read the section on creative thinking skills.	❯ You developed more specific ideas of how to apply your emotional intelligence.
❯ In the Get Analytical exercise, you honed your skills by analyzing a statement.	❯ In the Get Creative exercise, you brainstormed creative acts as well as new ideas about how to deal with a problem.	❯ In the Get Practical exercise, you generated practical ideas about how to improve your successful intelligence.
❯ You considered how to evaluate potential ideas and choices in the problem-solving and decision-making processes.	❯ You explored ways to brainstorm solutions and choices when solving a problem or making a decision.	❯ You explored practical ways to put solutions and choices to work when solving a problem or making a decision.

Word*for*Thought

A recently coined **Norwegian** verb—*kunnskaping*
(kun'-skahp-ping)—translates loosely as
"knowledging," which can be read as
developing knowledge and meaning that are
useful in school and work (and more important
than ever before in the global marketplace).[21]
Work to develop the analytical, creative, and
practical skills that can help you "knowledge"
your way to success.

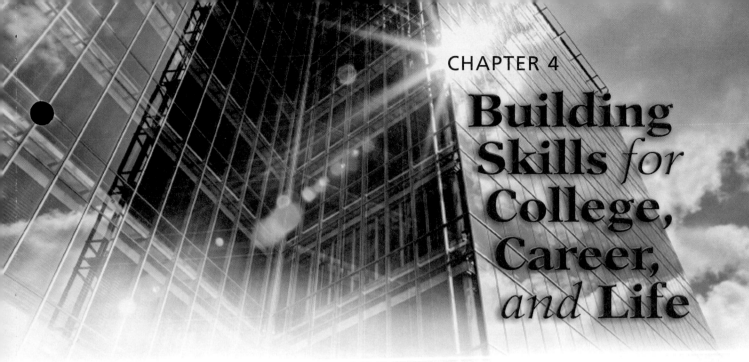

Building Skills *for* College, Career, *and* Life

Steps to Success

Make an Important Decision

BUILD BASIC SKILLS. List the steps of the decision-making process.

_____

_____

_____

_____

TAKE IT TO THE NEXT LEVEL. Think about how you would put the decision-making process to work on something that matters to you. Write an important long-term goal that you have, and define the decision that will help you fulfill it. Example: "My goal is to become a nurse. My decision: What to specialize in."

_____

_____

_____

_____

MOVE TOWARD MASTERY. Use a separate piece of paper to apply the decision-making process to your goal. Use the following steps to organize your thinking.

- *Examine needs and concerns.* What are your needs, and how do your values come into play? What is most needed in the health market, and how can you fulfill that need? What roadblocks might be involved? List everything you come up with. For example, the prospective nurse might list the following needs: "I need to feel that I'm helping people. I intend to help with the shortage of perinatal or geriatric nurses. I need to make a good living."

- *Generate options.* Ask questions to imagine what's possible. Where might you work? What might be the schedule and pace? Who might work with you? What would you see, smell, and hear on your job? What would you do every day? List, too, all of the options you know of. The prospective nurse, for example, might list perinatal surgery, neonatal intensive care unit, geriatric nursing in a hospital or in a retirement community, and so on.

- *Evaluate options.* Think about how well your options will fulfill your needs. For two of your options, write potential positive and negative effects (pros and cons) of each.

Option 1: _____

Potential pros: _____

Potential cons: _____

Option 2: _____

Potential pros: _____

Potential cons: _____

- *Imagine acting on your decision.* Describe one practical course of action, based on your thinking so far, that you might follow. List the specific steps you would take. For example, the prospective nurse might list actions to help determine what type of nursing suits him best, such as interning, summer jobs, academic goals, and talking to working nurses.

An additional practical action is to go to an actual job site and talk to people. The prospective nurse might go to a hospital, a clinic, and a health center at a retirement community. Get a feel for what the job is like day-to-day so that can be part of your decision.

Teamwork

Create Solutions Together

POWERFUL GROUP PROBLEM SOLVING

Goal: To experience problem solving as a group and to generate useful and relevant solutions.

Time on task: 30 minutes

Instructions: On a 3 × 5 card or a plain sheet of paper, each student in the class writes a school-related problem—this could be a fear, a challenge, a sticky situation, or a roadblock. Students hand these in without names. The instructor writes the list up on the board.

Divide into groups of two to four. Each group chooses one problem to work on (try not to have two groups working on the same problem). Use the empty problem-solving flowchart (Key 4.13) to fill in your work.

Analyze: Define and examine the problem. As a group, look at the negative effects and state your problem specifically. Write down the causes and examine them to see what's happening. Gather information from all group members, verify facts, and go beyond assumptions.

Create: Generate possible solutions. From the most likely causes of the problem, derive possible solutions. Record all the ideas that group members offer. Each group member should choose one possible solution to evaluate independently.

Analyze: Evaluate each solution. In thinking independently through the assigned solution, each group member should (a) weigh the positive and negative effects, (b) consider similar problems, and (c) describe how the solution affects the causes of the problem. Will your solution work?

Get practical: Choose a solution. Group members then come together, share observations and recommendations, and then take a vote: Which solution is the best? You may have a tie or want to combine two different solutions. Try to find the solution that works for most of the group. Then together come up with a plan for putting your solution to work.

To wrap up, think and write. What did you learn about problem solving from doing it in a group setting? What was different, easier, harder, the same?

WORK THROUGH A PROBLEM USING THIS **FLOWCHART**

DEFINE PROBLEM HERE:	ANALYZE THE PROBLEM

Use boxes below to list possible solutions:

POTENTIAL POSITIVE EFFECTS	SOLUTION #1	POTENTIAL NEGATIVE EFFECTS
List for each solution:		List for each solution:

	SOLUTION #2	

	SOLUTION #3	

Now choose the solution you think is best—circle it and make it happen.

ACTUAL POSITIVE EFFECTS	PRACTICAL ACTION	ACTUAL NEGATIVE EFFECTS
List for chosen solution:		List for chosen solution:

FINAL EVALUATION: Was it a good or bad solution?

Source: Based on heuristic created by Frank T. Lyman Jr. and George Eley, 1985.

Writing

Build Intrapersonal and Communication Skills

Record your thoughts on a separate piece of paper, in a journal, or electronically.

EMOTIONAL INTELLIGENCE JOURNAL

Make a wiser choice. Think about a decision you made that you wish you had handled differently. Describe the decision and what feelings resulted from it. Then, describe what you would do if you could approach the decision again, thinking about a mindset and actions that might produce more positive feelings and a better outcome.

REAL-LIFE WRITING

Address a problem. Think about a problem that you are currently experiencing in school—it could be difficulty with a course, a scheduling nightmare, or a conflict with a classmate. Write a letter—to an advisor, instructor, friend, medical professional, or anyone else who may help—that asks for help with your problem. Be specific about what you want and how the person to whom you are writing can help you. After you finish, consider sending your letter via mail or e-mail. Carefully assess the effect that it may have, and if you decide that it may help, send it. Be sure to have someone you trust review it for you before you send.

Personal Portfolio

Prepare for Career Success

GENERATE IDEAS FOR INTERNSHIPS

21st Century Learning Building Blocks

- Financial, Economic, Business, and Entrepreneurial Literacy
- Leadership and Responsibility
- Communication and Collaboration

Complete the following in your electronic portfolio or separately on paper.

Pursuing internships is a practical way to get experience, learn what you like and don't like, and make valuable connections. Even interning in a career area that you don't ultimately pursue can build skills that are useful in any career. The creative thinking skills you've built will help you generate ideas for where you might intern at some point during college.

First, use personal contacts to gather information about career fields. List two people here:

People whom I want to interview about their fields/professions, and why:

1. _____ Field: _____

   Because: _____

2. _____ Field: _____

   Because: _____

Talk to the people you have listed and take notes.

Next, look up each of these fields in the *Occupational Outlook Handbook* published by the U.S. Department of Labor (available at the library or online at http://stats.bls.gov/oco/home.htm). To get a better idea of whether you would want to intern in these fields, read OOH categories for each such as

Nature of the Work, Training, Working Conditions, Advancement, Job Outlook, Earnings, and so on. Take notes and compare the fields based on what you've learned.

Finally, consult someone in your school's career office about local companies that offer internships. Get specific information about internship job descriptions, timing (during the term, summer), and whether there is any financial compensation involved.

Analyze what you have learned from your reading, your interviews, and career office information. Write here the field or fields in which you would like to intern and why, and describe what practical action you plan to take to secure an internship within the next two years:

_____

_____

_____

_____

_____

_____

_____

_____

_____

_____

Social Networking

ESTABLISH YOUR HISTORY

Broaden your profile with information about any work history you have. Sign in to your LinkedIn account and click on "Edit My Profile." Then, fill in work information on the following (as applicable):

- Current (Click on "Current" and add information about your current employment: company name, job title, when you started working there, and description.)
- Past (Click on "Past" and add information about one or more past jobs: company name, job title, time period you worked, and description.)

If you have a lean or nonexistent work history, start thinking now about how to build that history while you are in school. Besides paid jobs in the workforce, other possibilities include internships, volunteering, and working on campus with faculty. Be sure to update your resumé and LinkedIn profile with work history as you build it.

■ *Answers to perception puzzles on p. 95:* First puzzle: A duck or a rabbit. Second puzzle: A face or a musician. Third puzzle: Lines or a letter.

Reading and Information Literacy

Learning from Print and Online Materials

What Would You Do?

Think about this problem as you read, and consider how you would approach it. This chapter focuses on reading in ways that help you take in information comprehensively, analyze it critically, and decide what to remember. It can help you with any reading struggle you need to address on your path to success.

Gary Montrose had no idea why he struggled in grade school, and neither did his family or teachers. He was the first to sit down during spelling bees and the last to turn in class exams, even though his hard work got him elected student body president at Palmdale High School. His guidance counselor told him that he "wasn't college material" and should consider going straight into a job at the local Lockheed assembly plant.

Determined to persevere, Gary enrolled at Antelope Valley College in Palmdale, California, and put his nose to the grindstone. After 2 years he was able to transfer to the University of California at Berkeley, but the confusing struggle remained, damaging his self-confidence and requiring survival strategies developed through experience. He avoided courses with in-class timed exams—an absolute terror—and looked for classes featuring papers he could write on his own time. He gave up 90 percent of a normal college student's social life and spent hours "unpacking" textbooks by reading the table of contents, chapter headings, tables, and charts. Knowing he was unlikely to complete any reading assignment without support, he needed to develop an idea of the scope of a book.

Despite graduating with high honors and a double major, Gary still lived with his "big secret," terrified about how slowly he read and wrote. Hoping for advice on what type of work he could suc-cessfully pursue, he went to the career center while in graduate school, where a series of tests showed he was functioning at a seventh-grade reading level. From those results he learned that he had a reading disability called *dyslexia* that causes difficulty with recognizing and understanding words. He began to see why he needed to put in so much extra time and effort to appear normal to the outside world. (To be continued . . .)

Gary's ability to move out of his comfort zone has turned learning into an adventure that he continues as a world-wide traveler. You'll learn more about Gary, and revisit his situation, within the chapter.

In this chapter, you'll explore answers to these questions:

> What sets you up for reading comprehension? p. 116

> How can SQ3R improve your reading? p. 119

> What strategies help with specific subjects and formats? p. 130

> How can you be an information literate reader and researcher? p. 136

> How can you respond critically to what you read? p. 139

 ANALYTICAL

 CREATIVE

 PRACTICAL

For each statement, circle the number that feels right to you, from 1 for "not at all true for me" to 5 for "very true for me."

▶ I make choices in when and how I read that help me boost focus and comprehension.	1 2 3 4 5
▶ I preview a text before studying it by skimming and scanning front matter, chapter elements, and back matter for clues about content and organization.	1 2 3 4 5
▶ I develop questions to guide me before I begin to read.	1 2 3 4 5
▶ I practice reciting what I've learned from the reading by working with a study partner, taking notes, using flash cards, or some other study technique.	1 2 3 4 5
▶ I use text note taking and highlighting to turn my texts into study tools.	1 2 3 4 5
▶ I have a process for reading on-screen assignments and articles.	1 2 3 4 5
▶ I prioritize my reading assignments so that I focus on what is most important.	1 2 3 4 5
▶ When I get a research or writing assignment, I go first to general references for an overview.	1 2 3 4 5
▶ I don't just rely on the Internet for research—I also consult library materials.	1 2 3 4 5
▶ I evaluate every Internet source for signs of bias, validity, credibility, and reliability.	1 2 3 4 5

Each of the topics in these statements is covered in this chapter. Note those statements for which you circled a 3 or lower. Skim the chapter to see where those topics appear, and pay special attention to them as you read, learn, and apply new strategies.

REMEMBER: *No matter how developed your reading and information literacy skills are, you can improve with effort and practice.*

"Successful intelligence is most effective when it balances all three of its analytical, creative, and practical aspects. It is more important to know when and how to use these aspects of successful intelligence than just to have them."

—Robert Sternberg

What sets you up for **reading comprehension?**

College reading assignments—textbook chapters or other materials—are often challenging, requiring more focus and new strategies to understand the material fully. In exchange for your extra effort, though, you stand to receive a broad and deep range of information and knowledge. Working hard to understand material in introductory-level texts also provides a more solid foundation for your understanding in advanced courses. Finally, if you are open to it, the new worlds reading reveals can bring you great satisfaction and even joy.

On any given day, you may have a variety of reading assignments, such as the following:

▶ An eighteen-page text chapter on the history of South African apartheid (world history)
▶ An original research study on the relationship between sleep deprivation and the development of memory problems (psychology)
▶ The first three chapters in John Steinbeck's classic novel *The Grapes of Wrath* (American literature)

▶ A technical manual on the design of computer anti-virus programs (computer science—software design)

To face this challenge, it's helpful to use specific reading techniques. Before you open a book or log onto your computer, how can you get ready to make the most of your reading?

Define your reading purpose

The first step in improving your reading comprehension is to ask yourself *why* you are reading particular material. With a clear purpose you can decide how much time and effort to expend on your assignments. Key 5.1 shows four common reading purposes. Depending on what your instructor expects, you may have as many as three reading purposes for one assignment, such as understanding, critical evaluation, and practical application.

Use the class syllabus to help define your purpose for each assignment. For example, if the syllabus shows that inflation is the topic of your next economics class lecture, read the assigned chapter with that focus in mind: mastering the definition of inflation, evaluating historical economic events that caused inflation, and so on. And keep open the possibility that any reading assignment with purposes 1, 2, or 3 may also bring you purpose 4—enjoyment.

Take an active and positive approach

Many instructors spend little or no time reviewing reading in class because they expect you to complete it independently. How can you approach difficult material actively and positively?

If you look carefully at your schedule, you may find useful segments of time in between classes. Try using such time for reading assignments.
© Spencer Grant/Photo Researchers

Key 5.1

ESTABLISH WHY YOU ARE READING A GIVEN PIECE OF MATERIAL

WHAT'S MY PURPOSE?	EXPLANATION
1. To understand	Read to comprehend concepts and details. Details help explain or support general concepts, and concepts provide a framework for details.
2. To evaluate analytically	Read with an open mind as you examine causes and effects, evaluate ideas, and ask questions that test arguments and assumptions. Evaluation develops a level of understanding beyond basic information recall (see pages 87 to 92 for more on this topic).
3. For practical application	Read to find information to help reach a specific goal. For instance, when you read a lab manual for chemistry, your goal is to learn how to do the lab experiment.
4. For pleasure	Read for entertainment, such as *Sports Illustrated* magazine or a mystery or romance novel.

► *Start with a questioning attitude.* Consider questions such as, How can I connect the reading to what I already know? Look at the chapter headings and ask yourself questions about what the material means and why it is being presented in this way.

► *Look for order.* Use SQ3R and the critical reading strategies introduced later in this chapter to discover patterns, logic, and relationships. Text cues—how the material is organized, outlines, bold terms, and more—help you anticipate what's coming next.

► *Have an open mind.* Be careful not to prejudge assignments as impossible or boring or a waste of time before you begin.

► *Plan for multiple readings.* Don't expect to master challenging material on the first pass. Get an overview of key concepts on the first reading. Use later readings to build your understanding, relate information to what you know, and apply information elsewhere. Gary accepted multiple readings as necessary to his success.

► *Get help.* If material is tough to understand, consult resources—instructors, study group partners, tutors, related texts, and websites—for help. Build a library of texts in your major and minor areas of study and refer to them when needed.

Choose the right setting

Where, when, and with whom you study has a significant effect on your success.

► *Choose locations that work.* Know yourself and choose settings that distract you least—in your room at home, at a library, outdoors, in an empty classroom, anywhere that works. Your schedule may restrict your choices. For example, if you can only study late at night when the libraries are closed, you will probably have to work at home; if you spend a good deal of your day commuting, mass transit may be your best study spot. Evaluate how effectively you focus. If you spend too much time time being distracted at a particular location, try someplace different.

► *Choose times that work.* Pay attention to your body's natural rhythms, and try to read during times when you tend to be most alert and focused. For example, although night owls are productive when everyone else is sleeping, morning people may have a hard time reading late at night. The times you choose depend, of course, on what your schedule allows.

PRIMARY SOURCES
Original documents, including academic journal articles and scientific studies.

SECONDARY SOURCES
Other writers' interpretations of primary source documents.

Learn to concentrate

Even well-written college textbooks may require a lot of focus, especially when you encounter complex concepts and new terms. Even greater focus is often necessary when assignments are from **primary sources** rather than **secondary sources.**

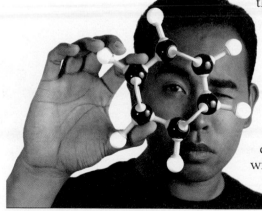

When you focus your attention on one thing and only one thing, you are engaged in the act of *concentration*. The following active-learning methods can help maintain focus as you study. Many involve tapping into your emotional and social intelligence.

► *Deal with internal distractions.* When worries come up, such as to-do list items for other projects, write them down to deal with later. Sometimes you may want to take a break to deal with what's bothering you. Exercise may help, or music may relieve stress; a snack can reduce hunger.

▶ *Take control of technology.* Web surfing, e-mailing, instant messaging, or downloading songs onto your iPod are reading distractions. Wait for breaks or after you finish your work to spend time checking texts or downloading.

▶ *Structure your work session.* Set realistic goals and a specific plan for dividing your time. Tell yourself, "I'm going to read 30 pages and then go online for 30 minutes."

▶ *Manage family obligations.* Set up activities or child care if you have kids. Tell them, if they are old enough to understand, what your education will mean to them and to you.

▶ *Plan a reward.* Have something to look forward to. You deserve it!

The strongest motivation to concentrate comes from within. When you see the connection between what you study and your short- and long-term goals, you will be better able to focus, to remember, to learn, and to apply.

Expand your vocabulary

As reading materials become more complex, your vocabulary influences how much you comprehend—and how readily you do so. When reading a textbook, the first "dictionary" to search is the end-of-book glossary that explains technical words and concepts. The definitions there are usually limited to the meanings used in the text. Standard dictionaries provide broader information such as word origin, pronunciation, part of speech, synonyms, antonyms, and multiple meanings. Buy a standard dictionary and investigate websites like dictionary.com. The suggestions in Key 5.2 will help you make the most of your dictionary.

How can SQ3R improve your reading?

Reading may look like a one-way street in which you, the reader, take in words the author has written. However, it is intended as an interactive communication. The author communicates ideas to you and invites your response. How can you respond? One answer is provided in the SQ3R reading strategy, which stands for *Survey, Question, Read, Recite,* and *Review.*[1] This straightforward technique helps readers take in, understand, and remember what they read. It encourages you to fulfill your side of interactive communication by asking questions, marking key ideas, introducing your own connections, and more.

As you move through the stages of SQ3R, you will skim and scan your text. **Skimming** refers to the rapid reading of such chapter elements as section introductions and conclusions, boldface or italicized terms, pictures and charts, and summaries. The goal of skimming is a quick construction of the main ideas. In contrast, **scanning** involves a careful search for specific information. You might use scanning during the SQ3R review phase to locate particular facts.

Just like many strategies presented to you throughout your college career, SQ3R works best if you adapt it to your own needs. Explore techniques, evaluate what works, and then make the system your own. As you become familiar with the system, keep in mind that SQ3R works best with textbook-based courses like science, math, social sciences, and humanities. SQ3R is not recommended for literature courses.

→ SKIMMING
Rapid, superficial reading of material to determine central ideas and main elements.

→ SCANNING
Reading material in an investigative way to search for specific information.

MAKE THE MOST
OF YOUR DICTIONARY

Use the word in the next 24 hours.

Not only does this demonstrate that you know how the word is used, but it also aids memorization.

Analyze word parts.

Many English words combine prefixes, roots, and suffixes. *Prefixes* are word parts added to the beginning of a root. *Suffixes* are added to the end of the root. The *root* is the central part or basis of a word around which prefixes and/or suffixes are added to produce different words. Recognizing these word parts can boost comprehension.

Read beyond the first definition.

Then think critically about which meaning suits the context of the word in question and choose the one that makes the most sense.

dic·tio·nary

Pronunciation; \ˈdik-shə-ˌner-ē, -ˌne-rē\

Function: *noun*

Inflected Form(s): *plural* **dic·tio·nar·ies**

Etymology: Medieval Latin *dictionarium,* from Late Latin *diction-, dictio* word, from Latin, speaking

Date: 1526

1. A reference source in print or electronic form containing words usually alphabetically arranged along with information about their forms, pronunciations, functions, etymologies, meanings, and syntactical and idiomatic uses.

2. A book giving information on particular subjects or on a particular class of words, names, or facts, usually arranged alphabetically: *a biographical dictionary; a dictionary of mathematics.*

3. (*computing*) An associative array, a data structure where each value is referenced by a particular key, analogous to words and definitions in a physical dictionary.

Say and spell new words to boost recall.

Listen to the pronunciation on a hand-held electronic or online dictionary. Then practice writing the word to verify that you know the spelling.

Restate the definition in your own words.

When you can do this with ease, you know that you understand the meaning and are not merely parroting a dictionary definition.

Step 1: Survey

Surveying, the first stage in SQ3R, is the process of previewing, or prereading, a book before you study it. Compare it to looking at a map before starting a road trip; determining the route and stops along the way in advance will save time and trouble while you travel. Gary made extensive use of the survey tools that most textbooks provide, including elements like the following that provide a big picture overview of the main ideas and themes.

■ *Front matter.* Skim the *table of contents* for the chapter titles, the main topics in each chapter and the order in which they will be covered, as well as special features. Then skim the *preface,* which is a personal note from the author that tells you what the book will cover and its point of view. For example, the preface for the American history text *Out of Many* states that it highlights "the experiences of diverse communities of Americans in the unfolding story of our country."[2] This tells you that cultural diversity is a central theme.

■ *Chapter elements.* Text chapters use various devices to structure the material and highlight content.

▶ *Chapter titles* establish the topic and often the author's perspective.
▶ *Chapter introductions or outlines* generally list objectives or key topics.
▶ *Level headings* (first, second, third), including those in question form, break down material into bite-size chunks.
▶ *Margin materials* can include definitions, quotes, questions, and exercises.
▶ *Tables, charts, photographs, and captions* illustrate important concepts in a visual manner.
▶ *Sidebars or boxed features* are connected to text themes and introduce extra tidbits of information that supplement the text.
▶ *Different styles or arrangements of type* (**boldface,** *italics,* underlining, larger fonts, bullet points, boxed text) can flag vocabulary or important ideas.
▶ *End-of-chapter summaries* review chapter content and main ideas.
▶ *Review questions and exercises* help you understand and apply content in creative and practical ways.

In Key 5.3, a typical page from the college textbook *Psychology: An Introduction,* by Charles G. Morris and Albert A. Maisto, how many elements do you recognize? How do these elements help you grasp the subject even before reading it?

■ *Back matter.* Some texts include a *glossary* that defines text terms, an *index* to help you locate topics, and a *bibliography* that lists additional readings.

Step 2: Question

The next step is to ask questions about your assignment. Using the *questioning* process that follows leads you to discover knowledge on your own, making an investment in the material and in your own memory.

Ask yourself what you know

Before you begin reading, think about—and summarize in writing if you can—what you already know about the topic, if anything. This step prepares you to apply what you know to new material. Building on current knowledge is especially important in your major, where the concepts you learn from intro courses prepare you for the higher-level material in classes to come later on.

Write questions linked to chapter headings

Next, examine the chapter headings and, on a separate page or in the text margins, write questions linked to them. When you encounter an assignment without headings, divide the material into logical sections and then develop questions based on what you think is the main idea of each section. There are no "correct" questions. Given the same headings, two students could create two different sets of questions. Your goal in questioning is to begin to think critically about the material.

Classical (or Pavlovian) conditioning The type of learning in which a response naturally elicited by one stimulus comes to be elicited by a different, formerly neutral stimulus.

Unconditioned stimulus (US) A stimulus that invariably causes an organism to respond in a specific way.

Unconditioned response (UR) A response that takes place in an organism whenever an unconditioned stimulus occurs.

Conditioned stimulus (CS) An originally neutral stimulus that is paired with an unconditioned stimulus and eventually produces the desired response in an organism when presented alone.

Conditioned response (CR) After conditioning, the response an organism produces when only a conditioned stimulus is presented.

you are experiencing insight. When you imitate the steps of professional dancers you saw last night on television, you are demonstrating observational learning. Like conditioning, cognitive learning is one of our survival strategies. Through cognitive processes, we learn which events are safe and which are dangerous without having to experience those events directly. Cognitive learning also gives us access to the wisdom of people who lived hundreds of years ago, and it will give people living hundreds of years from now some insight into our experiences and way of life.

Our discussion begins with *classical conditioning*. This simple kind of learning serves as a convenient starting point for examining what learning is and how it can be observed.

Classical Conditioning

How did Pavlov's discovery of classical conditioning help to shed light on learning?

Ivan Pavlov (1849–1936), a Russian physiologist who was studying digestive processes, discovered classical conditioning almost by accident. Because animals salivate when food is placed in their mouths, Pavlov inserted tubes into the salivary glands of dogs to measure how much saliva they produced when they were given food. He noticed, however, that the dogs salivated before the food was in their mouths: The mere sight of food made them drool. In fact, they even drooled at the sound of the experimenter's footsteps. This aroused Pavlov's curiosity. What was making the dogs salivate even before they had the food in their mouths? How had they learned to salivate in response to the sound of the experimenter's approach?

To answer these questions, Pavlov set out to teach the dogs to salivate when food was not present. He devised an experiment in which he sounded a bell just before the food was brought into the room. A ringing bell does not usually make a dog's mouth water but, after hearing the bell many times just before getting fed, Pavlov's dogs began to salivate as soon as the bell rang. It was as if they had learned that the bell signaled the appearance of food, and their mouths watered on cue even if no food followed. The dogs had been conditioned to salivate in response to a new stimulus—the bell—that would not normally have prompted that response (Pavlov, 1927). Figure 5–1, shows one of Pavlov's procedures in which the bell has been replaced by a touch to the dog's leg just before food is given.

Elements of Classical Conditioning

Generally speaking, **classical (or Pavlovian) conditioning** involves pairing an *involuntary* response (for example, salivation) that is usually evoked by one stimulus with a different, formerly neutral stimulus (such as a bell or a touch on the leg). Pavlov's experiment illustrates the four basic elements of classical conditioning. The first is an **unconditioned stimulus (US)**, such as food, which invariably prompts a certain reaction—salivation, in this case. That reaction—the **unconditioned response (UR)**—is the second element and always results from the unconditioned stimulus: Whenever the dog is given food (US), its mouth waters (UR). The third element is the neutral stimulus—the ringing bell—which is called the **conditioned stimulus (CS).** At first, the conditioned stimulus is said to be "neutral" with respect to the desired response (salivation), because dogs do not salivate at the sound of a bell unless they have been conditioned to react in this way by repeatedly presenting the CS and US together. Frequent pairing of the CS and US produces the fourth element in the classical conditioning process: the **conditioned response (CR).** The conditioned response is the behavior that the animal has learned in response to the conditioned stimulus. Usually, the unconditioned response and the conditioned

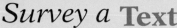

GET ANALYTICAL!

Survey a Text

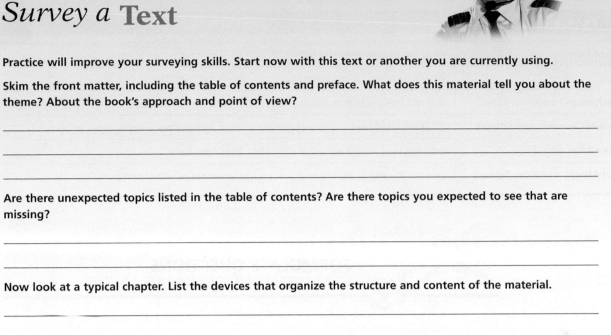

Practice will improve your surveying skills. Start now with this text or another you are currently using.

Skim the front matter, including the table of contents and preface. What does this material tell you about the theme? About the book's approach and point of view?

_____

_____

_____

Are there unexpected topics listed in the table of contents? Are there topics you expected to see that are missing?

_____

_____

Now look at a typical chapter. List the devices that organize the structure and content of the material.

_____

_____

After skimming the chapter, what do you know about the material? What elements helped you skim quickly?

_____

_____

Finally, skim the back matter. What elements can you identify?

_____

_____

How do you plan to use each of the elements you identified in your text survey when you begin studying?

_____

_____

Key 5.4 shows how this works. The column on the left contains primary and secondary headings from a section of *Out of Many*. The column on the right rephrases these headings in question form.

Use Bloom's Taxonomy to formulate questions

Questions can seek different types of answers and may require different levels of analytical thinking to solve. To help you understand and use different types of questions, consider the system educational psychologist Benjamin Bloom developed based on the idea that deeper learning occurs when the effort to understand is more rigorous.[3] Although some questions ask for a simple recall, said Bloom, others ask for higher thinking levels.

Key 5.5 shows the six levels of questions identified by Bloom: knowledge, understanding, application, analysis, synthesis, and evaluation. It also identifies

CREATE QUESTIONS
FROM HEADINGS

HEADINGS	QUESTIONS
The Meaning of Freedom	What did freedom mean for both slaves and citizens in the United States?
Moving About	Where did African Americans go after they were freed from slavery?
The African American Family	How did freedom change the structure of the African American family?
African American Churches and Schools	What effect did freedom have on the formation of African American churches and schools?
Land and Labor After Slavery	How was land farmed and maintained after slaves were freed?
The Origins of African American Politics	How did the end of slavery bring about the beginning of African American political life?

USE BLOOM'S TAXONOMY TO
FORMULATE QUESTIONS
AT DIFFERENT COGNITIVE LEVELS

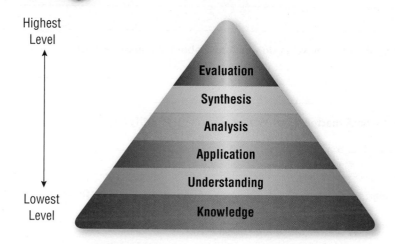

Highest Level

Lowest Level

Verbs That Indicate Each Level

1. **Knowledge:** average, define, duplicate, label, list, memorize, name, order, recognize, relate, recall, repeat, reproduce, state.

2. **Understanding:** classify, describe, discuss, explain, express, identify, indicate, locate, recognize, report, restate, review, select, translate.

3. **Application:** apply, choose, demonstrate, dramatize, employ, illustrate, interpret, operate, practice, schedule, sketch, solve, use, write.

4. **Analysis:** analyze, appraise, calculate, categorize, compare, contrast, criticize, differentiate, discriminate, distinguish, examine, experiment, question, test.

5. **Synthesis:** arrange, assemble, collect, compose, construct, create, design, develop, formulate, manage, organize, plan, prepare, propose, set up, write.

6. **Evaluation:** appraise, argue, assess, attach, choose, compare, defend, estimate, judge, predict, rate, score, select, support, value, evaluate.

verbs associated with each level. As you read, use these verbs to create specific questions that will help you learn. For instance, if you were to continue Key 5.4's process of creating questions based on the headings from *Out of Many,* the questions would change based on the level specified by Bloom's Taxonomy. See Key 5.6 for an example.

Step 3: Read

Your text survey and questions give you a starting point for *reading,* the first R in SQ3R. Retaining what you read requires an active approach.

▶ *Focus on the key points of your survey.* Pay special attention to points raised in headings, in boldface type, in the chapter objectives and summary, and in other emphasized text.
▶ *Focus on your Q-stage questions.* Read the material with the purpose of answering each question. Write down or highlight ideas and examples that relate to your questions.
▶ *Create text tabs.* Place plastic index tabs or adhesive notes at the start of each chapter so you can flip back and forth with ease.

Key 5.6 FOLLOW A QUESTION THROUGH THE STAGES OF BLOOM'S TAXONOMY

The Origins of African American Politics

Knowledge
- *List* three main characters of the early African American political scene.

Understanding
- *Explain* the struggles faced by African American politicians.

Application
- *Interpret* the impact of slavery on the early African American politicians.

Analysis
- *Compare* and *contrast* the Caucasian political environment of the time with the emerging African American politicians.

Synthesis
- *Arrange* the major events of the era as they corresponded with the emerging political movement.

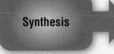
Evaluation
- *Rate* the effectiveness of the first African American political campaign and note any changes since.

▶ *Mark up your text.* Write notes in the margins, circle main ideas, or underline supporting details to focus on what's important. For an e-book, use the "Insert comments" feature. These cues will boost memory and help you study for exams. Here are some tips for *annotating*—taking marginal notes on the pages of your text:

- Use pencil so you can erase comments or questions that are answered later.
- Write your Q questions in the margins next to text headings.
- Mark critical sections with marginal notations such as "Def." for definition, "e.g." for helpful example, "Concept" for an important concept, and so on.
- Write notes at the bottom of the page connecting the text to what you learned in class or in research. You can also attach adhesive notes with your comments.

▶ *Highlight your text.* *Highlighting* involves the use of special markers or regular pens or pencils to flag important passages. When working with e-books, make note of the highlighting function, which allows you to overlay a color on important text. When used correctly, highlighting is an essential learning technique. However, experts agree that you will not learn what to highlight unless you *interact* with the material through surveying, questioning, reciting, and reviewing. Use the following tips to make highlighting a true learning tool:

- *Develop a system and stick to it.* Decide whether you will use different colors to highlight different elements, brackets for long passages, or pencil underlining.
- *Consider using a regular pencil or pen instead of a highlighter pen.* The copy will be cleaner and may look less like a coloring book.
- *Mark text carefully if you are using a rented book or a book to be resold.* Use pencil as often as possible and erase your marks at the end of the class. Write on sticky notes that you can remove. Make copies of important chapters or sections for marking. If you are renting, check with the rental service to see what they permit.
- *Read an entire paragraph before you begin to highlight, and don't start until you have a sense of what is important.* Only then put pencil or highlighter to paper as you pick out the main idea, key terms, and crucial supporting details and examples.
- *Avoid overmarking.* Too much color can be overwhelming. Try enclosing long passages with brackets and avoid underlining entire sentences, when possible.

Key 5.7, from an introduction to business textbook describing the concepts of target marketing and market segmentation, shows how to underline and take marginal notes.

Find the main idea

Understanding what you read depends on your ability to recognize *main ideas* and link other ideas to them. The main idea may appear in a **topic sentence** at the beginning of the paragraph followed by supporting details, or at the end of the paragraph with supporting details leading up to it. Sometimes, though, it is harder to figure out. When the main idea of a passage is unclear, use a three-step approach to decide what it is:[4]

1. *Search for the topic of the paragraph.* The topic of the paragraph is not the same as the main idea. Rather, it is the broad subject being discussed—for

TOPIC SENTENCE
A one- to two-sentence statement describing the main idea of a paragraph.

Chapter 10: Understanding Marketing Processes and Consumer Behavior　　　**297**

How does target marketing and market segmentation help companies sell product?

■ TARGET MARKETING AND MARKET SEGMENTATION

Marketers have long known that products cannot be all things to all people. Buyers have different tastes, goals, lifestyles, and so on. The emergence of the marketing concept and the recognition of consumer needs and wants led marketers to think in terms of **target markets**—groups of people with similar wants and needs. Selecting target markets is usually the first step in the marketing strategy.

Target marketing requires **market segmentation**—dividing a market into categories of customer types or "segments." Once they have identified segments, companies may adopt a variety of strategies. Some firms market products to more than one segment. General Motors *(www.gm.com)*, for example, offers compact cars, vans, trucks, luxury cars, and sports cars with various features and at various price levels. GM's strategy is to provide an automobile for nearly every segment of the market.

In contrast, some businesses offer a narrower range of products, each aimed toward a specific segment. Note that segmentation is a strategy for analyzing consumers, not products. The process of fixing, adapting, and communicating the nature of the product itself is called *product positioning*.

Definitions

target market
Group of people that has similar wants and needs and that can be expected to show interest in the same products

← *GM eg*

market segmentation
Process of dividing a market into categories of customer types

GM makes cars for diff. market segments

How do companies identify market segments?

Identifying Market Segments

By definition, members of a market segment must share some common traits that affect their purchasing decisions. In identifying segments, researchers look at several different influences on consumer behavior. Three of the most important are *geographic, demographic,* and *psychographic variables.*

What effect does geography have on segmentation strategies?

Geographic Variables Many buying decisions are affected by the places people call home. The heavy rainfall in Washington State, for instance, means that people there buy more umbrellas than people in the Sun Belt. Urban residents don't need agricultural equipment, and sailboats sell better along the coasts than on the Great Plains. **Geographic variables** are the geographical units, from countries to neighborhoods, that may be considered in a segmentation strategy.

These patterns affect decisions about marketing mixes for a huge range of products. For example, consider a plan to market down-filled parkas in rural Minnesota. Demand will be high and price competition intense. Local newspaper ads may be

Buying decisions influenced by where people live

geographic variables
Geographical units that may be considered in developing a segmentation strategy

— good eg —
selling parkas in Minnesota

Thought
Geographical variables change with the seasons

example, Apple CEO Steve Jobs, hate crimes on campus, or binge drinking on campus.

2. *Identify the aspect of the topic that is the paragraph's focus.* If the general topic is Steve Jobs, the author may focus on any of thousands of aspects of that topic, such as his cofounding of Apple Computer in 1976; his role in Pixar, a computer animation company; or his involvement in the development of the iPod portable music player.

3. *Find what the author wants you to know about that specific aspect.* This is the main idea or topic sentence. Whereas the topic establishes the subject, a topic sentence narrows down the purpose of the paragraph into one or two focused statements. Thus, although the topic of the paragraph might be Apple CEO Steve Jobs, the main idea, or topic sentence, might be, "In his role as CEO of Apple, Steve Jobs oversaw the creation of the iPod portable music player, which changed the way the world listens to and purchases music."

Step 4: Recite

Once you finish reading a topic, stop and answer the questions you raised in the Q stage of SQ3R. Even if you have already done this during the reading phase, do it again now—with the purpose of learning and committing the material to memory by *reciting* the answers.

You can say each answer aloud, silently speak the answers to yourself, "teach" the answers to another person, or write your ideas and answers in note form. Whatever recitation method you choose, make sure you know how ideas connect to one another and to the general concept being discussed.

Writing is often the most effective way to learn new material. Write responses to your Q-stage questions and use your own words to explain new concepts; save your writing as a study tool for review. Writing gives you immediate feedback: When it agrees with the material you are studying, you know the information. When it doesn't, you still need work with the text or a study partner.

Keep your learning styles in mind while exploring different strategies (see Chapter 3). For example, an intrapersonal learner may prefer writing, whereas an interpersonal learner may choose to recite answers aloud to a classmate. A logical-mathematical learner may benefit from organizing material into detailed outlines or charts, as opposed to a musical learner, who might chant information aloud to a rhythm.

When do you stop to recite? Waiting for the end of a chapter is too late; stopping at the end of one paragraph is too soon. The best plan is to recite at the end of each text section, right before a new heading. Repeat the question–read–recite cycle until you complete the chapter. If you fumble for thoughts, reread the section until you are on solid ground.

Step 5: Review

Reviewing, both immediately and periodically in the days and weeks after you read, will help you memorize, understand, and learn material. If you close the book after reading it once, chances are that you will forget almost everything, which is why students who read material for the first time right before a test don't tend to do too well. *Reviewing is your key to learning.*

Reviewing the same material in several sessions over time will also help you identify knowledge gaps. It's

Change the
CONVERSATION

Challenge yourself and your friends to ask—and answer—tough questions. Use the following to inspire discussion in pairs or groups.

▶ Understanding a text is essential to making good decisions, both in and out of the classroom. What other ways might reading skills impact your daily life?

▶ What steps do you take to ensure that you understand texts? Have those strategies worked for you so far? Why or why not?

▶ **CONSIDER THE CASE:** What step (or steps) from SQ3R were most helpful to Gary in dealing with his particular challenge? What step or steps do you think will be most helpful to you, and why?

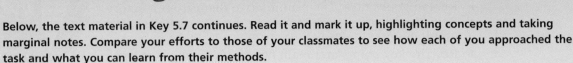

GET PRACTICAL!

Mark Up a Page to Learn a Page

Below, the text material in Key 5.7 continues. Read it and mark it up, highlighting concepts and taking marginal notes. Compare your efforts to those of your classmates to see how each of you approached the task and what you can learn from their methods.

---

298   Part IV: Understanding Principles of Marketing

effective, and the best retail location may be one that is easily reached from several small towns.

Although the marketability of some products is geographically sensitive, others enjoy nearly universal acceptance. Coke, for example, gets more than 70 percent of its sales from international markets. It is the market leader in Great Britain, China, Germany, Japan, Brazil, and Spain. Pepsi's international sales are about 15 percent of Coke's. In fact, Coke's chief competitor in most countries is some local soft drink, not Pepsi, which earns 78 percent of its income at home.

demographic variables
Characteristics of populations that may be considered in developing a segmentation strategy

Demographic Variables Demographic variables describe populations by identifying such traits as age, income, gender, ethnic background, marital status, race, religion, and social class. For example, several general consumption characteristics can be attributed to certain age groups (18–25, 26–35, 36–45, and so on). A marketer can, thus, divide markets into age groups. Table 10.1 lists some possible demographic breakdowns. Depending on the marketer's purpose, a segment can be a single classification (*aged* 20–34) or a combination of categories (*aged* 20–34, *married with children, earning* $25,000–$34,999). Foreign competitors, for example, are gaining market share in U.S. auto sales by appealing to young buyers (under age 30) with limited incomes (under $30,000). Whereas companies such as Hyundai *(www.hyundai.net),* Kia *(www.kia.com),* and Daewoo *(www.daewoos.com)* are winning entry-level customers with high quality and generous warranties, Volkswagen *(www.vw.com)* targets under-35 buyers with its entertainment-styled VW Jetta.[4]

psychographic variables
Consumer characteristics, such as lifestyles, opinions, interests, and attitudes, that may be considered in developing a segmentation strategy

Psychographic Variables Markets can also be segmented according to such **psychographic variables** as lifestyles, interests, and attitudes. Take, for example, Burberry *(www.burberry.com),* whose raincoats have been a symbol of British tradition since 1856. Burberry has repositioned itself as a global luxury brand, like Gucci *(www.gucci.com)* and Louis Vuitton *(www.vuitton.com).* The strategy, which recently resulted in a 31-percent sales increase, calls for attracting a different type of customer—the top-of-the-line, fashion-conscious individual—who shops at such stores as Neiman Marcus and Bergdorf Goodman.[5]

Psychographics are particularly important to marketers because, unlike demographics and geographics, they can be changed by marketing efforts. For example, Polish companies have overcome consumer resistance by promoting the safety and desirability of using credit rather than depending solely on cash. One product of changing attitudes is a booming economy and the emergence of a robust middle class.

TABLE 10.1
Demographic Variables

Age	Under 5, 5–11, 12–19, 20–34, 35–49, 50–64, 65+
Education	Grade school or less, some high school, graduated high school, some college, college degree, advanced degree
Family life cycle	Young single, young married without children, young married with children, older married with children under 18, older married without children under 18, older single, other
Family size	1, 2–3, 4–5, 6+
Income	Under $9,000, $9,000–$14,999, $15,000–$24,999, $25,000–$34,999, $35,000–$45,000, over $45,000
Nationality	African, American, Asian, British, Eastern European, French, German, Irish, Italian, Latin American, Middle Eastern, Scandinavian
Race	Native American, Asian, Black, White
Religion	Buddhist, Catholic, Hindu, Jewish, Muslim, Protestant
Sex	Male, female

---

natural to forget material between study sessions, especially if it's complex. When you come back after a break, you can focus on where you need the most help.

Examine the following reviewing techniques (more on these in Chapter 7). Try them all, and use the ones that work best for you. Try using more than one strategy when you study—switching among several different strategies tends to strengthen learning and memory.

- ▶ Reread your notes. Then summarize them from memory.
- ▶ Review and summarize in writing the text sections you highlighted or bracketed.
- ▶ Rewrite key points and main concepts in your own words. Create written examples that will help solidify the content in your mind.
- ▶ Answer the end-of-chapter review, discussion, and application questions.
- ▶ Reread the preface, headings, tables, and summary.
- ▶ Recite important concepts to yourself, or record and play them back on a tape player.
- ▶ Listen to MP3 audio recordings of your text and other reading materials on your IPod.
- ▶ Make flash cards with a word or concept on one side and a definition, examples, or other related information on the other. Test yourself.
- ▶ Quiz yourself, using the questions you raised in the Q stage.
- ▶ Discuss the concepts with a classmate or in a study group. Answer one another's Q-stage questions.
- ▶ Ask your instructor for help with difficult material.

Refreshing your knowledge is easier and faster than learning it the first time. Make a weekly review schedule and stick to it until you're sure you know everything.

GENERAL EDUCATION REQUIREMENTS Courses required for graduation in a variety of academic fields, including the humanities, social sciences, math, and science.

What strategies help with specific subjects and formats?

If your college has **general education requirements,** you may have to take a wide variety of courses to graduate. Knowing how to approach reading materials in different academic areas will help you learn.

Math and science

Math and science courses relate closely to one another, and almost all science courses require a base of math knowledge. Mathematical and scientific strategies help you develop thinking and problem-solving skills. In a world that is being transformed by new discoveries and technologies, a strong math and science background prepares you for tomorrow's jobs and can also help you create monthly budgets, choose auto insurance, understand illnesses, and more.

Math and science textbooks move *sequentially*. That is, your understanding of later material depends on how well you learned material in earlier chapters. Try the following strategies to get the most from your textbooks, and get extra help right away when you are confused.

■ *Interact with math material actively through writing.* Math textbooks are made up of problems and solutions. As you read, highlight important information and take notes on examples. Work out any missing problem steps on your pad or in the book. Draw sketches to help visualize the material. Try not to

GET CREATIVE!

Use SQ3R to Make a Connection

For this exercise, partner up with someone in your class. To begin, each of you will write a mini-biography—approximately three to five paragraphs—answering the following questions:

▶ Where are you from?

▶ How would you describe your family?

▶ How have they influenced the student you are today?

▶ What three facts or ideas about yourself would you like someone else to know?

Include a title that reflects your biography as a whole. Also, for each paragraph in the middle (not the first or last), provide a title "header" that tells the reader what to expect in the paragraph (for example, "My Childhood in Malaysia," "Daytime Student, Nighttime Employee," and so on).

Once you're finished, read over what you've written for spelling, punctuation, and clarity. Switch papers with your partner and read his or her biography. Using SQ3R:

1. *Survey:* Scan your partner's paper for any words that stand out or phrases that seem important. Circle or highlight anything you notice right away.

2. *Question:* Thinking about what you learned from your survey, write questions in the margins. Your questions should reflect what you expect to learn as you read.

3. *Read:* Read through the biography. Make notes in the margins when you find answers to your Q-stage questions. Use your pen to circle or underline main ideas.

4. *Recite:* Discuss what you learned from the paper with your partner. How accurate was your comprehension of the biography? Were there any areas that were not clear or that you misunderstood? If so, what might help in those cases?

5. *Review:* Summarize the biography of your partner in writing for yourself. Be sure to note any important information that relates to getting to know your partner. If there is time, solidify your review by reciting the summary aloud in front of the class. Introduce your partner to the class as if he or she had just joined, focusing on the most interesting and unique information from the biography.

Finally, discuss the impact of using SQ3R with your partner. How did it affect your comprehension of the biography? What might you try differently next time?

move on until you understand example problems and how they relate to the central ideas. Write down questions for your instructor or fellow students.

■ *Pay attention to formulas.* Math and science texts are filled with (formulas.) Focus on learning the main ideas behind each formula, and do problems to make sure your understanding sticks.

→ FORMULAS
General facts, rules, or principles usually expressed in mathematical symbols.

■ *Use memory strategies to learn science.* Science textbooks are packed with vocabulary specific to the field (for example, an environmental science text may refer to the *greenhouse effect, integrated waste management,* and the *law of limiting factors*). To remember what you read, use mnemonic devices, test yourself with flash cards, and rehearse aloud or silently (see Chapter 6).

student profile

Aneela Gonzales
Golden West College, Huntington Beach, California

About me:

I was born into a bicultural family: Hispanic American and Pakistani. My dad left the family when I was 3 months old and my mother became ill with cancer when I was 6. She passed away when I was 11, and the next few years were very difficult. I had to move to a new state to live with my aunt and uncle.

What I focus on:

Since I was a child I had dreamed of being a nurse. However, once I finally got to college to study nursing, remembering what I read was a problem and I was struggling to pass exams. I had to come up with specific techniques to help. One that worked for me is using different colored highlighters while I read (pink for somewhat important and yellow for very important), and then typing out all the very important points and reviewing that sheet several times. To figure out what to highlight I would pay close attention to what the instructor lectures about and I would reread those topics in the text.

Something else that I learned was important for me was to read in a quiet environment with few distractions. I read much better in the library with my phone off. When I didn't understand something I was reading I would go to the Tutoring Center. I also found it useful to talk about the reading one-on-one with another person. Finally, I realized that outside stresses, such as having to work to support myself through school, had an effect on my reading skills. Learning to manage my stress enabled me to better remember what I had read.

What will help me in the workplace:

I have just graduated college and started work as a nurse. I have much to read at work so it helps to apply some of the techniques I learned in college. First, I find it is important to find a quiet place to read. In addition, I first skim the material to find out if it is relevant for me; then I can slow down and read only those portions that I need. I find this saves me a lot of time.

Social sciences and humanities

Courses in the social sciences and humanities prepare you to be a well-rounded person, able and ready to fulfill your responsibilities to yourself, your family, and a free democracy. They also prepare you for 21st century jobs by focusing on critical thinking, civic and historic knowledge, and ethical reasoning. As you study these disciplines, look for themes with critical thinking as the foundation for your work. Build knowledge by using what you know to learn new material.

Themes

The National Council for the Social Studies (www.socialstudies.org) organizes the study of the social sciences and humanities under ten themes, providing "umbrellas" under which you can group ideas that you encounter in different classes and reading materials:

- ▶ Culture
- ▶ Time, continuity, and change
- ▶ People, places, and environment
- ▶ Individual development and identity
- ▶ Individuals, groups, and institutions
- ▶ Power, authority, and governance
- ▶ Production, distribution, and consumption
- ▶ Science, technology, and society
- ▶ Global connections
- ▶ Ideals and practices of citizenship

Look for these themes as you read, even if they are not spelled out. For example, as you read a chapter in a political science text on presidential politics, you might think of the history of presidential elections or how the Internet is changing electoral politics.

Think critically

Courses in the social sciences ask hard questions about ethics, human rights and freedoms, personal and community responsibility, looking at these topics over time and in different cultures. Critical thinking will help you maximize learning and understanding as you ask questions about what you read, think of material in terms of problems and solutions, look for evidence in arguments, consider possible bias of the writers, and examine big picture statements for solid cause-and-effect logic.

Literature

Even if you're not an English major, you will probably take one or more literature courses, exposing you to books that allow you to experience other times and cultures and understand how others react to the problems of daily life. Additionally, the thoughts and emotions you experience in reaction to what you read give you the opportunity to learn more about yourself.

Literature courses ask you to look at different literary elements to find meaning on various levels. As you read, use critical reading skills to consider the various aspects.

- ▶ *Character*. How do characters reveal who they are? How are the main characters similar or different? How do a character's actions change the course of the story?
- ▶ *Plot*. How would you evaluate the power of the story? Did it hold your interest?
- ▶ *Setting*. How does the setting relate to the actions of the major and minor characters?
- ▶ *Point of view*. How are the author's views expressed through characters' actions?
- ▶ *Style*. How would you describe the writing style?
- ▶ *Imagery*. How does the author use imagery as part of the theme?
- ▶ *Theme*. What is the goal of the work? What is it trying to communicate?

Visual aids

Many textbooks use tables, charts, drawings, maps, and photographs—all types of visual aids—to show, clarify, or summarize

Apply Different Intelligences to Concepts in Sociology

INTELLIGENCE	USE MI STRATEGIES TO BECOME A BETTER READER	APPLY MI READING STRATEGIES TO LEARN ABOUT SOCIAL GROUPS FOR YOUR INTRODUCTION TO SOCIOLOGY COURSE
Verbal-Linguistic	• Use the steps in SQ3R, focusing especially on writing Q-stage questions, summaries, and so on. • Make marginal text notes as you read.	• Summarize in writing the technical differences among social groups, categories, and crowds.*
Logical-Mathematical	• Logically connect what you are reading with what you already know. Consider similarities, differences, and cause-and-effect relationships. • Draw charts showing relationships and analyze trends.	• Create a table comparing and contrasting the characteristics of primary and secondary social groups.
Bodily-Kinesthetic	• Use text highlighting to take a hands-on approach to reading. • Take a hands-on approach to learning experiments by trying to recreate them yourself.	• Create an experiment that might turn a crowd of strangers into a social group joined together by a common problem.
Visual-Spatial	• Make charts, diagrams, or think links illustrating difficult ideas you encounter as you read. • Take note of photos, tables, and other visual aids in the text.	• Create a visual aid showing four primary mechanisms through which people with shared experiences, loyalties, and interests meet—for example, through school and business—and how initial contacts may lead to deep social group relationships.
Interpersonal	• Discuss reading material and clarify concepts in a study group. • Talk to people who know about the topic you are studying.	• Interview people who shared a difficult experience with a crowd of strangers—for example, people stuck in an elevator or train for an extended period—about how relationships changed as focus turned to a common problem.
Intrapersonal	• Apply concepts to your own life; think about how you would manage. • Try to understand your personal strengths and weaknesses to lead a study group on the reading material.	• After reading about the nature of primary groups, think about the nature of your personal family relationships and the degree to which family members are your key support system.
Musical	• Recite text concepts to rhythms or write a song to depict them. • Explore relevant musical links to the material.	• Listen to a rock concert that was performed in front of a live crowd. Then listen to the same music recorded in a studio. Think about performance differences that might link to the presence or absence of a crowd.
Naturalistic	• Tap into your ability to notice similarities and differences in objects and concepts by organizing reading materials into relevant groupings.	• Over the next few weeks, ask some close friends if you can have dinner with them and their families. After the visits, try to identify characteristics that all the families share. Create a chart to report your findings.

*For information on social groups, see John J. Macionis, *Sociology*, 11th ed., Upper Saddle River, NJ: Prentice Hall, 2007.

information in a form that is easy to read and understand. Pay attention to these elements as you are reading—often they contain important information not found elsewhere. Visual learners especially may benefit from information delivered in a format other than chapter text.

Certain types of visual aids—word and data tables as well as charts/graphs (pie, bar, or line)—are designed to compare information and statistics that show the following types of information:

▶ *Trends over time*. For example, the number of computers with Internet connections per household in 2010 compared to 2002
▶ *Relative rankings*. For example, the sizes of the advertising budgets of four major companies
▶ *Distributions*. For example, student performance on standardized tests by geographic area
▶ *Cycles*. For example, the regular upward and downward movement of the nation's economy as defined by periods of prosperity and recession

Online materials

Almost any student's success in college depends on being able to read both printed and on-screen material effectively. For some "digital natives" who have grown up with technology and the Internet, screen reading comes naturally and may even be preferable. Others may prefer printed materials they can hold in their hands and write on. For either group, the goal is to get the most out of what you must read online.

Screen readers tend to focus on heads and subheads, bullet points, and visuals, scanning material for the important points instead of staying focused through long paragraphs or articles.[5] They may also develop what Web researcher Jakob Nielsen calls *F-pattern reading*—reading across the line at the beginning of a document, then reading less and less of the full width of the line as you move down the page, and only seeing the left-hand text by the time you reach the bottom of the document.[6]

Nielsen suggests making the most of screen reading using a step-by-step process, which includes aspects of SQ3R:

1. *Skim through the article.* See whether it contains important ideas.
2. *Before reading in depth, save the article on your computer.* This gives you the ability to highlight and add notes, just as you would on a printed page.
3. *Survey the article.* Read the title, subtitle, headings, figures, charts, and tables.
4. *Come up with questions to guide your reading.* Ask yourself what general and specific information you want to learn from the article.
5. *Read the article in depth.* You have already judged that the material is important, so take it much slower than you would normally.
6. *Highlight and take notes.* Use the program's highlighter function and comment boxes.
7. *Print out articles you would rather study on paper.* Make sure the printouts include your highlighting and notes.
8. *Review your notes.* Combine them with your class notes and those on your printed text.

Finally, your awareness that screen reading skills are different from those needed to read printed textbooks will help you shift gears when picking up a book. Textbooks require close, slow reading that may seem like walking through mud after spending time on the Internet.

How can you be an information literate reader and researcher?

Although many students' first instinct is to power up the computer and start jumping around on Google, there is a wealth of research resources at your fingertips. Many of the materials you'll find in a library have been evaluated by librarians and researchers and are likely to be reliable—a definite time-saver when compared to the myriad of both credible and less-than-credible sources available online.

Map out the possibilities

To select the most helpful information for your research, you need to first know what is available to you. Sign up for a library orientation session. Familiarize yourself with the library resources shown in Key 5.8.

For a key advantage in any search for information, get to know a librarian. These professionals can assist you in locating unfamiliar or hard-to-find sources, navigating catalogs and databases, uncovering research shortcuts, and dealing with pesky equipment. Know what you want to accomplish before asking a question. At many schools, you can query a librarian via cell phone, e-mail, or instant messaging.

Key 5.8

GET TO KNOW **WHERE THINGS ARE** IN THE LIBRARY

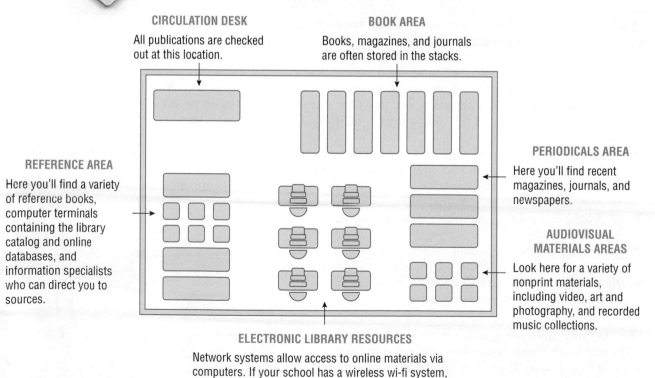

CIRCULATION DESK
All publications are checked out at this location.

BOOK AREA
Books, magazines, and journals are often stored in the stacks.

REFERENCE AREA
Here you'll find a variety of reference books, computer terminals containing the library catalog and online databases, and information specialists who can direct you to sources.

PERIODICALS AREA
Here you'll find recent magazines, journals, and newspapers.

AUDIOVISUAL MATERIALS AREAS
Look here for a variety of nonprint materials, including video, art and photography, and recorded music collections.

ELECTRONIC LIBRARY RESOURCES
Network systems allow access to online materials via computers. If your school has a wireless wi-fi system, you can conduct research anywhere on campus.

Conduct an information search

To avoid becoming buried in the sheer magnitude of resources available, use a practical, step-by-step search method. Key 5.9 shows how you start wide and then move in for a closer look at specific sources.

When using virtual or online catalogues, you will need to adjust your research methods. Searching library databases requires that you use a *keyword search*—an exploration that uses a topic-related natural language word or phrase as a point of reference to locate other information. To narrow your topic and reduce the number of "hits" (resources pulled up by your search), add more keywords. For example, instead of searching through the broad category "art," focus on "French art" or, more specifically, "19th century French art." Key 5.10 shows how to use the keyword system to narrow searches with what is called *Boolean logic*.

Be a critical Internet searcher

The *Internet*, a worldwide computer network, can connect you to billions of information sources. Unlike your college library collection or databases, Internet resources may not be evaluated by anyone who vouches for their quality. As a result, your research depends on critical thinking.

Much, although not all, research can be done using online databases. Get to know the databases and other resources that your school provides for you.
© Sarah Lyman Kravits

USE A STEP-BY-STEP SEARCH METHOD

Start with General Reference Works → Examples include encyclopedias, almanacs, dictionaries, and biographical references.

Move to Specialized Reference Works → Examples include encyclopedias and dictionaries that focus on a narrow field.

Use the Electronic Catalog to Locate Materials → Search the library catalog by author, title, or subject to learn where to locate specific books, periodicals, and journals. Most library catalogs are virtual and can be accessed by computers throughout the library. Ask a librarian for assistance, if needed.

Browse through Relevant Books and Articles → Using your results from the catalog search, dive in deeper by finding and accessing helpful information in books and articles related to your topic.

PERFORM AN **EFFECTIVE KEYWORD SEARCH** WITH BOOLEAN LOGIC

IF YOU ARE SEARCHING FOR...	DO THIS	EXAMPLE
A word	Type the word normally.	Aid
A phrase	Type the phase in its normal word order (use regular word spacing) or surround the phrase with quotation marks.	financial aid, "financial aid"
Two or more keywords without regard to order	Type the words in any order, surrounding the words with quotation marks. Use *and* to separate the words.	"financial aid" and "scholarships"
Topic A or topic B	Type the words in any order, surrounding the words with quotation marks. Use *or* to separate the words.	"financial aid" or "scholarships"
Topic A but not topic B	Type topic A first within quotation marks, and then topic B within quotation marks. Use *not* to separate the words.	"financial aid" not "scholarships"

Start with search engines

Among the most popular and effective search engines are Google (www.google .com) and Yahoo! (www.yahoo.com). Search engines aimed at academic audiences include the Librarian's Index to the Internet (www.lii.org) and INFOMINE (www.infomine.com). At these academic directories, someone has screened the sites and listed only those sources that have been determined to be reputable and regularly updated.

Additionally, your school may include access to certain nonpublic academic search engines in the cost of your tuition. Sites like LexusNexus, InfoTrac, GaleGroup, and OneFile are known for their credibility in the academic world as well as their vast amounts of information. Check with your school's library to see how to access these sites.

Use a search strategy

The World Wide Web has been called "the world's greatest library, with all its books on the floor." With no librarian in sight, you need to master a practical Internet search strategy.

1. *Use natural language phrases or keywords to identify what you are looking for.* University of Michigan professor Eliot Soloway recommends phrasing your search in the form of a question—for example, What vaccines are given to children before age 5? Then he advises identifying the important words in the question (vaccines, children, before age 5) as well as related words (polio, shot, pediatrics, and so on). This will give you a collection of terms to use in different combinations as you search.[7]
2. *Use a search engine to isolate valuable sites.* Enter your questions, phrases, and keywords in various combinations to generate lists of "hits." Vary word order to see what you can generate. If you get too many hits, try using fewer or more specific keywords.
3. *Skim sites to evaluate what seems most useful.* Check the synopsis of the site's contents, the content providers, and the purpose of the site. Does the site seem relevant, reputable, or biased in favor of a particular point of view? A site owned by a company will want to promote its new product rather than provide unbiased consumer information. Consider the purpose—a blog is apt to focus on opinion in contrast to an article

in a scholarly journal, which is likely to focus on facts and research findings.

4. *Save, or bookmark, the sites you want to focus on.* Make sure you can access them again. You may want to copy URLs and paste them into a separate document.

5. *When you think you are done, start over.* Choose another search engine and search again. Different systems access different sites.

The limitations of Internet-only research make it smart to combine Internet and library research. Search engines can't find everything, in part because not all sources are in digital format. The Internet also prioritizes current information. Furthermore, some digital sources that are not part of your library's subscription offerings cost money. Finally, Internet searches require electricity or battery power and an online connection. Consider printing out Internet materials that you know you will need to reference over and over again.

Your need to be an effective researcher doesn't stop at graduation—especially in a workplace dominated by information and media. The skills you develop as you do research for school projects will serve you well in any kind of job that requires you to use the Internet and other resources to find and evaluate information.

How can you respond critically to what you read?

With anything you read—trade books, journal and newspaper articles, Internet documents, primary sources, and even textbooks that are supposed to be as accurate as possible—it is crucial to be a questioning reader who does not simply accept material as truth. Critical reading involves questioning, analysis, and evaluation. Think of the reading process as an archaeological dig. First, you excavate a site and uncover the artifacts. Then you separate out what you've found, make connections among ideas, and evaluate what is important. This process allows you to focus on the most important materials.

Different purposes engage different parts of critical reading. When you are reading to learn and retain information or to master a skill, you *focus on important information* (analyzing and evaluating how the ideas are structured, how they connect, and what is most crucial to remember). When you are reading to search for truth, you *ask questions to evaluate arguments* (analyzing and evaluating the author's point of view as well as the credibility, accuracy, reliability, and relevancy of the material).

Focus on important information

Before determining how to respond to something you've read, ask yourself what is important and what you have to remember. According to Adam Robinson, co-founder of the *Princeton Review,* "The only way you can effectively absorb the relevant information is to ignore the irrelevant information."[8] The following tips will help you determine what is most important to focus on as you study. Check to see whether the information does the following:

▶ Contains headings, charts, tables, captions, key terms and definitions, or an introduction or summary (for a textbook, check mid-chapter or end-of-chapter exercises)

▶ Offers definitions, crucial concepts, examples, an explanation of a variety or type, critical relationships or comparisons

- Sparks questions and reactions as you read
- Surprises or confuses you
- Mirrors what your instructor emphasizes in class or in assignments

When trying to figure out what to study and what to skim, ask yourself whether your instructor would expect you to know the material. If you are unsure and the topic is not on your syllabus, e-mail your instructor and ask for clarification.

Ask questions to evaluate arguments

An *argument* refers to a persuasive case—a set of connected ideas supported by examples—that a writer makes to prove or disprove a point. Many scholarly books and articles, in print form or on the Internet, are organized around particular arguments (look for *claims*—arguments that appear to be factual but don't have adequate evidence to support them). Critical readers evaluate arguments and claims to determine whether they are accurate and logical. When quality evidence combines with sound logic, the argument is solid.

It's easy—and common—to accept or reject an argument according to whether it fits with your point of view. If you ask questions, however, you can determine the argument's validity and understand it in greater depth (see Key 5.11). Evaluating an argument involves looking at several factors:

EVIDENCE
Facts, statistics, and other materials that are presented in support of an argument.

- The quality of the **evidence** (facts, statistics, and other materials supporting an argument)
- Whether the evidence fits the idea concept
- The logical connections

Approach every argument with healthy skepticism. Have an open mind to assess whether you are convinced or have serious questions.

Evaluate every source

Evidence examination is important for all reading materials, but especially when you research on the Internet, because online resources vary widely in reliability. In fact, your Internet research is only as strong as your critical

ASK QUESTIONS LIKE THESE
TO **EVALUATE ARGUMENTS**

Key 5.11

EVALUATE THE VALIDITY OF THE EVIDENCE	DETERMINE WHETHER THE EVIDENCE SUPPORTS THE CONCEPT
Is the source reliable and free of bias?	Is there enough evidence?
Who wrote this and with what intent?	Do examples and ideas logically connect?
What assumptions underlie this material?	Is the evidence convincing?
Is this argument based on opinion?	Do the examples build a strong case?
How does this evidence compare with evidence from other sources?	What different and perhaps opposing arguments seem equally valid?

USE THE CARS TEST TO DETERMINE
INFORMATION QUALITY ON THE INTERNET

CREDIBILITY	ACCURACY	REASONABLENESS	SUPPORT
Examine whether a source is believable and trustworthy.	*Examine whether information is correct— i.e., factual, comprehensive, detailed, and up to date (if necessary).*	*Examine whether material is fair, objective, moderate, and consistent.*	*Examine whether a source is adequately supported with citations.*
What are the author's credentials? Look for education and experience, title or position of employment, membership in any known and respected organization, reliable contact information, biographical information, and reputation.	*Is it up to date, and is that important?* If you are searching for a work of literature, such as Shakespeare's play *Macbeth,* there is no "updated" version. However, you may want reviews of its latest productions. For most scientific research, you will need to rely on the most updated information you can find.	*Does the source seem fair?* Look for a balanced argument, accurate claims, and a reasoned tone that does not appeal primarily to your emotions.	*Where does the information come from?* Look at the site, the sources used by the person or group who compiled the information, and the contact information. Make sure that the cited sources seem reliable and that statistics are documented.
Is there quality control? Look for ways in which the source may have been screened. For example, materials on an organization's website have most likely been approved by several members; information coming from an academic journal has to be screened by several people before it is published.	*Is it comprehensive?* Does the material leave out any important facts or information? Does it neglect to consider alternative views or crucial consequences? Although no one source can contain all of the available information on a topic, it should still be as comprehensive as is possible within its scope.	*Does the source seem objective?* While there is a range of objectivity in writing, you want to favor authors and organizations who can control their bias. An author with a strong political or religious agenda or an intent to sell a product may not be a source of the most truthful material.	*Is the information corroborated?* Test information by looking for other sources that confirm the facts in this information—or, if the information is opinion, sources that share that opinion and back it up with their own citations. One good strategy is to find at least three sources that corroborate each other.
Is there any posted summary or evaluation of the source? You may find abstracts of sources (summary) or a recommendation, rating, or review from a person or organization (evaluation). Either of these—or, ideally, both—can give you an idea of credibility before you decide to examine a source in depth.	*For whom is the source written, and for what purpose?* Looking at what the author wants to accomplish will help you assess whether it has a bias. Sometimes biased information will not be useful for your purpose; sometimes your research will require that you note and evaluate bias (such as if you were to compare Civil War diaries from Union soldiers with those from Confederate soldiers).	*Does the source seem moderate?* Do claims seem possible, or does the information seem hard to believe? Does what you read make sense when compared to what you already know? While wild claims may turn out to be truthful, you are safest to check everything out.	*Is the source externally consistent?* Most material is a mix of both current and old information. External consistency refers to whether the old information agrees with what you already know. If a source contradicts something you know to be true, chances are higher that the information new to you may be inconsistent as well.
Signals of a potential lack of credibility: Anonymous materials, negative evaluations, little or no evidence of quality control, bad grammar or misspelled words	*Signals of a potential lack of accuracy:* Lack of date or old date, generalizations, one-sided views that do not acknowledge opposing arguments	*Signals of a potential lack of reasonableness:* Extreme or emotional language, sweeping statements, conflict of interest, inconsistencies or contradictions	*Signals of a potential lack of support:* Statistics without sources, lack of documentation, lack of corroboration using other reliable sources

Source: Robert Harris, "Evaluating Internet Research Sources," November 17, 1997, VirtualSalt (www.virtualsalt.com/evalu8it.htm).

thinking. Robert Harris, professor and Web expert, has developed an easy-to-remember system for evaluating Internet information called the CARS test for information quality (Credibility, Accuracy, Reasonableness, Support). Use the information in Key 5.12 to question any source you find as you conduct research. You can also use it to test the reliability of non-Internet sources.

Reading is the tool you will use over and over again to acquire information in school, on the job, and in life (to understand your 401(k) retirement plan, to learn about local and world news, to understand the fine print in a cell phone contract). Develop the ability to read with focus, purpose, and follow-through, and you will never stop enjoying the benefits.

Case Wrap-up

What happened to Gary? With perseverance and support, Gary has become a health care management and strategic planning consultant whose clients include state Medicaid directors and Fortune 500 insurance companies. However, he lives every day with the challenge of dyslexia. Because of the time and effort he needs to read, he has spent most of his adult life working in small private offices or a home office. He can't read directions fast enough to avoid wrong turns on highways and often makes spelling mistakes. The support of his wife, Lynne, a gifted writer and public speaker, has proven essential in his struggle to persevere. Armed with today's knowledge about learning differences, Gary and Lynne tested their children early and often and were able to provide their son with an academic environment that addressed his reading challenges. With their support, he has developed a soaring sense of self-confidence—the kind that Gary still strives for.

What does this story mean for you? Learning to be a productive member of society, with the gifts you are born with or can develop, is the name of the game. It also helps to have an understanding support system. Nearly everyone has a "big secret"—or perhaps a "small secret"—that causes challenges in school or on the job. Whether a learning disability like dyslexia, a negative attitude about a task like reading or math, or some other obstacle, it gets in the way as you strive for success. Think about one secret that you have, and put it in writing. Then write the name of a person whom you trust to support you. Finally, talk with this person and begin to come up with ideas of how you will address and manage your secret.

What effects go beyond your world? Reading is the essential success skill for the 21st century information-focused workplace. The more the world's citizens know how to read, the more they will be able to lead productive and successful lives. To start exploring what is happening in the promotion of literacy, go to www.roomtoread.org and explore what this organization is doing to build schools, stock libraries, and support education. Click on their "Get Involved" tab to see how to support their initiatives. Perhaps you will want to get involved yourself—or, if not, look into ways you can support literacy in your community, at your college, or even within your own family. Be a part of the solution.

Successful Intelligence *Wrap-up*

HERE'S HOW YOU HAVE BUILT SKILLS IN **CHAPTER 5** :

ANALYTICAL THINKING	CREATIVE THINKING	PRACTICAL THINKING
❯ You explored the steps of SQ3R and learned how to utilize strategies to boost your understanding of written materials.	❯ You learned about innovative ways to improve comprehension by studying in a way suitable to your personal needs.	❯ You developed highlighting and note-taking skills to help you in recalling important information after reading.
❯ In the Get Analytical exercise, you tried surveying and skimming a text to become familiar with the application of SQ3R.	❯ The section on getting ready to comprehend what you read may have inspired creative ideas about study locations, times, and motivators.	❯ In the Get Practical exercise, you practiced your highlighting abilities and learned new methods from other students.
❯ You explored the importance of evaluating online and hard copy sources.	❯ In the Get Creative exercise, you wrote a short personal biography.	❯ You studied different strategies that can be used to master different subject areas.

Word*for*Thought

Reading college textbooks may feel at times like the disorientation implied by the **Japanese** word *yokomeshi* (yo-ko-meh'-shee), which literally means "eating a meal sideways."[9] The word describes the Japanese learner's difficulty with a foreign language written horizontally, unlike Japanese script, which reads from top to bottom. You are not alone in trying to figure out what things mean. Keep your sense of humor and commit to the task, and it is likely to feel more comfortable over time.

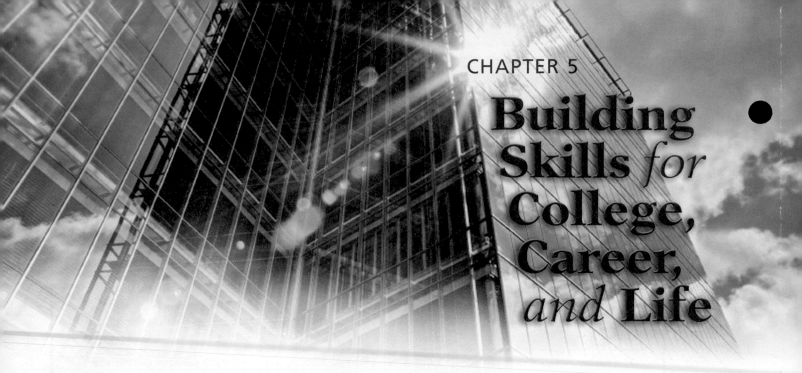

Building Skills *for* College, Career, *and* Life

Steps to Success

Study a Text Page

BUILD BASIC SKILLS. The facing page is from the chapter "Groups and Organizations" in the sixth edition of John J. Macionis's *Sociology*.[10] Skim the excerpt. Identify the headings on the page and the relationships among them. Mark primary-level headings with a numeral 1, secondary headings with a 2, and tertiary (third-level) headings with a 3.

TAKE IT TO THE NEXT LEVEL. Analyze the headings and text.

Which heading serves as an umbrella for the rest?

_____

What do the headings tell you about the content of the page?

_____

_____

_____

_____

Name three concepts that seem important to remember.

1. _____

2. _____

3. _____

Based on the three concepts you pulled out, write three study questions that you can review with an instructor, a teaching assistant, or a fellow student.

1. _____

2. _____

3. _____

SOCIAL GROUPS

Virtually everyone moves through life with a sense of belonging; this is the experience of group life. A social group refers to *two or more people who identify and interact with one another.* Human beings continually come together to form couples, families, circles of friends, neighborhoods, churches, businesses, clubs, and numerous large organizations. Whatever the form, groups encompass people with shared experiences, loyalties, and interests. In short, while maintaining their individuality, the members of social groups also think of themselves as a special "we."

Groups, Categories, and Crowds

People often use the term "group" imprecisely. We now distinguish the group from the similar concepts of category and crowd.

■ *Category.* A *category* refers to people who have some status in common. Women, single fathers, military recruits, homeowners, and Roman Catholics are all examples of categories.

Why are categories not considered groups? Simply because, while the individuals involved are aware that they are not the only ones to hold that particular status, the vast majority are strangers to one another.

■ *Crowd.* A *crowd* refers to a temporary cluster of individuals who may or may not interact at all. Students sitting in a lecture hall do engage one another and share some common identity as college classmates; thus, such a crowd might be called a loosely formed group. By contrast, riders hurtling along on a subway train or bathers enjoying a summer day at the beach pay little attention to one another and amount to an anonymous aggregate of people. In general, then, crowds are too transitory and impersonal to qualify as social groups.

The right circumstances, however, could turn a crowd into a group. People riding in a subway train that crashes under the city streets generally become keenly aware of their common plight and begin to help one another. Sometimes such extraordinary experiences become the basis for lasting relationships.

Primary and Secondary Groups

Acquaintances commonly greet one another with a smile and the simple phrase, "Hi! How are you?" The response is usually a well scripted, "Just fine, thanks, how about you?" This answer, of course, is often more formal than truthful. In most cases, providing a detailed account of how you are *really* doing would prompt the other person to beat a hasty and awkward exit.

Sociologists classify social groups by measuring them against two ideal types based on members' genuine level of personal concern. This variation is the key to distinguishing *primary* from *secondary* groups.

According to Charles Horton Cooley (1864–1929), a **primary group** is a *small social group whose members share personal and enduring relationships.* Bound together by primary relationships, individuals in primary groups typically spend a great deal of time together, engage in a wide range of common activities, and feel that they know one another well. Although not without periodic conflict, members of primary groups display sincere concern for each other's welfare. The family is every society's most important primary group.

Cooley characterized these personal and tightly integrated groups as *primary* because they are among the first groups we experience in life. In addition, the family and early play groups also hold primary importance in the socialization process, shaping attitudes, behavior, and social identity.

Source: John J. Macionis, *Sociology*, 6th ed., p. 145, © 1997 Prentice-Hall, Inc. Reproduced by permission of Pearson Education, Inc., Upper Saddle River, NJ.

MOVE TOWARD MASTERY. Read the excerpt, putting SQ3R to work. Using a marker pen, highlight key phrases and sentences. Write short marginal notes to help you review the material later. After reading this page thoroughly, write a short summary paragraph.

_____

_____

_____

_____

Teamwork

Create Solutions Together

FORM A STUDY GROUP

Goal: To organize a study group with the intent of preparing for an upcoming event.

Time on task: 30 minutes; ongoing

Instructions: Get together with three or four members of your class with whom you would like to form a group. These are your study group members. Do the following at the group's first meeting:

- *Set a specific goal.* Create a weekly schedule for reaching your goal—to prepare for an upcoming test, for example. Write everything down and give everyone a copy.
- *Talk about the specific ways you will work together.* Discuss which of the following methods you want to try in the group: pooling your notes; teaching each other difficult concepts; making up, administering, and grading quizzes for each other; creating study flash cards; using SQ3R to review required readings. Set specific guidelines for how group members will be held accountable.

As an initial group exercise, try the following:

- *Review the study questions that you wrote for the* Sociology *excerpt in the previous exercise.* Each person should select one question to focus on while reading (no two people should have the same question). Group members should then reread the excerpt individually, thinking about their questions as they read and answering them in writing.
- *When you finish reading critically, gather as a group.* Each person should take a turn presenting the question, the response or answer that was derived through critical reading, and other thoughts. Other members may then add to the discussion. Continue until everyone presents a concept.

Over several weeks, evaluate the different methods as a group, singling out those that were most helpful. Then incorporate them into your ongoing study sessions.

Writing

Build Intrapersonal and Communication Skills

Record your thoughts on a separate piece of paper, in a journal, or electronically.

EMOTIONAL INTELLIGENCE JOURNAL

Reading challenges. Which current course presents your most difficult reading challenge? Describe what makes the reading tough—type of material, length of assignments, level of difficulty, or something else. What feelings come up for you when you read, and what effect do they have on your reading? Describe techniques you learned in this chapter that can help you get into a growth mindset to read productively.

REAL-LIFE WRITING

Ask for help. Self-help plans often involve reaching out to others. Draft an e-mail to your instructor describing the difficulties in your challenging course as well as the specific help you need to move to the next step. Make sure that your message is clear and accurate, your grammar, spelling, and punctuation correct, and your tone appropriate. (See the Quick Start for guidelines on communicating with instructors.) *Whether you send the e-mail or not is up to you.* In either case, writing it will help you move forward in your reading improvement plan.

Personal Portfolio

Prepare for Career Success

READING SKILLS ON THE JOB

21st Century Learning Building Blocks

- Information Literacy
- Media Literacy
- ICT Literacy

Complete the following in your electronic portfolio or separately on paper.

Excellent reading skills are a requirement for almost every 21st century job. Employers expect that you will read independently to master new skills and keep up with change. Whether in print or electronic form, on-the-job reading will challenge you as does college reading. For example, sociology courses may involve reading textbooks, journals, and case studies, but actually working in the field requires that you keep on top of case reports, government regulations, court documents, and an unending stream of work-related e-mails.

Prepare yourself by honestly assessing your practical skills *right now.* Use the following list to rate your ability on a scale of 1 to 10, with 10 being the highest:

- Ability to concentrate, no matter the distractions
- Ability to use emotional triggers to learn and remember material
- Ability to define your reading purpose and use it to guide your focus and pace
- Ability to use specific vocabulary-building techniques to improve comprehension
- Ability to use every aspect of SQ3R to master content
- Ability to skim and scan
- Ability to use analytical thinking skills when reading
- Ability to use highlighting and notes to help you master content

For the two skill areas in which you rated yourself lowest, think about how you can improve. Make a problem-solving plan for each (you may want to use a flowchart like the one on page 111). Check your progress in one month and at the end of the term. Finally, write down how you anticipate using the reading skills you learned in this chapter in your chosen career.

Social Networking

INCLUDE YOUR EDUCATION

Information about your education is often important when networking for jobs. Sign in to your LinkedIn account and click on "Edit My Profile." Then, click on "Education" and fill in the following:

- Country
- State
- Degree (either attained or working toward)
- Field(s) of study
- Dates attended (Current students enter their graduation year.)
- Activities and societies
- Additional notes (Give any other information about your education that you think would be valuable to a contact or potential employer—awards, honors, details about your major, study abroad, and so on.)

If you have a previously earned degree at another institution, don't forget to fill in a separate Education field about that as well.

Listening and Note Taking

Taking In and Recording Information

What Would You Do?

Think about this problem as you read, and consider how you would approach it. *This chapter introduces you to listening and note-taking skills that will help you successfully take in, and write down, knowledge that you can use.*

*H*alfway through her first term in college, Maya Leanza is not feeling the connection she expected—neither to her coursework nor her school. She is working her way through a full load of core requirements, none of which really interests her. In fact, although she is not sure what her academic focus or major will be, after only half a term she is sure that it won't be in any of the departments of the courses she is taking now.

She and her study partner Ross have a once-a-week session on Tuesdays for their contemporary civilization class. When they met to prepare for the midterm, they exchanged sets of notes as planned. Looking at hers, Ross said, "Maya, did you miss some of class? You have about half as many pages as I do, and I'm having trouble following your notes." Maya responded, "No, I was there the whole time. Honestly, Ross, I'm trying to listen but nothing sticks. I'm just done, and we still have seven weeks to go." "Well, is it okay if we study from my notes? The midterm is Friday and I'm a little stressed," said Ross. Maya agreed, and they worked through Ross's notes and their textbook chapters for an hour.

When they were packing up, Ross said, "Maya, it's hard to get anywhere with this stuff unless you somehow believe it is important. Does it mean anything to you?" "I'm not sure," Maya said. "I feel like, what's the point?" "Well, try just thinking about why you are here," replied Ross. "Find some reason that will keep you going, even if it's just 'A degree will help me get a better job.'" Maya thought for a minute. "I'm not sure that's enough," she said. "I don't know what is enough, but I guess I'm wasting my time and money if I don't figure it out." (To be continued . . .)

Many students, at some point during college, feel disconnected from their coursework. You'll learn more about Maya, and revisit her situation, within the chapter.

In this chapter, you'll explore answers to these questions:

> How can you become a better listener? p. 150

> How can you improve your note-taking skills? p. 156

> What note-taking systems can you use? p. 160

> How can you take notes faster? p. 165

ANALYTICAL

CREATIVE

PRACTICAL

STATUS *Check*

▶ *How developed are your listening and note-taking skills?*

For each statement, circle the number that feels right to you,
from 1 for "not at all true for me" to 5 for "very true for me."

▶ I know and understand the stages of listening.	1 2 3 4 5
▶ I arrive early for class prepared to absorb information by having read the required text ahead of time.	1 2 3 4 5
▶ I ask questions during lectures and listen for verbal clues to understand important information.	1 2 3 4 5
▶ I understand the differences between internal and external distractions and work to control my learning environment whenever possible.	1 2 3 4 5
▶ I use different note-taking systems depending on my instructor's teaching styles and the material being taught.	1 2 3 4 5
▶ I know how to use visuals in my notes to clarify tough concepts discussed in class.	1 2 3 4 5
▶ I believe that good preparation is a necessary first step toward taking comprehensive notes.	1 2 3 4 5
▶ I use strategies to make sense of and record large class discussions.	1 2 3 4 5
▶ I review notes within 24 hours of taking them.	1 2 3 4 5
▶ I use shorthand to take notes faster.	1 2 3 4 5

Each of the topics in these statements is covered in this chapter. Note those statements for which you circled a 3 or lower. Skim the chapter to see where those topics appear, and pay special attention to them as you read, learn, and apply new strategies.

REMEMBER: *No matter how developed your listening and note-taking skills are, you can improve with effort and practice.*

"Successfully intelligent people find their path and then pursue it, realizing that there will be obstacles along the way and that surmounting these obstacles is part of their challenge."

—Robert Sternberg

LISTENING
A process that involves sensing, interpreting, evaluating, and reacting to spoken messages.

How can you become a better listener?

The act of *hearing* is not the same as the act of (listening.) *Hearing* refers to sensing spoken messages and sounds from their source. You can hear all kinds of things and not understand or remember any of them. Listening, however, is a communication process that starts with hearing but also includes focused thinking about what you hear. Listening is a learnable skill that engages your analytical, creative, and practical thinking abilities and extends far beyond the classroom, enhancing your ability to relate with work and school colleagues, friends, and family.

Know the stages of listening

Listening is made up of four stages that build on one another: sensing, interpreting, evaluating, and reacting. These stages take the message from the speaker to the listener and back to the speaker (see Key 6.1).

▶ During the *sensation* stage (also known as *hearing*) your ears pick up sound waves and transmit them to the brain. For example, you are sitting in class and hear your instructor say, "The only opportunity to make up last week's test is Tuesday at 5:00 P.M."

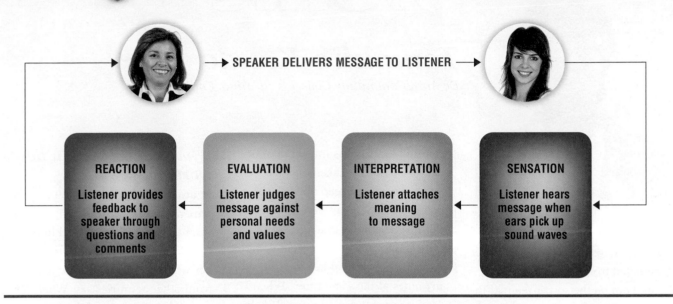

→ SPEAKER DELIVERS MESSAGE TO LISTENER →

REACTION	EVALUATION	INTERPRETATION	SENSATION
Listener provides feedback to speaker through questions and comments	Listener judges message against personal needs and values	Listener attaches meaning to message	Listener hears message when ears pick up sound waves

▶ In the *interpretation* stage, you attach meaning to a message. You understand what is said and link it to what you already know. You relate this message to your knowledge of the test, whether you need to make it up, and what you are doing on Tuesday at 5:00.

▶ In the *evaluation* stage, you evaluate the message as it relates to your needs and values. If the message goes against your values or does not fulfill your needs, you may reject it, stop listening, or argue in your mind with the speaker. In this example, if you need to make up the test but have to work Tuesday at 5:00, you may evaluate the message in an unfavorable way.

▶ The final stage of listening is a *reaction* to the message in the form of direct feedback. In a classroom, direct feedback often comes in the form of questions and comments. Your reaction, in this case, may be to ask the instructor if she can schedule another test time.

You will become a better listener by learning to recognize and manage listening challenges and becoming actively involved with the material.

Become an active listener

On the surface, listening seems like a passive activity. You sit back as someone else speaks. In reality, effective listening is an active process that involves the following factors.

■ *Be there.* Being an active listener requires that you show up on time—preferably a few minutes before class begins. Instructors often make important announcements in the first few minutes and may also summarize the last lecture.

Listening to other students can be as important as listening to instructors. These students may learn something useful from their fellow student's presentation.
© iStockPhoto

student profile

Tomohito Kondo

De Anza Community College, Cupertino, California

About me:

I came here in spring 2009 right after I graduated from my high school in Japan. I am on the soccer team at the college and I'm majoring in political science. I plan on transferring to a four-year university next fall.

What I focus on:

In college, most professors move from topic to topic when they want to, no matter where students may be in their note taking. To take good notes for yourself is important, but it can be so hard to take notes when you are trying to keep up with the professor. The point here is that you need to take notes that you can understand. I focus on listening and I write down several key words on my notes at the same time. When I read it over later, my keywords help me remember what the teacher was talking about. Even if your handwriting is really awful, it doesn't matter as long as you can read it. I think my note-taking skills help me not only to be successful in my classes, but also to save me time so I can enjoy the fun side of college life.

What will help me in the workplace:

At any time of your life, you need to remember key points. In my case, I want to be an international meeting coordinator, so I will have to remember whatever the representatives from other countries say. Whatever your job will be, the skill of taking notes helps you to remember the information, and it will help you to get into a better position. You want to move on to the next stage, right? Good listening and note-taking skills will give you a boost.

■ *Set purposes for listening.* Before every class, use your analytical intelligence to establish what you want to achieve, such as understanding a particular concept. Many instructors start a lecture with a statement of purpose, so listen carefully and write the purpose at the top of your notes to help you focus. If you read assignments and review previous notes before class, you may be able to follow along more easily. Come to class with ideas about how what you hear will help you achieve your goals (this would help Maya make her purpose for listening more personal).

■ *Focus on understanding.* Rather than taking notes on everything, record information only when you can say to yourself, "I get it!" If you miss important material, leave holes in your notes and return later. Your instructor may repeat the point you missed, or another comment may help you piece it together.

■ *Ask questions.* Active listeners ask analytical questions to clarify their understanding and to associate new ideas with what they already know. Questions like "What is this part of?" or "How is it similar to yesterday's topic?" signal active involvement. Get into the habit of jotting down your questions and coming back to them during a discussion period so they don't interfere with listening.

Manage listening challenges

Sitting in your classes, you probably have noticed a variety of not-so-academic activities that interfere with listening. Some people may be texting or surfing the Internet, some may be talking or sleeping, and some might just be daydreaming. In all of these cases the students are probably not absorbing much—or any—information from the instructor, and they may be distracting you from listening as well. Read on to see how to address these issues, and others, on your path to becoming a better listener.

Issue 1: Distractions that divide your attention

The common distractions that interfere with listening can be divided into *internal distractions* (worry, illness, fatigue, hunger, feeling too hot or too cold) and *external distractions* (chatting, computer use, any kind of movement or noise). Distractions like these nip away at you while you're trying to pay attention.

Fix 1: Focus, focus, focus

First of all, tell yourself you're in the class to learn and that you *really need* to know the material. You may even want to remind yourself of what you're paying to sit in this class. Find practical ways to minimize distractions.

▶ Sit near the front of the room.
▶ Move away from talkative classmates.
▶ Turn off your cell phone or put it on silent mode when in class.
▶ Get enough sleep to stay alert.
▶ Eat enough so you're not hungry—or bring small snacks if allowed.
▶ Try to put your worries aside during class.

The often overwhelming pace of modern life leads students to multitask (do several things at once), under the impression that multitasking can help them accomplish goals effectively in less time. Although you may think you can handle distractions because you are used to multitasking, recent research shows that multitasking actually *decreases* both memory power and performance. In a study at Stanford, low multitaskers actually outperformed high multitaskers on all tasks.[1] Try to keep your focus on one thing at a time.

Issue 2: Listening lapses

Even the most fantastic instructor can't make you listen. You and you alone can do that. If you decide that a subject is too difficult or uninteresting, you may tune out and miss what comes next, as Maya found out. You may also focus on certain points and shut out everything else. Either way, you run the risk of not being prepared and not making the most of your time.

Fix 2: An I-can-do-it attitude

▶ *Start with a productive mindset.* If the class is hard, that's all the more reason to pay attention. Instructors are generally more sympathetic to, and eager to help, students who've obviously been trying even when it's tough.
▶ *Concentrate.* Work to take in the whole message so you will be able to read over your notes later,

combine your class and text notes, and think critically about what is important. Making connections between ideas can alleviate the difficulty of the material in some cases and boredom if you're familiar with the concepts.

▶ *Refocus.* If you experience a listening lapse, try to get back into the lecture quickly instead of worrying about what you missed. After class, look at a classmate's notes to <u>fill in the gaps</u>.

▶ *Be aware.* Pay attention to **verbal signposts** to help organize information, connect ideas, and indicate what is important and what is not. See Key 6.2 for examples.

VERBAL SIGNPOSTS
Spoken words or phrases that call attention to information that follows.

Issue 3: Rushing to judgment

It's common to stop listening when you hear something you don't like or don't agree with. You react, and then your emotions take focus. Unfortunately, you can spend valuable class time thinking of all the reasons your instructor is wrong and miss everything else. The situation might not seem particularly bad that day, but when the test comes around, you may feel differently about having missed material.

Judgments also involve reactions to speakers themselves. If you do not like your instructors or have preconceived notions about their race, ethnicity, gender, physical characteristics, or disability, you may dismiss their ideas—and miss out on your opportunity to learn.

Fix 3: Recognize and correct your patterns

Although it can be human nature to stop listening when you react to a speaker or message, it can make listening a lot harder. College is about broadening your horizons and looking for what different people can teach you, even though they and their beliefs may differ from you and yours. So what do you do?

PAY ATTENTION TO
VERBAL SIGNPOSTS

SIGNALS POINTING TO KEY CONCEPTS	SIGNALS OF SUPPORT
A key point to remember . . .	A perfect example, . . .
Point 1, point 2, etc. . . .	Specifically, . . .
The impact of this was . . .	For instance, . . .
The critical stages in the process are . . .	Similarly, . . .

SIGNALS POINTING TO DIFFERENCES	SIGNALS THAT SUMMARIZE
On the contrary, . . .	From this you have learned, . . .
On the other hand, . . .	In conclusion, . . .
In contrast, . . .	As a result, . . .
However, . . .	Finally, . . .

▶ Recognize your pattern so you can change it. When you feel yourself reacting to something said in a lecture, stop and take a moment to breathe. Count to ten. Take one more breath and see how you feel.

▶ Know that you can't hear—and therefore can't learn anything from—others if you are filled with preconceived notions about them and their ideas. Put yourself in their shoes; would you want them to stop listening to you if they disagreed, or would you want to be heard completely?

▶ Stop it. It's as simple as that. Listen with an open mind even when you disagree or have a negative reaction to an instructor. Being open to the new and different, even when it makes you a bit uncomfortable, is part of what education is about.

Issue 4: Partial hearing loss and learning disabilities

If you have a hearing loss or a learning disability, listening effectively in class may prove challenging. As discussed in Chapter 3, learning disabilities can come in a variety of forms affecting different parts of cognition.

Fix 4: Get help

If you have a hearing loss, find out about available equipment. For example, listening to a taped lecture at a higher-than-normal volume can help you hear things you missed. Ask instructors if digitalized recordings are available for download to a computer or iPod. Meeting with your instructor outside of class to clarify your notes may also help, as will sitting near the front of the room.

If you have (or think you have) a learning disability, learn what services are available. Talk to your advisor and instructor about your problem, seek out a tutor, visit academic centers that can help (such as the writing center if you have a writing issue), scan the college website, or connect to the office for students with disabilities. Know that you can succeed and that people are there to help you.

Issue 5: Comprehension difficulties for speakers of other languages

If English isn't your first language, listening and understanding material in the classroom can be challenging, requiring concentration, dedication, and patience. Specialized vocabulary, informal language, and the rate of speech can add to the challenge.

Fix 5: Take a proactive approach to understanding

Talk to your instructor as soon as possible about your situation. Recognizing a need early and meeting to discuss it keeps your instructor informed and shows your dedication. In some cases, your professor will give you a list of key terms to review before class. During class, keep a list of unfamiliar words and phrases to look up later, but whenever possible, don't let these terms prevent you from understanding the main ideas. Focus on the main points of the lecture and plan to meet with classmates after class to fill gaps in your understanding. If, after several weeks, you're still having difficulties, consider enrolling in an English refresher course, getting a tutor, or visiting the campus advising center for more assistance. Be proactive about your education.

Listening isn't always easy and it isn't always comfortable. As poet Robert Frost once said, "Education is the

Discover Yourself as a Listener

Complete the following as you focus on your personal listening habits:

Analyze how present you are as a listener. Are you easily distracted, or can you focus well? Do you prefer to listen, or do you tend to talk?

_____

_____

When you are listening, what tends to distract you?

_____

_____

What happens to your listening skills when you become confused?

_____

_____

How do you react when you strongly disagree with something your instructor says—when you are convinced that you are right and your instructor is wrong?

_____

_____

Thinking about your answers, list two strategies from the chapter that will help you improve listening skills.

1. _____

2. _____

ability to listen to almost anything without losing your temper or your self-confidence." Keeping an open, engaged mind takes practice, but when excellent listening becomes second nature, you'll thank yourself for the work it took. Effective listening skills are the basis for effective note taking—an essential and powerful study tool.

How can you improve your note-taking skills?

Taking notes makes you an active class participant—even when you don't say a word—and provides you with study materials. What's on the line is nothing short of your academic success.

Class notes have two primary purposes: to serve as a record of what happened in class and to use for studying, alone and in combination with your text notes. Because it is virtually impossible to take notes on everything you hear, note taking encourages you to use your analytical intelligence to critically evaluate what is worth remembering. Exploring the strategies outlined next can help you prepare and take notes in class, review notes, and take notes on reading materials.

Prepare

Showing up for class on time is just the start. Here's more about preparing to take notes:

■ *Preview your reading material.* More than anything else you can do, reading assigned materials before class will give you the background to take effective notes. Check your class syllabi daily for assignment due dates and plan your reading time with these deadlines in mind.

Good listening powers note taking. When taking notes in class, stop to listen to the information before deciding what to write down.
© iStockPhoto

■ *Review what you know.* Taking 15 minutes before class to review your notes from the previous class and your reading assignment notes for that day will enable you to follow the lecture from the start.

■ *Set up your environment.* Find a comfortable seat, away from friends if sitting with them distracts you. Use a separate notebook for each course, and start a new page for each class. If you use a laptop, open the file containing your class notes right away. Be ready to write (or type) as soon as the instructor begins speaking.

■ *Gather support.* In each class, set up a support system with one or two students so you can look at their notes after an absence. Find students whose work you respect, as Maya did with Ross.

■ *Choose the best note-taking system.* Take these factors into account to select a system that works best in each class:

▶ *The instructor's style* (which will be clear after a few classes). In the same term, you may have an instructor who is organized and speaks slowly, another who jumps around and talks rapidly, and a third who goes off topic in response to questions. Be flexible as you adapt.
▶ *The course material.* You may decide that an informal outline works best for a highly structured lecture and that a think link (discussed later in the chapter) is right for a looser presentation. Try one note-taking system for several classes and then adjust if necessary.
▶ *Your learning style.* Choose strategies that make the most of your strengths and compensate for your weaknesses.

Examples of various note-taking systems, and a more thorough discussion, appear later in the chapter.

Record information effectively during class

The following practical suggestions will help you record what is important in a format that you can review later:

▶ *Start a new page or section for each new topic,* especially if your instructor jumps from topic to topic during a single class.
▶ *Record whatever your instructor emphasizes* by paying attention to verbal and nonverbal cues.
▶ *Write down all key terms and definitions* so that you can refer back to them easily.

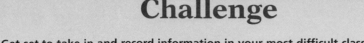

GET PRACTICAL!

Face a Note-Taking Challenge

Get set to take in and record information in your most difficult class.

Course name and date of class:

_____

Consult your syllabus, and then list what you have to read (text sections and/or other materials) before your next class:

_____

_____

Where will you sit in class to focus your attention and minimize distractions?

_____

Which note-taking system is best suited for the class and why?

_____

_____

Write the phone numbers and e-mail addresses of two classmates whose notes you can borrow if you miss a class or are confused about material:

_____

_____

▶ *Note relevant examples, applications, and links to other material* when you encounter difficult concepts.

▶ *Ask questions.* If your instructor allows questions during class, ask them. Chances are several other students have similar queries. If your instructor prefers to answer questions at the end of class, keep a separate sheet of paper to jot down questions as you think of them.

▶ *Write down every question your instructor raises,* because these questions may be on a test.

▶ *Be organized, but not fussy.* Remember that you can always improve your notes later.

▶ *Leave blank spaces between points* to make it easy see where one topic ends and another begins. (This suggestion does not apply if you are using a think link.)

▶ *Draw pictures and diagrams* to illustrate ideas.

▶ *Be consistent.* Use the same system to show importance—such as indenting, spacing, or underlining—on each page.

▶ *Record as much as you can if you have trouble understanding a concept.* Then leave space for an explanation and flag the margin with a large question mark. After class, try to clarify your questions by reading the text or ask a classmate or your instructor for help.

▶ *Consider that your class notes are only part of the picture.* You will learn best when you combine your text and class notes.

▶ *Go beyond the PowerPoint.* Increasingly, instructors are using computer software to present lectures in the classroom. Although it may be tempting to simply copy down what's written on the slide, realize that instructors usually show the main points, not the details that may be tested later. Take notes on what your instructor says about each main idea highlighted on a PowerPoint slide.

Finally, don't stop taking notes when your class engages in a discussion. Even though it isn't part of the instructor's planned presentation, it often includes important information. Key 6.3 has suggestions for how to make the most of discussions.

Review and revise

By their very nature, class notes require revision. They may be incomplete in some places, confusing in others, and illegible in still others. That is why it is critical to review and revise your notes as soon as possible after class. This will enable you to fill in gaps while the material is fresh, to clarify sloppy hand-writing, or to raise questions.

If you can review your notes within 24 hours of taking them down in class, you are likely to reactivate and strengthen the new neural pathways you created when you learned the material. Waiting longer than 24 hours can result in losing the information you worked so hard to record. Reviewing and revising your class notes prepares you for the vital step of combining class and text notes.

IMPROVE YOUR NOTES
DURING CLASS DISCUSSION

- Listen to everyone; you never know when something important will be said.

- Listen for threads that weave through comments. They may signal an important point.

- Listen for ideas the instructor likes and for encouraging comments, such as "You make a great point" or "I like your idea."

- Take notes when the instructor rephrases and clarifies a point.

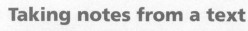

Change the CONVERSATION

Challenge yourself and your friends to ask—and answer—tough questions. Use the following to inspire discussion in pairs or groups.

▶ Think about what typically plays on your brain's "soundtrack" during a class meeting—words, music, anything that streams through. Be honest: How much of it relates to the class, and how much is unrelated? What effect does it have on your focus?

▶ When you have no interest in class material, how does it affect you—your behavior, your grades, your connection to others in the course, your commitment?

▶ **CONSIDER THE CASE:** Come up with a course of action for Maya that you think would help her get something out of her contemporary civilization class.

Taking notes from a text

Taking notes while reading a text follows the same basic principles as taking notes in class, but with a bit of an SQ3R twist. Although you won't be asking as many probing questions of the material, you'll need your skills in observation, as well as in recording and reviewing, to make it a success.

You might take notes from a text when the book is a library copy or borrowed from a classmate—or when you don't have enough room to take notes in the margin. In that case, it's best to start by identifying what you want to get from the notes. Are you looking for the basic topics from a chapter? An in-depth understanding of a particular concept? Once you've decided on the need, then you can identify the method.

Revisit the note-taking methods listed earlier in the chapter. Different note-taking approaches work best for different situations. For instance, mind maps work well to understand broad connections, overall relationships, or how your text works in relation to your instructor's lecture. On the other hand, formal outlines can make sense of complicated information in a structured way that can provide clarity. Try different approaches to see which ones work for you.

What note-taking systems can you use?

Now that you have gathered some useful note-taking strategies, take a look at different approaches to note taking. As you read, keep some questions in mind:

▶ What class or type of instruction would this system be best suited for? Why?
▶ How could I make use of this system?
▶ Which system seems most comfortable to me?
▶ What system might be most compatible with my learning style strengths? Why?

Outlines

Outlines use a standard structure to show how ideas interrelate. *Formal outlines* indicate idea dominance and subordination with Roman numerals, uppercase and lowercase letters, and numbers. In contrast, *informal outlines* show the same associations but replace the formality with a system of consistent indenting and dashes.

When a lecture seems well organized, an informal outline can show how ideas and supporting details relate while also indicating levels of importance. Key 6.4 shows how the structure of an informal outline helps a student take notes on the topic of tropical rain forests. The multiple intelligences table in this chapter (see page 162) is designed to help harness different learning approaches for an earth science course. Specifically, the table will suggest different note-taking strategies you can use to study the topic of tropical rain forests.

Tropical Rain Forests

What are tropical rain forests?
—Areas in South America and Africa, along the equator
—Average temperatures between 25° and 30° C (77°–86° F)
—Average annual rainfalls range between 250 to 400 centimeters (100 to 160 inches)
—Conditions combine to create the Earth's richest, most biodiverse ecosystem.
  –A biodiverse ecosystem has a great number of organisms coexisting within a defined area.
  –Examples of rain forest biodiversity
    –2½ acres in the Amazon rain forest has 283 species of trees
    –a 3-square-mile section of a Peruvian rain forest has more than 1,300 butterfly species and 600 bird species.
    –Compare this biodiversity to what is found in the entire U.S.—only 400 butterfly species and 700 bird species
How are humans changing the rain forest?
  —Humans have already destroyed about 40% of all rain forests.
    –They are cutting down trees for lumber or clearing the land for ranching or agriculture.
  —Biologist Edwin O. Wilson estimates that this destruction may lead to the extinction of 27,000 species.
  —Rain forest removal is also linked to the increase in atmospheric carbon dioxide, which worsens the greenhouse effect.
    –The greenhouse effect refers to process in which gases such as carbon dioxide trap the sun's energy in the Earth's atmosphere as heat resulting in global warning.
  —Recognition of the crisis is growing as are conservation efforts.

Source: Teresa Audesirk, Gerald Audesirk, and Bruce E. Byers. *Life on Earth,* 2nd ed. Upper Saddle River, NJ: Prentice Hall, 2000, pp. 660–662.

When an instructor's presentation is disorganized, it may be difficult to use an outline. Focus instead on taking down whatever information you can as you try to connect key topics. The Cornell system and other note-taking methods discussed next can be beneficial in such situations.

From time to time, an instructor may give you a guide, usually in outline form, to help you take notes in class. This outline, known as *guided notes,* may be on the board, projected onto a screen, or in a handout that you receive at the beginning of class. Because guided notes are usually general and sketchy, they require that you fill in the details.

Cornell T-note system

The *Cornell note-taking system,* also known as the *T-note system,* consists of three sections on ordinary notepaper.[2]

▶ *Notes,* the largest section, is on the right. Record your notes here in whatever form you choose. Skip lines between topics so you can clearly see where a section begins and ends.

▶ The *cue column* goes to the left of your notes. Leave it blank while you read or listen, and then fill it in later as you review. You might insert keywords or comments that highlight ideas, clarify meaning, add examples, link ideas, or draw diagrams. Many students use this column to raise questions, which they answer when they study.

▶ The *summary* goes at the bottom of the page. Here you reduce your notes to critical points, a process that will help you learn the material. Use this section to provide an overview of what the notes say.

MULTIPLE INTELLIGENCE STRATEGIES
for Note-Taking

Apply Different Intelligences to Concepts to Taking Notes in Earth Science

INTELLIGENCE	USE MI STRATEGIES TO IMPROVE YOUR NOTES	APPLY MI NOTE-TAKING STRATEGIES TO THE TOPIC OF TROPICAL RAIN FORESTS FOR AN EARTH SCIENCE COURSE
Verbal-Linguistic	• Rewrite your class notes in an alternate note-taking style to see connections more clearly. • Combine class and text notes to get a complete picture.	• Rewrite and summarize your reading and lecture notes to understand the characteristics of tropical rain forests.*
Logical-Mathematical	• When reviewing or rewriting notes, put information into a logical sequence. • Create tables that show relationships.	• Create a table comparing and contrasting the different species found in a typical rain forest.
Bodily-Kinesthetic	• Think of your notes as a crafts project that enables you to see "knowledge layers." Use colored pens to texture your notes. • Study with your notes spread in sequence around you so that you can see knowledge building from left to right.	• Fill a tube with 160 inches of water (that's 13⅓ feet!) to give you a physical sense of the annual rainfall in a rain forest. Or fill a bathtub with 10 inches of water and multiply by 16 to imagine rainfall totals. How would you react to living with so much rain? Take notes on your reaction.
Visual-Spatial	• Take notes using colored markers or pens. • Rewrite lecture notes in think link format, focusing on the most important points.	• As part of your notes, create a chart that covers the types of vegetation that grow in a rain forest. Use a different colored marker for each plant species.
Interpersonal	• Try to schedule a study group right after a lecture to discuss class notes. • Review class notes with a study buddy. Compare notes to see what the other missed.	• Interview someone you know who has visited a rain forest about what she saw, or interview a natural scientist at a museum about this environment. Use a different note-taking system for each person.
Intrapersonal	• Schedule some quiet time soon after a lecture to review and think about your notes. • As you review your notes, decide whether you grasp the material or need help.	• Think about the conflict between economic modernization and the preservation of rain forests in underdeveloped areas. Include your thoughts in your notes.
Musical	• To improve recall, recite concepts in your notes to rhythms. • Write a song that includes material from your class and text notes. Use the refrain to emphasize what is important.	• Use the Internet to find songs about the biodiversity of rain forests written by indigenous peoples who live in or near them. Then, use the song to remember key concepts. Take notes on what you find.
Naturalistic	• Notice similarities and differences in concepts by organizing material into natural groupings.	• If possible, visit a museum of natural history with exhibits of rain forests. Try to see common characteristics that make vegetation and species thrive in this environment. Take notes on your observations.

*For information on tropical rain forests, see Frederick Lutgens, Edward Tarbuck, and Dennis Tasa, *Foundations of Earth Science,* 5th ed., Upper Saddle River, NJ: Prentice Hall, 2008.

Create this note-taking structure before class begins. Picture an upside-down letter *T* as you follow these directions:

▶ Start with a sheet of 8½-by-11-inch lined paper. Label it with the date and lecture title.

▶ To create the cue column, draw a vertical line about 2½ inches from the left side of the paper. End the line about two inches from the bottom of the sheet.

▶ To create the summary area, start at the point where the vertical line ends (about two inches from the bottom of the page) and draw a horizontal line that spans the entire paper.

Key 6.5 shows how the Cornell system is used in a business course.

Key 6.5

THE **CORNELL SYSTEM** HAS SPACE FOR NOTES, COMMENTS, AND A SUMMARY

October 3, 2010, p. 1

Understanding Employee Motivation

Why do some workers have a better attitude toward their work than others?

Some managers view workers as lazy; others view them as motivated and productive.

Maslow's Hierarchy

self-actualization needs
(challenging job)
esteem needs
(job title)
social needs
(friends at work)
security needs
(health plan)
physiological needs
(pay)

Purpose of motivational theories
— To explain role of human relations in motivating employee performance
— Theories translate into how managers actually treat workers

2 specific theories
— Human resources model, developed by Douglas McGregor, shows that managers have radically different beliefs about motivation.
— Theory X holds that people are naturally irresponsible and uncooperative
— Theory Y holds that people are naturally responsible and self-motivated
— Maslow's Hierarchy of Needs says that people have needs in 5 different areas, which they attempt to satisfy in their work.
— Physiological need: need for survival, including food and shelter
— Security need: need for stability and protection
— Social need: need for friendship and companionship
— Esteem need: need for status and recognition
— Self-actualization need: need for self-fulfillment
Needs at lower levels must be met before a person tries to satisfy needs at higher levels.
— Developed by psychologist Abraham Maslow

Two motivational theories try to explain worker motivation. The human resources model includes Theory X and Theory Y. Maslow's Hierarchy of Needs suggests that people have needs in 5 different areas: physiological, security, social, esteem, and self-actualization.

Label a sheet of paper with the date and title of the lecture.

Create the cue column by drawing a vertical line about 2½ inches from the left side of the paper. End the line about 2 inches from the bottom of the sheet.

Create the summary area by starting where the vertical line ends (about 2 inches from the bottom of the page) and drawing a horizontal line across the paper.

Think links

A *think link,* also known as a *mind map* or *word web,* is a visual form of note taking that encourages flexible thinking. When you draw a think link, you use shapes and lines to link ideas with supporting details and examples. The visual design makes the connections easy to see, and shapes and pictures extend the material beyond words.

To create a think link, start by circling or boxing your topic in the middle of the paper. Next, draw a line from the topic and write the name of one major idea at the end of the line. Circle that idea. Then jot down specific facts related to the idea, linking them to the idea with lines. Continue the process, connecting thoughts to one another with circles, lines, and words. Key 6.6, a think link on the sociological concept "stratification," follows this structure.

Examples of think link designs include stair steps showing connected ideas that build toward a conclusion and a tree with trunk and roots as central concepts and branches as examples. Key 8.5 on page 221 shows another type of think link called a "jellyfish."

A think link may be difficult to construct in class, especially if your instructor talks quickly. If this is the case, transform your notes into think link format later when you review.

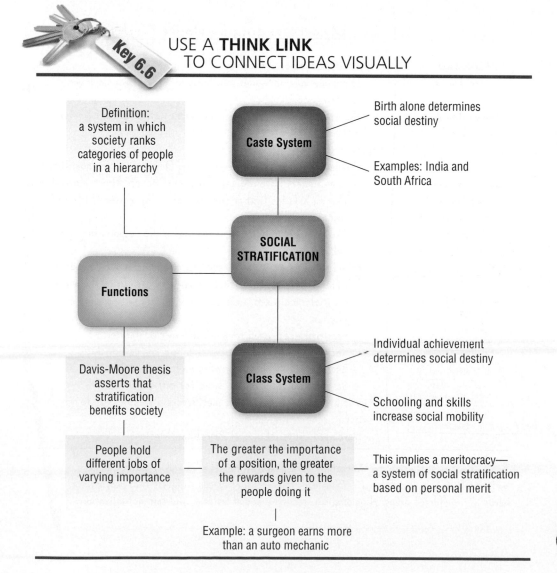

Key 6.6 USE A **THINK LINK** TO CONNECT IDEAS VISUALLY

Definition: a system in which society ranks categories of people in a hierarchy

Caste System
- Birth alone determines social destiny
- Examples: India and South Africa

SOCIAL STRATIFICATION

Functions
- Davis-Moore thesis asserts that stratification benefits society
- People hold different jobs of varying importance

Class System
- Individual achievement determines social destiny
- Schooling and skills increase social mobility

The greater the importance of a position, the greater the rewards given to the people doing it

This implies a meritocracy—a system of social stratification based on personal merit

Example: a surgeon earns more than an auto mechanic

Charting method

Sometimes instructors deliver information in such quantities and at such speeds that taking detailed notes becomes nearly impossible. In such situations, when a lot of material is coming at you very quickly, the charting method might prove quite useful. It is also excellent for classes presented chronologically or sequentially.

To create charting notes, look ahead in your syllabus to determine the topics of the day's lecture. Then separate your paper into distinct columns, such as definitions, important phrases, and key themes. As you listen to the lecture, this will eliminate excessive writing, help you track dialogues that can be easy to lose, and provide quick memorization tools by splitting material into relevant categories. Shown is a partial set of charting notes for a history class:

Time Period	Important People	Events	Importance
1969–1974	Richard Nixon	Watergate, Vietnam War	Ended Vietnam War, Opened relations with China, First president to resign

Other visual strategies

Other strategies that help organize information are especially useful to visual learners, although they may be too involved to complete during class. Use them when taking text notes or combining class and text notes for review.

▶ *Pictures and diagrams.* Copy any and all diagrams from the board and feel free to adapt your own. Make complex concepts into images or cartoons. The act of converting material into a visual display will activate both your bodily-kinesthetic attributes as well as your visual intelligence.

▶ *Timelines.* Use a timeline to organize information into chronological order. Draw a vertical or horizontal line on the page and connect each item to the line, in order, noting the dates and basic event descriptions.

▶ *Tables.* Use the columns and rows of a table to organize information as you condense and summarize your class and text notes.

▶ *Hierarchy charts.* Charts showing an information hierarchy can help you visualize how pieces fit together. For example, you can use a hierarchy chart to show ranks within a government bureaucracy or levels of scientific classification of animals and plants.

How can you take notes faster?

> SHORTHAND
> A system of rapid handwriting that employs symbols, abbreviations, and shortened words to represent words and phrases.

Personal (shorthand) is a practical intelligence strategy that enables you to write faster. Because you are the only intended reader, you can misspell and abbreviate words in ways that only you understand. A risk of using shorthand is that you might forget what your writing means. To avoid this problem, review your notes shortly after class and spell out words that are confusing.

Another risk is forgetting to remove shorthand from work you hand in. This can happen when you use the same system for class notes as you do when talking to friends online. For example, when students take notes in text message shorthand they may be so accustomed to omitting capitalization and punctuation, using acronyms, and replacing long words with creative contractions that they may forget to correct their final work.

The suggestions that follow will help you master shorthand. Many will be familiar and, in fact, you may already use many of them to speed up your e-mail and text messaging.

1. Use standard abbreviations in place of complete words.

w/, w/o	with, without	Cf	compare, in comparison to
ur	you are	Ff	following
→	means; resulting in	Q	question
←	as a result of	gr8	great
↑	increasing	Pov	point of view
↓	decreasing	<	less than
∴	therefore	>	more than
b/c	because	=	equals
≈	approximately	b&f	back and forth
+ or &	and	Δ	change
Y	why	2	to; two; too
no. or #	number	Afap	as far as possible
i.e.	that is,	e.g.	for example
cos	change of subject	c/o	care of
Ng	no good	lb	pound
POTUS	President of the United States	hx	history

2. Shorten words by removing middle vowels.

prps = purpose
lwyr = lawyer
cmptr = computer

3. Substitute word beginnings for entire words.

assoc = associate; association
info = information
subj = subject

4. Form plurals by adding *s* to shortened words.

prblms = problems
envlps = envelopes
prntrs = printers

5. Make up your own symbols and use them consistently.

b/4 = before
4tn = fortune
2thake = toothache

6. Use standard or informal abbreviations for proper nouns such as places, people, companies, scientific substances, events, and so on.

DC = Washington, D.C.
H_2O = water
Moz. = Wolfgang Amadeus Mozart

7. If you know that a word or phrase will be repeated, write it once and then establish an abbreviation for the rest of your notes. For example, the first time your political science instructor mentions the Iraq Study Group,

GET CREATIVE!

Craft Your Own Shorthand

Now that you've read through some suggestions for shorthand, it's time to customize it to your needs.

Identify a class in which you take a lot of notes or one in which you would like to begin taking better notes.

_____

Next, write ten terms that are used often in this class. For instance, if you were creating a list for your psychology class, you might include terms like *Sigmund Freud, child development,* or *neuropsychology.*

_____

_____

_____

_____

_____

Finally, create a list of shorthand terms for the items you chose. Be creative but remember that they should be easy for you to remember and use. Thus, your shorthand should not be longer or more complex than the word itself. Use numbers, symbols, or even small images (like a heart or smiley face). For the list of psychology terms, the shorthand might look like the following:

Sigmund Freud	=	SigFrd
Child development	=	ChDev
Neuropsychology	=	nro-psych

the 2006 bipartisan commission that issued recommendations to the president on the Iraq War, write the name in full. After that, use the initials ISG.

8. Write only what is essential. Include only the information nuggets you want to remember, even if your instructor says much more. Do this by paring down your writing. Say, for example, your instructor had the following to say on the subject of hate crimes.[3]

> After the terrorist attacks on September 11, 2001, law enforcement officials noted a dramatic shift in the nature of hate crimes. For the first time, replacing crimes motivated by race as the leading type of hate crime were crimes that targeted religious and ethnic groups and particularly Muslims.

Your shorthand notes might look something like this:

—After 9/11 HCs ▲ focus & targeted religious and ethnic groups, esp. Muslims.
—Reduction of HC based on race.

Case *Wrap-up*

What happened to Maya? With Ross's help, Maya passed the midterm. Afterward, she found herself once again "there but not there" in her contemporary civ class as well as others. Trying to find meaning in the coursework, she talked with her parents. Her mother commented that she was building incredible skills for life, because not having much interest in the material meant that she needed extra motivation, commitment, and responsibility to get through it successfully. This awakened a sense of pride in Maya. Determined to improve during the remaining weeks, she concentrated on finding a note-taking system that made sense to her and deliberately used it in her classes. She found that the structure actually helped her pay more attention, and her increased focus helped her notice some ideas that interested her more than she had expected.

What does this mean for you? Nearly every student has to fulfill core requirements as part of a degree program. Chances are that some—or even many—of the core courses you have to take will not be on your list of favorites. In many ways this is a useful exercise for life, in which you will rarely be able to choose your favorite job, most desired co-workers, ideal neighbors, or perfect day-to-day schedule. Sure, sometimes you may find a way to enjoy a particular course, even if the material doesn't inspire you. You may make friends in the class, develop a good relationship with the instructor, or get motivated by the simple fact that passing the course moves you toward your goal of graduation. However, just getting through it with your GPA intact can teach you a useful skill—how to take something valuable away from any experience.

What effects go beyond your world? Searching for meaning in your coursework or your working life can mean more than just fulfillment for you. The more interested, committed, and fulfilled you are, the more the benefits radiate out from you and affect others. Read the article "Meaningful Work" located at www.psychologytoday.com/blog/the-meaning-in-life/200905/work-youre-meant-do-or-just-paid-do. Reflect on what kind of job might fulfill the three criteria for meaningful work (it must make sense to you, have a point or goal, and serve the greater good in some way). Brainstorm ideas for work that you believe would have positive effects on others, going beyond your needs for a steady paycheck and personal fulfillment.

ANALYTICAL CREATIVE PRACTICAL

Successful Intelligence *Wrap-up*

HERE'S HOW YOU HAVE
BUILT SKILLS IN **CHAPTER 6** :

ANALYTICAL THINKING	CREATIVE THINKING	PRACTICAL THINKING
❯ You examined common challenges you face when listening.	❯ You developed new systems for note taking and how to apply them to your courses.	❯ You compiled practical tools for managing listening challenges.
❯ In the Get Analytical exercise, you analyzed your own listening skills to better understand your personal needs.	❯ In the Get Creative exercise, you brainstormed personal shorthand terms to speed up note taking.	❯ In the Get Practical exercise, you explored how to use note-taking systems in difficult situations.
❯ You explored note-taking systems and considered which would work best for you given certain locations and classes.	❯ You may have been inspired to think about new ways in which you might listen and receive information in classes.	❯ You learned shorthand techniques to add to your understanding of note-taking strategies.

Word *for* Thought

In **Swedish,** the word *lagom* (lagh'-ohm) refers to the place between extremes, the spot that is neither too much nor too little, but just right.[4] Think of the quest for lagom as you work to improve listening and note-taking skills. You can never hope to take in and record every word your instructor says—and that's okay. You are aiming for "just right."

Building Skills *for* College, Career, *and* Life

Steps to Success

Your Best Listening and Note-Taking Conditions

BUILD BASIC SKILLS. Think of a recent class in which you were *able to listen and take notes effectively.*

Describe the environment (course title, classroom setting, and so on):

_____

_____

_____

_____

Describe the instructor's style (lecture, group discussion, Q and A):

_____

_____

_____

_____

Describe your level of preparation and attitude toward the class:

_____

_____

_____

_____

Describe the note-taking style you generally use in the class and how effective it is for you:

_____

_____

_____

_____

Describe any barriers to effective listening that were present:

_____

_____

_____

_____

Now think of a recent class in which you found it *hard to listen and take notes.*

Describe the environment (course title, classroom setting, and so on):

_____

_____

_____

_____

Describe the instructor's style (lecture, group discussion, Q and A):

_____

_____

_____

Describe your level of preparation and attitude toward the class:

_____

_____

_____

_____

Describe the note-taking style you generally use in the class and how effective it is for you:

_____

_____

_____

_____

Describe any barriers to effective listening that were present:

_____

_____

_____

_____

TAKE IT TO THE NEXT LEVEL. Examine the two situations. From what you notice, identify three conditions that seem, for you, to be crucial for effective listening and note taking:

1. _____

2. _____

3. _____

MOVE TOWARD MASTERY. Think about the more difficult listening and note-taking situation. For each of the three conditions you named, describe either how you can make sure that condition occurs or how you can compensate for it if it is out of your control.

1. _____

_____

2. _____

_____

3. _____

_____

Teamwork

Create Solutions Together

TEAM UP TO TAKE NOTES

Goal: To create a note-taking team.

Time on task: One week; 30 minutes of review

Instructions: In your most demanding course, form a study group with two classmates. Ask everyone to gather together a week's worth of class notes so that you can review and compare the different versions. Focus on the following:

- Legibility (Can everyone read what is written?)
- Completeness (Did you all record the same information? If not, why not?)
- Organizational effectiveness (Does everyone get an idea of how ideas flow?)
- Value of the notes as a study aid (Will this help everyone remember the material?)

What did you learn? Use your insights to improve personal note-taking skills. As a bonus, exchange contact information with the two students. Contact them to swap notes in the future or form a study group.

Writing

Build Intrapersonal and Communication Skills

Record your thoughts on a separate piece of paper, in a journal, or electronically.

EMOTIONAL INTELLIGENCE JOURNAL

Understanding your needs and making changes. Think about a situation when you've had trouble taking effective notes. Was it the teacher's pace? The subject matter of the class? How did you feel about the situation, and what did you do? After you describe the situation, find and write three note-taking strategies discussed in this chapter that could help you in the future. How might they help you create a more positive outcome?

REAL-LIFE WRITING

Determining the best method for you. Over the next week, commit to trying at least two different types of note-taking systems in your classes. If possible, choose a different method for each subject. Prepare for your method before entering the class by readying your notebook with the correct formatting. Try to complete your classes using the new method. When the week is over, reflect on which style worked best for you and which would be the most beneficial going forward.

Personal Portfolio

Prepare for Career Success

LEARN MORE ABOUT CAREER SUCCESS

21st Century Learning Building Blocks

- Financial, Economic, Business, and Entreprencurial Literacy
- Information Literacy
- Media Literacy

Complete the following in your electronic portfolio or on separate paper.

Put your listening and note-taking skills to work as you investigate what brings success in the workplace. Write down a few potential career areas that interest you.

1. _____

2. _____

3. _____

Next, visit an Internet website that hosts user-loaded videos like YouTube.com. Perform a search for a career interview of your choice. You might try search terms like "marketing interview," "what's it like to be a dental technician?" or "what does a movie producer do?" When you've found a usable video (keep in mind that you're looking for credible, realistic information), practice one of the note-taking techniques discussed in this chapter.

Watch the video once all the way through, concentrating on main points and overall themes. Then, watch it again focusing on filling in gaps, understanding key terms and concepts, and gathering interesting extras. Remember to use shorthand when necessary.

After you've watched the video twice and taken thorough notes, write a one-page summary of the career for your portfolio. Include important information discussed in the video, such as the training required, salary expectations, daily duties, and so on. Keep the summary in your portfolio for future career searches.

Social Networking

BUILD CONTACTS

Begin to build, or continue to build, your network on LinkedIn. Sign in to your account and click on "Add Connections." Find and contact 10 people in one of the following ways:

- Enter the name of someone you know in the "People" field at the top of the screen to see whether that person has a LinkedIn account. If they do, click on "Add to network" to invite them to join your network.
- Use the "See Who You Already Know on LinkedIn" feature to search your e-mail contacts for people who have LinkedIn accounts.
- In the "Enter E-mail Addresses" box, enter the e-mail addresses of people you want to invite to your network. Each will receive an invitation, regardless of whether they are already LinkedIn members.

Think carefully about who you want as part of your network. Consider family, friends, and coworkers. Choose people who you believe will help you move forward toward your goals, and who you think may have interesting and useful networks themselves.

Memory and Studying

Retaining What You Learn

What Would You Do?

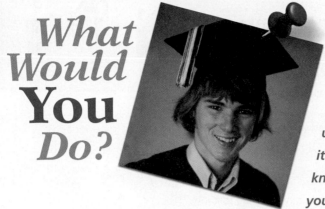

Think about this problem as you read, and consider how you would approach it. This chapter shows you how memory works and then helps you use it effectively as you study. Although it's easier to remember what you want to know, the strategies you learn will help you study materials no matter how you feel about them.

Norton Ewart struggled from fourth grade through high school. Overwhelmed by the work and the level of independence, he did the least amount of work possible and earned a C average. He enrolled in the liberal arts program at Mohawk Valley Community College in Utica, New York, out of a desire to please his parents. Uninterested in the coursework and not ready for the independence of college life, Norton hitchhiked home each weekend to work as a house-painter and left school 10 weeks later. He then moved to his aunt's house in Colorado, where he skied black diamond runs, worked as a ski technician, and tried to figure out who he was and what he wanted.

After two years, Norton decided he wanted to return to college and moved back home. Thinking he might follow the family path of engineering, as had three generations before him, he decided to pursue an associate's degree in math and science at Hudson Valley Community College in Troy, New York. Despite his newfound confidence and the fun of a state-of-the-art calculator his father had given him, he could not move on right away from his inconsistent study habits. He received Cs and Ds in calculus and physics courses during his first year.

Norton was behind, but for the first time he was determined to excel. He found himself enjoying the creativity and beauty of math and how the mind interacts with it. On the advice of an academic advisor, he spent a year in a civil technology program while retaking every calculus and physics course. Aware that he was more motivated when working with others, he put together a study group. His group of fellow engineering students called themselves the "Engineering Defense League" and met daily to work through problems, drill one another on formulas and problem-solving steps, and experience the struggle together. (To be continued . . .)

Skiing and working in Colorado gave Norton a sense of ownership of his success as well as a desire—and a reason—to get back to college. You'll learn more about Norton, and revisit his situation, within the chapter.

In this chapter, you'll explore answers to these questions:

> How does memory work? p. 176

> How can you remember what you study? p. 179

> What will help you remember math and science material? p. 191

> How can mnemonic devices boost recall? p. 192

> What study strategies help you put it all together? p. 196

ANALYTICAL

CREATIVE

PRACTICAL

For each statement, circle the number that feels right to you, from 1 for "not at all true for me" to 5 for "very true for me."

▶ I know that not everything that I hear and read will necessarily stay in my memory for long—or at all.　　1 2 3 4 5

▶ When I am studying, I try to choose what is most important to remember.　　1 2 3 4 5

▶ Through trial and error, I have figured out study locations and times that work best for me.　　1 2 3 4 5

▶ After a test or presentation is over, I retain much of what I had to know.　　1 2 3 4 5

▶ I write, rewrite, and summarize information to remember it.　　1 2 3 4 5

▶ I use flash cards and other active memory strategies to remember what I study.　　1 2 3 4 5

▶ I create mnemonic devices with images and associations as memory hooks.　　1 2 3 4 5

▶ I try to review material in several sessions over time rather than cram the night before a test.　　1 2 3 4 5

▶ If I find myself looking up something over and over again, I make an effort to memorize it.　　1 2 3 4 5

▶ I know how to study class and text notes effectively to prepare for tests.　　1 2 3 4 5

Each of the topics in these statements is covered in this chapter. Note those statements for which you circled a 3 or lower. Skim the chapter to see where those topics appear, and pay special attention to them as you read, learn, and apply new strategies.

REMEMBER: *No matter how developed your memory and studying skills are, you can improve with effort and practice.*

"Successfully intelligent people are aware of the circumstances under which they are able to function at their best. They create those circumstances and then use them to their maximum advantage."

—Robert Sternberg

How does memory work?

Memory anchors all learning and performance—on tests as well as at work. The information you remember—concepts, facts, processes, formulas, and more—is the raw material with which you think, write, create, build, and perform day-to-day in school and out. Tasks ranging from high-level chemistry experiments to running a load of laundry through the washing machine all require you to retain and use information in your memory.

Memorization also gives you the tools to tackle higher-level thinking, such as in Chapter 5's discussion of Bloom's taxonomy (see pp. 123–125). You need to recall and understand information before you can apply, analyze, synthesize, or evaluate it.

Through studying, you build your memory and use it to move toward your goals. This chapter provides a host of memory improvement techniques that you can make your own with a positive attitude and active involvement. The first step is exploring how memory works.

The information processing model of memory

Memory refers to the way the brain stores and recalls information or experiences that are acquired through the five senses. Although you take in thousands of pieces of information every second—everything from the shape and

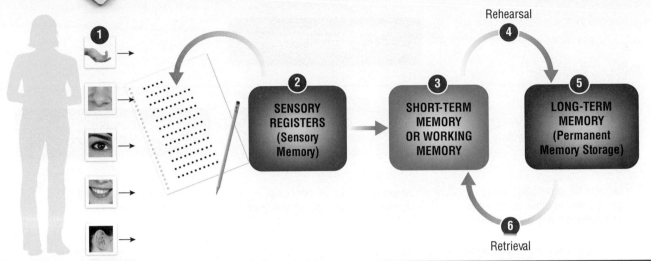

color of your chair to how your history text describes Abraham Lincoln's presidency—you remember few. Unconsciously, your brain sorts through stimuli and stores only what it considers important.

Key 7.1 illustrates how the brain forms lasting memories.

1. Raw information, gathered through the five senses, reaches the brain (for example, the tune of a song you're learning in your jazz ensemble class).

2. This information enters (sensory registers,) where it stays for only seconds. (As you play the notes for the first time, the sounds stop first in your auditory register.)

3. You then choose whether to pay attention to information in the sensory register. When you selectively look, listen, smell, taste, or feel the information, you move it into (short-term memory,) also known as *working memory*, which contains what you are thinking at any moment and from where information can be made available for further processing. (The part of the song that is your responsibility, for example, the clarinet solo, will likely take up residence in your working memory.) You can temporarily keep information in short-term memory through *rote rehearsal*—the process of repeating information to yourself or even out loud.

4. Information moves to (long-term memory) through focused, active rehearsal repeated over time. (As you practice the song in class and at home, your brain stores the tone, rhythm, and pace in your long-term memory, where you will be able to draw on it again.) Long-term memory stores everything you know from Civil War battle dates to the location of your grade school. As shown in Key 7.2, long-term memory has three separate storage houses. There are no limits to how much information long-term memory can hold or how long it is held, but most people retain memories of personal experiences and procedures longer than concepts, facts, formulas, and dates.

When you need a piece of information from long-term memory, the brain retrieves it and places it in short-term memory. On test day, this enables you to choose the right answer on a multiple-choice question or lay out a fact-based argument for an essay question.

> SENSORY REGISTER
> Brain filters through which sensory information enters the brain and is sent to short-term memory.

> SHORT-TERM MEMORY
> The brain's temporary information storehouse, in which information remains for a limited time (from a few seconds to half a minute).

> LONG-TERM MEMORY
> The brain's permanent information storehouse, from which information can be retrieved.

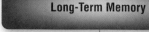
Long-Term Memory

Storage of Procedural Memory	Storage of Declarative Memory	Storage of Episodic Memory
Storage for information about procedures, in other words, how to do things—ride a bike, drive a car, tie your shoes. It can take a while to develop these memories, but they are difficult to lose.	Memories of facts, concepts, formulas, and so on. These are relatively easy to learn, but are easy to forget without continual review.	Memories of events linked to personal experiences.

$$x = \frac{-b \pm \sqrt{b^2 - 4ac}}{2a}$$

The movement of information in your brain, from short-term to long-term memory and then back again, strengthens the connections among neurons (brain cells). As you read in Chapter 1, learning happens and memories are built when neurons grow new dendrites and form new synapses. When you learn an algebra formula, for example, your brain creates new connections. Every time you review it, the connections get stronger.

Why you forget

Health issues and poor nutrition can cause memory problems. Stress is also a factor; research shows that even short-term stress can interfere with cell communication in the learning and memory regions of the brain.[1] However, *the most common reason that information fails to stay in long-term memory is ineffective studying*—not doing what you should to retain what you learn.

As Key 7.3 shows, retaining information requires continual review. You are still learning information 10 minutes after you hear it the first time. If you review the material over time—after 24 hours, a week, a month, 6 months, and more—you will retain the knowledge. If you do not review, the neural connections will weaken, and eventually you will forget. For Norton, a combination of unfocused listening and reading and a lack of consistent studying made it tough for him to retain important information.

In a classic study conducted in 1885, researcher Herman Ebbinghaus memorized a list of meaningless three-letter words such as CEF and LAZ. He then examined how quickly he forgot them. Within 1 hour, he had forgotten more than 50 percent of

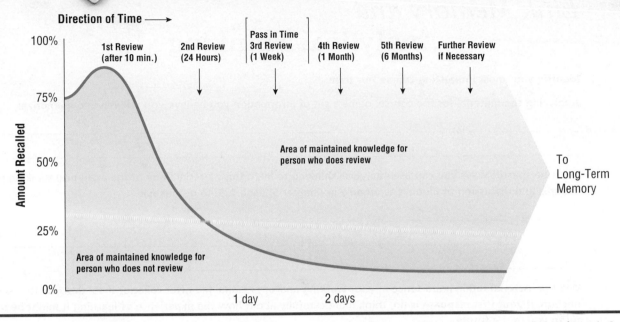

Source: From Tony Buzan, *Use Both Sides of Your Brain,* copyright © 1974, 1983, 1991 by Tony Buzan. Used by permission of Dutton, a division of Penguin Group (USA) Inc., and by kind permission of Tony Buzan, www.thinkbuzan.com.

what he had learned; after 2 days, he knew fewer than 30 percent of the memorized words. Although Ebbinghaus's recall of the nonsense syllables remained fairly stable after that, his experiment shows how fragile memory can be—even when you take the time and expend the energy to memorize information.[2]

Now that you know more about how memory works, get down to the business of how to retain the information you think is important—and provide that information when you need it.

How can you remember **what you study?**

Whatever you study—textbooks, course materials, notes, primary sources—your goal is to anchor important information in long-term memory so that you can use it, for both short-term goals like tests and long-term goals like being an information technology specialist. To remember what you study, you need to carefully figure out and use what works best for you. One great way to do this is with *journalists' questions*—the six questions journalists need to answer to write an effective newspaper story.

1. **When, Where, Who**—determine the times, places, and company (or none) that suit you.
2. **What, Why**—choose what is important to study, and set the rest aside.
3. **How**—find the specific tips and techniques that work best for you.

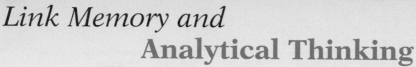

GET ANALYTICAL!

Link Memory and
Analytical Thinking

Identify your most interesting course this term.

Analyzing the material for the course, name a set of information you believe you will have to memorize:

_____

_____

Describe specific ways you can use analytical thinking to learn this material (look at the analytical thinking procedures and discussion of Bloom's taxonomy in Chapter 5, page 123, to get ideas):

_____

_____

_____

Will the material retain importance in your working and/or personal life after college? If so, describe the connection. If your first response is no, think more carefully about how the experience of learning it might be useful to you in the future.

_____

_____

When, where, and who:
Choosing your best setting

Figuring out the when, where, and who of studying is all about self-management. You analyze what works best for you, create ideas about how to put that self-knowledge to work, and use practical thinking to implement those ideas as you study.

When

The first part of *When* is "How Much." Having the right amount of time for the job is crucial. One formula for success is the simple calculation you have read about earlier in this book: *For every hour you spend in the classroom each week, spend at least 2 to 3 hours preparing for the class.* For example, if you are carrying a course load of fifteen credit hours, you should spend 30 hours a week studying outside of class. Check your syllabus for the dates reading assignments are due, and give yourself enough time to complete them.

The second part of *When* is "What Time." If two students go over their biology notes from 8 to 9 A.M., but one is a morning person who went to bed at 11 P.M. and the other is a night owl who hit the sack around 2 A.M., you can guess who has a greater chance of remembering the information. First, determine the time available to you in between classes, work, and other commitments. Then, thinking about when you function best, choose your study times carefully. You may not always have the luxury of being free during your peak energy times—but do the best you can.

The third part of *When* is "How Close to Original Learning." Because most forgetting happens right after learning, as you saw in Key 7.3, the review that helps you retain information most effectively happens close to when you first learn the material. If you can, review notes the same day you took them in class, make an organizer of important information from a text chapter shortly after you read it, or write a summary of a group study session within 24 hours of the meeting.

The final part of *When* is "When to Stop." Take a break, or go to sleep, when your body is no longer responding. Forcing yourself to study when you're not focused doesn't work.

Where

Where you study matters. As with time, consider your restrictions first—there may be only so many places available to you, within a reasonable travel distance, and open when you have study time free. Also, analyze previous study sessions. If you spent over 20 percent of your time blocking out distractions at a particular location, try someplace different.

Who

Some students prefer to study alone, and some in pairs or groups. Many mix it up, doing some kinds of studying—first reading, close reading, creating note sets—alone, and others—test review, problem sets—with one or more people. Some find that they prefer to study certain subjects alone and others with a group. For Norton, knowing he was going to work with others motivated him to be prepared, and sharing the work helped him learn.

Even students who study primarily alone can benefit by working with others from time to time. Besides the obvious benefit of greater communication and teamwork skills, group study enhances your ability to remember information in several ways:[3]

▶ Gets you to say what you know out loud, which solidifies your understanding

▶ Exposes you to the ideas of others and gets you thinking in different ways

▶ Increases the chance that all of the important information will be covered

▶ Motivates you to study in preparation for a group meeting

▶ Subjects you to questions about your knowledge, and maybe even some challenges, that make you clarify and build on your thinking

Instructors sometimes initiate student study groups, commonly for math or science courses, as peer-assisted study sessions or supplemental instruction. However, don't wait for your instructor—or for exam crunch time—to benefit from studying with others. As you begin to get to know students in your classes, start now to exchange phone numbers and e-mails, form groups, and schedule meetings. Here are some strategies for study group success:

▶ *Limit group size.* Groups of five or less tend to experience the most success.

The study location that works for you depends on your individual needs. This student has found he can concentrate best on his physical geology material if he reads it at a table in the library.
© Davis Barber/PhotoEdit

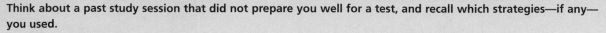

GET PRACTICAL!

Answer Your Journalists' Questions

Think about a past study session that did not prepare you well for a test, and recall which strategies—if any—you used.

Now, plan a study session that will take place within the next 7 days—one that will help you learn something important to know for one of your current courses. Answer the following questions to create your session:

When will you study, and for how long?

_____

Where will you study?

_____

Who will you study with, if anyone?

_____

What will you study?

_____

Why is this material important to know?

_____

How will you study it—what strategy (or strategies) do you plan to use?

_____

_____

How do you think the journalists' questions in this structure would have helped you get more from your previous study session?

_____

_____

The final step is putting this plan to work. Date you will use it: _____

▶ *Set long-term and short-term goals.* At your first meeting, determine what the group wants to accomplish, and set mini-goals at the start of the first meeting.

▶ *Determine a regular schedule and leadership rotation.* Determine what your group needs and what the members' schedules can handle. Try to meet weekly or, at the least, every other week. Rotate leadership among members willing to lead.

▶ *Create study materials for one another.* Give each person a task of finding a piece of information to compile and share with the group. Teach material to one another.

▶ *Share the workload and pool note-taking resources.* The most important factor is a willingness to work, not knowledge level. Compare notes with group members and fill in information you don't have.

▶ *Know how to be an effective leader.* The leader needs to define projects, assign work, set schedules and meeting goals, and keep people focused, motivated, and moving ahead.

▶ *Know how to be an effective participant.* Participants are "part owners" of the team process with a responsibility for, and a stake in, the outcome. Participants need to be organized, fulfill the tasks they promise to do, and stay open to discussion.

One final part of *Who* is dealing with "Who Might Be Distracting." You may have friends who want you to go out. You may have young children or other family members who need you. Think carefully about your choices. Do you want to head out with a group of friends you can see anytime, even if it compromises your ability to do well in an important course? Can you schedule your study time when your kids are occupied for an hour or so?

Tell your friends why studying is important to you. Friends who truly care about you are likely to support your goals. Tell your kids (if they are old enough to understand) what your education and eventual degree will mean to you—and to them. Children may be more able to cope if they see what lies at the end of the road. Key 7.4 shows some ways that parents or others caring for children can maximize their efforts.

What and why: Evaluating study materials

Even if you had hours of study time and boundless energy, you would be likely to go on overload if you studied every word and bit of information.

MANAGE CHILDREN
WHILE STUDYING

STUDYING WITH CHILDREN	STUDYING WITH INFANTS

- **Keep them up-to-date on your schedule.** Kids appreciate being involved, even though they may not understand entirely. Let them know when you have a big test or project due and what they can expect of you.

- **Find help.** Know your schedule and arrange for child care if necessary. Consider offering to help another parent in exchange for babysitting, hiring a sitter, or using a day care center.

- **Utilize techonology.** You may be able to have a study session over the phone, through instant messaging, by e-mail, or over social networking sites. Additionally, some sites offer tools that allow multiple users to work on a document or project remotely.

- **Be prepared and keep them active.** Consider keeping some toys, activities, or books that only come out during study time. This will make the time special for children.

- **Plan for family time.** Offset your time away from your children with plans to do something together such as a movie or ice cream. Children may be more apt to let you study when they have something to look forward to.

- **Utilize your baby's sleeping schedule.** Study at night if your baby goes to sleep early or in the morning if your baby sleeps late.

- **Make time in the middle.** Study during nap times if you aren't too tired yourself.

- **Talk to your baby.** Recite your notes to the baby. The baby will appreciate the attention, and you will get work done.

- **Keep them close.** Put your baby in a safe and fun place while you study, such as a playpen, motorized swing, or jumping seat.

Before you get ready to dive into your books and materials, engage your analytical thinking skills for a critical task: Decide *what* to study by examining *why* you need to know it. Here's how to accomplish this:

▶ *Choose materials to study.* Put away materials or notes you know you do not need to review. Then examine what's left. Within textbooks or other materials, which chapters or sections are important to know for your immediate goal (for example, to study for an upcoming test) and why? Thinking about the *Why* highlights your purpose and can increase your focus.

▶ *Prioritize materials.* First of all, there's no point in spending the bulk of your study time reviewing material you already know well. Determine what you need the most work on, and study that first. Almost every student has more steam at the beginning of a study session than at the end; plus, fatigue or an interruption may prevent you from covering everything.

▶ *Set specific goals.* Looking at what you need to cover and the time available, decide what you will accomplish—for example, reading a specific section in a certain textbook, reviewing three sets of class notes, and creating a study sheet from both the book and your notes. Make a list for reference and check things off as you go.

▶ *Within the sections you study, separate main points from unimportant details.* Ask yourself, "What is the most important information?" Highlight only the key points in your texts, and write notes in the margins about main ideas.

How: Using study strategies

After figuring out the *When, Where, Who, What,* and *Why* of studying, focus on the *How*—the strategies that will anchor the information you need in your brain (Key 7.5). You may already use several of them. Try as many as you can, and keep what works.

Have purpose, intention, and emotional connection

If you can remember the lyrics to dozens of popular songs but not the functions of the pancreas, perhaps emotion is involved. When you care about something, your brain responds differently, and you learn and remember more easily.

To achieve the same results in school, try to create a purpose and will to remember by a kind of emotional involvement with what you study. For example, an accounting student might think of a friend who is running a small business and needs to keep his records in order—to pay bills on time, to record income, to meet tax payments. Putting himself in the position of his friend's accountant, the student connects learning accounting principles with making a difference in a friend's life.

Put your notes to work

It is common to let notes sit in a notebook unread until just before midterms or finals. Even the most comprehensive, brilliant notes won't do you any good if you don't refer back to them. Regularly reread your notes in batches (for example, every one or two weeks) to build your recall of information. As you reread, do the following:

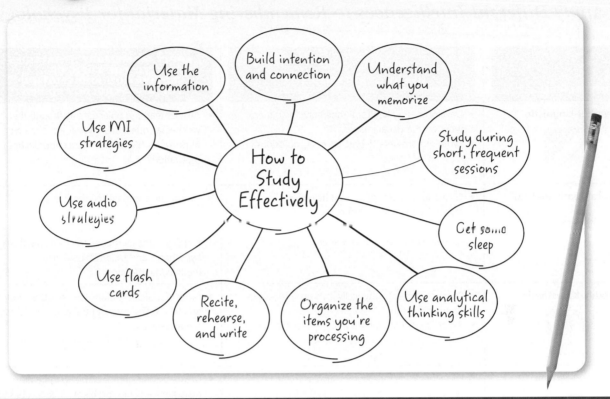

- ▶ Fill in any gaps or get help with trouble spots.
- ▶ Mark up your notes by highlighting main ideas and key supporting points.
- ▶ Add recall or practice test questions in the margins.
- ▶ Add relevant points from homework, text, and labwork into your notes.

Understand what you memorize

It sounds kind of obvious—but something that has meaning is easier to recall than something that makes little sense. This basic principle applies to everything you study. Figure out logical connections, and use these connections to help you learn. For example, in a plant biology course, memorize plants in family groups; in a history course, link events in a cause-and-effect chain.

When you are have trouble remembering something new, think about how the new idea fits into what you already know. A simple example: If you can't remember what a word means, look at the word's root, prefix, or suffix. Knowing that the root *bellum* means "war" and the prefix *ante* means "before" will help you recognize that *antebellum* means "before the war."

Study during short, frequent sessions

You can improve your chances of remembering material by learning it more than once. A pattern of short sessions—say, three 20-minute study sessions—followed by brief periods of rest is more effective than continual studying with little or no rest. Try studying on your own or with a classmate during breaks in

Apply Different Intelligences to Remembering Material for Psychology

INTELLIGENCE	USE MI STRATEGIES TO REMEMBER MORE EFFECTIVELY	APPLY MI MEMORY STRATEGIES TO THE TOPIC OF MOTIVATION AND EMOTION FOR A PSYCHOLOGY COURSE
Verbal-Linguistic	• Develop a story line for a mnemonic first; then work on the visual images. • Write out answers to practice essay questions.	• Answer learning objectives as though they were essay questions: "What are three types of needs?" "What are instinct approaches to motivation?"*
Logical-Mathematical	• Create logical groupings that help you memorize knowledge chunks. • When you study material in the middle, link it to what comes before and after.	• Group and compare the theories of emotion—the James-Lange theory, the Cannon-Bard theory, the Schachter-Singer and cognitive arousal theory, the facial feedback hypothesis, and Lazarus's cognitive-mediational theory.
Bodily-Kinesthetic	• Reenact concepts physically if you can to solidify them in memory. • Record information onto a digital recorder and listen as you walk between classes.	• Model facial expressions with another student and take turns guessing the emotion behind the expression.
Visual-Spatial	• Focus on visual mnemonics such as mental walks. • Use markers to add color to the images you use in your mnemonics.	• Create a colorful mnemonic to remember maladaptive eating problems such as obesity, anorexia nervosa, and bulimia.
Interpersonal	• Do flash card drills with a study partner. • Recite important material to a study partner.	• Working with a study partner, recite and explain Maslow's hierarchy of needs to each other.
Intrapersonal	• Listen to an audio podcast that reviews test material. • Create vocabulary cartoons and test yourself on the material.	• Understand incentive approaches by considering what kind of external stimuli create incentive for you.
Musical	• Play music while you brainstorm ideas. • Create a mnemonic in the form of a musical rhyme.	• Write a rap that lists and explains the different approaches to understanding motivation.
Naturalistic	• Organize what you have to learn so you see how everything fits together. • Sit outside and go through your flash cards.	• Make a chart organizing explanatory details of the three elements of emotion—physiology, behavior, and subjective experience.

*For information on motivation and emotion, see Saundra K. Ciccarelli and Glenn E. Meyer, *Psychology*. Upper Saddle River, NJ: Prentice Hall, 2006.

your schedule. Although studying between classes isn't for everyone, you may find that it can help you remember more.

In addition, scheduling regular, frequent review sessions over time will help you retain information more effectively. If you have 2 weeks before a test, set up study sessions three times per week instead of putting the final 2 days aside for hours-long study marathons.[4]

When you study for a test with a classmate, you can help each other understand difficult concepts as well as fill in the holes in each other's notes.
© Shutterstock

Get your body ready

Even though sleep may take a back seat with all you have to do in crunch times, research indicates that shortchanging your sleep during the week impairs your ability to remember and learn, even if you try to make up for it by sleeping all weekend.[5] Sleep improves your ability to remember what you studied before you went to bed. So does having a good breakfast. Even if you're running late, grab enough food to fill your stomach.

Use analytical thinking skills

Analytical, or critical, thinking encourages you to associate new information with what you already know. Imagine you have to remember information about the signing of the Treaty of Versailles, which ended World War I. How can critical thinking help?

▶ Recall everything that you know about the topic.
▶ Think about how this event is similar to other events in history.
▶ Consider what is different and unique about this treaty in comparison to other treaties.
▶ Explore the causes that led up to this event, and look at the event's effects.
▶ Evaluate how successful you think the treaty was.

This critical exploration makes it easier to remember the material you are studying.

Organize the items you are processing

▶ *Divide material into manageable sections.* Master each section, put all the sections together, and then test your memory of all the material.
▶ *Use the chunking strategy.* Chunking increases the capacity of short-term and long-term memory. For example, though it is hard to remember these ten digits—4808371557—it is easier to remember them in three chunks—480 837 1557. In general, try to limit groups to ten items or fewer. The 8-day study plan in Key 7.6 relies on chunking.
▶ *Use organizational tools.* Rely on an outline, a think link, or another organizational tool to record material with logical connections among the elements (see Chapter 6 for more on note taking).
▶ *Be mindful when studying more than one subject.* When studying for several tests at once, avoid studying two similar subjects back-to-back. Your memory may be more accurate when you study history after biology rather than chemistry after biology.
▶ *Notice what ends up in the middle—and practice it.* When studying, you tend to remember what you study first and last. The weak link is likely

CHUNKING
Placing disconnected information into smaller units that are easier to remember.

STUDY PLAN SUCCESS
DEPENDS ON A GOOD MEMORY

DAY 8 (IN EIGHT DAYS, YOU'LL BE TAKING A TEST)

PLANNING DAY

- List everything that may be on the exam. (Check your syllabus and class notes; talk with your instructor.)
- Divide the material into four learning chunks.
- Decide on a study schedule for the next 7 days—when you will study, with whom you will study, the materials you need, and so on.

DAY 7 (COUNTDOWN: SEVEN DAYS TO GO)

- Use the techniques described in Chapters 7 and 8 to study chunk A.
- Memorize key concepts, facts, formulas, and so on that may be on the test.
- Take an active approach to learning: take practice tests, summarize what you read in your own words, use critical thinking to connect ideas.

DAY 6 (COUNTDOWN: SIX DAYS TO GO)

- Use the same techniques to study chunk B.

DAY 5 (COUNTDOWN: FIVE DAYS TO GO)

- Use the same techniques to study chunk C.

DAY 4 (COUNTDOWN: FOUR DAYS TO GO)

- Use the same techniques to study chunk D.

DAY 3 (COUNTDOWN: THREE DAYS TO GO)

- Combine and review chunks A and B.

DAY 2 (COUNTDOWN: TWO DAYS TO GO)

- Combine and review chunks C and D.

DAY 1 (COUNTDOWN: ONE DAY TO GO)

PUT IT ALL TOGETHER: REVIEW CHUNKS A, B, C, AND D

- Take an active approach to review all four chunks.
- Make sure you have committed every concept, fact, formula, process, and so on to memory.
- Take a timed practice test. Write out complete answers so that concepts and words stick in your memory.
- Create a sheet with important information to memorize (again) on test day.

TEST DAY—DO YOUR BEST WORK

- Look at your last-minute study sheet right before you enter the test room so that difficult information sticks.
- As soon as you get your test, write down critical facts on the back of the paper.

Source: Adapted from the University of Arizona. "The Eight-Day Study Plan." (http://ulc.arizona.edu/documents/8day_074.pdf)

to be what you study midway. Knowing this, try to give this material special attention.

Recite, rehearse, and write

Repetition is a helpful memory tool. The more you can repeat, and the more ways you can repeat, the more likely you are to remember. Reciting, rehearsing, and writing help you diversify your repetition and maximize memory.

When you *recite* material, you repeat key concepts aloud, summarizing them in your own words, to aid memorization. *Rehearsing* is similar to reciting but is done silently. *Writing* is reciting on paper. The following steps represent one way to benefit from these strategies:

▶ Focus as you read on *main ideas,* which are usually found in the topic sentences of paragraphs (see Chapter 5). Then recite, rehearse, or write the ideas down.

▶ Convert each main idea into a keyword, phrase, or visual image—something easy to recall that will set off a chain of memories bringing you back to the original material. Write each keyword or phrase on an index card.

▶ One by one, look at the keywords on your cards and recite, rehearse, or write all the associated information you can recall. Check your recall against the original material.

These steps are part of the process of consolidating and summarizing lecture and text notes as you study—a key study strategy explored later in this chapter.

Reciting, rehearsing, and writing involve more than rereading material and then parroting words out loud, in your head, or on paper. Because rereading does not necessarily require involvement, you can reread without learning. However, you cannot help but think and learn when you convert text concepts into key points, rewrite main ideas as keywords and phrases, and assess what you know and what you still need to learn.

Use flash cards

Flash cards give you short, repeated review sessions that provide immediate feedback. Either find an online site on which you can create electronic flash cards or use the front of a 3-by-5-inch index card to write a word, idea, or phrase you want to remember. Use the back for a definition, explanation, example, or other key facts. Key 7.7 shows two flash cards used to study for a psychology exam.

FLASH CARDS HELP YOU MEMORIZE IMPORTANT FACTS

Key 7.7

Theory

- Definition: Explanation for a phenomenon based on careful and precise observations

- Part of the scientific method

- Leads to hypotheses

Hypothesis

- Prediction about future behavior that is derived from observations and theories

- Methods for testing hypotheses: case studies, naturalistic observations, and experiments

The following suggestions can help you make the most of your flash cards:

► *Use the cards as a self-test.* As you go through them, create two piles—the material you know and the material you are learning.
► *Carry the cards with you and review frequently.* You'll learn the most if you start using cards early in the course, well ahead of exam time.
► *Shuffle the cards and learn the information in various orders.* This will help you avoid putting too much focus on some items and not enough on others.
► *Test yourself in both directions.* First, look at the terms and provide the definitions or explanations. Then turn the cards over and reverse the process.
► *Reduce the stack as you learn.* Eliminate cards when you know them well. As the pile shrinks, your motivation may grow. Do a final review of all the cards before the test.

Use audio strategies

Although audio strategies can benefit all students, they are especially useful if you learn best through hearing.

► *Create audio flash cards.* Record short-answer study questions by leaving 10 to 15 seconds blank after questions, so you can answer out loud. Record the correct answer after the pause to give yourself immediate feedback. For example, part of a recording for a writing class might say, "Three elements that require analysis before writing are . . . [10–15 second pause] . . . topic, audience, and purpose."
► *Use podcasts.* An increasing amount of information is presented in podcasts—knowledge segments that are downloadable to your computer or MP3 player. Ask your instructors if they intend to make any lectures available in podcast format.

Use learning styles strategies

Look back to your MI and Personality Spectrum assessments in Chapter 3. Identify your strongest areas and locate study techniques applicable for each. For example, if you scored high in bodily-kinesthetic, try reciting material aloud while standing or walking. Be open to trying something new—even if it sounds a little odd to begin with. Effective studying is about finding what works, often by any means necessary.

Use the information

In the days after you learn something new, try to use the information in every way you can. Apply it to new situations and link it to problems. Explain the material to a classmate. Test your knowledge to make sure the material is in long-term memory. "Don't confuse recognizing information with being able to recall it," says learning expert Adam Robinson. "Be sure you can recall the information without looking at your notes for clues. And don't move on until you have created some sort of sense-memory hook for calling it back up when you need it."[6]

What will help you remember math and science material?

The strategies you've just explored apply to all sorts of academic areas. However, recalling what you learn in math and science courses can demand particular attention and some specific techniques, as Norton really found out the second time around.

■ ***Review processes and procedures.*** Much of math and science work involves knowing how to work through each step of a proof, a problem-solving process, or a lab experiment. Review your class notes as soon as possible after each class. Look at your notes with the textbook alongside and compare the lecture information to the book. Fill in missing steps in the instructor's examples before you forget them. You may want to write the instructor's examples in the book next to the corresponding topics.

■ ***Do problems, problems, and more problems.*** Working through problems provides examples that will help you understand concepts and formulas. Plus, becoming familiar with a group of problems and related formulas will help you apply what you know to similar problems on other assignments and tests.

■ ***Fight frustration with action.*** If you are stuck on a problem, go on to another one. If you repeatedly get a wrong answer, look at the steps you've taken and see whether anything doesn't make sense. If you hit a wall, take a break to clear your head. If you have done the assigned homework but still don't feel secure, do additional problems or ask for help.

■ ***Work with others.*** Working with one or more classmates can be particularly helpful when trying to figure out math and science problems. Do as much homework as you can on your own, and then meet to discuss it and work through additional problems. Be open to other perspectives, and ask others how they arrived at answers, especially if they used different approaches. When the work is really tough, try to meet daily, as Norton's study group did.

■ ***Focus on learning styles.*** Use strategies that activate your strengths. A visual learner might draw pictures to illustrate problems, and an interpersonal learner might organize a study group. Musical learners might create songs describing math concepts. Barbara Aaker wrote 40 songs for her students at the Community College of Denver to help musical learners retain difficult concepts. Key 7.8 presents one of her algebra songs.

■ ***Strive for accuracy.*** Complete a step of an algebra problem or biology lab project inaccurately, and your answer will be incorrect. In class, the consequences of inaccuracy are reflected in low grades. In life, the consequences could show in a patient's health or in the strength of a bridge. Check over the details of your work and always try to get it exactly right.

Because many math and science courses require you to memorize sets and lists of information, one key tool

Change the CONVERSATION

Challenge yourself and your friends to ask—and answer—tough questions. Use the following to inspire discussion in pairs or groups.

▶ All students experience the frustration of working hard to remember something that seems unimportant and irrelevant to their lives. How do you handle this? How *should* you handle it?

▶ What memorization techniques do you resist trying? Is it because they seem too unrelated to the information—or too goofy? What would you be willing to try out just to see whether it works?

▶ **CONSIDER THE CASE:** How do you respond when, like Norton, you have no interest in what you are studying? Do you attempt to find meaning, do the minimum, give up? How do the people in your life advise you to proceed—and what do you think of the advice?

"HOW MUCH IS THAT _X_ IN THE EQUATION?"

(to the tune of "How Much Is That Doggie in the Window?")

How much is that _x_ in the equation?
What value will make it be true?
To find the _x_ and get the solution
The numbers attached we **undo.**

The **connector** is plus or minus seven,
To find _x_ we have to **undo.**
Just write below both sides—make it even.
We **undo** to find the _x_ value.

If multiply or divide is showing,
The **connector** tells what has been done.
To **undo** is where we still are going—
We're trying to get _x_ alone.

Source: Reprinted with permission. Barbara Aaker, *Mathematics: The Musical,* Denver: Crazy Broad Publishing, 1999.

is the *mnemonic device.* As you will see next, mnemonic devices create sense-memory hooks that are difficult to forget.

How can mnemonic devices
boost recall?

MNEMONIC DEVICES
Memory techniques that
use vivid associations and
acronyms to link new
information to what
you already know.

Certain performers entertain audiences by remembering the names of 100 strangers or flawlessly repeating 30 ten-digit numbers. Although these performers probably have superior memories, they also rely on memory techniques, known as **mnemonic devices** (pronounced neh-MAHN-ick), for assistance. Mnemonics include visual images and associations and acronyms.

Mnemonics depend on vivid associations (relating new information to other information) that engage your emotions. Instead of learning new facts by *rote* (repetitive practice), associations give you a "hook" on which to hang these facts and retrieve them later. Mnemonics make information unforgettable through unusual mental associations and visual pictures.

Resource Link: See Ch. 7 PowerPoint Slides 12–14 for a section overview. For practice with mnemonics, have students complete the memory techniques practice activity, MyStudentSuccessLab, Memory/Studying topic. *(Time: 20–25 minutes)*

Mnemonics take time and effort to create, and you'll have to be motivated to remember them. Because of this, use them only when necessary—for instance, to distinguish confusing concepts that consistently trip you up. Also know that no matter how clever they are and how easy they are to remember, mnemonics usually do not contribute to understanding. Their objective is to help you memorize.

Craft Your Own Mnemonic

Create a mnemonic to help you remember some facts.

Identify a group of facts that you have to memorize—for example, the names of all the world's major religions or a series of elements in the periodic table.

_____

_____

Now create your own mnemonic to remember the grouping, using any of the devices in this chapter. Write the mnemonic here (or, if you need more space, use separate paper).

_____

_____

_____

Describe your mnemonic. Is it focused on images or sounds—or both? Is it humorous, ridiculous, or colorful?

_____

_____

Considering your learning style preferences, describe why you think this particular device will help you retain the information.

_____

_____

_____

Create visual images and associations

Turning information into mental pictures helps improve memory, especially for visual learners. To remember that the Spanish artist Picasso painted *The Three Women,* you might imagine the women in a circle dancing to a Spanish song with a pig and a donkey (*pig-asso*). The best images involve bright colors, three dimensions, action scenes, inanimate objects with human traits, and humor.

As another example, say you are trying to learn some Spanish vocabulary, including the words *carta, libro,* and *dinero.* Instead of relying on rote learning, you might come up with mental images such as those in Key 7.9.

Use visual images to remember items in a list

With the *mental walk* strategy, you imagine storing new ideas in familiar locations. Say, for example, that on your next biology test you have to remember the body's major endocrine glands. To do this, think of your route to the library.

SPANISH WORD	DEFINITION	MENTAL IMAGE
carta	letter	A person pushing a shopping cart filled with letters into a post office.
dinero	money	A man eating lasagna at a diner. The lasagna is made of layers of money.
libro	book	A pile of books on a table at a library.

You pass the college theater, the science center, the bookstore, the cafeteria, the athletic center, and the social science building before reaching the library. At each spot along the way, you "place" a concept you want to learn. You then link the concept with a similar-sounding word that brings to mind a vivid image (see Key 7.10):

▶ At the campus theater, you imagine bumping into the actor Brad *Pitt* (pituitary gland).
▶ At the science center, you visualize a body builder with bulging *thighs* (thyroid gland).
▶ At the campus bookstore, you envision a second body builder with his *thighs* covered in *mus*tard (thymus gland).
▶ In the cafeteria, you bump into *Dean Al* (adrenal gland).
▶ At the athletic center, you think of the school team, the Panthers— nicknamed the Pans—and remember the sound of the cheer *"Pans-R-Us"* (pancreas).
▶ At the social science building, you imagine receiving a standing *ovation* (ovaries).
▶ And at the library, you visualize sitting at a table taking a *test* that is *easy* (testes).

Make acronyms

Another helpful association method involves acronyms. In history class, you can remember the Allies during World War II—Britain, America, and Russia—with the acronym BAR. This is an example of a *word acronym,* because the first letters of the items you want to remember spell a word. The word (or words) spelled don't necessarily have to be real words. See Key 7.11 for an acronym—the name Roy G. Biv—that will help you remember the colors of the spectrum.

Other acronyms take the form of an entire sentence, in which the first letters of the words in the sentence stand for the first letters of the memorized terms. This is called a *list order acronym.* When astronomy students want to remember the list of planets in order of distance from the sun (Mercury, Venus, Earth, Mars, Jupiter, Saturn, Uranus, and Neptune), they might learn the sentence *My very elegant mother just served us nectarines.*

Suppose you want to remember the names of the first six U.S. presidents. You notice that the first letters of their last names—Washington, Adams, Jefferson, Madison, Monroe, and Adams—together read W A J M M A. To remember

ACRONYM
A word formed from the first letters of a series of words created to help you remember the series.

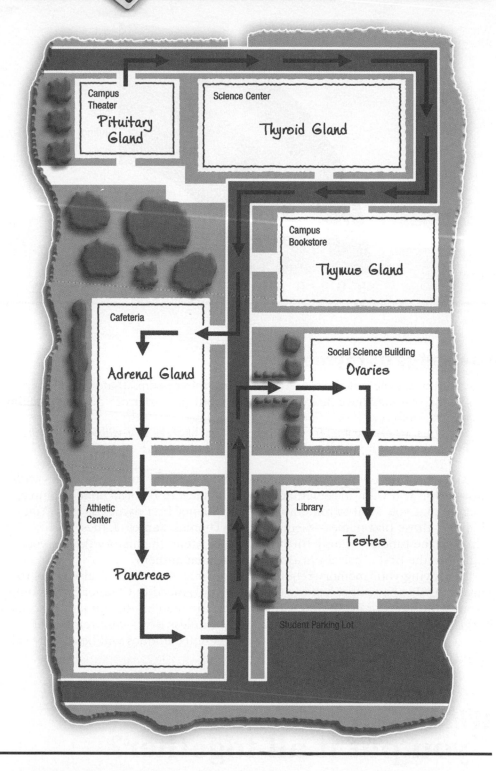

them, first you might insert an *e* after the *j* and create a short nonsense word—*wajemma*. Then to make sure you don't forget the nonsense word, visualize the six presidents sitting in a row and wearing pajamas.

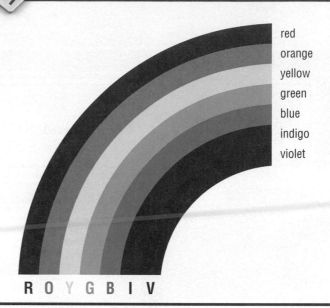

red
orange
yellow
green
blue
indigo
violet

R O Y G B I V

Use songs or rhymes

Some of the classic mnemonic devices are rhyming poems that stick in your mind. One you may have heard is the rule about the order of *i* and *e* in spelling:

> Spell *i* before *e*, except after *c*, or when sounded like *a* as in *neighbor* and *weigh*. Four exceptions if you please: *either, neither, seizure, seize.*

Make up your own poems or songs, linking familiar tunes or rhymes with information you want to remember. Thinking back to the *wajemma* example, imagine that you want to remember the presidents' first names as well. You might set those first names—George, John, Thomas, James, James, and John—to the tune of "Happy Birthday." Or to extend the history theme, you might use the first musical phrase of the national anthem.

Improving your memory requires energy, time, and work. It also helps to master SQ3R, the textbook study technique introduced in Chapter 5. By going through the steps in SQ3R and using the specific memory techniques described in this chapter, you will be able to learn more in less time—and remember what you learn long after exams are over. These techniques will be equally valuable when you start a career.

What study strategies help you put it all together?

Especially in the later stages of review, strategies that help you combine and condense information are crucial. Such strategies help you relate information to what you know, connect information in new ways, and boost your ability to use it to think analytically and creatively—especially important for essay exams.

student profile

Alexis Zendejas
Brigham Young University, Provo, Utah

About me:

I am a Native American woman from Omaha, Nebraska, and am excited to be attending BYU (Brigham Young University) this fall. I am the seventh of eight children. Growing up in a big family was a lot of fun as well as challenging; my personal goal was to keep up with my older brothers and sisters educationally and mentally. I know that I can count on my family to help me achieve my aspirations. I plan to major in business marketing with a minor in American history. After completing my undergraduate degree I hope to earn a joint juris doctorate (law degree) and master's of business administration (MBA).

What I focus on:

When I first started high school, I didn't have to work that hard to do well in class. That all changed junior year when I took three advanced placement classes and three honors classes. Studying got tougher. I actually had to apply myself after school, not just finish my assigned homework and be done with school until 7:45 the next morning.

Here is how I approach studying. If my brain is fried after a day of classes, I give myself a short break, setting a time to return to my studies. When I go back, I start by reading my notes from my classes for about 15 minutes or sometimes a bit longer, depending on the class and my ability to understand what was learned. My extra workload requires this extra effort. I work hard to focus and not let myself get distracted during my study time. I do take breaks, however—just short 10-minute breaks to get a drink of water, listen to a song, or move around. I also make and use a lot of flash cards (flash cards are my studying salvation!) for subjects where repetitive learning is required to grasp the words and their meanings. However, it's important to apply what you've learned after memorizing from the flash cards. For example, I would make flash cards for Spanish, then speak the vocabulary words in my day-to-day speech (you may think this approach odd at first but it will pay off).

What will help me in the workplace:

One of my sisters works in a law firm and I see that she has to do a lot of research. It's easy to imagine that all a lawyer does is work in a courtroom pleading the case to a judge or showcase evidence to persuade a grand jury, but I see her spending more time gathering information she needs. I know that the study skills I practice will come in handy during my intended career whenever I need to learn and focus.

Create a summary of reading material

When you summarize main ideas in your own words, you engage analytical thinking, considering what is important to include as well as how to organize and link it together. To construct a summary, focus on the main ideas and examples that support them. Don't include your own ideas or evaluations at this point. Your summary should simply condense the material, making it easier to focus on concepts and interrelationships when you review.

Use the following suggestions for creating effective summaries:

▶ Organize your summary by subject or topic—a textbook chapter, for example, or an article.
▶ Before you summarize, identify the main ideas and key supporting details by highlighting or annotating the material.
▶ Wherever possible, use your own words. When studying a technical subject with precise definitions, you may have little choice but to use text wording.
▶ Try to make your writing simple, clear, and brief. Eliminate less important details.
▶ Consider creating an outline of your notes or the portion of the text so you can see how ideas relate to one another.
▶ Include information from tables, charts, photographs, and captions in your summary; these visual presentations may contain important information not written in the text.
▶ Combine word-based and visual note-taking forms that effectively condense the information, such as a concept map, timeline, chart, or outline.
▶ Use visual strategies such as a color-coding system to indicate different ideas or different-colored pens to indicate levels of importance for information.

Combine class and reading notes into a master set

Studying from either text or class notes alone is not enough; your instructor may present material in class that is not in your text or may gloss over topics that your text covers in depth. The process of combining class and text notes enables you to see patterns and relationships among ideas, find examples for difficult concepts, and much more. It takes time, but pays off enormously because it strengthens memory and offers a more cohesive and connected study tool.

Some students may prefer to act quickly, combining class and reading notes as close to that class meeting as possible so the material is fresh. Others may prefer to use this strategy nearer to midterm or finals time.

Follow these steps to combine your class and text notes into a master note set:

MASTER NOTE SET ←
A complete, integrated note set that contains both class and text notes.

■ *Step 1: Focus on what's important by condensing to the essence.* Reduce your combined notes so they contain only main ideas and key supporting details, such as terms, dates, formulas, and examples. (Eliminating the repetition you are likely to find in your notes will also help reduce the material.) Tightening and summarizing forces you to critically evaluate which ideas are most important and to rewrite your notes with only this material. As you begin to study, move back and forth between the full set and the reduced set. Key 7.12 shows a comprehensive outline and a reduced key-term outline of the same material.

■ *Step 2: Recite what you know.* As you approach exam time, use the terms in your bare-bones notes as cues for reciting what you know about a topic. Many students assume that they know concepts simply because they understand what they read. This type of passive understanding doesn't necessarily mean that they can recreate the material on an exam or apply it to problems. Make the process more active by reciting out loud during study sessions, writing your responses on paper, making flash cards, or working with a partner.

Different Views of Freedom and Equality in the American Democracy

I.   U.S. democracy based on 5 core values: freedom and equality, order and stability, majority rule, protection of minority rights, and participation.

   A. U.S. would be a "perfect democracy" if it always upheld these values.

   B. U.S. is less than perfect, so it is called an "approaching democracy."

II.   Freedom and Equality

   A. Historian Isaiah Berlin defines freedom as either positive or negative.

      1. Positive freedoms allow us to exercise rights under the Constitution, including right to vote.

      2. Negative freedoms safeguard us from government actions that restrict certain rights, such as the right to assemble. The 1st Amendment restricts government action by declaring that "Congress shall make no law . . ."

   B. The value of equality suggests that all people be treated equally, regardless of circumstance. Different views on what equality means and the implications for society.

      1. Equality of opportunity implies that everyone has the same chance to develop inborn talents.

         a. But life's circumstances—affected by factors like race and income—differ. This means that people start at different points and have different results. E.g., a poor, inner-city student will be less prepared for college than an affluent, suburban student.

         b. It is impossible to equalize opportunity for all Americans.

      2. Equality of result seeks to eliminate all forms of inequality, including economic differences, through wealth redistribution.

   C. Freedom and equality are in conflict, say text authors Berman and Murphy: "If your view of freedom is freedom from government intervention, then equality of any kind will be difficult to achieve. If government stays out of all citizen affairs, some people will become extremely wealthy, others will fall through the cracks, and economic inequality will multiply. On the other hand, if you wish to promote equality of result, then you will have to restrict some people's freedoms—the freedom to earn and retain an unlimited amount of money, for example."*

KEY-TERM OUTLINE OF THE SAME MATERIAL

Different Views of Freedom and Equality in the American Democracy

I.   America's 5 core values: freedom and equality, order and stability, majority rule, protection of minority rights, and participation.

   A. "Perfect democracy"

   B. "Approaching democracy"

II.   Value #1—Freedom and equality

   A. Positive freedoms and negative freedoms

   B. Different views of equality: equality of opportunity versus equality of result

   C. Conflict between freedom and equality centers on differing views of government's role

*Larry Berman and Bruce Allen Murphy, *Approaching Democracy: Portfolio Edition*, Upper Saddle River, NJ: Prentice Hall, 2005, pp. 6–8.

■ Step 3: Use critical thinking. Now reflect on ideas in the following ways as you review your combined notes:

▶ Brainstorm examples from other sources that illustrate central ideas. Write down new ideas or questions that come up as you review.
▶ Think of ideas from your readings or from class that support or clarify your notes.
▶ Consider how your class notes differ from your reading notes and why.
▶ Apply concepts to questions at the ends of text chapters, to problems posed in class, or to real-world situations.

■ Step 4: Create study sheets. Putting your master notes in their shortest, most manageable (and portable) form, a study sheet is a one-page synthesis of all key points on one theme, topic, or process. Use critical thinking skills to organize information into themes or topics that you will need to know on an exam. On an individual study sheet, include the related lecture and text page references, a quick summary, possible questions on the topic, key terms, formulas, dates, people, examples, and so on.

■ Step 5: Review and review again. To ensure learning and prepare for exams, review your condensed notes, study sheets, and critical thinking questions until you know every topic cold.

Try to vary your review methods, focusing on active involvement. Recite the material to yourself, have a Q and A session with a study partner, or create and take a practice test. Another helpful technique is to summarize your notes in writing from memory after reviewing them. This will tell you whether or not you'll be able to recall the information on a test.

Resource Link: See Ch. 7 PowerPoint Slides 16–18 to discuss the case, Change the Conversation, and the case wrap-up.

Activity (journal): Ask students to write a responsive essay to the word *ngarong*. Ask them to describe how they plan on helping their ngarong do their work (by going to bed earlier or getting a new pillow) and what they hope to achieve from a good night's rest.

Case Wrap-up

What happened to Norton? With increased effort and help from his study group, Norton did well in his courses the second time around and returned to the pre-engineering program, later transferring to Union College where he graduated with a bachelor's in electrical engineering. He was hired by Hewlett-Packard after college and worked his way up to management over 20 years. One of several jobs there took him to Boeblingen, Germany, on international assignment for 3 years. His current work in the area of product management, defining high-tech products to address what the market wants and needs, combines his passion for engineering, business, and new technologies. He is still an expert skier and has learned to become just as successful in his personal life and career as he is when playing outdoors.

What does this mean for you? No student can spend every second of class time taking courses that are meaningful and inspiring. You will always experience different levels of motivation and interest for different courses. Your challenge is to find a way to do the work well when your interest doesn't provide the energy. Choose the course you are taking right now that interests you the least. Make three lists with the following headers: "Study Strategies That Can Help," "How I Will Use What I Learn in This Course," and "How I Will Reward Myself If I Persist in This Course." Then fill each list with as many items as you can. Refer to the lists whenever your focus or motivation begin to slip over the course of the term.

What effects go beyond your world? Anywhere you turn, from your immediate neighborhood to a country halfway around the world, you can find organizations looking for support. The demands of your everyday life may be so pressing that you cannot see how you will have the time to help out. Think about a person, place, thing, idea, or situation that has grabbed your attention and sparked your interest and emotion—your version of Norton's H-P calculator. Find an organization that relates to it and investigate to see how you can help in some small way. One action now, no matter how small, can help. Who knows? Maybe you can make time for more action in the future.

Successful Intelligence *Wrap-up*

HERE'S HOW YOU HAVE BUILT SKILLS IN **CHAPTER 7** :

ANALYTICAL THINKING	CREATIVE THINKING	PRACTICAL THINKING
➤ You analyzed why memory strategies work—and why people forget.	➤ You began thinking of places, times, and modes of studying that might suit you best.	➤ You explored strategies you can put to work to remember what you study, including specific strategies for math and science.
➤ You learned how analyzing your personal tendencies can help you design the most effective study plan.	➤ You considered different ways to use mnemonic devices to boost recall.	➤ You learned about how to create summaries of notes and text readings as well as helpful study sheets.
➤ In the Get Analytical exercise, you explored how analytical thinking will help you retain information for one of your courses.	➤ In the Get Creative exercise, you came up with your own mnemonic device for some information you need to remember.	➤ In the Get Practical exercise, you developed a study plan based on journalists' questions.

Word*for*Thought

Research shows that sleep helps solidify information in memory. In the Dyak language, spoken in **Borneo,** a figure called a *ngarong* (nn-ga'-rawng) or "dream-helper" comes to sleepers and helps clarify ideas. Let your ngarong have a chance to do his or her good work—get some sleep.[7]

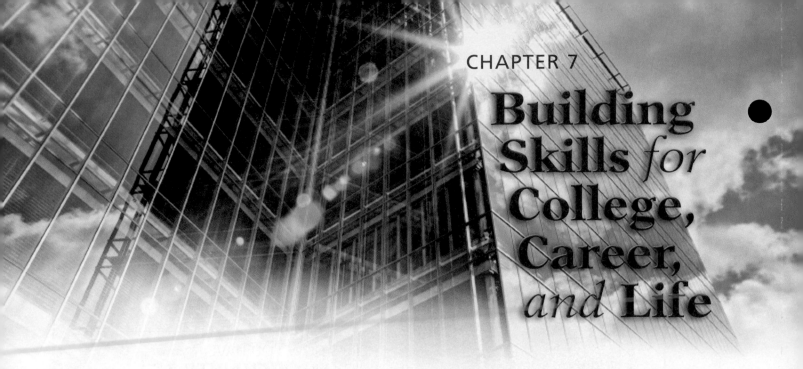

Building Skills *for* College, Career, *and* Life

Steps to Success

Evaluate Your Memory

BUILD BASIC SKILLS. Under each of these classifications of information in long-term memory, write down an example from your personal experience:

Episodic memory (events). Example: I remember the first time I conducted an experiment in chemistry class.

_____

_____

Declarative memory (facts). Example: I know that the electoral college must vote before a new U.S. president is officially elected.

_____

_____

Procedural memory (motion). Example: I know how to type without looking at the keyboard.

_____

_____

TAKE IT TO THE NEXT LEVEL.

Which type of information (events, facts, motion) is easiest for you to remember? Why?

_____

_____

_____

Which type of information is hardest for you to remember? Why?

_____

_____

MOVE TOWARD MASTERY. Address the type of information you find *most difficult* to remember.

Name an example from your life of some information in this category that you need to be able to recall and use.

_____

_____

_____

Name two approaches from the chapter that you believe will help you strengthen it.

1. _____

2. _____

Now give both a try. Circle the one that worked best.

Teamwork

Create Solutions Together

ASSESS AND BUILD YOUR MEMORY POWER

Goal: To improve your ability to remember.

Time on Task: 15 minutes

Instructions: Gather as a class if there are fewer than twenty people, or divide into two groups if there are more. Proceed according to the following steps (you'll need a timer or a cell phone that can act as one):

- Each person in your group should place at least one item on a table (try to avoid repeats). Try to reach a total of fifteen items—from your backpack or bag, study area, home, or classroom— anything small enough to easily fit on the table. Find something that will cover them all—a jacket or newspaper, for example—and place it over the items. Let them stay covered for at least 10 minutes before beginning the activity. Alternatively, the instructor can gather fifteen items ahead of time.
- Allow 1 minute for everyone to look at the items, using the watch or cell phone timer.
- When the time is up, cover the items. Each person should list as many as possible on a sheet of paper.

Compare your lists to the actual items. Talk as a group about the results and about what you did and didn't remember. Describe your observations here.

_____

_____

_____

_____

_____

Now repeat the exercise using a mnemonic device in the following steps:

- Talk as a group about ways to remember more items, considering different mnemonic devices or strategies. Together, choose a device or strategy to try.
- Create a new group of fifteen items (if you can't swap out all of them, exchange as many as you can) and cover them.
- Uncover and allow 1 minute of observation as before, but focus on the mnemonic device as you look at the items.
- When time is up, cover again and make a new list.
- Think and talk about the difference between the two experiences. Write your findings here.

_____

_____

_____

_____

_____

_____

_____

_____

_____

_____

_____

_____

_____

_____

Writing

Build Intrapersonal and Communication Skills

Record your thoughts on a separate piece of paper, in a journal, or electronically.

EMOTIONAL INTELLIGENCE JOURNAL

How feelings connect study success. Think about how you were feeling when you were most able to recall and use information in a high-stress situation—a test, a workplace challenge, a group presentation. What thought, action, or situation put you in this productive mindset that helped you succeed? Did you go for a run? talk to your best friend? take 30 minutes for yourself? Create a list of thoughts or actions you can call on when you will be faced with a challenge to your memory and want the best possible outcome.

REAL-LIFE WRITING

Combining class and text notes. Choose a course for which you have a test coming up in the next 4 weeks. Create a master set of notes for that course combining one week's classes and reading assignments (make sure it is material you need to know for your test). Your goal is to summarize and connect all the important information covered during the period.

Personal Portfolio

Prepare for Career Success

MEMORY AND NETWORKING

21st Century Learning Building Blocks

- Communication and Collaboration
- Social and Cross-Cultural Skills

Complete the following in your electronic portfolio or separately on paper.

Your ability to remember people you meet or interact with in the workplace—their names, what they do, other relevant information about them—is an enormous factor in your career success.

Consider this scenario: You are introduced to your supervisor's new boss, someone who is in a position to help you advance in the company, and you both exchange small talk for a few minutes. A week later you run into him outside the building. If you greet him by name and ask whether his son is over the case of the flu he had, you have made a good impression that is likely to help you in the future. If you call him by the wrong name, realize your mistake, and slink off to work, you may have set up a bit of a hurdle for yourself as you try to get ahead.

Using what you know about memory strategies and what works for you, set up a system to record and retain information about people you meet whom you want to remember. For your system, decide on a tool (address book, set of notecards, electronic organizer, computer file), what to record (name, phone, e-mail, title, how you met, important details), and how you will update. Choose a tool that you are most likely to use and that will be easy for you to refer to and update.

Tool of choice: _____

Information to record:

_____

When to record and how often to check or update:

_____

Get started by putting in information for all the people you consider to be important networking contacts at this point—family, friends, instructors and advisors, or work colleagues and supervisors. Make this the start of a database that will serve you throughout your career.

Social Networking

REMEMBER INFORMATION ABOUT YOUR CONTACTS

Use LinkedIn to connect with the list of important contacts you just developed—sign in to your account and invite them to join your network using any of the methods from the Chapter 6 exercise.

When at least three of these contacts have responded by joining your network, use the LinkedIn "My Connections" area to fill in helpful information about them that you want to remember.

- Click on "My Connections."
- Choose a name from your connections list and click on "view and edit details" beneath that person's name.
- Fill in any relevant information—phone, address, website, birthday, and notes about your contact with this person.

Test Taking

Showing What You Know

What Would You Do?

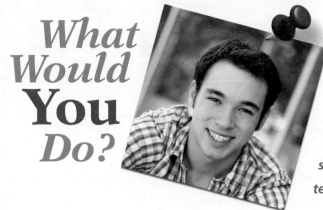

Think about this problem as you read, and consider how you would approach it. This chapter helps you use preparation, persistence, and strategy to conquer test anxiety fears, show what you know, and learn from test mistakes.

Teo Velez is working toward an associate's degree in nursing. Although hoping to finish in 2 years, he struggled in two particular required courses and has to repeat them during a fifth term. His advisor called him in for a meeting.

Sitting down in Mr. Sorrenti's office, Teo spoke first: "I know why I'm here. I have to repeat Nursing II and Pharmacology. I just couldn't make it happen; the tests killed me." "I talked to your professors," said Mr. Sorrenti. "Both of them said you were on your game in class time and with projects. But your test scores brought everything down too far in both cases. Do you have problems memorizing that kind of material?"

"No, actually . . . it's just . . . I have terrible text anxiety," replied Teo. "Always have. It's worst when it comes to lists, terms, sets of things that I should be able to memorize straight up. All the stuff for the two courses I failed, really." Mr. Sorrenti thought for a moment. "Well, Teo, the fact that you can pinpoint the issue is a huge step in the right direction. What do you think causes the anxiety?"

"Oh, I'm not really sure, but if a test is coming up that I think will be a problem, I get so freaked out that I can't even study for it. Then the night before I go crazy cramming all this information into my head, and I show up exhausted for the test, and my brain goes blank, and I get shaky and my palms sweat, and I screw up the test, and then I just tell myself it was because I didn't prepare properly, and I try to forget it ever happened."

"You know, you are setting yourself up for failure," said Mr. Sorrenti. "It's a vicious cycle. You are nervous, you don't study, and then you don't succeed in part because you don't have the knowledge. If you gave yourself a chance by preparing well, you might find ways to settle down at test time and see what you are really capable of."

Teo looked at him. "Sounds great, but easier said than done," he replied. (To be continued . . .)

Tests are a reality that all students have to deal with. You'll learn more about Teo, and revisit his situation, within the chapter.

In this chapter, you'll explore answers to these questions:

> How can preparation improve test performance? p. 208

> How can you work through test anxiety? p. 214

> What general strategies can help you succeed on tests? p. 216

> How can you master different types of test questions? p. 222

> What can you learn from test mistakes? p. 228

ANALYTICAL

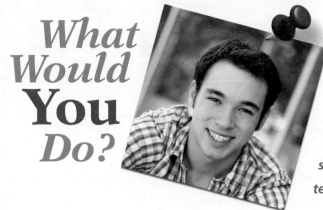
CREATIVE

PRACTICAL

STATUS *Check*

▶ *How prepared are you for taking tests?*

For each statement, circle the number that feels right to you, from 1 for "not at all true for me" to 5 for "very true for me."

▶ I use strategies to help me predict what will be on tests.	1 2 3 4 5
▶ I actively prepare and review before taking exams.	1 2 3 4 5
▶ I do anything to avoid cramming.	1 2 3 4 5
▶ When I recognize signs of test anxiety, I use relaxation methods to calm down.	1 2 3 4 5
▶ I read test directions before beginning.	1 2 3 4 5
▶ I use certain strategies to answer questions I'm unsure of.	1 2 3 4 5
▶ I don't think cheating is worth the price.	1 2 3 4 5
▶ I know the difference between objective and subjective questions and how to answer each.	1 2 3 4 5
▶ I look for action verbs when answering essay questions.	1 2 3 4 5
▶ I learn from my testing mistakes and actively grow from them.	1 2 3 4 5

Each of the topics in these statements is covered in this chapter. Note those statements for which you circled a 3 or lower. Skim the chapter to see where those topics appear, and pay special attention to them as you read, learn, and apply new strategies.

REMEMBER: *No matter how prepared you are for taking tests, you can improve with effort and practice.*

"Successfully intelligent people seek to perform in ways that not only are competent but distinguish them from ordinary performers. They realize that the gap between competence and excellence may be small but the greatest rewards, both internal and external, are for excellence."

—Robert Sternberg

How can preparation improve test performance?

Although you may dread taking tests and exams, consider this: *The goal of a test is to see what you have learned.* Every day that you are learning—by attending class, staying on top of assignments, completing readings and projects, and participating in class discussions—you are preparing for tests. The following strategies, specific to tests, put your analytical, creative, and practical thinking skills into action to help you be as prepared as possible.

Identify test type and what you will be expected to know

Before you begin studying, take practical steps to find out as much as you can about the test, including the following:

▶ *Topics that will be covered.* Will the test cover everything since the term began or will it be more limited?
▶ *Material you will be tested on.* Will the test cover only what you learned in class and in the text or will it also include outside readings?

► *Types of questions.* Will the questions be objective (multiple choice with only one correct answer, multiple choice with more than one correct answer, true/false, sentence completion), subjective (essay), or a combination?

► *Supplemental information you may be able to have.* Is the test open book (meaning you can use your class text)? Open note (meaning you can use any notes you've taken)? Both? Or neither? Are you able to work with a partner on any part of it? Is it a take-home exam? Will you be expected to complete part or all of it online?

Instructors routinely answer questions like these. If you are unsure, ask for clarification. Chances are, some other students are wondering the same thing.

As you begin thinking about the test, remember that not all tests are created equal—a quiz is not as important as a midterm or final, although accumulated grades on small quizzes add up and can make a difference in your final grade. Plan and prioritize your study time and energy according to the value of the quiz or test. Consult your syllabus for test and quiz dates and times.

Here are other practical strategies for predicting what may be on a test.

► *Use your textbook.* Check features such as summaries, vocabulary terms, and study questions for clues about what's important to remember.

► *Listen at review sessions.* Many instructors offer review sessions before midterms and finals. Bring your questions to these sessions and listen to the questions others ask.

► *Make an appointment to see your instructor.* Spending a few minutes talking about the test one-on-one may clarify misunderstandings and help you focus on what to study.

► *Get information from people who already took the course.* Try to get a sense of test difficulty, whether tests focus primarily on assigned readings or class notes, what materials are usually covered, and the types of questions that are asked.

► *Examine old tests, if the instructor makes them available.* You may find old tests in class, online, or on reserve in the library. Old tests will help you answer questions like the following:

- Do tests focus on examples and details, general ideas and themes, or a combination?
- Are the questions straightforward or confusing and sometimes tricky?
- Will you be asked to apply principles to new situations and problems?

After taking the first exam in a course, you will have a better idea of what to expect.

Part of successful test preparation is knowing when to stop. To avoid overload, study in shorter segments over a period of time, and get the sleep you need before test day.
© Alvis Upitis/Image Bank/Getty Images

Determine where and how the test will be given

Where you take a test can affect your performance. For instance, a take-home exam may sound like an easy A, but distractions like children and TV can threaten your focus. Similarly, if you miss a test date and need to make it up, you may find yourself taking an exam in a testing center. Being prepared for the stresses of your environment will help you manage test time.

student profile

Kevin Ix

Bergen Community College, Paramus, New Jersey

About me:

After high school, I attended college for three semesters studying to become an electrician. Later, with the way the housing market has been plummeting and the direction the economy is heading, I decided a business major made a lot more sense. I am now working toward a degree in business. I keep myself busy during the summer months with one full-time and one part-time job.

How I faced a challenge:

Taking the time to read directions has never been a strong point of mine. Whether it's setting up a new television or taking a final exam, my initial reaction is to jump right into the task without paying attention to the instructions. On one particular occasion I remember being given a test and started answering the questions without even glancing at the directions. At the end of the test, the teacher began collecting the exams and occasionally gave out a laugh as she made her way around the room. As it turned out, the directions on the top of the test clearly read, "If you're reading these directions, please do not fill in the answer sheet." Certainly this test was more focused on testing our ability to follow directions than on the curriculum. Needless to say, while I wasn't the only one to make this foolish mistake, I did not fare too well on that particular test! I work to combat my tendencies by paying careful attention to directions.

What will help me in the workplace:

The expression "measure twice, cut once" was commonly instilled into our minds while I was enrolled at my former technical college. If you didn't pay particular attention to measurements and directions, your mistake could become extremely expensive in material costs. This simple saying reminds me to focus on directions because, as I have learned over time, simply glancing at directions can lead to various forms of costly mistakes.

Online tests, like open book tests, may seem easier than tests in the classroom. In reality, due to the wide amount of information available at your fingertips, online tests are generally more challenging and require strong critical thinking skills. You may be able to Google factual information about a topic, but test questions will probably ask you to analyze and evaluate situations related to that information.

Create a study schedule and checklist

If you establish a plan ahead of time and write it down, you are more likely to follow it. Use journalists' questions to map out a study plan.

▶ Ask *what* and *why* to decide what you will study. Go through your notes, texts, related primary sources, and handouts, and set aside materials you don't need. Then prioritize the remaining materials to focus on the information most likely to be on the exam.

▶ Ask *when*, *where*, and *who*—and use the time management and goal-setting skills from Chapter 2—to prepare a schedule. Consider all of the relevant factors—your study materials, who you will study with, the number of days until the test, and the time and place you can study each day. Note study sessions in your planner ahead of time.

▶ Ask *how* to figure out what strategies you will use.

A comprehensive *checklist* will help you organize and stay on track as you prepare. Use the checklist to assign specific tasks to particular study times and sessions. Try out the checklist in Key 8.1 or create your own.

Use reading and studying strategies

Put what you have learned about thinking, reading, memory, and studying in Chapters 4, 5, and 7 into action to give yourself the best shot at remembering material.

▶ *Think analytically.* College exams often ask you to analyze and apply material in more depth than you experienced in high school. For example, your history instructor may ask you to place a primary source in its historical context. Prepare for these challenges as you study by continually asking analytical thinking questions (see Chapter 4) and using the higher levels of Bloom's taxonomy (see Chapter 5).

▶ *Use SQ3R.* This reading method provides an excellent structure for reviewing your reading materials (see Chapter 5).

▶ *Employ strategies from* how *questions.* Use flash cards, audio strategies, chunking, or anything else that suits you and the material you are studying (see pages 184–190).

▶ *Create mnemonic devices.* Memory strategies help make what you review stick.

▶ *Actively review your combined class and text notes.* Summaries and master sets of combined text and class notes provide comprehensive study tools.

Make and take a pretest

Use end-of-chapter text questions to create your own pretest. If your course doesn't have an assigned text, develop questions from notes and assigned readings. Old homework problems will also help target areas that need work. Some texts also provide a website with online activities and pretests designed to help you review material. Keep in mind that the same test-preparation skills you learn in college will help you do well on standardized tests for graduate school.

Answer your questions under test-like conditions—in a quiet place where you can see a clock to tell you when to quit, with no books or notes (unless the exam is open book). This type of low-pressure test experience may help people like Teo calm test-taking fears.

Prepare for final exams

Studying for final exams, which usually take place the last week of the term, is a major commitment that requires careful time management. Your college may schedule study days (also called a *reading period*) between the end of classes

PREPARE FOR A TEST

Complete the following checklist for each exam to define your study goals, get organized, and stay on track:

Course: _____ Instructor: _____

Date, time, and place of test: _____

Type of test (Is it a midterm or a minor quiz?): _____

What instructor said about the test, including types of test questions, test length, and how much the test counts toward your final grade:

_____

_____

Topics to be covered on the test, in order of importance (information should also come from your instructor):

1. _____

2. _____

3. _____

4. _____

5. _____

Study schedule, including materials you plan to study (texts, class notes, homework problems, and so forth) and dates you plan to complete each:

Material   **Completion Date**

1. _____   _____

2. _____   _____

3. _____   _____

4. _____   _____

5. _____   _____

Materials you are expected to bring to the test (textbook, sourcebook, calculator, etc.):

_____

_____

_____

Special study arrangements (such as planning study group meeting, asking the instructor for special help, getting outside tutoring):

_____

_____

_____

Life-management issues (such as rearranging work hours):

_____

_____

_____

_____

Source: Adapted from Ron Fry, *"Ace" Any Test,* 3rd ed., Franklin Lakes, NJ: Career Press, 1996, pp. 123–124.

Write Your Own Test

Use the tips in this chapter to predict the material that will be covered, the types of questions that will be asked (multiple choice, essay, etc.), and the nature of the questions (a broad overview of the material or specific details).

Then be creative. Your goal is to write questions that your instructor is likely to ask—interesting questions that tap what you have learned and make you think about the material in different ways. Go through the following steps:

1. Write the questions you come up with on a separate sheet of paper.

2. Use what you have created as a pretest. Set up test-like conditions—a quiet, timed environment—and see how you do.

3. Evaluate your pretest answers against your notes and the text. How did you do?

_____

_____

4. Finally, after you take the actual exam, evaluate whether you think this exercise improved your performance. Would you use this technique again? Why or why not?

_____

_____

and the beginning of finals. Lasting from a day or two to several weeks, this period gives you time to prepare for exams and finish papers.

End-of-year studying requires flexibility. Libraries are often packed, and students may need to find alternative locations. Consider outdoor settings (if weather permits), smaller libraries (many departments have their own libraries), and empty classrooms. Set up times and places that will provide the atmosphere you need.[1]

Prepare physically

Most tests ask you to work at your best under pressure, so try to get a good night's sleep before the exam. Sleep improves your ability to remember what you studied before you went to bed.

Eating a light, well-balanced meal including protein (eggs, milk, yogurt, meat and fish, nuts, or peanut butter) will keep you full longer than carbohydrates alone (breads, candy, or pastries). When time is short, don't skip breakfast—grab a quick meal such as a few tablespoons of peanut butter, a banana, or a high-protein granola bar.

Make the most of last-minute cramming

Cramming—studying intensively and around the clock right before an exam—often results in information going into your head and popping right back out when the exam is over. *If learning is your goal, cramming will not help you reach it.* The reality, however, is that you are likely to cram for tests, especially midterms and finals, from time to time in your college career. You may also cram if, like Teo, anxiety leads you to avoid studying. Use these hints to make the most of this study time:

▶ *Focus on crucial concepts.* Summarize the most important points and try to resist reviewing notes or texts page by page.

▶ *Create a last-minute study sheet to review right before the test.* Write down key facts, definitions, and formulas on a single sheet of paper or on flash cards.

▶ *Arrive early.* Review your study aids until you are asked to clear your desk.

After the exam, evaluate how cramming affected your performance. Did it help, or did it load your mind with disconnected details? Did it increase or decrease anxiety at test time? Then evaluate how cramming affected your recall. Within a few days, you will probably remember very little—a reality that will work against you in advanced courses that build on the knowledge being tested and in careers that require it. Think ahead about how you can start studying earlier next time.

How can you work through test anxiety?

A certain amount of stress can be a good thing. You are alert, ready to act, and geared up to do your best. Some students, however, experience incapacitating stress before and during exams, especially midterms and finals. Test anxiety can cause sweating, nausea, dizziness, headaches, and fatigue. It can reduce concentration and cause you to forget everything you learned. Sufferers may get lower grades because their performance does not reflect what they know or because, as in Teo's case, their fear has affected their ability to prepare effectively.

Prepare well and have a positive attitude

Being prepared—both by reviewing material and following a detailed study plan—is the most essential way to ready yourself for an academic showdown. Only by knowing the material as best you can will you have reason to believe in your ability to pass the test. The other key tool is a positive attitude that says, "I know this material and I'm ready to show it."

Anxiety is defined as an emotional disturbance, meaning that it tends to be based on an imagined risk rather than an actual one, and often leads you away from your goals rather than toward them.[2] With this in mind, think metacognitively about your anxiety over a test:

▶ Look at the risk you *think* you are facing—and compare it with the *actual* risk. Consider the possibility that you may be more prepared than you realize.

▶ Look at your goal for this test. Identify the physical and mental responses caused by your anxiety, and note how they are affecting your ability to reach that goal.

Use the strategies in Key 8.2 to be both prepared and positive.

Math anxiety

For some students, math exams cause more anxiety than other academic challenges. A form of test anxiety, *math anxiety* is often based on common misconceptions about math, such as the notion that an ability to think quantitatively is an inborn talent some people have and others don't or that men are better at math than women. Students who feel that they can't do math may give up without asking for help. At exam time, they may experience test anxiety symptoms that reduce their ability to concentrate and leave them feeling defeated.

The test anxiety strategies just discussed will also help combat math anxiety. In addition, math anxiety sufferers should focus heavily on problem-solving

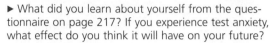

Change the CONVERSATION

Challenge yourself and your friends to ask—and answer—tough questions. Use the following to inspire discussion in pairs or groups.

▶ What did you learn about yourself from the questionnaire on page 217? If you experience test anxiety, what effect do you think it will have on your future?

▶ Which suggestions for reducing test anxiety are you likely to use? How do you think they will help you feel more comfortable at test time? What other ways can you think of for improving your performance?

▶ **CONSIDER THE CASE:** If you were Ten's advisor, what would you tell him to do first in order to get ready to handle tests next term? If he claimed he was doomed to freeze up on tests no matter what, how would you try to help him shake off that attitude?

 USE STRATEGIES TO **BUILD A POSITIVE ATTITUDE** AND GET PREPARED

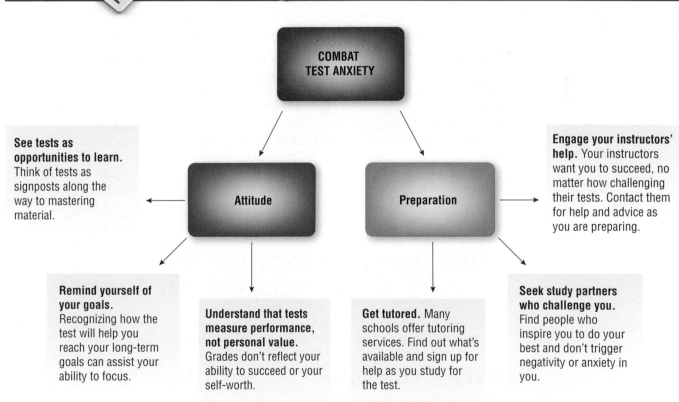

COMBAT TEST ANXIETY

Attitude

Preparation

See tests as opportunities to learn. Think of tests as signposts along the way to mastering material.

Remind yourself of your goals. Recognizing how the test will help you reach your long-term goals can assist your ability to focus.

Understand that tests measure performance, not personal value. Grades don't reflect your ability to succeed or your self-worth.

Get tutored. Many schools offer tutoring services. Find out what's available and sign up for help as you study for the test.

Engage your instructors' help. Your instructors want you to succeed, no matter how challenging their tests. Contact them for help and advice as you are preparing.

Seek study partners who challenge you. Find people who inspire you to do your best and don't trigger negativity or anxiety in you.

techniques, as in the math and science study strategies on page 191, and should also seek help from instructors and tutors early and often.

Test time strategies

When test time comes, several strategies may help you manage and calm test anxiety.

▶ *Manage your environment.* Make a conscious effort to sit away from students who might distract you. If it helps, listen to relaxing music on an MP3 player while waiting for class to begin.

▶ *Use positive self-talk.* Tell yourself that you can do well and that it is normal to feel anxious, particularly before an important exam.

▶ *Practice relaxation.* Close your eyes, breathe deeply and slowly, and visualize positive mental images like getting a good grade. Or try a more physical tensing-and-relaxing method:[3]

1. Put your feet flat on the floor.
2. With your hands, grab underneath the chair.
3. Push down with your feet and pull up on your chair at the same time for about 5 seconds.
4. Relax for 5 to 10 seconds.
5. Repeat the procedure two or three times.
6. Relax all your muscles except those actually used to take the test.

▶ *Bring a special object.* You may have an object that has special meaning for you—a photograph, a stone or crystal, a wristband, a piece of jewelry, a hat. Bring it along and see if it provides comfort or inspiration at test time. Use it to get focused and to calm yourself during the test.

Test anxiety and the returning student

If you're returning to school after years away, you may wonder how well you will handle exams. To deal with these feelings, focus on what you have learned through life experience, including the ability to handle work and family pressures. Without even thinking about it, you may have developed many time management, planning, organizational, and communication skills needed for college success.

In addition, your life experiences will give real meaning to abstract classroom ideas. For example, workplace relationships may help you understand social psychology concepts, and refinancing your home mortgage may help you grasp a key concept in economics—how the actions of the Federal Reserve Bank influence interest rate swings.

What general strategies can help you succeed on tests?

Even though every test is different, certain general strategies will help you handle almost all tests, from short-answer to essay exams.

Test day strategies

▶ *Choose the right seat.* Find a seat that will put you in the right frame of mind and minimize distractions. Choose a place near a window, next to a wall,

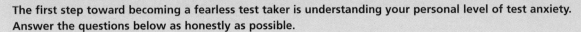

GET PRACTICAL!

Assess Test Anxiety with the Westside Test Anxiety Scale

The first step toward becoming a fearless test taker is understanding your personal level of test anxiety. Answer the questions below as honestly as possible.

Rate how true each of the following is of you, from "Always true" to "Never true." Use the following 5 point scale. Circle your answers.

5 = Always true; 4 = Usually true; 3 = Sometimes true; 2 = Seldom true; 1 = Never true

1. The closer I am to a major exam, the harder it is for me to concentrate on the material.	5 4 3 2 1
2. When I study for my exams, I worry that I will not remember the material on the exam.	5 4 3 2 1
3. During important exams, I think that I am doing awful or that I may fail.	5 4 3 2 1
4. I lose focus on important exams, and I cannot remember material that I knew before the exam.	5 4 3 2 1
5. I remember answers to exam questions only after the exam is already over.	5 4 3 2 1
6. I worry so much before a major exam that I am too worn out to do my best on the exam.	5 4 3 2 1
7. I feel out of sorts or not really myself when I take important exams.	5 4 3 2 1
8. I find that my mind sometimes wanders when I am taking important exams.	5 4 3 2 1
9. After an exam, I worry about whether I did well enough.	5 4 3 2 1
10. I struggle with written assignments, or avoid doing them, because I want them to be perfect.	5 4 3 2 1

Sum of the 10 questions: _____

Now divide the sum by 10. Write it here. _____ This is your test anxiety score.

Compare your score against the following scale. How does your level of test anxiety rate? In general, students that score a 3.0 or higher on the scale tend to have more test anxiety than normal and may benefit from seeking additional assistance.

1.0–1.9 Comfortably low test anxiety

2.0–2.4 Normal or average test anxiety

2.5–2.9 High normal test anxiety

3.0–3.4 Moderately high (some items rated 4—high)

3.5–3.9 High test anxiety (half or more of the items rated 4—high)

4.0–5.0 Extremely high anxiety (items rated 4—high and 5—extreme)

Reflect on your results. Do they show a high level of test anxiety? A normal level? Based on what you've learned about yourself, select anxiety-reducing strategies that you will use when studying for or taking your next test. Record your plan on a sheet of paper or computer file.

Source: Used by permission of Richard Driscoll.

MULTIPLE INTELLIGENCE STRATEGIES
for Test Preparation

Apply Different Intelligences to Preparing for a Geometry Exam

INTELLIGENCE	USE MI STRATEGIES TO IMPROVE TEST PREPARATION	APPLY MI TEST-PREP STRATEGIES TO STUDY FOR A TEST ON GEOMETRIC SHAPES AND MEASUREMENT*
Verbal-Linguistic	• Write test questions your instructor might ask. Answer the questions and then try rewriting them in a different format (essay, true/false, and so on). • Underline important words in review or practice questions.	• Underline important vocabulary words in the chapter. Then make a set of flash cards, with the word on one side and the definition on the other. Test yourself.
Logical-Mathematical	• Logically connect what you are studying with what you know. Consider similarities, differences, and cause-and-effect relationships. • Draw charts that show relationships and analyze trends.	• Create a table that highlights the similarities and differences among polygons, circles, and three-dimensional shapes. Use columns to note qualities such as number of sides, number of angles, measurement of angles, formulas that apply consistently, and special features (for example, in a rectangle, all angles are right angles).
Bodily-Kinesthetic	• Use text highlighting to take a hands-on approach to studying. • Create a sculpture, model, or skit to depict a tough concept that will be on the test.	• Use pencils, Popsicle sticks, pipe cleaners, containers, or other materials to create the shapes on which you will be tested.
Visual-Spatial	• Make charts, diagrams, or think links illustrating concepts. • Make drawings related to possible test topics.	• Draw illustrations that represent all of the postulates (statements assumed to be true) in the chapter.
Interpersonal	• Form a study group to prepare for your test. • In your group, come up with possible test questions. Then use the questions to test each other's knowledge.	• With a study partner, work through the exercise set on polygons and circles. Try either working through problems together or having partners "teach" problems to each other.
Intrapersonal	• Apply concepts to your own life; think about how you would manage. • Brainstorm test questions and then take the sample "test" you developed.	• Reread the "Geometry Around Us" material in your text to reinforce your understanding of how geometry functions in the real world. Write two additional ideas about how geometry relates to your world.
Musical	• Recite text concepts to rhythms or write a song to depict them. • Explore relevant musical links to reading material.	• Write a song that helps you remember the types of triangles and their definitions.
Naturalistic	• Try to notice similarities and differences in objects and concepts by organizing your study materials into relevant groupings.	• Create a table or visual organizer that arranges all of the types of two- and three-dimensional shapes into logical groupings.

*For information on geometric shapes and measurement, see Gary L. Musser, Lynn E. Trimpe, and Vikki R. Maurer, *College Geometry: A Problem-Solving Approach with Applications,* 2nd ed., Upper Saddle River, NJ: Pearson/Prentice Hall, 2008.

or in the front row so you can look into the distance. Know yourself: For many students, it's smart to avoid sitting near friends.

▶ *Write down key facts.* Before you even look at the test, write down key information, including formulas, rules, and definitions, that you don't want to forget. (Use the back of the question sheet so your instructor knows that you made these notes after the test began.)

▶ *Start with the big picture.* Spend a few minutes at the start gathering information about the questions—how many of which types are in each section, along with their point values. Use this information to schedule your time. Take level of difficulty into account as you parcel out your time. For example, if you think you can do the short-answer questions in 45 minutes and sense that the writing section will take longer, you can budget 1 hour and 15 minutes for the essay.

▶ *Directions count, so read them.* Reading test directions carefully can save you trouble. For example, you may be required to answer only one of three essay questions, or you may be penalized for incorrect responses to short-answer questions.

▶ *Mark up the questions.* Mark up instructions and keywords to avoid careless errors. Circle (**qualifiers**) such as *always, never, all, none, sometimes,* and *every;* verbs that communicate specific instructions; and concepts that are tricky or need special attention.

▶ QUALIFIERS
Words and phrases that can alter the meaning of a test question and thus require careful attention.

▶ *Be precise when taking a machine-scored test.* Use the right pencil (usually a no. 2) on machine-scored tests, and mark your answer in the correct space, filling it completely. Periodically check answer numbers against question numbers to make sure they match.

▶ *Work from easy to hard.* Begin with the easiest questions and answer them quickly without sacrificing accuracy. This will boost your confidence and leave more time for harder questions. Mark tough questions as you reach them, and return to them after answering the questions you know.

▶ *Watch the clock.* If you are worried about time, you may rush through the test and have time left over. When this happens, check over your work instead of leaving early. If, on the other hand, you are falling behind, be flexible about the best use of the remaining time.

▶ *Take a strategic approach to questions you cannot answer.* Key 8.3 has ideas to consider when you face questions that stump you.

▶ *Use special techniques for math tests.* Use the general test-taking strategies presented in this chapter as well as the techniques in Key 8.4 to achieve better results on math exams.

Maintain academic integrity

You're starting on a test when your cell phone vibrates. Your friend, who has this same class the day before, has sent you a text with answers to the multiple-choice sections. Although cheating has the immediate gain of possibly passing a test or getting a few free answers, its long-term consequences aren't so beneficial. If you cheat, you run the risk of being caught and subsequently disciplined (which can include expulsion), not to mention that you probably will not actually learn the material. Cheating that goes on your record can also damage your ability to get a job.

In recent years, cheating has become high-tech, with students using their cell phones, iPods, personal digital assistants (PDAs), graphing calculators, and Internet-connected laptops to share information through text messaging or to search the Internet. Because this type of cheating can be difficult to discover when exams are administered in large lecture halls, some instructors ban all electronic devices from the room.

Valid concerns can put students under great pressure: "I have to do well on the final. I am in a constant time crunch. I need a good grade to qualify for the next course in my major. I can't risk failing because I'm

Key 8.3 UNDERSTAND **WHAT TO DO** IF YOU DON'T KNOW THE ANSWER

Ask for clarification. → Sometimes a simple rewording will make you realize that you do know the material.

Skip the question and come back to it later. → Letting your subconscious mind work on the question sometimes can make a difference.

Build logical connections. → Take a calculated risk by using what you already know about the topic.

Bring up a "mental map" of your notes. → Remembering where material was covered in your notes and text may jog your memory about content.

Just start writing. → The act of writing about related material may help you recall the targeted information. You may want to do this kind of writing on a spare scrap of paper, think about what you've written, and then write your final answer on the test paper or booklet.

Key 8.4 TRY THESE TECHNIQUES TO SUCCEED ON **MATH EXAMS**

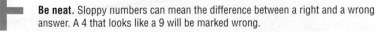

Read through the exam first. When you receive an exam, read through every problem quickly and make notes on how you might attempt to solve the problems.

Analyze problems carefully. Categorize problems according to type. Take the "givens" into account, and write down any formulas, theorems, or definitions that apply. Focus on what you want to find or prove.

Estimate to come up with a "ballpark" solution. Then work the problem and check the solution against your estimate. The two answers should be close. If they're not, recheck your calculations.

Break the calculation into the smallest possible pieces. Go step-by-step and don't move on to the next step until you are clear about what you've done so far.

Recall how you solved similar problems. Past experience can provide valuable clues.

Draw a picture to help you see the problem. Visual images such as a diagram, chart, probability tree, or geometric figure may help clarify your thinking.

Be neat. Sloppy numbers can mean the difference between a right and a wrong answer. A 4 that looks like a 9 will be marked wrong.

Use the opposite operation to check your work. Work backward from your answer to see if you are right.

Look back at the question to be sure you did everything. Did you answer every part of the question? Did you show all required work?

already in debt and I have to graduate and get a job." Compounded, these worries can often drive students to thoughts of academic dishonesty. In the end, the choice is yours. Remember that there is often more than one solution to the problem and that every possible solution has potential positive and negative effects. Key 8.5 shows you some choices and potential consequences of cheating on a final exam.

Your decisions will have lasting impacts on your future and your life. The next time you are tempted to break the rules of academic integrity, remember: *You are responsible for your own choices and the consequences of your actions.*

THINK THROUGH THE **CONSEQUENCES** OF CHEATING

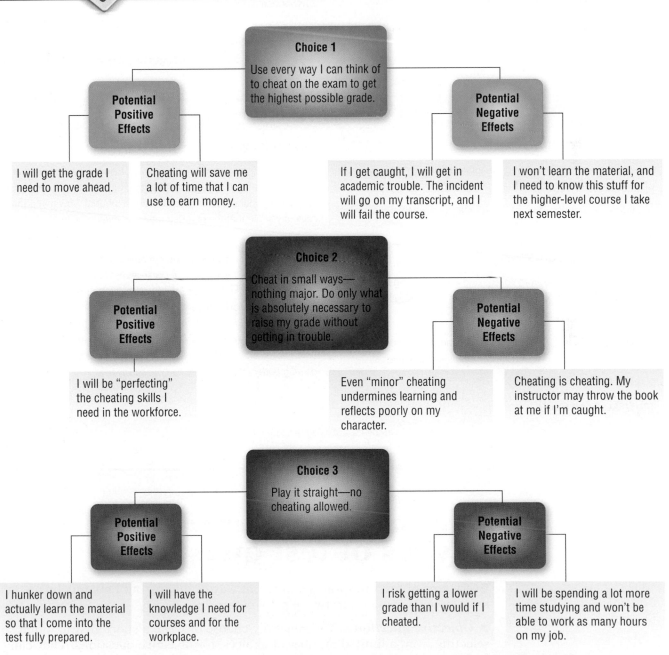

Choice 1
Use every way I can think of to cheat on the exam to get the highest possible grade.

Potential Positive Effects

I will get the grade I need to move ahead.

Cheating will save me a lot of time that I can use to earn money.

Potential Negative Effects

If I get caught, I will get in academic trouble. The incident will go on my transcript, and I will fail the course.

I won't learn the material, and I need to know this stuff for the higher-level course I take next semester.

Choice 2
Cheat in small ways—nothing major. Do only what is absolutely necessary to raise my grade without getting in trouble.

Potential Positive Effects

I will be "perfecting" the cheating skills I need in the workforce.

Potential Negative Effects

Even "minor" cheating undermines learning and reflects poorly on my character.

Cheating is cheating. My instructor may throw the book at me if I'm caught.

Choice 3
Play it straight—no cheating allowed.

Potential Positive Effects

I hunker down and actually learn the material so that I come into the test fully prepared.

I will have the knowledge I need for courses and for the workplace.

Potential Negative Effects

I risk getting a lower grade than I would if I cheated.

I will be spending a lot more time studying and won't be able to work as many hours on my job.

**FROM CHAPTER 29, "THE END OF IMPERIALISM,"
IN WESTERN CIVILIZATION: A SOCIAL AND CULTURAL HISTORY, 2ND EDITION**

- **MULTIPLE-CHOICE QUESTION**

  India's first leader after independence was:

  A. Gandhi   B. Bose   C. Nehru   D. Sukharno

  (answer: C)

- **FILL-IN-THE-BLANK QUESTION**

  East Pakistan became the country of _____ in 1971.

  A. Burma   B. East India   C. Sukharno   D. Bangladesh

  (answer: D)

- **TRUE/FALSE QUESTION**

  The United States initially supported Vietnamese independence.

  T   F

  (answer: false)

- **ESSAY QUESTION**

  Answer one of the following:

  1. What led to Irish independence? What conflicts continued to exist after independence?

  2. How did Gandhi work to rid India of British control? What methods did he use?

**FROM CHAPTER 6, "UNEMPLOYMENT AND INFLATION,"
IN MACROECONOMICS: PRINCIPLES AND TOOLS, 3RD EDITION**

- **MULTIPLE-CHOICE QUESTION**

  If the labor force is 250,000 and the total population 16 years of age or older is 300,000, the labor-force participation rate is

  A. 79.5%   B. 83.3%   C. 75.6%   D. 80.9%

  (answer: B)

- **FILL-IN-THE-BLANK QUESTION**

  Mike has just graduated from college and is now looking for a job, but has not yet found one. This causes the employment rate to _____ and the labor-force participation rate to _____.

  A. increase; decrease   C. stay the same; stay the same
  B. increase; increase   D. increase; stay the same

  (answer: C)

- **TRUE/FALSE QUESTION**

  The Consumer Price Index somewhat overstates changes in the cost of living because it does not allow for substitutions that consumers might make in response to price changes.   T   F   *(answer: true)*

- **ESSAY QUESTION**

  During a press conference, the Secretary of Employment notes that the unemployment rate is 7.0%. As a political opponent, how might you criticize this figure as an underestimate? In rebuttal, how might the secretary argue that the reported rate is an overestimate of unemployment?

  (Possible answer: The unemployment rate given by the secretary might be considered an underestimate because discouraged workers, who have given up the job search in frustration, are not counted as unemployed. In addition, full-time workers may have been forced to work part-time. In rebuttal, the secretary might note that a portion of the unemployed have voluntarily left their jobs. Most workers are unemployed only briefly and leave the ranks of the unemployed by gaining better jobs than they had previously held.)

How can you master different types of test questions?

Every type of test question is a different way of finding out how much you know. Questions fall into two general categories.

■ *Objective questions.* You generally choose or write a short answer, often selecting from a limited number of choices, for objective questions. They can include multiple-choice, fill-in-the-blank, matching, and true/false questions.

- **MATCHING QUESTION**

You are learning new words and your teacher asks you to think of an object similar to or related to the words he says. His words are listed below. Next to each word, write a related word from the list below.

el reloj	el cuaderno	el pupitre	una computadora
el televisor	la tiza	el lápiz	la mochila

1. el escritorio _____

2. el bolígrafo _____

3. la videocasetera _____

4. la pizarra _____

5. el libro _____

(answers: 1. el pupitre; 2. el lápiz; 3. el televisor; 4. la tiza; 5. el cuaderno)

- **ESSAY QUESTION**

Your mother always worries about you and wants to know what you are doing with your time in Granada. Write a short letter to her describing your experience in Spain. In your letter, you should address the following points:

1. What classes you take

2. When and where you study

3. How long you study every day

4. What you do with your time (mention three activities)

5. Where you go during your free time (mention two places)

- **MULTIPLE-CHOICE QUESTION**

What units are bonded together to make a strand of DNA?

A. chromatids B. cells C. enzymes D. nucleotides
E. proteins *(answer: D)*

- **FILL-IN-THE-BLANK QUESTION**

In a normal DNA molecule, adenine always pairs with _____ and cytosine always pairs with _____.

(answers: thymine, guanine)

- **TRUE/FALSE QUESTION**

Errors never occur in DNA replication, because the DNA polymerases edit out mistakes. T F

(answer: false)

- **MATCHING QUESTIONS**

Match the scientists and the approximate time frames (decades of their work) with their achievements.

Column 1

_____ 1. Modeled the molecular structure of DNA

_____ 2. Generated X-ray crystallography images of DNA

_____ 3. Correlated the production of one enzyme with one gene

Column 2

_____ A. George Beadle and Edward Tatum, 1930s and 1940s

_____ B. James Watson and Francis Crick, 1950s

_____ C. Rosalind Franklin and Maurice Wilkins, 1950s

(answers 1–B; 2–C; 3–A)

Sources: [*Western Civilization* test items] Margaret L. King, *Western Civilization: A Social and Cultural History,* 2nd ed., Upper Saddle River, NJ: Pearson Education, Inc., 2003. Questions from *Instructor's Manual and Test Item File* by Dolores Davison Peterson. Used with permission. [*Macroeconomics* test items] Arthur O'Sullivan and Steven M. Sheffrin, *Macroeconomics: Principles and Tools,* 3rd ed., Upper Saddle River, NJ: Pearson Education, Inc., 2003. Questions from *Test Item File 2* by Linda Ghent. Used with permission. [*Mosaicos* test items] Matilde Olivella de Castells, Elizabeth Guzmán, Paloma Lupuerta, and Carmen García, *Mosaicos: Spanish as a World Language,* 3rd ed., Upper Saddle River, NJ: Pearson Education, Inc., 2002. Questions from *Testing Program* by Mark Harpring. Used with permission. [*Biology* test items] David Krogh, *Biology: A Guide to the Natural World,* 2nd ed., Upper Saddle River, NJ: Pearson Education, Inc., 2002. Questions from *Test Item File* edited by Dan Wivagg. Used with permission.

■ *Subjective questions.* Demanding the same information recall as objective responses, subjective questions also require you to plan, organize, draft, and refine a response. All essay questions are subjective.

Key 8.6 shows samples of real test questions from Western civilization, macroeconomics, Spanish, and biology college texts published by Pearson Education. Included are exercises and multiple-choice, true/false, fill-in-the-blank, matching, and essay questions. Analyzing the types, formats, and complexities of these questions will help you gauge what to expect when you take your exams.

Look also at the Multiple Intelligence Strategies for Test Preparation on page 218. Harness the strategies that fit your learning strengths to prepare for geometry exams.

Note that some suggestions are repeated in the following sections, in order to reinforce the importance of these suggestions and their application to different types of test questions.

Multiple-choice questions

Multiple-choice questions are the most popular type of question on standardized tests. The following analytical and practical strategies will help you answer them:

▶ *Read the directions carefully and try to think of the answer before looking at the choices.* Then read the choices and make your selection.

▶ *Underline keywords and significant phrases.* If the question is complicated, try to break it down into small sections that are easy to understand.

▶ *Make sure you read every word of every answer.* Focus especially on qualifying words such as *always, never, tend to, most, often,* and *frequently.* Look also for negatives in a question ("Which of the following is *not* . . .").

▶ *When questions are linked to a reading passage, read the questions first.* This will help you focus on the information you need to answer the questions.

The following examples show the kinds of multiple-choice questions you might encounter in an introductory psychology course (the correct answer follows each question):

1. Arnold is at the company party and has had too much to drink. He releases all of his pent-up aggression by yelling at his boss, who promptly fires him. Arnold normally would not have yelled at his boss, but after drinking heavily he yelled because

   a. parties are places where employees are supposed to be able to "loosen up"

   b. alcohol is a stimulant

   c. alcohol makes people less concerned with the negative consequences of their behavior

   d. alcohol inhibits brain centers that control the perception of loudness   *(answer: C)*

2. Which of the following has not been shown to be a probable cause of or influence in the development of alcoholism in our society?

   a. intelligence

   b. culture

   c. personality

   d. genetic vulnerability   *(answer: A)*

3. Geraldine is a heavy coffee drinker who has become addicted to caffeine. If she completely ceases her intake of caffeine over the next few days, she is likely to experience each of the following *except:*

   a. depression

   b. lethargy

   c. insomnia

   d. headaches   *(answer: C)*

Source: Gary W. Piggrem and Charles G. Morris, *Test Item File for Understanding Psychology,* 3rd ed., © 1996 Prentice-Hall, Inc. Reprinted by permission of Pearson Education, Inc., Upper Saddle River, NJ.

True/false questions

Read true/false questions carefully to evaluate what they are asking. Look for absolute qualifiers (such as *all, only,* or *always,* which often make an otherwise true statement false) and conservative qualifiers (*generally, often, usually,* or *sometimes,* which often make an otherwise false statement true). For example, "The grammar rule '*i* before *e* except after *c*' is *always* true" is false, whereas "The grammar rule '*i* before *e* except after *c*' is *usually* true" is true.

Be sure to read *every* word of a true/false question to avoid jumping to an incorrect conclusion. Common problems in reading too quickly include missing negatives (*not, no*) that would change your response and deciding on an answer before reading the complete statement.

The following examples show the kinds of true/false questions you might encounter in an introductory psychology course (the correct answer follows each question):

Are the following questions true or false?

1. Alcohol use is clearly related to increases in hostility, aggression, violence, and abusive behavior.   *(true)*

2. Marijuana is harmless.   *(false)*

3. Simply expecting a drug to produce an effect is often enough to produce the effect.   *(true)*

4. Alcohol is a stimulant.   *(false)*

Source: Gary W. Piggrem and Charles G. Morris, *Test Item File for Understanding Psychology,* 3rd ed., © 1996 Prentice-Hall, Inc. Reprinted by permission of Pearson Education, Inc., Upper Saddle River, NJ.

Matching questions

Matching questions ask you to match the terms in one list with the entries in another list. For example, the directions may tell you to match a communicable disease with the microorganism that usually causes it. The following strategies will help you handle these questions.

▶ *Make sure you understand the directions.* The directions tell you whether each answer can be used only once (common practice) or more than once.

▶ *Work from the column with the longest entries.* The column on the left usually contains terms to be defined or questions to be answered, with the column on the right for definitions or answers. As a result, entries on the right are usually longer than those on the left. Reading those items only once will save time.

▶ *Start with the matches you know.* On your first run-through, pencil in these matches. When you can use an answer only once, you may have to adjust if you rethink a choice.

▶ *Finally, tackle the matches you're not sure of.* Think back to your class lectures, text notes, and study sessions as you try to visualize the correct response. If one or more phrases seem to have no correct answer and you can use answers only once, consider the possibility that one of your sure-thing answers is wrong.

Fill-in-the-blank questions

Fill-in-the-blank questions, also known as *sentence completion questions,* ask you to supply one or more words or phrases to complete the sentence. These strategies will help you make successful choices.

▶ *Be logical.* Insert your answer; then reread the *sentence from beginning* to end to be sure it makes sense and is factually and grammatically correct.

▶ *Note the lengths and number of the blanks.* If two blanks appear right after one another, the instructor is probably looking for a two-word answer. If a blank is longer than usual, the correct response may require additional space.

▶ *If there is more than one blank and the blanks are widely separated, treat each one separately.* Answering each as if it were a separate sentence-completion question increases the likelihood that you will get at least one answer correct.

▶ *If you are uncertain, guess.* Have faith that after hours of studying, the correct answer is somewhere in your subconscious mind and that your guess is not completely random.

The following examples show fill-in-the-blank questions you might encounter in an introductory astronomy course (correct answers follow questions):

1. A _____ is a collection of hundreds of billions of stars. *(galaxy)*

2. Rotation is the term used to describe the motion of a body around some _____. *(axis)*

3. The solar day is measured relative to the sun; the sidereal day is measured relative to the _____. *(stars)*

4. On December 21, known as the _____ _____, the sun is at its _____ _____. *(winter solstice; southernmost point)*

Source: Eric Chaisson and Steve McMillan, *Astronomy Today,* 3rd ed., 1999. Reprinted by permission of Pearson Education, Inc., Upper Saddle River, NJ.

Essay questions

Essay questions ask you to express your knowledge and views in a less structured way than short-answer questions. With freedom of thought and expression comes the challenge to organize your ideas and write well under time pressure. The following steps—basically a shortened version of the writing process (see Appendix A)—will help you plan, draft, revise, and edit your responses.

1. *Read every question.* Decide which to tackle (if there's a choice). Use critical thinking to identify exactly what the question is asking.

2. *Map out your time.* Schedule how long to allot for each answer, remembering that things don't always go as planned. Above all, be flexible.

3. *Focus on action verbs.* Key 8.7 shows verbs that tell you what to do to answer the question. Underline action verbs and use them to guide your writing.

4. *Plan.* Think about what the question is asking and what you know. On scrap paper, outline or map your ideas and supporting evidence. Then develop a thesis statement that defines your content and point of view. Don't skimp on planning. Not only does planning result in a better essay, but it also reduces stress because it helps you get in control.

5. *Draft.* Note the test directions before drafting your answer. Your essay may need to be of a certain length, for example, or may need to take a certain format. Use the following guidelines as you work:

- State your thesis, and then get right to the evidence that backs it up.
- Structure your essay so that each paragraph presents an idea that supports the thesis.

FOCUS ON **ACTION VERBS**
IN ESSAY TESTS

ANALYZE—Break into parts and discuss each part separately.

COMPARE—Explain similarities and differences.

CONTRAST—Distinguish between items being compared by focusing on differences.

CRITICIZE—Evaluate the issue, focusing on its problems or deficiencies.

DEFINE—State the essential quality or meaning.

DESCRIBE—Paint a complete picture; provide the details of a story or the main characteristics of a situation.

DIAGRAM—Present a drawing, chart, or other visual.

DISCUSS—Examine completely, using evidence and often presenting both sides of an issue.

ELABORATE ON—Start with information presented in the question, and then add new material.

ENUMERATE/LIST/IDENTIFY—Specify items in the form of a list.

EVALUATE—Give your opinion about the value or worth of a topic and justify your conclusion.

EXPLAIN—Make meaning clear, often by discussing causes and consequences.

ILLUSTRATE—Supply examples.

INTERPRET—Explain your personal views and judgments.

JUSTIFY—Discuss the reasons for your conclusions or for the question's premise.

OUTLINE—Organize and present main and subordinate points.

PROVE—Use evidence and logic to show that a statement is true.

REFUTE—Use evidence and logic to show that a statement is not true or tell how you disagree with it.

RELATE—Connect items mentioned in the question, showing, for example, how one item influenced another.

REVIEW—Provide an overview of ideas and establish their merits and features.

STATE—Explain clearly, simply, and concisely.

SUMMARIZE—Give the important ideas in brief, without comments.

TRACE—Present a history of a situation's development, often by showing cause and effect.

- Use clear language and tight logic to link ideas to your thesis and to create transitions between paragraphs.
- Look back at your planning notes periodically to make sure you cover everything.
- Wrap it up with a short, to-the-point conclusion.

6. *Revise.* Although you may not have the time to rewrite your entire answer, you can improve it with minor changes. Check word choice, paragraph structure, and style. If you notice anything missing, use editing marks to neatly insert it into the text. When you're done, make sure your response is the best possible representation of your ideas.

As you check over your essay, ask yourself questions about it:

- Have I answered the question?
- Does my essay begin with a clear thesis statement, and does each paragraph start with a strong topic sentence that supports the thesis?
- Have I provided the support necessary in the form of examples, statistics, and relevant facts to prove my argument, organized with tight logic?
- Have I covered all the points in my original outline or map?
- Is my conclusion an effective wrap-up?

7. *Edit.* Check for mistakes in grammar, spelling, punctuation, and usage. Correct language—and neat, legible handwriting—leaves a positive impression and helps your grade.

Key 8.8 shows a student's completed response to an essay question on body language, including the word changes and inserts she made while revising the draft.

To answer an essay question for a communications test, one student created the planning outline shown in Key 8.9 (p. 231). Notice how abbreviations and shorthand help the student write quickly.

Neatness is crucial. No matter how good your ideas are, if your instructor can't read them, your grade will suffer. If your handwriting is a problem, try printing or skipping every other line, and be sure to write on only one side of the page. Students with illegible handwriting might ask to take the test on a computer.

The purpose of a test is to see how much you know, not merely to get a grade. Embrace this attitude to learn from your mistakes.

What can you learn from test mistakes?

Evaluating their test results will help these students understand their performance as well as learn from their mistakes.
© Sarah Lyman Kravits

Congratulations! You've finished the exam, handed it in, and gone home to a well-deserved night of sleep. At the next class meeting you've returned refreshed, rejuvenated, and ready to accept a high score. As you receive the test back from your instructor, you look wide-eyed at your grade. *How could that be?*

No one aces every test. And no one understands every piece of the material perfectly. Making mistakes on tests and learning from them is as much a part of your academic experience as studying, taking notes, working with others, and yes, even getting good grades. After all, if you never made any mistakes, what would you have to learn from?

The most important idea to remember when moving on from a bad grade is not to beat yourself up about it. Instead, benefit from it by looking realistically at what you could have done better. With exam in hand, consider the following areas to identify what you can correct—and perhaps change the way you study for, or take, your next exam.

QUESTION: Describe three ways that body language affects interpersonal communication.

Body language plays an important role in interpersonal communication and helps shape the impression you make. Two of the most important functions of body language are to contradict and reinforce verbal statements. When body language contradicts verbal language, the message ~~conveyed~~ delivered by the body is dominant. For example, if a friend tells you that she is feeling "fine," but her posture is slumped, and her facial expression troubled, you have every reason to wonder whether she is telling the truth. If the same friend tells you that she is feeling fine and is smiling, walking with a bounce in her step, and has direct eye contact, her body language is ~~telling the truth.~~

The nonverbal cues that make up body language also have the power to add shades of meaning. Consider this statement: "This is the best idea I've heard all day." If you were to say this three different ways—in a loud voice while standing up; quietly while sitting with arms and legs crossed and looking away; and while ~~maintaining~~ maintaining eye contact and taking the receiver's hand—you might send three different messages.

Finally, the impact of nonverbal cues can be greatest when you meet someone for the first time. When you meet someone, you tend to make assumptions based on nonverbal behavior such as posture, eye contact, gestures, and speed and style of movement.

In summary, nonverbal communication plays a ~~crucial~~ crucial role in interpersonal relationships. It has the power to send an accurate message that may ~~destroy~~ belie the speaker's words, offer shades of meaning, and set the tone of a first meeting.

Margin notes:

, especially when
you meet someone
for the first time

her eye contact
minimal,

accurately reflecting
and reinforcing her
words.

Although first
impressions emerge
from a combination
of nonverbal cues,
tone of voice, and
choice of words,
nonverbal elements
(cues and tone)
usually come
across first and
strongest.

■ *Ask yourself global questions that may help you identify correctable patterns.*
Honest answers can help you change the way you study for the next exam.

▶ What were your biggest problems? Did you get nervous, misread the question, fail to study enough, study incorrectly, or focus on memorizing material instead of on understanding and applying it?

Write to the Verb

Focusing on the action verbs in essay test instructions can mean the difference between giving instructors what they want and answering off the mark. Start by getting to know action verbs a little better.

Choose five verbs from Key 8.7 that you've seen used in essay questions. In the spaces below, write out what the verb inspires you to do *without reusing the verb*.

Verb 1: _____ makes me _____.

Verb 2: _____ makes me _____.

Verb 3: _____ makes me _____.

Verb 4: _____ makes me _____.

Verb 5: _____ makes me _____.

Now that you have a few favorites, put them to work.

Start by writing down a topic you have learned about in this text—for example, the concept of successful intelligence or different barriers to listening.

_____

_____

_____

Put yourself in the role of instructor. Write an essay question on this topic, using one of the action verbs in Key 8.7 to frame the question. For example, "List the three aspects of successful intelligence" or "Analyze the classroom-based challenges associated with internal barriers to listening."

_____

_____

_____

_____

Now choose three other action verbs from Key 8.7. Use each one to rewrite your original question.

1. _____

2. _____

3. _____

Finally, analyze how each new verb changes the focus of the essay.

1. _____

_____

2. _____

_____

3. _____

_____

- Did your instructor's comments clarify where you slipped up? Did your answer lack specificity? Did you fail to support your thesis well? Was your analysis weak?
- Were you surprised by the questions? For example, did you expect them all to be from the lecture notes and text instead of from your notes and supplemental readings?
- Did you make careless errors? Did you misread the question or directions, blacken the wrong box on the answer sheet, skip a question, or write illegibly?
- Did you make conceptual or factual errors? Did you misunderstand a concept? Did you fail to master facts or concepts?

■ ***Rework the questions you got wrong.*** Based on instructor feedback, try to rewrite an essay, recalculate a math problem from the original question, or redo questions following a reading selection. If you discover a pattern of careless errors, redouble your efforts to be more careful, and save time to double-check your work.

■ ***After reviewing your mistakes, fill in your knowledge gaps.*** If you made mistakes because you didn't understand important concepts, develop a plan to learn the material.

■ ***Talk to your instructor.*** Focus on specific mistakes on objective questions or a weak essay. The fact that you care enough to review your errors will make a good impression. If you are not sure why you were marked down on an essay, ask what you could have done better. If you feel that an essay was unfairly graded, ask for a rereading. When you use your social intelligence and approach your instructor in a nondefensive way, as Teo did, you are likely to receive help.

■ ***Rethink the way you studied.*** Make changes to avoid repeating your errors. Use the varied techniques in *Keys to Success* to study more effectively so that you can show yourself and your instructors what you are capable of doing. The

CREATE AN **INFORMAL OUTLINE** DURING ESSAY TESTS

Key 8.9

> Essay question: Describe three ways in which body language affects interpersonal communication.
>
> Roles of BL in IC
>
>   1. To contradict or reinforce words
>   —e.g., friend says "I'm fine"
>   2. To add shades of meaning
>   —saying the same sentence in 3 diff. ways
>   3. To make lasting 1st impression
>   —impact of nv cues and voice tone greater than words
>   —we assume things abt person based on posture, eye contact, etc.

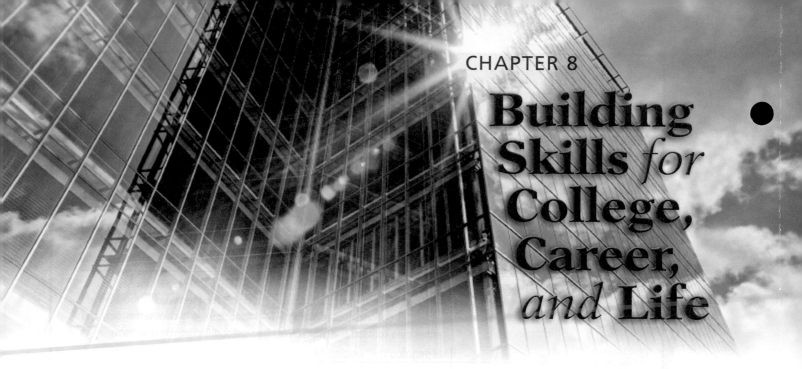

Building Skills *for* College, Career, *and* Life

Steps to Success

Prepare Effectively for Tests

Take a careful look at your performance on and preparation for a recent test.

BUILD BASIC SKILLS. Think about how you did on the test.

Were you pleased or disappointed with your performance and grade? Why?

_____

_____

Circle any of the listed problems that you experienced on this exam. If you experienced one or more problems not listed here, write them in the blank spaces provided.

- Incomplete preparation
- Fatigue
- Feeling rushed during the test
- Shaky understanding of concepts
- Poor guessing techniques
- Feeling confused about directions
- Test anxiety
- Poor essay organization or writing

_____

_____

_____

Now for each problem you identified, think about why you made mistakes.

TAKE IT TO THE NEXT LEVEL. Be creative about test-preparation strategies.

If you had all the time and materials you needed, how would you have prepared for this test? Describe briefly what your plan would be and how it would address your problem(s).

- Did your instructor's comments clarify where you slipped up? Did your answer lack specificity? Did you fail to support your thesis well? Was your analysis weak?
- Were you surprised by the questions? For example, did you expect them all to be from the lecture notes and text instead of from your notes and supplemental readings?
- Did you make careless errors? Did you misread the question or directions, blacken the wrong box on the answer sheet, skip a question, or write illegibly?
- Did you make conceptual or factual errors? Did you misunderstand a concept? Did you fail to master facts or concepts?

■ *Rework the questions you got wrong.* Based on instructor feedback, try to rewrite an essay, recalculate a math problem from the original question, or redo questions following a reading selection. If you discover a pattern of careless errors, redouble your efforts to be more careful, and save time to double-check your work.

■ *After reviewing your mistakes, fill in your knowledge gaps.* If you made mistakes because you didn't understand important concepts, develop a plan to learn the material.

■ *Talk to your instructor.* Focus on specific mistakes on objective questions or a weak essay. The fact that you care enough to review your errors will make a good impression. If you are not sure why you were marked down on an essay, ask what you could have done better. If you feel that an essay was unfairly graded, ask for a rereading. When you use your social intelligence and approach your instructor in a nondefensive way, as Teo did, you are likely to receive help.

■ *Rethink the way you studied.* Make changes to avoid repeating your errors. Use the varied techniques in *Keys to Success* to study more effectively so that you can show yourself and your instructors what you are capable of doing. The

CREATE AN **INFORMAL OUTLINE** DURING ESSAY TESTS

Key 8.9

Essay question: Describe three ways in which body language affects interpersonal communication.

Roles of BL in IC

  1. To contradict or reinforce words
    —e.g., friend says "I'm fine"

  2. To add shades of meaning
    —saying the same sentence in 3 diff. ways

  3. To make lasting 1st impression
    —impact of nv cues and voice tone greater than words
    —we assume things abt person based on posture, eye contact, etc.

earlier in the term you make positive adjustments the better, so make a special effort to analyze and learn from early test mistakes.

■ *If you fail a test, don't throw it away.* Use it to review troublesome material, especially if you will be tested on it again. You might also want to keep it as a reminder that you can improve. When you compare a failure to later successes, you'll see how far you've come.

Case *Wrap-up*

What happened to Teo? Mr. Sorrenti went through the aspects of test anxiety with Teo—how it creates an unrealistic view of risk, puts him off his goal path, and creates problematic physical effects and behaviors. He helped him combat each aspect with an action. To ease risk as well as see it more realistically, Teo set up a regular study schedule. To focus on his goal, he created a written set of goals for this term and beyond. Finally, Mr. Sorrenti gave him some ideas for how to combat test-time jitters. At this point halfway through the term, Teo is doing better at studying regularly. For his first exam last week he got seven hours of sleep beforehand, arrived early to stretch and breathe, and kept a picture of his girlfriend on the desk as a reminder of his plan for a successful life. He is waiting for his test grade, feeling hopeful.

What does this mean for you? What creates anxiety for you? Even if you don't experience test anxiety, you likely have some idea, situation, or issue to which you react with more than a healthy and productive fear. Take a look at the article on anxiety at www.counseling.mtu.edu/anxiety_management.html. Think about what you would like to be able to handle productively rather than anxiously. Write out a specific plan to address each aspect of anxiety for your particular situation.

What effects go beyond your world? Anxiety and high stress are unwelcome but real features of modern society in many countries. In fact, modern science has discovered that high stress is related to aging. The body's cells have small pieces of DNA called *telomeres* that become shorter each time the cell divides, ultimately getting so short that they prevent the cell from dividing anymore. Do a little research on people, societies, or groups who find ways to alleviate stress. What can you learn from them that will help you keep your telomeres as long as they can be? What about your life's goals will allow you to help others face and overcome anxiety?

ANALYTICAL   CREATIVE   PRACTICAL

Successful Intelligence *Wrap-up*

HERE'S HOW YOU HAVE BUILT SKILLS IN **CHAPTER 8** :

ANALYTICAL THINKING 	**CREATIVE THINKING**	**PRACTICAL THINKING**
❯ You examined test-preparation techniques with an eye toward what works best for you.	❯ In reading about test anxiety, you encountered a different perspective of tests as opportunities to learn rather than contests that you win or lose.	❯ You gathered specific test-preparation techniques. You learned specific ways to calm test anxiety and attack objective test questions.
❯ In the Get Analytical exercise, you wrote a series of original essay questions, analyzing the effect that different action verbs had on what the questions were asking.	❯ With the Get Creative exercise, you produced your own pretest that will help you assess if you have mastered crucial material.	❯ In the Get Practical exercise, you used a test anxiety instrument to gauge your level of testing stress and plan for productive solutions in the future.
❯ You investigated specific ways to maximize your chances of answering objective and subjective test questions correctly.	❯ The scheduling and study techniques may have inspired you to create a personal study schedule and regimen that help you make the most of your time.	❯ You expanded your knowledge of how to use planning tools, such as a keyword outline, to help you write test essays.

Word*for*Thought

In **Polish,** *hart ducha* (hahrt doo'-cha) means "strength of will" to overcome life's challenges.[4] In college, instructors challenge you on tests to demonstrate what you know and what you can do. Both before and during each test, call on your hart ducha to help you work hard and reach your academic potential.

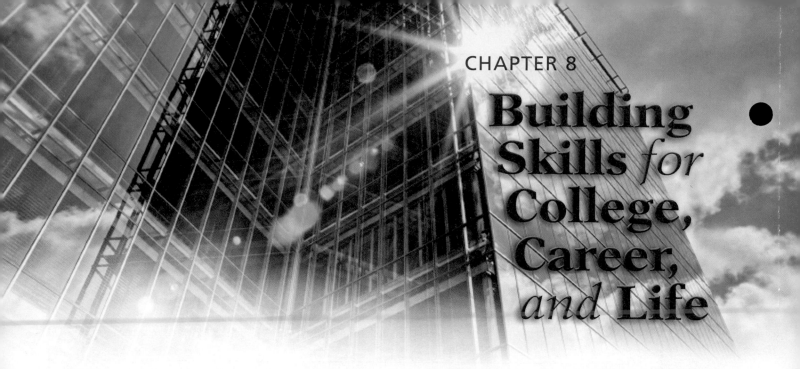

Building Skills *for* College, Career, *and* Life

Steps to Success

Prepare Effectively for Tests

Take a careful look at your performance on and preparation for a recent test.

BUILD BASIC SKILLS. Think about how you did on the test.

Were you pleased or disappointed with your performance and grade? Why?

_____

_____

Circle any of the listed problems that you experienced on this exam. If you experienced one or more problems not listed here, write them in the blank spaces provided.

- Incomplete preparation
- Fatigue
- Feeling rushed during the test
- Shaky understanding of concepts
- Poor guessing techniques
- Feeling confused about directions
- Test anxiety
- Poor essay organization or writing

_____

_____

_____

Now for each problem you identified, think about why you made mistakes.

TAKE IT TO THE NEXT LEVEL. Be creative about test-preparation strategies.

If you had all the time and materials you needed, how would you have prepared for this test? Describe briefly what your plan would be and how it would address your problem(s).

Now think back to your actual test preparation—the techniques you used and the amount of time you spent. Describe the difference between your ideal study plan and what you actually did.

_____

_____

_____

MOVE TOWARD MASTERY. Improve your chances for success on the next exam by coming up with specific changes in your preparation.

What I did this time but do not intend to do next time:

_____

_____

What I did not do this time but intend to do next time:

_____

_____

Teamwork

Create Solutions Together

PREPARE FOR A TEST

Goal: To discover preparation strategies as a group and explore their effectiveness.

Time on task: 20 minutes in the group (after individual preparation)

Instructions: Form a study group with two or three other students. When your instructor announces the next exam, ask study group members to record everything they do to prepare for the exam, including the following:

- Learning what to expect on the test (topics and material that will be covered, types of questions that will be asked)
- Examining old tests
- Creating and following a study schedule and checklist
- Using SQ3R to review material
- Taking a pretest
- Getting a good night's sleep
- Doing last-minute cramming
- Mastering general test-taking strategies
- Mastering strategies for handling specific types of test questions

After the exam, come together to compare preparation strategies. What important differences can you identify in the routines followed by group members? How did learning styles play a role in those differences? How do you suspect that different routines affected test performance and outcome? On a separate piece of paper or on a computer file, for your own reference, write down what you learned from the test-preparation habits of your study mates that may help you as you prepare for upcoming exams.

Writing

Build Intrapersonal and Communication Skills

Record your thoughts on paper, in a journal, or electronically.

EMOTIONAL INTELLIGENCE JOURNAL

Test types. What type of test do you feel most comfortable with, and what type brings up more negative feelings? Thinking of a particular situation involving the test type that challenges you, describe how it made you feel and how that feeling affected your performance. Discuss ways in which you might be able to shift your mindset in order to feel more confident about this type of test.

REAL-LIFE WRITING

Ask your instructor for feedback on a test. Nearly every student has been in the position of believing that a response on an essay exam was graded unfairly. The next time this happens to you—when you have no idea why you lost points or disagree with the instructor's assessment of your work—draft a respectful e-mail to your instructor explaining your position and asking for a meeting to discuss the essay. (See the e-mail etiquette guidelines in the Quick Start.) Use clear logic to defend your work and refer back to what you learned in class and in the text. It is important to address specifically any comments or criticisms the instructor made on the test paper. Before sending the e-mail, analyze your argument: Did you make your case effectively or was the instructor correct? When you have the meeting, the work you did on the e-mail will prepare you to defend your position.

Personal Portfolio

Prepare for Career Success

ON-THE-JOB TESTING

21st Century Learning Building Blocks

- Information Literacy
- Initiative and Self-Direction
- Productivity and Accountability

Complete the following in your electronic portfolio or separately on paper.

You will probably encounter different tests throughout your career. For example, if you are studying to be a nurse you are tested on subjects like anatomy and pharmacology. After you graduate you will be required to take certification and recertification exams that gauge your mastery of the latest information in different aspects of nursing.

Some postgraduate tests are for entry into the field; some test proficiency on particular equipment; some move you to the next level of employment. Choose one career you are thinking about and investigate what tests are involved as you advance through different career stages.

Use the accompanying grid to organize what you find. You'll be searching for the following information:

- The name of the test
- When the test is taken and if it needs to be retaken
- What it covers
- How you can prepare
- Web resources like pretests, websites, or review materials

TEST NAME	WHEN TAKEN	WHAT IT COVERS	PREPARATION	WEB RESOURCES

Social Networking

ESTABLISH YOUR PRIVACY

Informed users of technology take advantage of tools that help them control it. You are in charge of what you allow people to view and send you on LinkedIn. Sign in to your account, click on "Settings" at the top of the screen, and look over the categories under "Privacy Settings." Establish the settings you prefer by clicking on each of the subheads and following the instructions:

- Research Surveys
- Connections Browse
- Profile Views
- Viewing Profile Photos

- Profile and Status Updates
- Service Provider Directory
- Partner Advertising
- Authorized Applications

Consider your privacy settings carefully. Find the balance that will keep your information as private as you want it to be, but also allow you to benefit from what LinkedIn can do for you when it shares your information.

chapter 9

Diversity and Communication

Making Relationships Work

What Would You Do?

Think about this problem as you read, and consider how you would approach it. This chapter focuses on the diversity of today's student body, effective communication with others, and connecting with others.

In her native Philippines, Gaile Edrozo was on track to earn a biology degree and begin medical school. However, financial difficulties derailed her plans. Needing more opportunity to work, she and her family came to the United States in 2004. Gaile enrolled as a nursing student at Highline Community College in the fall of 2004. She was considered an international student at that time because she had not yet become a U.S. citizen.

Even as Gaile got started toward a productive goal, the financial burden of her education caused excessive stress and sleepless nights. The cost of her education was too high for her family to manage, even with the many sacrifices her parents were making. Even more frightening was the possibility that Gaile would lose her immigration status if she were unable to stay in school and would have to return to the Philippines alone, without her family.

Gaile felt overcome with fear that her dream to become a nurse and have a career she loved, as well as to contribute to her family financially, would be taken away as it had been in the Philippines. She threw herself into her schoolwork, hoping to be eligible for scholarships or other aid. However, none of the scholarships she explored was available to an international student. Sensing it was time to reach out for help, Gaile took the advice of fellow

students and registered for Honors 100, a course at Highline for both citizens and international students that helps students explore scholarship opportunities, prepare portfolio and resumé materials, and look at four-year institutions. She hoped her instructor could help her avoid losing her dream a second time. (To be continued . . .)

Connecting with others opens up possibilities and can help you live your dreams. You'll learn more about Gaile, and revisit her situation, within the chapter.

In this chapter, you'll explore answers to these questions:

> How can you develop cultural competence? p. 240

> How can you communicate effectively? p. 247

> How do you make the most of personal relationships? p. 253

ANALYTICAL

CREATIVE

PRACTICAL

Source: Adapted from Highline College Honors Scholar Program Success Stories, with permission from Louise Gaile Edrozo.

For each statement, circle the number that feels right to you, from 1 for "not at all true for me" to 5 for "very true for me."

▶ I am constantly working to develop cultural competence.	1 2 3 4 5
▶ I seek to incorporate diverse people and cultures into my life.	1 2 3 4 5
▶ I believe even positive stereotypes can hurt my ability to get to know someone.	1 2 3 4 5
▶ I understand the difference between tolerating those different from me and accepting and celebrating those differences.	1 2 3 4 5
▶ I am able to adjust to different communication styles when necessary.	1 2 3 4 5
▶ I pay attention to and interpret meaning from nonverbal and body language.	1 2 3 4 5
▶ I use positive relationship strategies to strengthen my personal connections.	1 2 3 4 5
▶ I know the warning signs of destructive or hostile relationships.	1 2 3 4 5
▶ I am aware of common date rape drugs and know how to protect myself.	1 2 3 4 5
▶ I manage electronic communication effectively and do not let it run my life.	1 2 3 4 5

Each of the topics in these statements is covered in this chapter. Note those statements for which you circled a 3 or lower. Skim the chapter to see where those topics appear, and pay special attention to them as you read, learn, and apply new strategies.

REMEMBER: *No matter how developed your cultural competence and communication skills are, you can improve with effort and practice.*

"Successfully intelligent people question assumptions and encourage others to do so. We all tend to have assumptions about the way things are or should be . . . but creatively intelligent people question many assumptions that others accept, eventually leading others to question those assumptions as well."

—Robert Sternberg

How can you **develop cultural competence?**

A century ago it was possible to live an entire lifetime surrounded only by people from your own culture. Not so today. American society consists of people from a multitude of countries and cultural backgrounds. In fact, in the 2000 census, U.S. citizens described themselves in terms of sixty-three different racial categories, compared with only five in 1990.[1] Cable television, the Internet, and the global marketplace have increased cultural awareness.

What *diversity* means

Differences among people

On an interpersonal level, *diversity* refers to the differences among people and among groups that people are a part of. Differences in gender, skin color, ethnicity and national origin, age, and physical characteristics are most obvious. Differences in cultural and religious beliefs and practices, education, sexual orientation, socioeconomic status, family background, and marital and parental status are less visible but no less significant.

Differences within people

Another layer of diversity lies within each person. Among the factors defining this layer are personality traits, learning style, strengths and weaknesses, and natural talents and interests. No one else has been or will ever be exactly like you.

In college, at work, and as you go about your daily life you are likely to meet people who reflect America's growing diversity, including the following:

- Bi- or multiracial individuals
- People from families with more than one religious tradition
- Nonnative English speakers, like Gaile, who may have emigrated from outside the United States
- Students older than the "traditional" 18- to 22-year-old
- People living with various kinds of disabilities
- Gay, lesbian, bisexual, or transgender individuals
- People practicing different lifestyles—often expressed in the way they dress or their interests, friends, or leisure activities

Interacting effectively with all kinds of people is the goal of *cultural competence*—the ability to understand and appreciate differences among people and adjust behavior in ways that enhance, rather than detract from, relationships and communication. Cultural competence is crucial to both school and life success. According to the National Center for Cultural Competence, developing cultural competence is based on five actions:[2]

When you share goals with someone, personal differences may fade into the background. This teacher and student share a goal of repairing an internal computer component.
© David Barber/PhotoEdit

1. Valuing diversity
2. Identifying and evaluating personal perceptions and attitudes
3. Being aware of what happens when different cultures interact
4. Building knowledge about other cultures
5. Using learning to adapt to diverse cultures that are encountered

In developing cultural competence, you learn practical skills that enable you to connect to others, bridging the gap between who you are and who they are.[3]

Action 1: Value diversity

Valuing diversity means having a basic respect for the differences among people and an understanding of what is positive about those differences. No one likes everyone they meet, but if you value diversity, you treat people with tolerance and respect whether you like them or not, avoiding assumptions and granting them the right to think, feel, and believe without being judged. This attitude helps you to take emotionally intelligent actions, as shown in Key 9.1.

It is important to note that valuing diversity is about more than just passive *tolerance* of the world around you (not causing conflict but not seeking harmony either). Moving further than that, toward *acceptance*, you value diversity by actively working toward teamwork and friendship, celebrating differences as an enriching part of life.

APPROACH DIVERSITY WITH EMOTIONAL INTELLIGENCE

YOUR ROLE	SITUATION	CLOSED-MINDED RESPONSE	EMOTIONALLY INTELLIGENT RESPONSE
Fellow student	For an assignment, you are paired with a student old enough to be your mother.	You assume the student will be clueless about the modern world. You get ready to react against her preaching about how to do the assignment.	You acknowledge your feelings but try to get to know the student as an individual. You stay open to what you can learn from her experiences and realize you have things to offer as well.
Friend	You are invited to dinner at a friend's house. When he introduces you to his partner, you realize that he is gay.	Uncomfortable with the idea of two men in a relationship, you pretend you have a cell phone call and make an excuse to leave early. You avoid your friend after that.	You have dinner with the two men and make an effort to get to know more about them, individually and as a couple. You compare your immediate assumptions to what you learned about them at dinner.
Employee	Your new boss is of a different racial and cultural background than yours.	You assume that you and your new boss don't have much in common. Thinking he will be distant and uninterested in you, you already don't like him.	You acknowledge your stereotypes but work to set them aside so that you can build a relationship with your boss. You adapt to his style and make an effort to get to know him better.

Action 2: Identify and evaluate personal perceptions and attitudes

Bringing the first and second parts of emotional intelligence into play, you identify perceptions and attitudes by noticing your feelings about others and then you evaluate these attitudes by looking at the effect they have on you and on others. Many who value the *concept* of diversity experience negative feelings about the *reality* of diversity in their own lives. This disconnect often reveals prejudices and stereotypes.

Prejudice

Almost everyone has some level of **prejudice** that involves prejudging others, usually on the basis of characteristics such as gender, race, sexual orientation, disability, and religion. People judge others without knowing anything about them because of factors like the following:

PREJUDICE
A preconceived judgment or opinion formed without just grounds or sufficient knowledge.

▶ *Influence of family and culture.* Children learn attitudes—including intolerance, superiority, and hate—from their parents, peers, and community.
▶ *Fear of differences.* It is human to fear and to make assumptions about the unfamiliar.
▶ *Experience.* One bad experience with a person of a particular race or religion may lead someone to condemn all people with the same background.

STEREOTYPE
A standardized mental picture that represents an oversimplified opinion or uncritical judgment.

Stereotypes

Prejudice is usually built on **stereotypes**—assumptions made, without proof or critical thinking, about the characteristics of a person or group of people, based on factors such as the following:

BOTH POSITIVE AND NEGATIVE STEREOTYPES **MASK UNIQUENESS**

POSITIVE STEREOTYPE	NEGATIVE STEREOTYPE
Women are nurturing.	Women are too emotional for business.
African Americans are great athletes.	African Americans struggle in school.
Hispanic Americans are family oriented.	Hispanic Americans have too many kids.
White people are successful in business.	White people are cold and power hungry.
Gay men have a great sense of style.	Gay men are overly effeminate.
People with disabilities have strength of will.	People with disabilities are bitter.
Older people are wise.	Older people are set in their ways.
Asian Americans are good at math and science.	Asian Americans are poor leaders.

▶ *Desire for patterns and logic.* People often try to make sense of the world by using the labels, categories, and generalizations that stereotypes provide.

▶ *Media influences.* The more people see stereotypical images—the airhead beautiful blonde, the jolly fat man—the easier it is to believe that stereotypes are universal.

▶ *Laziness.* Labeling group members according to a characteristic they seem to have in common takes less work than asking questions about who each individual really is.

Stereotypes derail personal connections and block effective communication; pasting a label on a person makes it hard to see the real person underneath. Even stereotypes that seem "positive" may be untrue and get in the way of perceiving uniqueness. Key 9.2 lists some of the "positive" and "negative" stereotypes often heard in media or conversations.

To identify attitudes that hinder cultural competence, ask analytical questions about your own ideas and beliefs:

▶ How do I react to differences?

▶ What prejudices or stereotypes come to mind when I see people, in real life or the media, who are a different color than I am? From a different culture? Making different choices?

▶ Where do my prejudices and stereotypes come from?

▶ Are these prejudices fair? Are these stereotypes accurate?

▶ What harm can having these prejudices and believing these stereotypes cause?

With the knowledge you build as you answer these questions, move on to the next stage: looking carefully at what happens when people from different cultures interact.

GET CREATIVE!

Expand Your Perception of Diversity

The ability to respond to people as individuals requires that you become more aware of the diversity that is not always on the surface. Start by examining your own uniqueness. Brainstorm ten words or phrases that describe you. The challenge: Keep references to your ethnicity or appearance (brunette, Cuban American, wheelchair dependent, and so on) to a minimum, and fill the rest of the list with characteristics others can't see at a glance (laid-back, only child, 24 years old, drummer, marathoner, interpersonal learner, and so on).

1. _____
2. _____
3. _____
4. _____
5. _____

6. _____
7. _____
8. _____
9. _____
10. _____

Next, pair up with a classmate you do not know well. List on a separate sheet of paper any characteristics you know about him or her—chances are most of them will be visible. Then talk with the classmate. As you talk, you should round out your lists about each other with what you have discovered from your conversation. Finally, answer two questions.

What stands out to you about what you learned about your classmate, and why?

_____

_____

What about your description of yourself would you like people to focus on more often, and why?

_____

_____

Action 3: Be aware of what happens when cultures interact

Interaction among people from different cultures can promote learning, build mutual respect, and broaden perspectives. However, as history has shown, such interaction can also produce problems caused by lack of understanding, prejudice, and stereotypic thinking. At their mildest, these problems create roadblocks that obstruct relationships and communication. At their worst, they set the stage for acts of discrimination and hate crimes.

Discrimination

DISCRIMINATION
Denying equal access to employment, educational, and housing opportunities or treating people as second-class citizens.

Federal law says that you cannot be denied basic opportunities and rights because of your race, creed, color, age, gender, national or ethnic origin, religion, marital status, potential or actual pregnancy, or potential or actual illness or disability (unless the illness or disability prevents you from performing required tasks and unless accommodations are not possible). Despite these legal protections, **discrimination** is common and often appears on college campuses. Members of campus clubs may reject prospective members because of religious differences or race, for example, or instructors and students may judge one another according to their weight, accent, or body piercings.

Hate crimes

When prejudice turns violent, it often manifests itself in *hate crimes*—actions motivated by a hatred of a specific characteristic thought to be possessed by the victim, usually based on race, ethnicity, or religious or sexual orientation. Because hate crime statistics include only reported incidents, they tell just a part of the story—many more crimes likely go unreported by victims fearful of what might happen if they contact authorities.

Focusing on the positive aspects of intercultural interaction starts with understanding the ideas and attitudes that lead to discrimination and hate crimes. With this awareness, you will be better prepared to push past negative possibilities and open your mind to positive outcomes. Dr. Martin Luther King Jr. believed that careful thinking could change attitudes.

> The tough-minded person always examines the facts before he reaches conclusions: in short, he postjudges. The tender-minded person reaches conclusions before he has examined the first fact; in short, he prejudges and is prejudiced. . . . There is little hope for us until we become tough minded enough to break loose from the shackles of prejudice, half-truths, and down-right ignorance.[4]

Action 4: Build cultural knowledge

The successfully intelligent response to discrimination and hate, and the next step in your path toward cultural competence, is to gather knowledge. You have a personal responsibility to learn about people who are different from you, including those you are likely to meet on campus. What are some practical ways to begin?

- ▶ *Read* newspapers, books, magazines, and websites that expose you to different perspectives.
- ▶ *Ask questions* of all kinds of people, about themselves and their traditions.
- ▶ *Observe* how people behave, what they eat and wear, how they interact with others.
- ▶ *Travel internationally* to unfamiliar places where you can experience different ways of living.
- ▶ *Travel locally* to equally unfamiliar but close-by places where you will encounter a variety of people.
- ▶ *Build friendships* with fellow students or co-workers you would not ordinarily approach.

Some colleges have international exchange programs that can help you appreciate the world's cultural diversity. Engaging with students from other countries—whether they have come to your college or you have chosen to study abroad—can provide a two-way learning experience, helping each of you learn about each other's culture.

Building knowledge also means exploring yourself. Talk with family, read, and seek experiences that educate you about your own cultural heritage; then share what you know with others.

Action 5: Adapt to diverse cultures

Here's where you put cultural competence to work and bring in the final stage of emotional intelligence—taking action with the intent of bringing about a

positive outcome. Choose actions that feel right to you, that cause no harm, and that make a difference, however small. Let the following suggestions inspire your own creative ideas about how you can relate to others.

▶ *Look past external characteristics.* If you meet a woman with a disability, get to know her. She may be an accounting major, a daughter, and a mother. She may love baseball, politics, and science fiction novels. These characteristics—not just her physical person—describe who she is.

▶ *Move beyond your feelings.* Engage your emotional intelligence to note what different people make you feel, and then examine the potential effect of those feelings. By working to move beyond feelings that could lead to harmful assumptions and negative outcomes, you will improve your chance for successful communication.

▶ *Put yourself in other people's shoes.* Ask questions about what other people feel, especially if there's a conflict. Offer friendship to someone new who is adjusting to your school community.

▶ *Adjust to cultural differences.* When you understand someone's way of being and put it into practice, you show respect and encourage communication. For example, if a study group member takes offense at a particular kind of language, avoid it when you meet.

▶ *Climb over language barriers.* When speaking with someone who is struggling with your language, choose words the person is likely to know, avoid slang expressions, be patient, and use body language to fill in what words can't say. Invite questions, and ask them yourself.

▶ *Help others.* There are countless ways to make a difference, from providing food or money to a neighbor in need to sending relief funds over the Internet to nations devastated by natural disasters. Every act, no matter how small, makes the world that much better. Remember Gaile's story and how she needs help to complete her education, which will enable her to help others as a nurse.

▶ *Stand up against prejudice, discrimination, and hate.* When you hear a prejudiced remark, notice discrimination taking place, or suspect a hate crime, ask questions about how to encourage a move in the right direction. You may choose to make a comment or to get help by approaching an authority such as an instructor or dean. Support organizations that encourage tolerance.

▶ *Recognize that people everywhere have the same basic needs.* Everyone loves, thinks, hurts, hopes, fears, and plans. When you are trying to find common ground with diverse people, remember that you are united first through your essential humanity.

Just as there is diversity in skin color and ethnicity, there is also diversity in the way people communicate. Effective communication helps people of all cultures make connections.

Change the CONVERSATION

Challenge yourself and your friends to ask—and answer—tough questions. Use the following to inspire discussion in pairs or groups.

▶ What stereotypes seem to stay in your head whether or not you want them to? For each one you can name, identify a person who reinforces it *and* a person who contradicts it.

▶ Has a point of difference ever kept you from connecting with someone? What makes you hesitate? What might you gain from overcoming your hesitation?

▶ **CONSIDER THE CASE:** Fellow students gave Gaile advice that led her to the course that helped her most. When have fellow students helped you—or not helped—when you needed it? When have you chosen to help—or to avoid—someone who needed support?

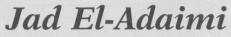

student profile

Jad El-Adaimi
California Polytechnic State University, San Luis Obispo, California

About me:
I went to school in Lebanon. Then I came to Cupertino, California, where I went to De Anza College and attained my A.S. degree in biological sciences. After two years and a degree I transferred to Cal Poly in San Luis Obispo and graduated in June of 2010 with a B.S. in molecular and cellular biology. I started my master's program in September of 2010.

How I faced a challenge:
I grew up in Lebanon, where almost everyone was Lebanese. I was open and friendly with everyone, but had never lived with those from other cultures. When I came to college in the U.S. that all changed. I met people from around the world. I worked and studied with people from different backgrounds. In the beginning I felt disconnected and tried finding friends from my regional area. This did not help me adjust, but instead made me feel homesick. As soon as I started broadening my perspective of cultures and communicating with everyone, everything changed. We learn from everyone around us. I started being less secluded and more outgoing and close with people from all over the U.S. and the world, which included learning a few words from each language, eating their food, celebrating some of their holidays, and respecting their traditions. I think that broadening my communication allowed me to adjust to different cultures and people and helped me transfer successfully from De Anza to Cal Poly.

What will help me in the workplace:
We build our personality and experiences through the people around us. When you start a new job you will be meeting new people. Learn to adjust to everyone and accept them for who they are within your limits. This way you can do your work at the highest standard and still maintain a social aspect and enjoy your workplace. Accepting people or at least adjusting to them in some manner will help in any situation.

How can you communicate effectively?

Spoken communication that is clear promotes success at school and work or in personal relationships. Thinking communicators analyze and adjust to communication styles, learn to give and receive criticism, analyze and make practical use of body language, and work through communication problems.

Adjust to communication styles

When you speak, your goal is for listeners to receive the message as you intended. Problems arise when one person has trouble "translating" a message

Communication with others is essential to every school and work goal, from team projects to study groups to on-the-job collaborations.
© Shutterstock

coming from someone using a different communication style. Your knowledge of the Personality Spectrum (see Chapter 3) will help you understand and analyze the ways diverse people communicate.

Identifying your styles

Successful communication depends on understanding your personal style and becoming attuned to the styles of others. The following styles are associated with the four dimensions of the Personality Spectrum. No one style is better than another. As you read, keep in mind that these are generalizations—individuals will exhibit a range of variations within each style.

■ **Thinkers communicate by focusing on facts and logic.** As speakers, they tend to rely on logical analysis to communicate ideas and prefer quantitative concepts to conceptual or emotional approaches. As listeners, they often do best with logical messages. Thinkers may also need time to process what they have heard before responding. Written messages—on paper or via e-mail—are useful because creating them allows time to put ideas together logically.

■ **Organizers communicate by focusing on structure and completeness.** As speakers, they tend to deliver well-thought-out, structured messages that fit into an organized plan. As listeners, they often appreciate a well-organized message that defines practical tasks in concrete terms. As with Thinkers, a written format is often an effective form of communication to or from an Organizer.

■ **Givers communicate by focusing on concern for others.** As speakers, they tend to cultivate harmony, analyzing what will promote closeness in relationships. As listeners, they often appreciate messages that emphasize personal connection and address the emotional side of an issue. Whether speaking or listening, Givers often favor in-person talks over written messages.

■ **Adventurers communicate by focusing on the present.** As speakers, they focus on creative ideas, tending to convey a message as soon as the idea arises and then move on to the next activity. As listeners, they appreciate up-front, short, direct messages that don't get sidetracked. Like Givers, Adventurers tend to communicate and listen more effectively in person.

What is your style? Use this information as a jumping-off point for your self-exploration. Just as people tend to demonstrate characteristics from more than one Personality Spectrum dimension, communicators may demonstrate different styles.

Put your knowledge of communication styles to use

Compare these communication styles to your own tendencies and also consider how others seem to respond to you. Your practical thinking skills can help you figure out what works well for you. However, you are only half of any communication picture. Your creative skills will help you shift your perspective to think about the other person's thoughts and feelings and what might work best interacting with that person's communication style.

- ■ **Speakers adjust to listeners.** Listeners may interpret messages in ways you never intended. Think about practical solutions to this kind of problem as you read the following interaction involving a Giver (instructor) and Thinker (student):

  > *Instructor:* "Your essay didn't communicate any sense of your personal voice."
  >
  > *Student:* "What do you mean? I spent hours writing it. I thought it was on the mark."

  - ▶ *Without adjustment:* The instructor ignores the student's need for detail and continues to generalize. Comments like "You need to elaborate," "Try writing from the heart," or "You're not considering your audience" might confuse or discourage the student.
  - ▶ *With adjustment:* Greater logic and detail will help. For example, the instructor might communicate better by saying, "You've supported your central idea clearly, but you didn't move beyond the facts into your interpretation of what they mean. Your essay reads like a research paper. The language doesn't sound like it is coming directly from you."

- ■ **Listeners adjust to speakers.** As a listener, improve understanding by being aware of differences and translating messages so they make sense to you. The following example with an Adventurer (employee) and an Organizer (supervisor) shows how adjusting can pay off.

  > *Employee:* "I'm upset about the e-mail you sent me. You never talked to me directly and you let the problem build into a crisis. I haven't had a chance to defend myself."

  - ▶ *Without adjustment:* If the supervisor is annoyed by the employee's insistence on direct personal contact, he or she may become defensive: "I told you clearly what needs to be done. I don't know what else there is to discuss."
  - ▶ *With adjustment:* In an effort to improve communication, the supervisor responds by encouraging the in-person exchange that is best for the employee. "Let's meet after lunch so you can explain to me how you believe we can improve the situation."

In addition to the Personality Spectrum, multiple intelligences can also provide clues about communication style. The multiple intelligences table in this chapter (see p. 250) presents different communication strategies suggested for use in a study group for a criminal justice course.

Knowing yourself is an important aspect of successful communication. However, adapting to differences between yourself and others, such as generational differences, is essential as well.

Adjust to communication styles between generations

Like other groupings of people, generations come with personal and lifestyle characteristics that can affect intergenerational communication. Being able to recognize and adapt to differences caused by generation gaps can help you communicate successfully. Key 9.3 contains helpful communication tips for interacting with people of different ages.

MULTIPLE INTELLIGENCE STRATEGIES
for Communication

Apply Different Intelligences to Improve a Criminal Justice Study Group

INTELLIGENCE	USE MI STRATEGIES TO IMPROVE COMMUNICATION	APPLY MI COMMUNICATION STRATEGIES TO LEARN ABOUT THE U.S. COURT SYSTEM*
Verbal-Linguistic	• Find opportunities to express your thoughts and feelings to others—either in writing or in person. • Listening to words is at least as important as speaking them.	• Divide your group or pair into two parts. One person or subgroup should teach the historical development of the state court system. The other should teach the historical development of the federal court system.
Logical-Mathematical	• Allow yourself time to think through a problem before discussing it. Write out an argument on paper and rehearse it. • When communicating with others whose styles are not as logic-focused, ask specific questions to learn the facts you need.	• Ask questions to evaluate the effectiveness of the state and federal court systems: What works well? Where are the breakdowns? What improvements could you suggest?
Bodily-Kinesthetic	• Have an important talk while walking, running, or performing a task that does not involve concentration. • Work out to burn off excess energy before having an important discussion.	• Assign roles for group members to arrange a courtroom "set" in the classroom. Choose a case to recreate and perform a "mock trial" to illustrate an example of how a trial works in a state or federal court.
Visual-Spatial	• Make a drawing or diagram of points you want to communicate during an important discussion. • If you are in a formal classroom or work setting, use visual aids to explain your main points.	• In a pair or group, each individual or group half draws a diagram—one showing the structure of the state court system and one showing the structure of the federal court system.
Interpersonal	• If you tend to dominate group conversation, focus more on listening. • If you tend to prioritize listening to others, work on becoming more assertive about expressing your opinion.	• Select a landmark Supreme Court case. In a pair or group, each person or half of the group should argue one side of the case. Give everyone time to communicate clearly.
Intrapersonal	• Be as clear as possible when expressing what you know about yourself, and recognize that not all communicators may be self-aware. • When you have a difficult encounter, take time alone to decide how to communicate more effectively next time.	• Select the court system topic or segment that you know you will comprehend best. Suggest that you handle that topic or segment when the group divides up material for each group member to learn and present to the others.
Musical	• Before communicating difficult thoughts or feelings, work through them by writing a poem or song. • Be sensitive to the rhythms of a conversation. Sense when to voice your opinion and when to hang back.	• Create a song or rhythmic mnemonic device together that helps you remember the vocabulary associated with the court system, such as *appeal, jurisdiction,* and *judicial review.*
Naturalistic	• Use your ability to recognize patterns to evaluate communication situations. Employ patterns that work well and avoid those that do not. • When appropriate, make an analogy from the natural world of plants or animals to clarify a point in a conversation.	• In a pair or group, talk through the process of how a trial moves from the lowest state level all the way to the Supreme Court. Make a timeline that shows the pattern of how the case progresses.

*For information on the federal court system, see Frank Schmalleger, *Criminal Justice Today: An Introductory Text for the Twenty-First Century,* Upper Saddle River, NJ: Prentice Hall, 2005.

GENERATION	COMMUNICATION STYLE	COMMUNICATION CHALLENGES	TIPS FOR COMMUNICATING
Baby Boomers (1946–1964)	• Focus on personal growth and achievement • Politically correct • Inclined to use both face-to-face and electronic communication	• Can easily misunderstand instant electronic communication (texts, IMs, blogs, etc.) • Uncomfortable with conflict • Judgmental	• Be open and direct (baby boomers are the "show me" generation) • Use face-to-face or electronic communication • Provide details
Generation X (1965–1980)	• Casual • Pragmatic • Skeptical • Unimpressed by authority • Use e-mail	• Impatient • Cynical • Communication can be limited to e-mail or other noninteractive forms of communication	• Use e-mail as primary communication • Ask for feedback • Keep it short to hold attention • Use an informational style
Generation Y or Millennials (1980–1994)	• Value self-expression over self-control • Respect must be earned • Comfortable with online communication • Spend a lot of time online	• Overly focused on accessing information electronically • Teaching older generations to use technology erodes sense of respect for elders • Inexperience dealing with people	• Use e-mail, voice mail, and texts • Communicate with visuals • Use humor • Respect their knowledge • Encourage them to break rules when thinking

Note: The majority of people from all generations prefer face-to-face communication to written or electronic communication.

Source: Some information from a table on different generations by Greg Hammil, "Mixing and Managing Four Generations of Employees." *FDU Magazine,* Winter/Spring 2005 (www.fdu.edu/newspubs/magazine/05ws/generations.htm)

Know how to give and take criticism

Criticism can be either constructive or unconstructive. **Constructive criticism** is a practical problem-solving strategy, involving goodwill suggestions for improving a situation. In contrast, unconstructive criticism focuses on what went wrong, doesn't offer alternatives that might help solve the problem, and is often delivered negatively, creating bad feelings.

> CONSTRUCTIVE
> CRITICISM
> Criticism that promotes improvement or development.

When offered constructively, criticism can help bring about important changes. Consider a case in which someone has continually been late to study group sessions. Which comment from the group leader would better encourage a change in behavior?

> ▶ *Constructive.* The group leader talks privately with the student: "I've noticed that you've been late a lot. We count on you to contribute. Is there a problem that is keeping you from being on time? Can we help?"
>
> ▶ *Unconstructive.* The leader watches the student arrive late and says, in front of everyone, "If you can't start getting here on time, there's really no point in your coming."

At school, instructors criticize classwork, papers, and exams. On the job, criticism may come from supervisors, co-workers, or customers. No matter the source, constructive comments can help you grow. Be open to what you hear, and remember that most people want you to succeed.

■ *Offering constructive criticism.* Use the following strategies to increase its effectiveness:

> ▶ *Criticize the behavior, not the person.* Avoid personal attacks. "You've been late to five group meetings" is preferable to "You're lazy."
> ▶ *Define the specific problem.* Try to focus on the facts, backing them up with specific examples and minimizing emotions.
> ▶ *Suggest new approaches and offer help.* Talk about practical ways to handle the situation. Brainstorm creative options. Help the person feel supported.
> ▶ *Use a positive approach and hopeful language.* Express your belief that the person can turn the situation around.

■ *Receiving criticism.* When on criticism's receiving end, use the following techniques:

> ▶ *Analyze the comments.* Listen carefully and then evaluate what you hear. What does it mean? What is the intent? Try to let unconstructive comments go without responding.
> ▶ *Ask for suggestions on how to change your behavior.* Be open to what others say.
> ▶ *Summarize the criticism and your response.* The goal is for all to understand the situation.
> ▶ *Use a specific strategy.* Apply problem-solving skills to analyze the problem, brainstorm ways to change, choose a strategy, and take practical action to make it happen.

Criticism, as well as other thoughts and feelings, may be communicated nonverbally. You will become a more effective communicator if you understand body language.

Understand body language

Body language has an extraordinary capacity to express people's real feelings through gestures, eye movements, facial expressions, body positioning and posture, touching behaviors, vocal tone, and use of personal space. Why is it important to know how to analyze body language?

> ▶ *Nonverbal cues shade meaning.* What you say can mean different things depending on body positioning or vocal tone. The statement "That's a great idea" sounds positive. However, said while sitting with your arms and legs crossed and looking away, it may communicate that you dislike the idea. Said sarcastically, the tone may reveal that you consider the idea a joke.

> ▶ *Cultures use body language differently.* In the United States, for example, looking away from someone may be a sign of anger or distress; in Japan, the same behavior is usually a sign of respect.
> ▶ *Nonverbal communication strongly influences first impressions.* First impressions emerge from a combination of verbal and nonverbal cues. Nonverbal elements, including tone of voice, posture, eye contact, and speed and style of movement, usually come across first and strongest.

Although reading body language is not an exact science, the following practical strategies will help you use it to improve communication.

GET ANALYTICAL!

Give Constructive Criticism

Think of a situation that could be improved if you were able to offer constructive criticism to a friend or family member. Describe the situation and name the improvement you seek:

_____

_____

Imagine that you have a chance to speak to this person. First describe the setting—time, place, atmosphere—where you think you would be most successful:

_____

_____

Now develop your "script." Analyze the situation and decide on the most constructive approach. Use a separate sheet of paper to freewrite what you would say. Keep in mind the goal your communication seeks to achieve.

Finally, if you can, make your plan a reality. Will you do it?   Yes_____   No _____

If you have the conversation, was it worth it?   Yes_____   No _____

▶ *Pay attention to what is said through nonverbal cues.* Focus on your tone, your body position, and whether your cues reinforce or contradict your words. Then do the same for those with whom you are speaking. Look for the level of meaning in the physical.

▶ *Adjust behavior based on cultural differences.* In cross-cultural conversation, discover appropriate behavior by paying attention to what the other person does and by noting how others react to what you do. Then consider changes based on your observations.

▶ *Adjust body language to the person or situation.* What body language might you use when making a presentation in class? Meeting with your advisor? Confronting an angry co-worker? Think through how to use your physicality to communicate successfully.

One of the primary goals of successful communication is to build and maintain good relationships with family, friends, and others you encounter in daily life. All of the communication and cultural competence strategies you've read will contribute to that goal. Read on for more ways to navigate your relationships successfully.

How do you make the most of personal relationships?

Personal relationships with friends, classmates, spouses and partners, and parents can be sources of great satisfaction and inner peace. Good relationships can motivate you to do your best in school and on the job. When conflict arises or relationships fall apart, however, it can affect your ability to function in all areas of your life. Relationships have enormous power.

The following straightforward approaches can help make your personal relationships as good as they can be while also showing how to manage problems when things move in the wrong direction.

Use positive relationship strategies

When you devote time and energy to education, work, and activities, results are more likely to be positive. The same is true of human connections. Here are a few ways to nurture relationships:

▶ *Approach people and conversations with emotional intelligence.* The more you can notice feelings, understand what they mean, and handle them in ways that bring people closer to you instead of pushing them away, the better your relationships will be.

▶ *If you want a friend, be a friend.* If you treat others with the kind of loyalty and support that you appreciate, you are likely to receive the same in return.

▶ *Spend time with people you respect and admire.* Life is too short to hang out with people who bring you down or encourage you to ignore your values.

▶ *Work through tensions.* Negative feelings can fester when left unspoken. Get to the root of a problem by discussing it, compromising, forgiving, and moving on.

▶ *Take risks.* It can be frightening to reveal your deepest dreams and frustrations, to devote yourself to a friend, or to fall in love. However, if you open yourself up, you stand to gain the incredible benefits of companionship, which for most people outweigh the risks.

▶ *Find a dating pattern that suits you.* Some students date exclusively and commit early. Some students prefer to socialize in groups. Some students date casually. Be honest with yourself—and others—about what you want in a relationship.

▶ *If a relationship fails, find ways to cope.* When an important relationship becomes strained or breaks up, analyze the situation and choose practical strategies to move on. Some people need time alone; others want to be with friends and family. Some need a change of scene whereas others let off steam with exercise or other activities. Whatever you do, believe that in time you will emerge stronger from the experience.

Plug into communication technology without losing touch

Modern technology has revolutionized the way people communicate. Not even 30 years ago, the telephone, mail, and telegrams were the only alternatives to speaking in person. Today, you can call or text on a mobile phone; you can write a note via e-mail, instant message, or Twitter; you can communicate through blogs and chat rooms; and you can learn about one another on social networking sites such as Facebook.

Younger students, who grew up with technology, tend to use it most. A recent Kaiser Family Foundation study found that 8- to 18-year-olds averaged 6½ hours a day in various media interactions, including texting, cell phones, and networking sites. AOL reports that among Americans aged 16 to 21, 66 percent prefer instant messaging to e-mail.[5]

ELECTRONIC COMMUNICATION HAS POSITIVE AND NEGATIVE EFFECTS

Advantages of electronic communication	Disadvantages of electronic communication
Able to communicate faster.	Easy to reveal too much personal information, which can impact jobs or careers.
Able to communicate with more people at a time.	Easy to misunderstand or misinterpret messages.
Can build communication and multitasking skills.	Can be addictive and negatively impact study time.
Can build confidence for face-to-face situations.	Can limit interpersonal abilities and face-to-face interaction skills.

Although communication technologies allow you to communicate faster, more frequently, and with more people than ever before, they also have drawbacks. Key 9.4 shows some positive and negative aspects of communication technology. Keep in mind that revealing too much about yourself on social networking sites may cause trouble, because many employers check these sites for information about prospective job candidates.[6] See Appendix B for more information on social networking and media.

Notable among the problems with electronic communication is that it can hamper your ability to communicate in person and make friends. As freeing as it may be to communicate electronically in an anonymous, faceless environment, real life demands the ability to interact effectively face-to-face. The ideal is to communicate electronically to enhance real-time interaction rather than replace it, but this ideal can be tough to achieve.

Ultimately, you will develop your own personal communication "recipe," consisting of how—and how much—you want to communicate. Analyze situations carefully, think creatively, and make practical decisions about how to move forward. How do you prefer to communicate with others? What forms of communication do you overuse, and what effects result?

If you're concerned about the time you spend using forms of electronic communication, consider keeping a time journal. Any time you use an electronic device, log the time you start and stop. Review the log after a week, and think about any changes you need to make to bring your life back into balance.

Whether online or in person, conflict occurs within nearly every relationship. It can cause anger and, if taken too far, even violence. With effort, you can manage conflict and anger (and stay away from those who cannot).

Manage conflict

Conflicts, both large and small, arise when there is a clash of ideas or interests. You may have small conflicts with a housemate over a door left unlocked. You may have major conflicts with your partner about finances or with an instructor about a failing grade. Conflict, as unpleasant as it can be, is a natural element in the dynamic of getting along with others. Prevent it when you can—and when you can't, use problem-solving strategies to resolve it.

Conflict prevention strategies

Some strategies can help you to prevent conflict from starting in the first place.

■ **Send "I" messages.** "I" messages communicate your needs rather than attacking someone else. Creating these messages involves some simple rephrasing: "You didn't lock the door!" becomes "I was worried when I came home and found the door unlocked." "I" statements soften the conflict by highlighting the effects that the other person's actions have on you, rather than focusing on the person or the actions themselves.

■ **Be assertive.** Most people tend to express themselves in one of three ways—aggressively, assertively, or passively. *Aggressive* communicators focus primarily on their own needs and can become impatient when needs are not satisfied. *Passive* communicators focus primarily on the needs of others and often deny themselves power, causing frustration. *Assertive* communicators are able to declare and affirm their opinions while respecting the rights of others to do the same. Assertive behavior strikes a balance between aggression and passivity and promotes the most productive communication. Key 9.5 contrasts these three communication styles.

What can aggressive and passive communicators do to move toward a more assertive style? Aggressive communicators might take time before speaking, use "I" statements, listen to others, and avoid giving orders. Passive communicators might acknowledge anger, express opinions, exercise the right to make requests, and know that their ideas and feelings are important.

Conflict resolution

All too often, people deal with conflict through *avoidance* (a passive tactic that shuts down communication) or *escalation* (an aggressive tactic that often leads to fighting). Conflict resolution demands calm communication, motivation, and careful thinking. Use analytical, creative, and practical thinking skills to apply the problem-solving plan from Chapter 4 when things heat up.

Key 9.5 ASSERTIVENESS FOSTERS
SUCCESSFUL COMMUNICATION

AGGRESSIVE	ASSERTIVE	PASSIVE
Blaming, name-calling, and verbal insults: "You created this mess!"	Expressing oneself and letting others do the same: "I have thoughts about this—first, what is your opinion?"	Feeling that one has no right to express anger: "No, I'm fine."
Escalating arguments: "You'll do it my way, no matter what it takes."	Using "I" statements to defuse arguments: "I am uncomfortable with that choice and want to discuss it."	Avoiding arguments: "Whatever you want to do is fine."
Being demanding: "Do this."	Asking and giving reasons: "Please consider doing it this way, and here's why . . ."	Being noncommittal: "I'm not sure what the best way to handle this is."

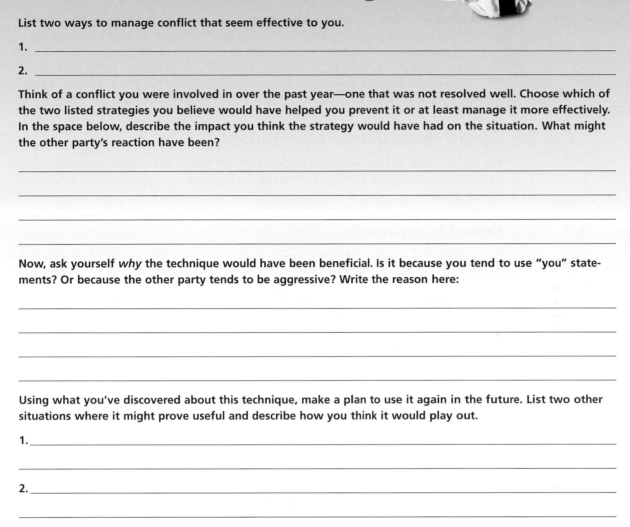

GET PRACTICAL!

Conflict Prevention Strategies

List two ways to manage conflict that seem effective to you.

1. _____

2. _____

Think of a conflict you were involved in over the past year—one that was not resolved well. Choose which of the two listed strategies you believe would have helped you prevent it or at least manage it more effectively. In the space below, describe the impact you think the strategy would have had on the situation. What might the other party's reaction have been?

_____

_____

_____

_____

Now, ask yourself *why* the technique would have been beneficial. Is it because you tend to use "you" statements? Or because the other party tends to be aggressive? Write the reason here:

_____

_____

_____

_____

Using what you've discovered about this technique, make a plan to use it again in the future. List two other situations where it might prove useful and describe how you think it would play out.

1. _____

_____

2. _____

_____

Trying to calm anger is an important part of resolving conflict. All people get angry at times—at people, events, and themselves. However, excessive anger can contaminate relationships, stifle communication, and turn friends and family away.

Manage anger

Strong emotions can get in the way of happiness and success. It is hard to concentrate on American history when you are raging over a nasty e-mail or a bad grade. Psychologists report that angry outbursts may actually make things worse. When you feel yourself losing control, try some of these practical anger management techniques.

▶ *Try to calm down.* Breathe. Slowly repeat a phrase like "Take it easy" or "Relax."

- *Change your environment.* Take a break from what's upsetting you. Take a walk, go to the gym, or see a movie. Come up with a creative idea that will help you settle down.
- *Think before you speak.* When angry, people tend to say the first thing that comes to mind, even if it's hurtful. Instead, wait until you are in control before you say something.
- *Problem-solve.* Instead of blowing up, analyze a challenging situation, make a plan, and begin. Even if it doesn't work, making the effort may help cool your anger.
- *Get help if you need it.* If you can't keep your anger in check, you may need the help of a counselor. Many schools provide professional mental health services to students.

Avoid destructive relationships

On the far end of the spectrum of conflict and anger are relationships that turn destructive. Knowing the facts about the following situations will help you to avoid them.

Sexual harassment

Both men and women can be victims, although the most common targets are women. There are two basic types of sexual harassment:

- *Quid pro quo harassment* refers to a request for a sexual activity in exchange for something else. "If you don't do X for me, I will fail you/fire you/make your life miserable."
- *Hostile environment harassment* indicates any situation in which sexually charged remarks, behavior, or items cause discomfort. Examples include lewd jokes and pornography.

If you feel degraded by anything that goes on at school or work, address the person responsible or speak to a dean or supervisor. College administrators will enforce rules against sexual harassment but they first have to know that an incident took place.

Violent relationships

Violent relationships among students do occur.[7] One in five students has experienced and reported at least one violent incident while dating, from being slapped to more serious violence. Although relationship violence can happen to anyone at any age, women in their teens and twenties are more likely to be victims than older women. One theory is that they are more uneasy about leaving destructive relationships or may believe that violence is normal.[8]

Analyze your situation and use problem-solving skills to come up with practical options. If you see warning signs such as controlling behavior, unpredictable mood swings, personality changes associated with alcohol and drugs, and outbursts of anger, consider ending the relationship. If you are being abused, call a shelter or abuse hotline or seek counseling at school or at a

KNOW ABOUT
DATE RAPE DRUGS

	APPEARANCE	EFFECT ON DRINK	RESPONSE
Rohypnol	A small white or green-gray pill. It can be round or oval.	Looks different. Dye in the pill causes clear liquids to turn bright blue and dark drinks to turn cloudy. However, there are pills available without dye.	Feelings similar to drunkenness: You may have trouble standing, your speech may slur, or you may pass out.
GHB	A colorless liquid, white powder, or a pill.	Tastes slightly salty. Often, it will be mixed with a sweet, fruity drink to mask the saltiness.	Dizziness, tremors, sweating, a slowed heart rate, and dream-like feelings.
Ketamine	A white powder or clear liquid.	Tastes normal. Ketamine is odorless and colorless.	Distorted perceptions of sight and sound, out-of-body experiences, impaired motor control, and problems breathing.

community center. If you believe that your life is in danger, get out and obtain a restraining order that requires your abuser to stay away from you.

Rape and date rape

Any intercourse or anal or oral penetration by a person against another person's will is defined as rape. Rape is primarily an act of rage and control, not sex. Acquaintance rape, or *date rape,* refers to sexual activity during an arranged social encounter that is against one partner's will, including situations where one partner is too drunk or drugged to give consent. Date rapists sometimes sedate victims with odorless, tasteless drugs like rohypnol, GHB, or ketamine, which are difficult to detect in a drink. See Key 9.6 for more information on each.

Prevention is the first line of defense. Communicate—clearly and early—what you want and don't want to do. Keep a cell phone handy. Avoid substances that impair awareness. Maintain control of your drink at all times (drink from a container you open, or watch your drink being mixed, and avoid open-source containers like punch bowls or trash cans). If you feel drunk without having had alcohol, or you notice stronger effects than usual, get help immediately.

If you are raped, whether by an acquaintance or a stranger, seek medical attention immediately. Talk to a friend or counselor. Consider reporting the incident to the police or to campus officials. And continue to get help through counseling, a rape survivor group, or a hotline.

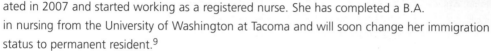

Case Wrap-up

What happened to Gaile? Gaile's Honors 100 course instructor Dr. Barbara Clinton, also the head of the Highline honors program, helped her see the positive in her challenges and express those strengths in her portfolio and resumé. After Gaile shared her financial concerns, Dr. Clinton helped her find—and win—scholarships for which she was eligible. With the confidence she gained from her mentor, Gaile got employment authorization from the Immigration and Naturalization Service and worked as a critical care nurse technician while finishing her studies. She graduated in 2007 and started working as a registered nurse. She has completed a B.A. in nursing from the University of Washington at Tacoma and will soon change her immigration status to permanent resident.[9]

What does this story mean for you? Everyone needs a person who can help to bring out strengths, give helpful information, and provide support and encouragement. Who could you find to be for you what Gaile considers Dr. Clinton—a resource for life? Make two lists, each with at least five people's names (friends, family, faculty, work acquaintances, anyone you know personally). One lists people whom you know well and are confident already support you and care about you. The other lists people you don't know as well but admire and feel that you could learn from. Choose one person from each list and brainstorm a short paragraph about what you think you need from that person as a mentor.

What effects go beyond your world? Your needs are important—and so are the needs of others. Reach beyond your world to mentor someone who could use your help. Check out www.mentoring.org as a start to find out more about what mentoring involves and what kinds of programs are already in place for people who want to mentor someone. Look into a program from that website, a program at your college or in your community, or start making more regular contact with someone in need on your own. Your presence will make a difference—both to the person you mentor as well as yourself.

Successful Intelligence *Wrap-up*

HERE'S HOW YOU HAVE
BUILT SKILLS IN **CHAPTER 9** :

ANALYTICAL THINKING	CREATIVE THINKING	PRACTICAL THINKING
• You examined how prejudice and racism can negatively affect your ability to communicate with a diverse population.	• You explored how shifting your perspective can help you adjust to different communication styles.	• You explored practical actions that help you to adapt to diverse cultures.
• In the Get Analytical exercise, you developed a script to tackle situations in need of constructive criticism and analyzed its effectiveness.	• In the Get Creative exercise, you looked at yourself and others from a new perspective and took action against the preconceptions of stereotypes.	• In the Get Practical exercise, you put conflict prevention strategies to work.
• You explored the positive and negative effects of using communication technology.	• You explored different possibilities for what body language may be communicating.	• You reviewed how to protect yourself against damaging relationships and avoid dangerous social situations.

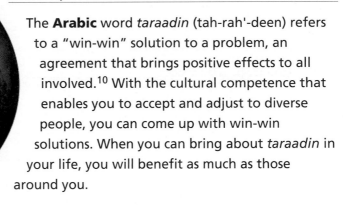

Word*for* Thought

The **Arabic** word *taraadin* (tah-rah'-deen) refers to a "win-win" solution to a problem, an agreement that brings positive effects to all involved.[10] With the cultural competence that enables you to accept and adjust to diverse people, you can come up with win-win solutions. When you can bring about *taraadin* in your life, you will benefit as much as those around you.

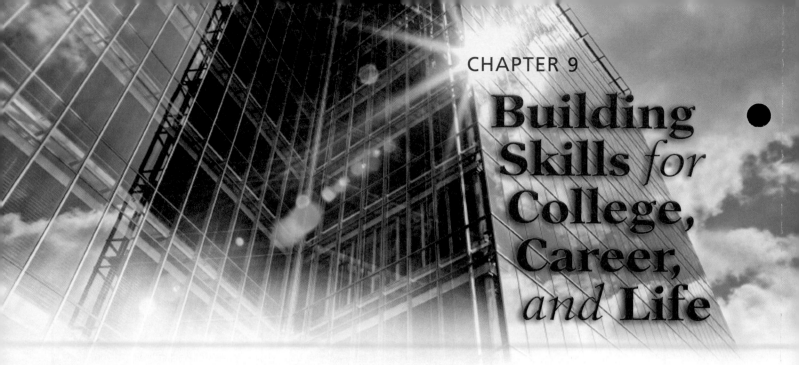

Building Skills for College, Career, and Life

Steps to Success

Make a Difference

BUILD BASIC SKILLS. Looking again at the five actions for cultural competence earlier in this chapter, reread the suggestions for Action 5: Adapt to Diverse Cultures on pages 245–246. For the three strategies listed here, give a real-life version (something you've done or know someone else has done). For example, by choosing to wear a blindfold for an entire day as part of a "Blind for a Day" experience, students are putting themselves in other people's shoes.

Look past external characteristics: _____

_____

Put yourself in other people's shoes: _____

_____

Help others in need: _____

_____

TAKE IT TO THE NEXT LEVEL. Make these strategies into personal plans. Rewrite any of them as specific actions you are willing to take in the next 6 months. For example, "Help others in need" might become "Sign up as a tutor for the Writing Center."

1. _____

2. _____

3. _____

MOVE TOWARD MASTERY. Choose one plan that you will put into action in the next 30 days (or even tomorrow, if you can). Choose wisely—recall your knowledge of SMART goals and pick the one that is most attainable and realistic. Circle your choice. Describe the goal of your plan—how you want to make a difference.

_____

_____

_____

_____

_____

Finally, do it. (Check here when you can honestly say you have taken your planned action.) ☐

Teamwork

Create Solutions Together

PROBLEM SOLVING CLOSE TO HOME

Goal: To work as a group on solving a real and relevant problem.

Time on task: 10 minutes as a group; 20 minutes as a class

Instructions: Divide into groups of two to five students. Assign one group member to take notes. Discuss the following questions, one at a time:

1. What are the three largest problems your school or community faces with regard to how people get along with and accept others?
2. What could we do to deal with these three problems? (At this point, if the group prefers, focus on one problem of your choosing.)
3. What can each individual student do to make improvements? (Talk specifically about what you think you can do.)

When all groups have finished, gather as a class and hear each group's responses. Observe the variety of problems and solutions. Notice whether more than one group came up with one or more of the same problems. If there is time, one person in the class, together with your instructor, could gather the responses to question 3 into an organized document that you can send to your school or local paper.

Writing

Build Intrapersonal and Communication Skills

Record your thoughts on paper, in a journal, or electronically.

EMOTIONAL INTELLIGENCE JOURNAL

Your experience with prejudice. Have you ever been discriminated against or experienced any other type of prejudice? Have you been on the other end and acted with prejudice yourself? Describe what happened and your feelings about the situation (if you have no personal experience, describe a situation you have seen or heard about). Outline an emotionally intelligent response that you feel would bring something positive or helpful out of the situation.

REAL-LIFE WRITING

Improve communication. Few students make use of the wealth of ideas and experience that academic advisors can offer. Think of a question you have—regarding a specific course, major, or academic situation—that your advisor might help you answer. Craft an e-mail in appropriate language to your advisor, and send it. Then, to stretch your communication skills, rewrite the same e-mail twice more: once in a format you would send to an instructor and once in a format appropriate for a friend. Send either or both of these if you think the response would be valuable to you.

Personal Portfolio

Prepare for Career Success

WRITE A JOB INTERVIEW COVER LETTER

21st Century Learning Building Blocks

- Communication and Collaboration
- Financial, Economic, Business, and Entrepreneurial Literacy
- Leadership and Responsibility

Complete the following in your electronic portfolio or on separate sheets of paper.

To secure a job interview, you will have to put your communication skills to the test—on paper—by creating a cover letter to accompany your resumé. With this key communication tool, you can pull your best selling points out of your resumé and highlight them to a potential employer.

For your portfolio, write a one-page, three-paragraph cover letter to a prospective employer, describing your background and explaining your value to the company. Be creative—you may use fictitious names, but select a career and industry that interest you. Use the format shown in Key 9.7.

Introductory paragraph: Start with a statement that convinces the employer to read on. You might name a person the employer knows who told you to write or refer to something positive about the company that you read in the newspaper or on the Internet. Identify the position for which you are applying, and tell the employer that you are interested in working for the company.

Middle paragraph: Sell your value. Try to convince the employer that hiring you will help the company in some way. Center your "sales effort" on your experience in school and the workplace. If possible, tie your qualifications to the needs of the company. Refer indirectly to your enclosed resumé.

Final paragraph: Close with a call to action. Ask the employer to call you, or tell the employer to expect your call to arrange an interview.

Exchange your first draft with a classmate. Read each other's letter and make marginal notes to improve impact and persuasiveness, writing style, grammar, punctuation, and spelling. Discuss and then make corrections. Create a final draft for your portfolio.

Social Networking

CONTROL YOUR COMMUNICATION

Many people these days are overwhelmed by the volume of electronic communication that comes their way each day. Make sure that LinkedIn is more helpful than overwhelming by establishing how you want to be contacted. Sign in to your account and proceed as follows:

- Click on "Edit My Profile."
- Scroll to the bottom, and click on the Edit button next to "Contact Settings."
- Indicate what type of messages you would like to accept on LinkedIn.
- Indicate what kinds of opportunities you are looking to receive from the network you are building.
- If you choose, include advice to users contacting you. (For example, if you feel like it will take too much time to accept InMail as well as manage your regular e-mail, you can instruct users to contact you using your regular e-mail account.)

First name Last name
1234 Your Street
City, ST 12345

November 1, 2008

Ms. Prospective Employer
Prospective Company
5432 Their Street
City, ST 54321

Dear Ms. Employer:

On the advice of Mr. X, career center advisor at Y College, I am writing to inquire about the position of production assistant at KWKW Radio. I read the description of the job and your company on the career center's employment-opportunity bulletin board, and I would like to apply for the position.

I am a senior at Y College and will graduate this spring with a degree in communications. Since my junior year when I declared my major, I have wanted to pursue a career in radio. For the last year I have worked as a production intern at KCOL Radio, the college's station, and have occasionally filled in as a disc jockey on the evening news show. I enjoy being on the air, but my primary interest is production and programming. My enclosed resumé will tell you more about my background and experience.

I would be pleased to talk with you in person about the position. You can reach me anytime at 555/555–5555 or by e-mail at xxxx@xx.com. Thank you for your consideration, and I look forward to meeting you.

Sincerely,

Sign Your Name Here

First name Last name

Enclosure(s) *(use this notation if you have included a resumé or other item with your letter)*

Wellness and Stress Management

Staying Healthy in Mind and Body

What Would You Do?

Think about this problem as you read, and consider how you would approach it. This chapter examines ways to manage stress through health maintenance, handle physical and mental health issues, and make effective decisions about substances and sex.

Joe Martin grew up in the housing projects of Miami, Florida, in an environment in which six of his friends died—either from drug involvement or murder—by the time he was in high school. No one in his family even considered going to college. Although he had friends and family members who were in prison or caught up in crime and drugs, his mother reminded him to never accept the situation. He knew things could be different, but wasn't sure how.

Joe planned to join the military after high school. However, when he was a senior, he had a change of heart. Looking at his college-bound friends, he decided that if they could go to college, so could he. When he told the Navy recruiter he wanted to attend school, the man said he was not college material. With his low SAT scores, the recruiter said, "they won't let you drive by college, let alone get in."

This challenge lit a fire under Joe and got him applying to colleges. Having barely passed high school and dogged by those low SAT scores, he got turned down by so many schools he lost count. Finally he was accepted at Okaloosa Walton Junior College, thanks to open enrollment. His first day at Okaloosa was literally his first day ever on a college campus. He was completely ignorant of the college culture and social life. He didn't drink and, due to his childhood experience, jumped when he heard noises and was nervous. He had taken on two jobs to pay for his education. Joe wasn't sure how he was going to handle the stress of college. (To be continued . . .)

Joe's determination to move beyond the past has led him to build a healthy life with his son. You'll learn more about Joe, and revisit his situation, within the chapter.

In this chapter, you'll explore answers to these questions:

> How can focusing on health help you manage stress? p. 268

> How can you make effective decisions about alcohol, tobacco, and drugs? p. 279

> How can you make effective decisions about sex? p. 284

ANALYTICAL

CREATIVE

PRACTICAL

STATUS *Check*

▶ *How effectively do you maintain your personal wellness?*

"Successfully intelligent people are flexible in adapting to the roles they need to fulfill. They recognize that they will have to change the way they work to fit the task and situation at hand, and then they analyze what these changes will have to be and make them."

—Robert Sternberg

How can focusing on health
help you manage stress?

Going to school, working full- or part-time, raising children, participating in activities, doing an internship, volunteering—it can add up to a lot of time and stress. If you're feeling high levels of *stress*—the physical or mental strain that occurs when your body reacts to pressure—you're not alone. Stress levels tend to be high among college students.

Dealing with stress can be an everyday challenge. The greater your stress, the greater the toll it may take on your health and on your ability to achieve your goals. However, this doesn't mean that you should try to get rid of *all* stress. Moderate stress can actually be helpful, motivating you to do well on tests, finish assignments on time, and prepare for presentations. Key 10.1, based on research conducted by Drs. Robert M. Yerkes and John E. Dodson, shows that stress can be helpful or harmful, depending on how much you experience.

Psychologists T. H. Holmes and R. H. Rahe found that stress is linked to both positive *and* negative changes. Key 10.2 is an adaptation of their stress-rating scale, designed for college students. Based on events you've encountered within the last year, it delivers a "stress score" that indicates your likelihood of having or developing a stress-related health problem. Knowing the factors that create stress can help you learn to handle demands and ongoing pressures.

STRESS LEVELS CAN HELP OR HINDER PERFORMANCE

Key 10.1

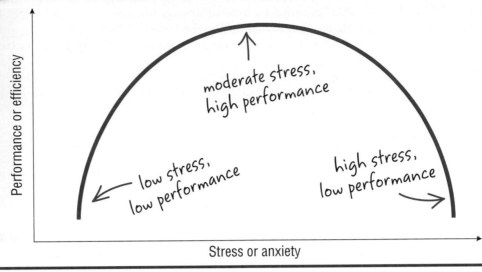

Performance or efficiency (vertical axis)

moderate stress, high performance

low stress, low performance

high stress, low performance

Stress or anxiety

Source: From *Your Maximum Mind* by Herbert Benson M.D., copyright © 1987 by Random House, Inc. Used by permission of Crown Publishers, a division of Random House, Inc.

USE THIS ASSESSMENT TO DETERMINE YOUR "STRESS SCORE"

Key 10.2

Add up the number of points corresponding to the events you have experienced in the past 12 months.

1. Death of a close family member	_____ 100	
2. Death of a close friend	_____ 73	
3. Divorce between parents	_____ 65	
4. Jail term	_____ 63	
5. Major personal injury or illness	_____ 63	
6. Marriage	_____ 58	
7. Firing from a job	_____ 50	
8. Failing an important course	_____ 47	
9. Change in health of a family member	_____ 45	
10. Sex problem	_____ 44	
11. Serious argument with close friend	_____ 40	
12. Change in financial status	_____ 39	
13. Change in major	_____ 39	
14. Trouble with parents	_____ 39	
15. New girlfriend or boyfriend	_____ 37	

16. Increase in work load at school	_____ 37
17. Outstanding personal achievement	_____ 36
18. First quarter/semester in college	_____ 36
19. Change in living conditions	_____ 31
20. Serious argument with an instructor	_____ 30
21. Lower grades than expected	_____ 29
22. Change in sleeping habits	_____ 29
23. Change in social activities	_____ 29
24. Change in eating habits	_____ 28
25. Chronic car trouble	_____ 26
26. Change in the number of family gatherings	_____ 26
27. Too many missed classes	_____ 25
28. Change of college	_____ 24
29. Dropping more than one class	_____ 23
30. Minor traffic violations	_____ 20

Total: _____

If your score is 300 or higher, you are at high risk for developing a health problem. If your score is between 150 and 300, you have a 50 percent chance of experiencing a serious health change within 2 years. If you score is below 150, you have a 30 percent chance of a serious health change.

Source: Paul Insel and Walton Roth, *Core Concepts in Health* (4th ed.). Palo Alto, CA: Mayfield Publishing Company, 1985, p. 29.

Being as physically and mentally healthy as possible is a crucial stress management tool. You are making a difference in your health, recent studies say, by simply being in school. Scientists and researchers who study aging report that statistically, more education is linked to longer life. Some potential causes for this link may be that education teaches cause-and-effect thinking, helping people to plan ahead and make better choices for their health, and that educated people tend to be better equipped to **delay gratification**, reducing risky behavior.[1]

No one is able to make healthy choices and delay gratification all the time. However, you can pledge to do your best to maintain your physical and mental health.

Eat well

Making intelligent choices about what you eat can lead to more energy, better general health, and an improved quality of life. However, this is easier said than done, for two reasons in particular. One is that the *food environment* in which most people live—characterized by an overabundance of unhealthful food choices combined with the cheaper pricing of many of the worst alternatives—does not support people's efforts to choose well.[2]

The second reason is that college life can make it tough to eat right. Students spend hours sitting in class or studying and tend to eat on the run; students may also build social events around food or eat as a reaction to stress. Many new students find that the "freshman fifteen"—referring to the fifteen pounds that freshmen tend to gain in the first year of school—is an unpleasant reality.

Healthy eating requires *balance* (varying your diet) and *moderation* (eating reasonable amounts). Key 10.3 presents some ways to incorporate both into your life.

To get a good picture of where you are and where you want to be, evaluate your eating habits, understand obesity and its effects, and target your ideal weight.

■ *Evaluate your eating habits.* Evaluate a day's food intake by writing down everything that you ate during the previous day and calculating the total calories. You may even want to log in a week's worth of eating. Go to http://mypyramid.gov for guidance about the types and amounts of food you should be getting. The same site also has a tool with which you can create a food guide customized to your age, gender, and habitual level of physical activity. If your eating habits fall short of your ideal plan, make changes in your eating and exercise to move in a more healthful direction.

■ *Understand the effects of obesity.* The term obese refers to having a BMI of thirty or over (overweight refers to having a BMI of twenty-five to twenty-nine). The overweight and obese make up the majority of the U.S. population, with 66 percent currently falling into these two groups.[3] Obesity is a major risk factor in the development of adult-onset diabetes, coronary heart disease, high blood pressure, stroke, cancer, and other illnesses. Additionally, studies have shown that overweight job applicants tend to be reviewed more negatively during interviews, and that overweight employees tend to be paid less than normal weight people in the same jobs and have a reduced chance of promotion.[4]

■ *Target your ideal weight.* The Centers for Disease Control has information about weight ranges.

CREATE POSITIVE
FOOD HABITS

- Vary what you eat, focusing on fruits and vegetables
- Choose foods with limited fat, cholesterol, and trans fats
- Replace sugary snacks with fresh or dried fruit
- Keep healthy snacks within reach
- Limit calorie-heavy alcoholic drinks and sugar-heavy soda
- Notice and reduce portion sizes
- Plan meals and minimize late-night eating sprees
- Substitute other activities for stress-related eating
- Get help from weight-loss organizations and on-campus support

The **body mass index (BMI)** calculator at www.cdc.gov/healthyweight/ assessing/bmi/index.html can help you see whether you fall within a healthy range or would be considered overweight or obese. If you want to lose weight, set a reasonable goal and work toward it at a pace of approximately 1 to 2 pounds a week. You may also want to consult health professionals, enroll in a reputable and reasonable weight-loss program, and incorporate regular exercise into your life. Striving for the goal of reducing your BMI will improve not only your physical well-being but your mental health as well.

> BODY MASS INDEX (BMI)
> The ratio of your weight to your height.

Get exercise

Being physically fit enhances your general health, increases your energy, and helps you cope with stress. During physical activity, the brain releases endorphins, chemical compounds that have a positive and calming effect on the body. Regular exercise builds discipline, time management, and motivation that can also contribute to academic success.

Always check with a physician before beginning an exercise program, and adjust your program to your physical needs and fitness level. If you don't currently exercise, walking daily is a good way to begin.

student profile

Kelly Thompson
Colorado State University, Fort Collins

About me:

I am a sophomore attending Colorado State University. I always played sports growing up and I have always been very active. Coming to college has changed my active lifestyle; I find it more difficult to be active because I am so busy academically.

What I focus on:

School can be stressful and time-consuming. I have had to learn how to prioritize my active lifestyle and my academics. It is hard having time to stay active, but I make time to work out. Gradually, I changed my lifestyle and started going to bed earlier. Waking up an hour earlier creates more time for me to work out, which helps me to be more productive with the rest of my day. I plan ahead of time. I organize my calendar with tests and due dates at the beginning of the semester. I have now learned how to prioritize my time in order to be academically successful and maintain the active lifestyle that I love and that keeps me balanced.

What will help me in the workplace:

Being organized and able to prioritize will be useful in the workplace when managing various events and business projects. Planning upfront in order to keep ahead of the workplace pace will help me to maintain a high performance level at work and still have time for an active lifestyle in my off hours. I look forward to creating a working lifestyle that is productive and healthy.

Types of exercise

There are three general categories of exercise: cardiovascular, strength, and flexibility (see Key 10.4). The type you choose depends on your exercise goals, available equipment, your time and fitness level, and other factors.

Some exercises, such as lifting weights or biking, fall primarily into one category. Others, like power yoga, combine elements of two or all three. For maximum benefit, try alternating exercise methods through *cross-training* (alternating types of exercise and combining elements from different types of exercise). For example, if you lift weights, use a stationary bike for cardiovascular work and build stretching into your workout.

Make exercise a priority

Busy students often have trouble getting to the gym, even when there is a fully equipped athletic center on campus. Use these ideas to help make exercise a priority, even in the busiest weeks:

▶ Walk to classes and meetings. When you reach your building, use the stairs.
▶ Use your school's fitness facilities.

VARY YOUR **EXERCISE ACTIVITIES** AMONG THESE THREE TYPES OF TRAINING

Cardiovascular Training

- Strengthens your heart and lungs
- Examples: swimming, running, skating, aerobic dancing, and biking

Strength Training

- Strengthens different muscle groups
- Examples: weight machines, free weights, push-ups, and abdominal crunches

Flexibility Training

- Increases muscle flexibility
- Examples: yoga and stretching exercises such as dynamic, ballistic, static active, and static passive

▶ Play team recreational sports at school or in your community.
▶ Take up swing or ballroom dancing.
▶ Find activities you can do outside of a club, such as running or pickup basketball.
▶ Work out with friends or family to combine socializing and exercise.

Being fit is a lifelong pursuit that is never "done." Furthermore, because your body is constantly changing, reevaluate your exercise program on a regular basis to maximize its benefits. Finally, remember that being healthy is part of your personal responsibility. Think preventatively about your well-being and take charge of your choices.

Get enough sleep

College students are often sleep deprived. While research indicates that students need 8 to 9 hours of sleep a night to function well, studies show that students average 6 to 7 hours—and often get much less.[5] Inadequate sleep hinders your ability to concentrate, raises stress levels, and makes you more susceptible to illness. It can also increase your risk of auto accidents. According to Dr. Tracy Kuo at the Stanford Sleep Disorders Clinic, "A sleepy driver is just as dangerous as a drunk driver."[6]

Students, overwhelmed with responsibilities, often feel that they have no choice but to prioritize schoolwork over sleep. Some stay up regularly until the

If you overload on caffeine, it can become less effective and may disrupt your sleep patterns. Choose your coffee breaks carefully and try to avoid drinking caffeine late at night.
© Shutterstock

wee hours of the morning to study. Others pull "all-nighters" from time to time to get through a tough project or paper.

For the sake of your health and your GPA, find a way to get enough sleep. Look for such tell-tale symptoms of sleep deprivation as being groggy in the morning, dozing off during the day, or needing caffeine to make it through the day. Sleep expert Gregg D. Jacobs has the following practical suggestions for improving sleep habits:[7]

▶ *Reduce consumption of alcohol and caffeine.* Caffeine may keep you awake, especially if you drink it late. Alcohol causes you to sleep lightly, making you feel less rested when you awaken.

▶ *Exercise regularly.* Regular exercise, especially in the afternoon or early evening, promotes sleep.

▶ *Take naps.* Taking short afternoon naps can reduce the effects of sleep deprivation.

▶ *Be consistent.* Try to establish somewhat regular times to wake up and go to bed.

▶ *Manage your environment.* Wear something comfortable, turn down the lights, and keep the room cool. Use earplugs, soft music, or white noise if you're dealing with outside distractions.

Sleep is crucial for both stress reduction and normal development. The multiple intelligences table on the facing page presents different strategies for managing the stress of writing a final paper in a human development course, many of which involve time management tools that will help a student avoid writing the whole paper during a last-minute all-nighter.

Stay safe

Staying safe is another part of staying well and reducing stress. Crime is a reality on campus as it is in any community. Alcohol- and drug-related offenses may occur more frequently than other crimes on campus. By law, colleges are required to report crime statistics yearly. Check www.securityoncampus.org for a link to statistics by school and for other helpful information.

Making intelligent choices is a crucial part of staying safe. Take these practical measures to prevent incidents that jeopardize your well-being.

▶ *Be aware of safety issues.* Every college has its particular issues—problematic areas of the campus, particular celebrations that get out of hand, and bad habits such as students propping open security doors. With awareness, you can steer clear of problems and even work to improve them.

▶ *Avoid situations that present clear dangers.* Don't walk or exercise alone at night, especially in isolated areas. Don't work or study alone in a building. If a person looks suspicious, contact someone who can help. In Joe's case, he needed to leave his neighborhood entirely in order to take his life in a more positive direction.

▶ *Avoid drugs or overuse of alcohol.* Anything that impairs judgment makes you vulnerable to assault. Avoid driving while impaired or riding with someone who has taken drugs or alcohol.

▶ *Avoid people who make you uneasy.* If a fellow student gives you bad feelings, avoid situations that place you alone together. Speak to an instructor if you feel threatened.

MULTIPLE INTELLIGENCE STRATEGIES
for Stress Management

Apply Different Intelligences to Reduce the Stress of Writing a Final Paper in Human Development

INTELLIGENCE	USE MI STRATEGIES TO MANAGE STRESS	APPLY MI STRESS-MANAGEMENT STRATEGIES TO HANDLE A FINAL PAPER ON THE STAGES OF PHYSICAL DEVELOPMENT IN INFANCY*
Verbal-Linguistic	• Keep a journal of what situations, people, or events cause stress. • Write letters or e-mail friends about your problems.	• Early in the writing process, summarize in writing the different reflex reactions common in normal newborns.
Logical-Mathematical	• Think through problems using a problem-solving process, and devise a detailed plan. • Analyze the negative and positive effects that may result from a stressful situation.	• Analyze the functions of each of the six different states of being in infants: crying, waking activity, alert activity, drowsiness, irregular sleep, and regular sleep.
Bodily-Kinesthetic	• Choose a physical activity that helps you release tension—running, yoga, team sports—and do it regularly. • Plan physical activities during free time—go for a hike, take a bike ride, go dancing with friends.	• When you need a break from writing or research, re-create the classic experiment to test infants' depth perception, known as the "visual cliff."
Visual-Spatial	• Enjoy things that appeal to you visually—visit an exhibit, see an art film, shoot photos with your camera. • Use a visual organizer to plan out a solution to a stressful problem.	• Create a visual aid comparing the development of a full-term infant with that of a premature infant.
Interpersonal	• Talk with people who care about you and are supportive. • Shift your focus by being a good listener to others who need to talk about their stresses.	• Interview the parents of a premature infant to learn about the special challenges the family faced during the first year.
Intrapersonal	• Schedule downtime when you can think through what is causing stress. • Allow yourself 5 minutes a day of meditation where you visualize a positive way in which you want a stressful situation to resolve.	• Separate your scheduled working times over a period of weeks so that you have time to contemplate individual development topics in between sessions.
Musical	• Listen to music that relaxes, inspires, and/or energizes you. • Write a song about what is bothering you.	• Listen to lullabies from different countries. Compare and contrast melody and rhythm. Link observations to what you know about infants' auditory systems.
Naturalistic	• See whether the things that cause you stress fall into categories that can give you helpful ideas about how to handle situations. • If nature is calming for you, interact with it—spend time outdoors, watch nature-focused TV, read books or articles on nature or science.	• Visit the newborns at your local hospital during visiting hours. Search for common characteristics—for example, reflex responses and states of wakefulness or sleep. Create a chart to report your findings.

*For information on the newborn, see Robert S. Feldman, *Child Development*, 4th ed., Upper Saddle River, NJ: Prentice Hall, 2007.

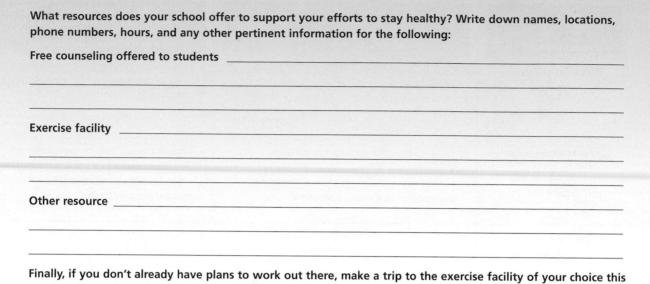

GET PRACTICAL!

Find Health Resources

What resources does your school offer to support your efforts to stay healthy? Write down names, locations, phone numbers, hours, and any other pertinent information for the following:

Free counseling offered to students _____

_____

_____

Exercise facility _____

_____

_____

Other resource _____

_____

_____

Finally, if you don't already have plans to work out there, make a trip to the exercise facility of your choice this week and see what it has to offer.

▶ *Be wary of dangers online.* Don't give out personal information online to people whom you don't know well. If you have a MySpace or Facebook page, be careful about the text and photos you post. If you feel that someone is harassing you on e-mail or IM, contact an advisor or counselor who can help you address the problem.

▶ *Review your immunizations.* Your safety and well-being in college also depends on your ability to adequately fight off infections, diseases, and anything else that could put off your education. Be aware of your medical records and make it a point to check your vaccine schedule regularly. Not only will you be protecting yourself, but you'll be protecting your fellow students too. College students living on campus should pay particular notice to the meningococcal meningitis vaccine, and women under 26 should look into the HPV (human papillomavirus) vaccine.

However, it is not enough to have a healthy body. Your well-being also depends on a healthy mind.

Address mental health issues

Staying positive about who you are, making hopeful plans for the future, and building resilience to cope with setbacks will all help you target positive mental health. However, some people experience emotional disorders that make it more difficult than usual to cope with life's stressful situations. If you recognize

KNOW THE **CAUSES AND SYMPTOMS** OF DEPRESSION

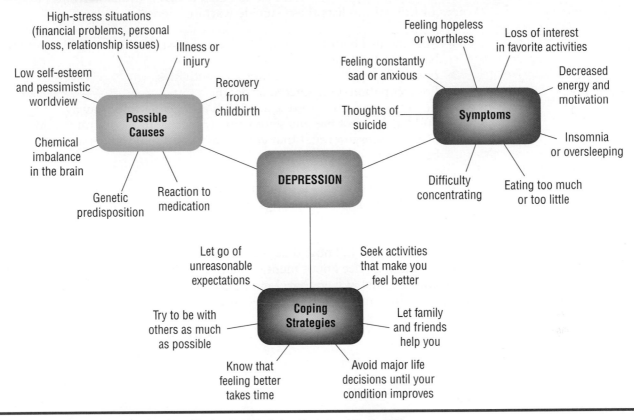

Possible Causes
- High-stress situations (financial problems, personal loss, relationship issues)
- Illness or injury
- Low self-esteem and pessimistic worldview
- Recovery from childbirth
- Chemical imbalance in the brain
- Genetic predisposition
- Reaction to medication

DEPRESSION

Symptoms
- Feeling hopeless or worthless
- Loss of interest in favorite activities
- Feeling constantly sad or anxious
- Decreased energy and motivation
- Thoughts of suicide
- Insomnia or oversleeping
- Difficulty concentrating
- Eating too much or too little

Coping Strategies
- Let go of unreasonable expectations
- Seek activities that make you feel better
- Try to be with others as much as possible
- Let family and friends help you
- Know that feeling better takes time
- Avoid major life decisions until your condition improves

Source: Depression, National Institutes of Health publication 02-3561, National Institutes of Health, 2002.

yourself in any of the following descriptions, take practical steps to improve your health. Most student health centers and campus counseling centers provide both medical and psychological help or referrals for students with emotional disorders.

Depression

Almost everyone has experienced sadness after setbacks such as the end of a relationship or failing a course. However, a *depressive disorder* is an illness, not a mental state that can be escaped by trying to "snap out of it." It is also fairly common among college students. Recent research reports that nearly half of surveyed students reported feelings of depression at some point, with over 30 percent saying that the level of depression made it difficult to function at times.[8] Key 10.5 shows possible causes of depression as well as some typical symptoms.

If you recognize some of these symptoms in yourself, seek help from a professional. Depression requires a medical evaluation and is treatable. Most student health centers and campus counseling centers provide both medical and psychological help or referrals for students with emotional disorders. For some people, adequate sleep, a regular exercise program, a healthy diet, and the passage of time are enough to lessen stress and ease the disorder. For others, medication is important.

At its worst, depression can lead to suicide. SAVE (Suicide Awareness Voices of Education) lists these suicide warning signs:[9]

▶ Statements about hopelessness or worthlessness: "The world would be better without me."
▶ Loss of interest in people, things, or activities.
▶ Preoccupation with suicide or death.
▶ Visiting or calling family and friends and giving things away.
▶ Sudden sense of happiness or calm. (A decision to commit suicide often brings a sense of relief that convinces others that the person "seemed to be on an upswing.")

If you recognize these symptoms in someone you know, begin talking with the person about his or her feelings. Then do everything you can to convince the individual to see a doctor or mental health professional. Don't keep your concerns a secret; sound an alarm that may save a life. If you recognize these symptoms in yourself, know that you can find help if you reach out.

For general advice about mental health issues, see Campus Mental Health: Know Your Rights! at www.bazelon.org/l21/rightsguide.htm. The right help can change—or, in some cases, even save—your life.

Eating disorders

Every year, millions of people develop serious and sometimes life-threatening *eating disorders*, including anorexia nervosa, bulimia, and binge eating disorder. Negative effects of these disorders range from fertility and obesity issues to digestive tract and other organ damage, heart failure, and even death. There are three basic types of eating disorders:[10]

▶ *Anorexia nervosa.* People with anorexia nervosa restrict their eating and become dangerously underweight. They may also engage in overexercising, vomiting, and abuse of diuretics and laxatives. Anorexia nervosa is often linked to excessive anxiety and perfectionism.

▶ *Bulimia nervosa.* People with bulimia engage in "binge episodes," which involve eating excessive amounts of foods and feeling out of control. Following the binge, the person feels remorseful and attempts to purge the calories through self-induced vomiting, laxative abuse, excessive exercise, or fasting.

▶ *Binge eating disorder.* Binge eating disorder is the most common eating disorder. People with this condition eat large amounts of food and feel out of control, similar to those with bulimia, but they do not purge after a binge episode. They also tend to eat unusually fast, eat in secret, eat until they feel uncomfortably full, and feel ashamed of their eating behavior.

The stresses of college lead some students to experiment with alcohol, tobacco, and other potentially addictive substances. Although these substances may alleviate stress temporarily, they have potentially serious consequences.

How can you make *effective decisions* about alcohol, tobacco, and drugs?

Abusing alcohol, tobacco, and drugs adds significantly to stress levels and can cause financial struggles, emotional traumas, family and financial upheaval, health problems, and even death. As you read the information in this section, think about the effects of your actions on yourself and others, and continually look for new and better ways to make positive, life-affirming choices.

When you can take a break, try out different ways to have fun. These students escape to some open space for a picnic.
© Jeff Greenberg/Photo Researchers

Alcohol

Alcohol is a depressant and the most frequently abused drug on campus. Even a few drinks affect thinking and muscle coordination. Heavy drinking can damage the liver, the digestive system, and brain cells and also impair the central nervous system. Prolonged use can lead to (addiction,) making it seem impossible to quit. In addition, alcohol contributes to the deaths of 75,000 people every year through both alcohol-related illnesses and accidents involving drunk drivers.[11]

> ADDICTION
> The compulsive need for a habit-forming substance.

According to the Centers for Disease Control (CDC), your tolerance and reaction to alcohol can depend on a variety of factors, including but not limited to age, gender, race or ethnicity, physical condition, the amount of food consumed before drinking, how quickly alcohol is consumed, use of drugs or prescription medications, and family history.[12] Key 10.6 shows the varying levels of drinking behaviors defined by the CDC.

Of all alcohol consumption, *binge drinking* (see Key 10.6) is associated with the greatest problems. Consistently an issue on college campuses, students who binge drink are more likely to miss classes, perform poorly, experience physical problems (memory loss, headache, stomach issues), become depressed, and engage in unplanned or unsafe sex.[13]

If you drink, think carefully about the effects on your health, safety, and academic performance. The Get Analytical exercise on page 281, a self-test, will help you analyze your habits.

Tobacco

The 2007 National Survey on Drug Use and Health (NSDUH) found that nearly 25.6 percent of full-time college students reported smoking at least once in the month before they were surveyed, and 41.2 percent of students attending less than full time had smoked at least once within the previous month.[14]

Many students use tobacco as a stress reliever and then become hooked on nicotine, a highly addictive drug found in all tobacco products.

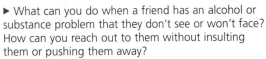

Change the CONVERSATION

Challenge yourself and your friends to ask—and answer—tough questions. Use the following to inspire discussion in pairs or groups.

▶ What can you do when a friend has an alcohol or substance problem that they don't see or won't face? How can you reach out to them without insulting them or pushing them away?

▶ Sometimes friends are calming—and sometimes they increase stress. How can you decide when to turn to a friend and when to turn away?

▶ **CONSIDER THE CASE:** Imagine you are an experienced student meeting Joe when he began college. How would you help him adjust and manage stress? Discuss at least three helpful actions.

UNDERSTAND LEVELS OF
ALCOHOL CONSUMPTION

Key 10.6

		Men	Women
Moderate Drinking	Lower-risk drinking pattern equaling "having no more than 1 drink per day for women and no more than 2 drinks per day for men."	🍷🍷 per day	🍷 per day
Heavy Drinking	For men, heavy drinking is typically defined as consuming an average of more than 2 drinks per day. For women, heavy drinking is typically defined as consuming an average of more than 1 drink per day.	🍷🍷 + per day	🍷 + per day
Binge Drinking	"A pattern of alcohol consumption that brings the blood alcohol concentration (BAC) level to 0.08% or above . . . usually corresponds to 5 or more drinks on a single occasion for men or 4 or more drinks on a single occasion for women, generally within about 2 hours."	🍷🍷🍷🍷🍷 in 2 hrs.	🍷🍷🍷🍷 in 2 hrs.

Source: www.cdc.gov/alcohol/index.htm

Nicotine's immediate effects may include an increase in blood pressure and heart rate, sweating, and throat irritation. Long-term effects may include high blood pressure, bronchitis and emphysema, stomach ulcers, heart disease, and cancer.

In recent years, the health dangers of **secondhand smoke** have been recognized. Living with smokers or being around them on a regular basis is linked to about 3,000 lung cancer deaths and 46,000 heart disease deaths per year in nonsmokers.[15] This awareness has led many colleges (and local jurisdictions) to ban smoking in classrooms and other public spaces and even in dorm rooms. More and more companies, aware of the risk, are banning smoking in the workplace or even refusing to hire people who smoke.[16]

If you smoke regularly, you can quit with motivation, perseverence, and outside help. The following tips provide practical suggestions for quitting:[17]

> ► Get support and encouragement from a health care provider, a "quit smoking" program, a support group, and friends and family.
> ► Keep a "smoking journal" to learn more about what leads you to smoke and how you can avoid the temptation.
> ► Set goals. Set a quit date and tell people who care about you. Make and keep medical appointments.
> ► Try a nicotine patch or nicotine gum, and be sure to use it consistently.
> ► Remove tobacco products from your environment—home, car, workplace—and avoid situations that increase your desire to smoke, such as being around other smokers and drinking heavily.
> ► Find other ways to keep busy and lower stress, such as exercise or other activities you enjoy.

The positive effects of quitting—increased life expectancy, lung capacity, and energy, as well as significant financial savings—may inspire any smoker to

SECONDHAND SMOKE
Smoke in the air exhaled by smokers or given off by cigarettes, cigars, or pipes.

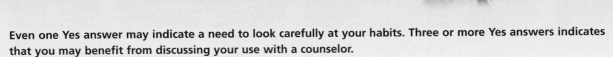

Evaluate Your Substance Use

Even one Yes answer may indicate a need to look carefully at your habits. Three or more Yes answers indicates that you may benefit from discussing your use with a counselor.

Within the Last Year:

Y   N   1.   Have you tried to stop drinking or taking drugs but found that you couldn't do so for long?

Y   N   2.   Do you get tired of people telling you they're concerned about your drinking or drug use?

Y   N   3.   Have you felt guilty about your drinking or drug use?

Y   N   4.   Have you felt that you needed a drink or drugs in the morning—as an "eye-opener"—in order to cope with a hangover?

Y   N   5.   Do you drink or use drugs alone?

Y   N   6.   Do you drink or use drugs every day?

Y   N   7.   Have you found yourself regularly thinking or saying "I need" a drink or any type of drug?

Y   N   8.   Have you lied about or concealed your drinking or drug use?

Y   N   9.   Do you drink or use drugs to escape worries, problems, mistakes, or shyness?

Y   N   10. Do you find you need increasingly larger amounts of drugs or alcohol in order to achieve a desired effect?

Y   N   11. Have you forgotten what happened while drinking or using drugs because you had a blackout?

Y   N   12. Have you spent a lot of time, energy, or money getting alcohol or drugs?

Y   N   13. Has your drinking or drug use caused you to neglect friends, your partner, your children, or other family members, or caused other problems at home?

Y   N   14. Have you gotten into an argument or a fight that was alcohol or drug related?

Y   N   15. Has your drinking or drug use caused you to miss class, fail a test, or ignore schoolwork?

Y   N   16. Have you been choosing to drink or use drugs instead of attending social events or performing other activities you used to enjoy?

Y   N   17. Has your drinking or drug use affected your efficiency on the job or caused you to fail to show up at work?

Y   N   18. Have you continued to drink or use drugs despite any physical problems or health risks that your use has caused or made worse?

Y   N   19. Have you driven a car or performed any other potentially dangerous tasks while under the influence of alcohol or drugs?

Y   N   20. Have you had a drug- or alcohol-related legal problem or arrest (possession, use, disorderly conduct, driving while intoxicated, etc.)?

Source: Adapted from the Criteria for Substance Dependence and Criteria for Substance Abuse in the *Diagnostic and Statistical Manual of Mental Disorders,* Fourth Edition, published by the American Psychiatric Association, Washington, D.C., and from materials entitled "Are You an Alcoholic?" developed by Johns Hopkins University.

make a lifestyle change. If you're interested in quitting, the Centers for Disease Control provides a website with quitting resources at www.cdc.gov/tobacco/quit_smoking/how_to_quit/index.htm.

   In order to assess the level of your potential addiction, you may want to take the self-test in the exercise on this page, replacing the words *alcohol* or *drugs* with *cigarettes* or *smoking*. Think about your results, weigh your options, and make a responsible choice.

DRUGS HAVE
POTENT EFFECTS ON THE USER

DRUG	DRUG CATEGORY	USERS' EFFECTS	POTENTIAL PHYSICAL EFFECTS, SHORT-TERM AND LONG-TERM	DANGER OF DEPENDENCE
Cocaine (also called *coke, blow, snow*) **and crack cocaine** (also called *crack* or *rock*)	Stimulant	Alert, stimulated, excited, energetic, confident	Nervousness, mood swings, sexual problems, stroke or convulsions, psychoses, paranoia, coma at large doses	Strong
Alcohol	Depressant	Sedated, relaxed, loose	Impaired brain function; impaired reflexes and judgment; cirrhosis; impaired blood production; greater risk of cancer, heart attack, and stroke	Strong with regular, heavy use
Marijuana and hashish (also called *pot, weed, herb*)	Cannabinol	Euphoric, mellow, little sensation of time, paranoid	Impaired judgment and coordination, bronchitis and asthma, lung and throat cancers, anxiety, lack of energy and motivation, hormone and fertility problems	Moderate
Heroin (also called *smack, dope, horse*) **and codeine**	Opiates	Warm, relaxed, without pain, without anxiety	Infection of organs, inflammation of the heart, convulsions, abscesses, risk of needle-transmitted diseases such as hepatitis and HIV	Strong with heavy use
Lysergic acid diethylamide (LSD) (also called *acid, blotter, trips*)	Hallucinogen	Heightened sensual perception, hallucinations, distortions of sight and sound, little sense of time	Impaired brain function, paranoia, agitation and confusion, flashbacks	Insubstantial
Hallucinogenic mushrooms (psilocybin mushrooms or *Amanita muscaria*) (also called *shrooms, magic mushrooms*)	Hallucinogen	Strong emotions, hallucinations, distortions of sight and sound, "out of body" experience	Paranoia, agitation, poisoning	Insubstantial
Glue, aerosols (also called *whippets, poppers, rush*)	Inhalants	Giddy, lightheaded, dizzy, excited	Damage to brain, liver, lungs, and kidneys; suffocation; heart failure	Insubstantial
Ecstasy (also called *X, XTC, vitamin E*)	Stimulant	Heightened sensual perception, relaxed, clear, fearless	Fatigue, anxiety, depression, heart arrhythmia, hyperthermia from lack of fluid intake during use	Insubstantial
Ephedrine (also called *chi powder, zest*)	Stimulant	Energetic	Anxiety, elevated blood pressure, heart palpitations, memory loss, stroke, psychosis, insomnia	Strong
Gamma hydroxyl butyrate (GHB) (also called *G, liquid ecstasy, goop*)	Depressant	Uninhibited, relaxed, euphoric	Anxiety, vertigo, increased heart rate, delirium, agitation	Strong
Ketamine (also called *K, Special K, vitamin K*)	Anesthetic	Dreamy, floating, having an "out of body" sensation, numb	Neuroses, disruptions in consciousness, reduced ability to move	Strong

DRUG	DRUG CATEGORY	USERS EFFECTS	POTENTIAL PHYSICAL EFFECTS, SHORT-TERM AND LONG-TERM	DANGER OF DEPENDENCE
OxyContin (also called *Oxy, OC, legal heroin*)	Analgesic (containing opiate)	Relaxed, detached, without pain or anxiety	Overdose death can result when users ingest or inhale crushed time-release pills, or take them in conjunction with alcohol or narcotics	Moderate, with long-term use
Anabolic steroids (also called *roids, juice, hype*)	Steroid	Increased muscle strength and physical performance, energetic	Stunted growth, mood swings, male-pattern baldness, breast development (in men) or body hair development (in women), mood swings, liver damage, insomnia, aggression, irritability	Insubstantial
Methamphetamine (also called *meth, speed, crank*)	Stimulant	Euphoric, confident, alert, energetic	Seizures, heart attack, strokes, vein damage (if injected), sleeplessness, hallucinations, high blood pressure, paranoia, psychoses, depression, anxiety, loss of appetite	Strong, especially if taken by smoking

Source: SafetyFirst, Drug Policy Alliance (www.safety1st.org/drugfacts.html).

Drugs

Illicit drug use is a perennial problem on college campuses. The NSDUH reports that over 37 percent of college students surveyed had used illicit drugs in the year prior to the survey.[18] College students may use drugs to relieve stress, be accepted by peers, or just try something new.

In most cases, the negative consequences of drug use outweigh any temporary high. Drug use violates federal, state, and local laws, and you may be arrested, tried, and imprisoned for possessing even a small amount of drugs. You can jeopardize your reputation, your student status, and your ability to get a job if you are caught using drugs or if drug use impairs your performance. Finally, long-term drug use can damage your body and mind. Key 10.7 has comprehensive information about the most commonly used illicit drugs.

You are responsible for analyzing the potential consequences of what you introduce into your body. Joe, looking at those consequences, chose to walk in another direction. Ask questions like the following:

▶ Why do I want to do this?
▶ Am I taking drugs to escape from other problems?
▶ What positive and negative effects might my behavior have?
▶ Why do others want me to take drugs, and what do I really think of these people?
▶ How would my drug use affect the people in my life?

Use the self-test on page 281 to assess your relationship with drugs. If you believe you have a problem, read the following section on steps that can help you get your life back on track.

Facing addiction

If you think you may be addicted, seek help through counseling and medical services, detoxification centers, and support groups. Because substances often cause physical changes and psychological dependence, habits are tough to break and quitting may involve a painful withdrawal. Asking for help isn't an admission of failure but a courageous move to reclaim your life.

Even one Yes answer on the self-test may indicate that you need to evaluate your alcohol or drug use and to monitor it more carefully. If you answered Yes to three or more questions, you may benefit from talking to a professional about your use and the problems it may be causing.

Working through substance abuse problems can lead to restored health and self-respect. Helpful resources can provide guidance for generating options and developing practical plans for recovery.

> ▶ *Counseling and medical care.* You can find help from school-based, private, government-funded, or workplace-sponsored resources. Ask your school's counseling or health center, your personal physician, or a local hospital for a referral.
> ▶ *Detoxification ("detox") centers.* If you have a severe addiction, you may need a controlled environment where you can separate yourself completely from drugs or alcohol.
> ▶ *Support groups.* The effectiveness of Alcoholics Anonymous (AA) has led to other support groups for addicts such as Overeaters Anonymous (OA) and Narcotics Anonymous (NA).

Part of being physically and mentally healthy involves thinking through sexual decisions and being aware of sexually transmitted infections that can derail your plans. The decisions you make now have consequences for the rest of your life.

How can you make effective decisions about sex?

What sexuality means to you and the role it plays in your life are personal choices. However, the physical act of sex can go beyond the private realm. Individual sexual conduct can result in an unexpected pregnancy or exposure to *sexually transmitted diseases or infections* (STDs and STIs). These consequences affect everyone involved in the sexual act and, often, their families.

Just as your success in school depends on your ability to manage time, your success in school can also depend on making choices that maintain health and safety—yours as well as those of the person with whom you are involved. Analyze sexual issues carefully, weighing the positive and negative effects of your choices. Ask questions like the following:

> ▶ Is this what I really want? Does it fit with my values?
> ▶ Do I feel ready or do I feel pressured? Does this choice cause stress for me?
> ▶ Is this the right person/moment/situation? Does my partner truly care for me and not just for what we might be doing? Will this enhance or damage our emotional relationship?
> ▶ Do I have what I need to prevent pregnancy and exposure to STIs? If not, is having unprotected sex worth the risk?

GET CREATIVE!

Find More Fun

Sometimes, college students get involved in potentially unsafe activities because it seems like there isn't anything else to do. Use your creativity to find enjoyable activities to choose from when you hang out with friends. Check your resources: What possibilities can you find at your student union, student activities center, college or local arts organizations, athletic organizations, various clubs, nature groups? Could you go hiking? Paint pottery? Check out a baseball game? Run a 5K? Try a new kind of cuisine? Volunteer at a children's hospital ward? See a play?

Expand your horizons. List ten specific activities available to you.

1. _____
2. _____
3. _____
4. _____
5. _____

6. _____
7. _____
8. _____
9. _____
10. _____

Birth control

Using *birth control* is a choice, and it is not for everyone. For some, using any kind of birth control goes against religious or personal beliefs. Others may want to have children. Many sexually active people, however, choose one or more methods of birth control.

Evaluate the pros and cons of each option for yourself and your partner. Consider cost, ease of use, reliability, comfort, and protection against STIs. Communicate with your partner and together make a choice that is comfortable for both of you. For more information, check your library, the Internet, or a bookstore; talk to your doctor; or ask a counselor at the student health center. Key 10.8 describes established methods, with effectiveness percentages and STI prevention based on proper and regular use.

Sexually transmitted infections

STIs spread through sexual contact (intercourse or other sexual activity that involves contact with the genitals). All are highly contagious. The only birth control methods that offer protection are the male and female condoms (latex or polyurethane only), which prevent skin-to-skin contact. Have a doctor examine any irregularity or discomfort as soon as you detect it. Key 10.9 describes common STIs.

AIDS and HIV

The most serious STI is AIDS (acquired immune deficiency syndrome), caused by the human immunodeficiency virus (HIV). AIDS has no cure and can result in death. Medical science continues to develop drugs to combat

MAKE AN **EDUCATED DECISION**
ABOUT BIRTH CONTROL

METHOD	APPROXIMATE EFFECTIVENESS	PREVENTS STIs?	DESCRIPTION
Abstinence	100%	Only if no sexual activity occurs	Just saying no. No intercourse means no risk of pregnancy. However, alternative modes of sexual activity can still spread STIs.
Condom	85% (95% with spermicide)	Yes, if made of latex	A sheath that fits over the penis or within the vagina and prevents sperm from entering the vagina.
Diaphragm, cervical cap, or shield	85%	No	A bendable rubber cap that fits over the cervix and pelvic bone inside the vagina (the cervical cap and shield are smaller and fit over the cervix only). The diaphragm and cervical cap must be fitted initially by a gynecologist. All must be used with a spermicide.
Oral contraceptives (the Pill)	99% with perfect use, 92% for typical users	No	A dosage of hormones taken daily by a woman, preventing the ovaries from releasing eggs. Side effects can include headaches, weight gain, and increased chances of blood clotting. Various brands and dosages; must be prescribed by a gynecologist.
Injectable contraceptives (Depo-Provera)	97%	No	An injection that a woman must receive from a doctor every few months. Possible side effects may resemble those of oral contraceptives.
Vaginal ring (NuvaRing)	92%	No	A ring inserted into the vagina that releases hormones. Must be replaced monthly. Possible side effects may resemble those of oral contraceptives.
Spermicidal foams, jellies, inserts	71% if used alone	No	Usually used with diaphragms or condoms to enhance effectiveness, they have an ingredient that kills sperm cells (but not STIs). They stay effective for a limited period of time after insertion.
Intrauterine device (IUD)	99%	No	A small coil of wire inserted into the uterus by a gynecologist (who must also remove it). Prevents fertilized eggs from implanting in the uterine wall. May or may not have a hormone component. Possible side effects include increased or abnormal bleeding.
Tubal ligation	Nearly 100%	No	Surgery for women that cuts and ties the fallopian tubes, preventing eggs from traveling to the uterus. Difficult and expensive to reverse. Recommended for those who do not want any, or any more, children.
Vasectomy	Nearly 100%	No	Surgery for men that blocks the tube that delivers sperm to the penis. Like tubal ligation, difficult to reverse and only recommended for those who don't want any, or any more, children.
Rhythm method	Variable	No	Abstaining from intercourse during the ovulation segment of the woman's menstrual cycle. Can be difficult to time and may not account for cycle irregularities.
Withdrawal	Variable	No	Pulling the penis out of the vagina before ejaculation. Unreliable, because some sperm can escape in the fluid released prior to ejaculation. Dependent on a controlled partner.

Source: MayoClinic.com (www.mayoclinic.com/health/birth-control/BI99999/PAGE=BI00020)

DISEASE	SYMPTOMS	HEALTH PROBLEMS IF UNTREATED	TREATMENTS
Chlamydia	Discharge, painful urination, swollen or painful joints, change in menstrual periods for women	Can cause pelvic inflammatory disease (PID) in women, which can lead to sterility or ectopic pregnancies; infection; miscarriage or premature birth.	Curable with full course of antibiotics; avoid sex until treatment is complete.
Gonorrhea	Discharge, burning while urinating	Can cause PID, swelling of testicles and penis, arthritis, skin problems, infections.	Usually curable with antibiotics; however, certain strains are becoming resistant to medication.
Genital herpes	Blisterlike itchy sores in the genital area, headache, fever, chills	Symptoms may subside and then reoccur, often in response to high stress levels; carriers can transmit the virus even when it is dormant.	No cure; some medications, such as Acyclovir, reduce and help heal the sores and may shorten recurring outbreaks.
Syphilis	A genital sore lasting 1 to 5 weeks, followed by a rash, fatigue, fever, sore throat, headaches, swollen glands	If it lasts over 4 years, it can cause blindness, destruction of bone, insanity, or heart failure; can cause death or deformity of a child born to an infected woman.	Curable with full course of antibiotics.
Human papilloma virus (HPV, or genital warts)	Genital itching and irritation, small clusters of warts	Can increase risk of cervical cancer in women; virus may remain in body and cause recurrences even when warts are removed.	Treatable with drugs applied to warts or various kinds of wart removal surgery. Vaccine (Gardasil) newly available; most effective when given to women before exposure to HPV.
Hepatitis B	Fatigue, poor appetite, vomiting, jaundice, hives	Some carriers will have few symptoms; others may develop chronic liver disease that may lead to other diseases of the liver.	No cure; some will recover, some will not. Bed rest may help ease symptoms. Vaccine is available.

AIDS and related illnesses. Although the drugs can slow the progression of the infection and extend life expectancy, there is currently no known cure.

People acquire HIV through sexual relations, by sharing hypodermic needles for drug use, and by receiving infected blood transfusions. You cannot become infected except through blood, semen, or vaginal fluid contact with one of your own fluids. Breastmilk is the only other fluid that can carry the disease. Therefore, it is unlikely you can contract HIV from toilet seats, hugging, kissing, or sharing a glass. Other than not having sex at all condoms are the best defense against AIDS. Always use a latex condom, because natural skin condoms may let the virus pass through. Avoid petroleum jelly, which can destroy latex. Be wary of "safe sex fatigue," which leads young and healthy people to be less vigilant about using condoms for every sexual encounter. Although some people dislike using condoms, it's a small price to pay for preserving your life.

To be safe, have an HIV test done at your doctor's office or at a government-sponsored clinic. Your school's health department may also administer HIV tests, and home HIV tests are available over the counter.

Consider requiring that any sexual partner be tested as well. If you are infected, inform all sexual partners and seek medical assistance. If you're interested in contacting support organizations in your area, call the National AIDS Hotline at 1-800-342-AIDS.

Case Wrap-up

What happened to Joe? The stress of what Joe had left behind made college seem full of promise by contrast. Driven to succeed, he prioritized his work—and ended up with a 4.0 his very first semester. Feeling a new sort of stress from the challenge of maintaining this success, he worked hard through the rest of his experience, refusing drink and drugs. He socialized "strategically," making friends in groups that he joined, so that he could have fun in the context of something he wanted to accomplish. He finished community college, transferred to the University of West Florida, and graduated at the top of his class with a bachelor's degree. After college, a motivational speaker helped him realize he could make a living by communicating important ideas—by teaching and talking—to students growing up in poverty. Now, having earned master's and doctoral degrees and spoken to more than a quarter of a million people about student success through courses, speeches, books, and recorded programs, he can reach students all over the globe through his website, Real World University. As a professor and educational consultant, he is driven to help students aim for wellness and make the most of their gifts and talents.

What does this mean for you? Joe worked hard to move away from environments, people, and situations that he thought would not allow him to realize his dreams. Think about an environment, person, or situation that is causing you stress and preventing you from truly living well. Consider ways in which you can move away. Be creative—your move may not be all at once, it may not be right away, and it may not follow a logical progression. Thinking about the benefit you may receive can help you take the first step.

What effects go beyond your world? One person making positive changes sets an example for people connected to that person—an example that, if others follow, can have an effect that stretches through many different networks of people. Joe Martin's website at www.rwuniversity.com is his way of putting his positive changes out there for others to think about and follow if they choose. Be bold and make a change that your friends will notice. Drink less, sleep more, reduce late-night junk food fests, start seeing a counselor regularly for a mental health issue—whatever is important for your wellness. If some question your choice—maybe because they miss you at the parties, for example—be right up front with them about what you are doing and why. Maybe you will inspire others to think—and even to follow your lead.

Successful Intelligence *Wrap-up*

HERE'S HOW YOU HAVE BUILT SKILLS IN **CHAPTER 10** :

ANALYTICAL THINKING	CREATIVE THINKING	PRACTICAL THINKING
❯ You explored how focusing on your health can help you manage your stress levels.	❯ By reading about the ways stress impacts your well-being, you became inspired to think broadly about fun ways to reduce the effect of stress on your health.	❯ Understanding that a healthy level of stress is helpful in many situations, you devised easy, everyday methods to use it effectively.
❯ You questioned how to make calculated, informed decisions about alcohol, tobacco, drugs, and sex.	❯ You explored the controversies surrounding alcohol, sex, and tobacco, which inspired you to find your method of coping.	❯ Learning about the realities of drugs, tobacco, alcohol, and sex allowed you to think practically about how these topics can affect your life.
❯ By evaluating your level of substance abuse in the Get Analytical exercise, you noted whether you need to seek help, stay aware, or keep on the same track.	❯ By brainstorming fun outlets in the Get Creative exercise, you made a plan to avoid potentially dangerous activities you may have sought out of boredom.	❯ By developing your list of helpful resources in the Get Practical exercise, you devised a roadmap toward becoming and staying healthy.

Word*for*Thought

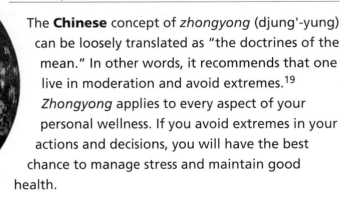

The **Chinese** concept of *zhongyong* (djung'-yung) can be loosely translated as "the doctrines of the mean." In other words, it recommends that one live in moderation and avoid extremes.[19] *Zhongyong* applies to every aspect of your personal wellness. If you avoid extremes in your actions and decisions, you will have the best chance to manage stress and maintain good health.

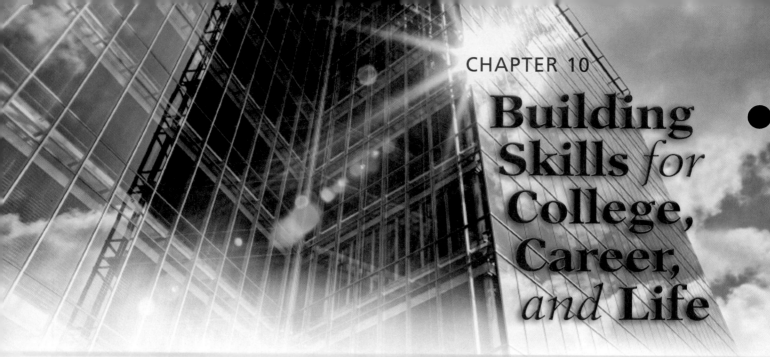

Building Skills *for* College, Career, *and* Life

Steps to Success

Move Toward Better Health

BUILD BASIC SKILLS. Pick a topic—eating, drinking, sleeping, sexual activity—that holds some kind of issue for you. Describe your behavior and your attitude toward what you do.

Example

Issue: binge drinking

Behavior: I binge drink probably once a week.

Attitude: I don't think it's any big deal. I like using it to escape.

Your turn

Issue:

_____

_____

Behavior:

_____

_____

Attitude:

_____

_____

Question to think about: Is it worth it?

TAKE IT TO THE NEXT LEVEL. To examine whether your behavior is a problem, note positive and negative effects. To continue the example:

> *Positive effects:* I have fun with my friends. I feel confident, accepted, social.

> *Negative effects:* I feel foggy the next day. I miss class. I'm irritable.

Your turn

Positive effects:

_____

_____

Negative effects:

_____

_____

MOVE TOWARD MASTERY. Based on the effects of your behavior, think about what you want to be different and why. Then come up with changes you could make. For example, the binge drinker might consider cutting back on one drinking outing a week and investigating one new social activity that does not involve drinking.

How you might change your behavior:

_____

_____

_____

How you might change your attitude:

_____

_____

_____

Positive effects you think these changes would have:

_____

_____

_____

Choose two actions to take—one that would improve your attitude and one that would improve your behavior—that you think would have the most positive effect for you. Commit to these actions with specific plans and put positive change in motion.

Attitude improvement plan:

_____

_____

_____

Behavior improvement plan:

_____

_____

_____

Teamwork

Create Solutions Together

ACTIVELY DEAL WITH STRESS

Goal: To benefit from different ideas about how to cope with stress.

Time on task: 5 minutes by yourself, 10 minutes in discussion with the class, and 20 minutes in groups

Instructions: Complete Part One first by yourself and then with the class; for Part Two, get into four groups and follow the steps.

Part One: By yourself, look back at the Holmes-Rahe scale on page 269. Note the stressors you have experienced in the past year and tally your "stress score." In a class discussion, identify the four stressors from the scale most commonly experienced by the members of the class.

Part Two: Once the class has identified the four biggest stressors, divide into four groups according to each person's most important stressor (redistribute some people if the group sizes are unbalanced). Each group should address the following points:

- Discuss the particular stressor and its effects on people.
- Brainstorm solutions and strategies, making sure to include choices that relate to wellness (eating, sleeping, exercise, substances).
- List your best coping strategies and present them to the class.

Groups may want to make extra copies of the lists so that every member of the class has four, one for each stressor.

Writing

Build Intrapersonal and Communication Skills

Record your thoughts on paper, in a journal, or electronically.

EMOTIONAL INTELLIGENCE JOURNAL

Addiction. Discuss how you feel about addiction in any form—to alcohol, drugs, food, sex, the Internet, gambling—whether or not it you have had direct or indirect experience with it. Imagine that a close friend or family member has a dangerous addiction of some kind. Use your emotional intelligence to describe how you would address the problem with that person in order to have the best possible outcome.

REAL-LIFE WRITING

Health on campus. Think about what you consider to be the most significant health issue at your school—safety, alcohol or drug abuse, smoking, weight management, or another problem. Write a 500-word editorial for your school paper on the topic, describing the details of the problem and proposing one or more solutions. For example, if weight control is a problem, you might suggest changing the contents of the drink vending machines in the student union. When you are done, consider submitting your editorial to the paper (have an instructor or peer review it before you send it in).

Personal Portfolio

Prepare for Career Success

WELLNESS AT WORK

21st Century Learning Building Blocks
- Initiative and Self-Direction
- Critical Thinking and Problem Solving
- Information Literacy

Complete the following in your electronic portfolio or separately on paper.

In the working world, mental and physical health is a big issue, in part because many companies are putting pressure on their employees to do more in less time. Resulting issues such as increased work burdens, late nights, and keeping your cell phone on for work calls on weekends or at off hours create a great deal of stress for workers. In addition, health care costs are on the rise for companies, in terms of both paying for health insurance and dealing with the cost of lost work time when employees are out sick.

Taking responsibility for your health early is not only good for your body, but it can also make you a more valuable employee. Knowing your health risks and how to prevent them lets employers know that you value your job enough to protect it. Part of that knowledge comes from getting routine screenings from a doctor or health clinic. Health screenings test various aspects of your health for normalcy and can highlight potential threats. Below is a list of health attributes doctors test in a screening. Using the Internet or your library, research the listed items. For each, describe first why the item is important to your overall health. Then, include information about what the normal range is for this item, and what numbers (high, low, or both) indicate a risk. Finally, describe what steps you can take to improve if you have high-risk results for this item.

- Hemoglobin
- Hematocrit
- Glucose
- Potassium
- Chloride
- Magnesium
- Calcium
- Iron
- Cholesterol

Social Networking

FILL OUT YOUR PROFILE

LinkedIn helps you see how much of your profile you have completed. Use the information it gives you to make your profile even more complete—and therefore more useful. Plus the closer you get to your goal (completing the profile), the less stress!

- Sign in to your account and click on "Profile."
- Look at the bar on the right side of the screen that shows "profile completeness." Note your percentage.
- Below that, read the list of "Profile Completion Tips" that it recommends.
- Click on "Why do this?" to get an even better idea of how the site can help you.
- Finally, act on LinkedIn's recommendations to increase your profile completeness percentage. With the knowledge that a higher percentage may help you grow your network more effectively, aim to hit 75 percent or higher.

Managing Money

Living Within Your Means

What Would You Do?

Think about this problem as you read, and consider how you would approach it. This chapter helps you get to know yourself as a money manager. It offers thoughtful strategies for using money wisely in the present so that you have more financial stability in the future.

Alina Brown uses her father's old laptop for schoolwork and got a wireless card so that she could research on the Internet, receive e-mail, and do her banking online. Two weeks ago, Alina got an e-mail that said her bank account was locked. The e-mail instructed her to click on a link to go to a site where she could unlock the account. She read the e-mail, followed the directions, and was satisfied that she had solved the problem.

The next day, Alina got a call from her bank. After seeing two fairly large withdrawals the day before, the bank officer wanted to confirm they were authorized. Alina reported that she had made no withdrawals, and after some further questioning the officer let her know that she had fallen victim to an e-mail "phishing" scam.

Then she got a call from her father, a co-signer on the account. "Alina, I just got a call from the bank and—" "Dad, listen, it isn't my fault, it was an e-mail scam," Alina quickly responded. "There's still some money left and the bank moved it to a new account." "SOME money? Not enough to cover your tuition that's due in a month!" her father said. "This isn't like getting your credit card stolen, where the card company gives back your money. What made you think that e-mail was

real?" Alina paused. "Well, uh, when I clicked on the link it sent me to a site that looked exactly like our bank. I just entered my information like it told me to do, like I've done before on the bank's website." "Alina. You can't believe everything you read. How carefully did you think before giving out such important information? I really don't know what we're going to do." (To be continued . . .)

Rapidly changing technology has brought new challenges to money management. You'll learn more about Alina, and revisit her situation, within the chapter.

In this chapter, you'll explore answers to these questions:

> What does money mean in your life? p. 296

> How can you create and use a budget? p. 299

> How can you increase income through work and financial aid? p. 304

> What will help you use credit cards wisely? p. 309

> How can you plan for a solid financial future? p. 314

ANALYTICAL

CREATIVE

PRACTICAL

For each statement, circle the number that feels right to you, from 1 for "not at all true for me" to 5 for "very true for me."

▶ I am aware of my personal views on money spending and saving.	1 2 3 4 5
▶ I know how much money I have to spend each month.	1 2 3 4 5
▶ I know the difference between things that I want and things that I need, and I shop accordingly.	1 2 3 4 5
▶ I control my spending by using a monthly budget.	1 2 3 4 5
▶ I successfully balance my responsibilities at work and at school.	1 2 3 4 5
▶ I understand the benefits and responsibilities of financial aid.	1 2 3 4 5
▶ I know the current interest rates on my credit cards.	1 2 3 4 5
▶ I know my credit rating and its potential effect on my financial future.	1 2 3 4 5
▶ I add to a savings account or CD regularly.	1 2 3 4 5
▶ I have begun planning for my retirement.	1 2 3 4 5

Each of the topics in these statements is covered in this chapter. Note those statements for which you circled a 3 or lower. Skim the chapter to see where those topics appear, and pay special attention to them as you read, learn, and apply new strategies.

REMEMBER: *No matter how effectively you manage your money, you can improve with effort and practice.*

"Successfully intelligent people have the ability to delay gratification. People who are unable to delay gratification seek rewards for achieving short-term goals but miss the larger rewards they could receive from accomplishing more important, long-term goals."

—Robert Sternberg

What does **money mean** *in your life?*

According to the American Psychological Association, nearly three out of four people in the United States cite money as the number one stressor in their lives.[1] Adding the high cost of college tuition to the normal list of financial obligations means that, for the vast majority of college students, money is tight. This situation is especially true for self-supporting students, who may have to cover living and family expenses in addition to funds for tuition, books, and other college fees.

Thinking analytically, creatively, and practically about money management can help relieve money-related stress and increase control. Start first by analyzing who you are as a money manager and examining the relationship between your money and your time.

How you perceive and use money

Your spending and saving behavior and attitudes about money reflect your values, goals, and self-image. You might spend your money as soon as you earn it, or you might save for the future. You might charge everything, make cash purchases only, or do something in between. You might handle finances online, as Alina prefers to do. You might measure your success in life in

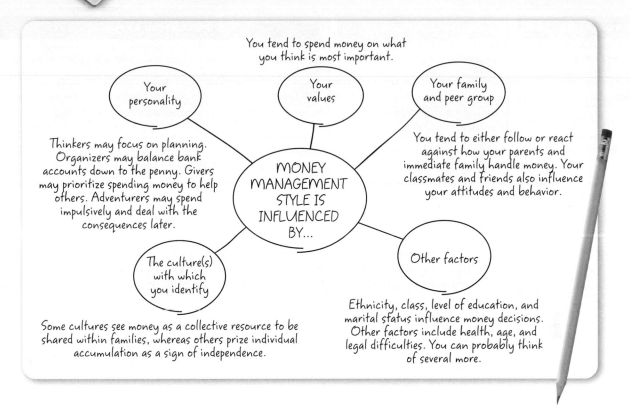

You tend to spend money on what you think is most important.

Your personality

Your values

Your family and peer group

MONEY MANAGEMENT STYLE IS INFLUENCED BY...

Thinkers may focus on planning. Organizers may balance bank accounts down to the penny. Givers may prioritize spending money to help others. Adventurers may spend impulsively and deal with the consequences later.

You tend to either follow or react against how your parents and immediate family handle money. Your classmates and friends also influence your attitudes and behavior.

The culture(s) with which you identify

Other factors

Some cultures see money as a collective resource to be shared within families, whereas others prize individual accumulation as a sign of independence.

Ethnicity, class, level of education, and marital status influence money decisions. Other factors include health, age, and legal difficulties. You can probably think of several more.

terms of how much money you have or define your worth in nonmaterial terms. As you analyze who you are as a money manager, consider the influences in Key 11.1.

Money coach Connie Kilmark notes that you cannot change how you handle money until you analyze your attitudes and behaviors. "If managing money was just about math and the numbers, everyone would know how to manage their finances sometime around the fifth grade," she says.[2] When you take an honest look at how you feel about money, you can make more effective financial decisions based on what works best for you.

Needs versus wants

When spending money, people often confuse what they *need* with what they *want*. True needs are few and basic: food, water, air, shelter (rent or mortgage as well as home maintenance costs and utilities), family and friends, and some mode of transportation. Everything else is technically a want—something you would like to have but can live without. When people spend money on those wants, they often find that they don't have enough cash available for needs. You may want to spend $1,000 on a flat-screen TV, but you might regret the purchase if your car suddenly breaks down and needs a $1,000 transmission repair.

Check your spending for purpose. What do you buy with your money? Are the items you purchase necessary? When you do spend on a want rather than a need, are you doing so thoughtfully by planning the added expense into your monthly budget? If you get a clear idea of what you want and what you need,

DAY-TO-DAY EXPENSE	APPROXIMATE COST	POTENTIAL SAVINGS
Gourmet coffee	$4 per day, 5 days a week, totals $20 per week	$80 per month; $960 for the year. Invested in a 5 percent interest account for a year, the total would amount to over $1,000.
Alcohol	Two drinks plus tip total about $20 per night; two nights per week amounts to $40 per week	$160 per month; $1,920 for the year. Invested in a 5 percent interest account for a year, the total would amount to over $2,000.
Ordering in meals	$15 per meal, twice per week, totals $30 per week	$120 per month; $1,440 for the year. Invested in a 5 percent interest account for a year, the total would amount to nearly $1,550.

you can think through spending decisions more effectively. This is not to say that you should never spend money on wants. The main goal is to make sure that you satisfy your needs first, and then see how much money is left over for your wants.

How your time relates to money

When you spend money that came to you in a paycheck, you exchange the time you spent earning it for a product or service. For example, you are thinking about purchasing a $200 cell phone. If you have a job that pays you $10 an hour after taxes, you would have spent 20 hours of work—a full week at a part-time job—on the phone purchase. Ask yourself: Is it worth it? If the answer is no, put the money away and use it for something that is of more value to you. Every hour you work has a value—consider how to exchange those hours for what matters most to you.

The relationship between time and money becomes clear when you examine how long it takes to earn money while tracking your day-to-day expenses and then compare the results. Key 11.2 shows how reducing regular expenses can make a difference.

Going to college may cost more hours of work than almost anything else you purchase, and it takes hours away from your day that you might otherwise spend earning money. It is an expensive investment. However, you are spending tuition and time to better your chances of long-term financial success. Your finances may be tight now, but they are likely to improve in the years ahead (remember, statistics show that college graduates tend to earn more in the workplace than nongraduates). You are making a sound investment in your future.

What you give up to get something, in economic terms, is called *opportunity cost*. For most students, the opportunity cost of going to college is worth it. The multiple intelligences table in this chapter (see page 315) is designed to clarify the concept of opportunity cost through descriptions of different budgeting strategies.

You make financial decisions nearly every day. Managing your income and expenses, juggling work and school, handling credit card use, and financing your education require frequent money management actions. Engage your successful intelligence as you use analytical, creative, and practical skills to set and achieve both short- and long-term financial goals.

How can you create and use a budget?

Creating a practical monthly (budget) that works is essential for living within your means (in other words, not spending more than you earn). You gather information about your resources (money flowing in) and expenditures (money flowing out) and *analyze* the difference. Next, you come up with *creative ideas* about how you can make changes. Finally, you take *practical action* to adjust spending or earning so that you come out even or ahead. Because many expenses are billed monthly, most people use a month as a unit of time when budgeting.

Your biggest expense right now is probably the cost of your education, including tuition and perhaps room and board. However, that expense may not hit you fully until after you graduate and begin to pay back your student loans. (Financial aid options will be explored later in the chapter.) For now, include in your budget only the part of the cost of your education you are paying while you are in school.

> → BUDGET
> A plan to coordinate resources and expenditures; a set of goals regarding money.

Figure out what you earn

To determine what is available to you on a monthly basis, start with the money you earn in a month's time at any regular job. Then, if you have savings set aside for your education or any other source of income, determine how much of it you can spend each month and add that amount. If you have a grant for the entire year, for example, divide it by 12 (or by how many months you are in school over the course of a year) to see how much you can use each month.

Figure out what you spend

First, note regular monthly expenses like rent, phone, and cable (look at past checks and electronic debits to estimate what the month's bills will be). Some expenses, like automobile and health insurance, may be billed once or twice a year. In these cases, divide the yearly cost by 12 to see how much you spend every month. Then, over a month's time, record cash or debit card expenditures in a small notebook—anything over five dollars. Be sure to count smaller purchases if they are frequent (for example, one or two pricey coffees a day add up over time). Added together, your regular expenses and other expenditures will show how much you spend in a month. Key 11.3 lists common sources of income as well as customary expenses for students.

Use the total of all your monthly expenses as a baseline for other months, realizing that your expenditures will vary depending on what is happening in your life and even the season (for example, the cost to heat your home may be much greater in the winter than in the summer).

A note about technology: One advantage to managing your bank and credit accounts online, as Alina does, is that you can quickly access information about what you are earning and spending over a period of time. Even though she is experiencing a downside—the increased need to protect online account access—she chose to access her accounts this way so she could stay on top of her spending more effectively. Personal finance software programs, such as Quicken, are

UNDERSTAND WHERE MONEY COMES FROM . . . AND **WHERE IT GOES**

Common Sources of Income	Common Expenses
• Take-home pay from a full-time or part-time job • Take-home pay from summer and holiday employment • Money earned from work-study or paid internship • Money from parents or other relatives • Scholarships • Grants • Loans	• Rent or mortgage • Tuition you are paying now • Books and other course materials • Utilities (electric, gas, oil, water) • Telephone (cell phone and/or land line) • Food • Clothing, toiletries, household supplies • Child care • Transportation and auto expenses (gas, maintenance, service) • Credit cards and other payments on credit (car payment) • Insurance (health, auto, homeowner's or renter's, life) • Entertainment (cable TV, movies, eating out, books and magazines, music downloads) • Computer-related expenses, including online service costs • Miscellaneous expenses

also a useful way to track spending and saving as well as categorize expenses (you can create reports about how much you spend on groceries in a one-month period, for example, or how much you earned from work in a year's time).

Evaluate the difference

Focusing on the particular month you are examining, subtract your monthly expenses from your monthly income. Ideally, you have money left over—to save or to spend. However, if you are spending more than you take in, ask some focused questions.

▶ *Examine your expenses.* Did you forget to budget for recurring expenses such as the cost for semiannual dental visits? Or was your budget derailed by an emergency expense?

▶ *Examine your spending patterns and priorities.* Did you spend money wisely during the month, or did you overspend on luxuries?

▶ *Examine your income.* Do you bring in enough money? Do you need another source?

Adjust expenses or earnings

If you are spending more than you are earning, you can either earn more or spend less. To increase income, consider taking a part-time job, increasing hours at a current job, or finding scholarships or grants. To decrease spending, reduce or cut purchases you don't need to make. In addition, work to save money in small ways on a day-to-day basis. Small amounts can eventually add up to big savings. Key 11.4 has some suggestions for cutting corners.

Key 11.5 shows a sample budget of an unmarried student living with two other students in off-campus housing with no meal plan. Included are all regular and out-of-pocket expenses with the exception of tuition, which the student will pay back after graduation in student loan payments. In this case, the student is $523 over budget. How would you make up the shortfall?

Call on your dominant multiple intelligences when planning your budget. For example, logical-mathematical learners may choose a classic detail-oriented budgeting plan, visual learners may want to create a budget chart, and bodily-kinesthetic learners may want to make budgeting more tangible by dumping receipts into a big jar and tallying them at the end of the month. Personal finance software can accommodate different types of learners with features such as written reports (verbal-linguistic, logical-mathematical) and reports in graphic formats (visual).

LOOK FOR WAYS TO TRIM YOUR SPENDING

- Share living space
- Rent movies or borrow them from friends or the library
- Eat at home more often
- Use grocery and clothing coupons from the paper or online
- Take advantage of sales, buy store brands, and buy in bulk
- Find play and concert tickets that are discounted for students
- Walk or use public transportation
- Bring lunch from home
- Shop in secondhand or consignment stores or swap clothing with friends
- Communicate via e-mail or snail mail
- Ask a relative to help with child care, or create a babysitting co-op
- Reduce electricity costs by cutting back on air conditioning and switching to compact fluorescent bulbs (CFLs) in your lamps at home

EXAMINE HOW ONE STUDENT MAPPED OUT A MONTHLY BUDGET

- Wages: $12 an hour (after taxes) × 20 hours a week = $240 a week × $4\frac{1}{3}$ weeks (one month) = $1,039
- Monthly withdrawals from savings (from summer earnings) = $200
- Total income per month = $1,239

MONTHLY EXPENDITURES	
School-related expenses (books, supplies, any expense not covered by financial aid)	$80
Public transportation	$90
Phone	$92
Food (groceries and takeout)	$285
Credit card payments	$100
Rent (including utilities)	$650
Entertainment (music, movies, tickets to events)	$90
Miscellaneous expenses, including clothing and personal items	$375
Total monthly spending:	$1,762
$1,239 (income) − $1,762 (expenses) = −$523	*$523 over budget*

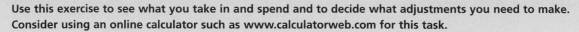

GET PRACTICAL!

Map Out Your Budget

Use this exercise to see what you take in and spend and to decide what adjustments you need to make. Consider using an online calculator such as www.calculatorweb.com for this task.

Step 1: Estimate your current expenses in dollars per month, using the accompanying table. This may require tracking expenses for a month if you don't already keep a record of your spending. The grand total is your overall monthly expenses. If any expense comes only once a year, enter it in the "Annual Expenses" column and divide by 12 to get your "Monthly Expenses" figure for that item.

EXPENSES	MONTHLY EXPENSES	ANNUAL EXPENSES
Education		
Books		
Tuition and fees		
Computer, supplies, lab		
Housing		
Dorm, rent, mortgage		
Utilities		
Phone including long distance, cell phone		
Cable TV, Internet		
Electricity, gas		
Water, garbage		
Transportation and Travel		
Car payment		
Auto insurance, maintenance and repairs, registration, emissions inspections		
Gas, public transportation, parking permits, tolls		
Vacation trips, trips home		
Food: Groceries, cafeteria meal plan, eating out, snacks		
Health		
Health insurance		
Gym, equipment, sports, fitness		
Medical, dental, prescriptions		
Personal		
Entertainment including CDs, socializing		
Laundry		

EXPENSES (CONTINUED)	MONTHLY EXPENSES	ANNUAL EXPENSES
Clothing		
Household supplies, furnishings		
Credit card payments		
Student loan or other loan repayment		
Donations: charity, church, gifts		
Child care		
Other: emergencies, hobbies		
TOTAL EXPECTED EXPENSES		

Step 2: **Calculate your average monthly income. As with expenses, if any source of income arrives only once a year, enter it in the "Annual" column and divide by 12 to get the monthly figure. For example, if you have a $6,000 scholarship for the year, your monthly income would be $500 ($6,000 divided by 12).**

INCOME/RESOURCES	MONTHLY INCOME	ANNUAL
Employment (assume 28% average income tax)		
Family contribution		
Financial assistance: grants, federal and other loans		
Scholarships		
Interest and dividends		
Other gifts, income, and contributions		
TOTAL EXPECTED INCOME		

Step 3: **Subtract the grand total of your monthly expenses from the grand total of your monthly income.**

INCOME PER MONTH	
EXPENSES PER MONTH	−
DIFFERENCE (INCOME OR EXPENSE)	=

Step 4: **If you have a negative cash flow, what would you change? You can increase income, decrease spending, or both. List two ideas about how to get your cash flow back in the black.**

1. _____

2. _____

Source: Adapted from Julie Stein, California State University, East Bay.

How can you increase income *through work and financial aid?*

The cost of education leads most students to seek additional dollars through work, financial aid, or both.

► According to a 2007 survey, nearly 50 percent of college freshmen add a job to their scheduled weekly responsibilities to earn money for tuition.[3]
► Statistics from the U.S. Department of Education show that in 2007–2008, fully two-thirds of undergraduates received some type of financial aid.[4]

Read on to find ways to get as much help as possible from these income sources.

Juggle work and school

If you want or need a job, try to work in a way that doesn't completely derail you from your academic work and goals. Think analytically and creatively, and come up with a practical plan that suits your situation.

Establish your needs

Think about what you need from a job. Ask questions like the following:

► How much money do I need to make—weekly, per term, for the year?
► What time of day is best for me? Should I consider night or weekend work?
► Can my schedule handle a full-time job, or should I look for part-time work?
► Do I want hands-on experience in a particular field?
► How flexible a job do I need?
► Can I, or should I, find work at my school or as part of a work-study program?

Analyze the impact

Working while in school has positive and negative effects. Think through these pros and cons when considering or evaluating any job:

PROS OF WORKING WHILE IN SCHOOL	CONS OF WORKING WHILE IN SCHOOL
• General and career-specific experience	• Time commitment that reduces available study time
• Developing contacts	• Reduced opportunity for social and extracurricular activities
• Enhanced school performance (although full-time work can be problematic, working up to 15 hours a week may actually improve efficiency)	• Having to shift gears mentally from work to classroom
• Money earned	• Stretching yourself too thin; fatigue

Create and choose options

With the information you have gathered and analyzed, you can look carefully at what is available on and off campus and apply for the job or jobs that suit your needs best. Continue to evaluate after you start a job. If it doesn't benefit you as much as you had anticipated, consider making a change, either in that job or by changing jobs. Also, even if you are not currently working, keep the option open. Alina, for example, might have to add a part-time job to her responsibilities to make up the money she lost to the online scam.

Your goal is to earn the money you need without derailing your education. If you make careful choices about work and about how to schedule your life around it, you can reach that goal.

Explore and apply for financial aid

Financing your education—alone or with the help of your family—involves gathering financial information and making decisions about what you can afford and how much help you need. You will need to work around various roadblocks, such as the following, that stand in the way of getting help:

■ *Students don't apply.* One recent report indicated that almost 40 percent of full-time community college students do not fill out a federal aid application, including 29 percent of students with incomes under $10,000 per year. These students may be intimidated by the application process or simply believe that they won't qualify for aid.[5]

■ *The economy has an effect.* When the economy is struggling, private banks are less likely to grant loans, and federal programs like Pell Grants have less money. Also, in tough economic times, more students apply for grants like the Pell (see Key 11.6), with the result that more people will get smaller pieces of the pie.

■ *Colleges vary in what they offer.* State colleges provide fewer opportunities for aid when their funding is reduced. Additionally, concerned about students' ability to pay back loans, some smaller colleges have stopped offering federal loans to their students.

Find your way around these roadblocks by becoming informed about what is available to you and proactive about going out and getting it.

Types of aid

Aid comes in the form of student loans, grants, and scholarships. *Never assume you are not eligible for aid.* Almost all students are eligible for some kind of need-based or merit-based financial assistance. The federal government administers the primary loan and grant programs, although many private sources may offer grants and scholarships as well.

■ *Student loans.* Student loan recipients are responsible for paying back the amount borrowed, plus interest, according to a payment schedule that may stretch over a number of years. The federal government administers or oversees all student loans. To receive aid from a federal program, you must be a citizen or eligible noncitizen enrolled in a program that meets government requirements.

Your school can help you wade through paperwork for grants, loans, or scholarships. This student gets help from someone in the financial aid office as she prepares applications.

© Mary Ann Chastain/AP Images

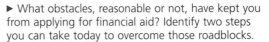

Change the CONVERSATION

Challenge yourself and your friends to ask—and answer—tough questions. Use the following to inspire discussion in pairs or groups.

▶ What obstacles, reasonable or not, have kept you from applying for financial aid? Identify two steps you can take today to overcome those roadblocks.

▶ How good are you at differentiating between needs and wants and on prioritizing needs?

▶ Everyone has a weak spot; some people like new clothes, whereas others like fancy restaurants (or just hate to cook). It's hard to do without things that help you cope. What can you do to make financial sacrifice seem worth the perceived feelings of deprivation?

▶ **CONSIDER THE CASE:** Technology has come to play a large part in money management. What practical skills was Alina missing when she mistook the e-mail as legitimate? How might she protect her money online in the future?

GET TO KNOW FEDERAL
LOAN AND GRANT PROGRAMS

Key 11.6

GRANTS	LOANS
• **Pell** (need based, available to undergraduates with no other degrees) • **Federal Supplemental Educational Opportunity,** or FSEOG (need based, only available at participating schools) • **Work-study** (need based, paying an hourly wage for selected jobs)	• **Perkins** (for those with exceptional financial need) • **Stafford** (for students enrolled at least half-time) • **PLUS** (available to students claimed as dependents by their parents)

Source: http://studentaid.ed.gov/PORTALSWebApp/students/english/index.jsp

■ *Grants.* Unlike student loans, grants do not require repayment. Grants funded by federal, state, or local governments as well as private organizations, are awarded to students who show financial need.

Key 11.6 lists federal grant and loan programs. Additional information about each is available in various federal student aid publications, which you can find at your school's financial aid office, request by phone (800-433-3243), or access online (http://studentaid.ed.gov/PORTALSWebApp/students/english/publications.jsp).

■ *Scholarships.* Scholarships are awarded to students who show talent or ability in specific areas (academic achievement, sports, the arts, citizenship, or leadership). They may be financed by government or private organizations, employers (yours or your parents'), schools, religious organizations, local and community groups, credit unions, or individuals. They do not require repayment.

Looking for aid

Here are five actions to take in your quest to pay for college.[6]

■ *Ask, ask, ask.* Visit the financial aid office—more than once. Ask what you are eligible for. Alert the office to any money problems, such as a change in your financial situation. Search libraries and the Web, including your school's website, for information on everything that is possible.

■ *Seek government aid.* Fill out the Free Application for Federal Student Aid (FAFSA) form electronically. The form can be found through your college's financial aid office or website, via www.fafsa.ed.gov, or on the U.S. Department

of Education's website at www.ed.gov/finaid.html. You will create a personal portfolio—called "MyFSA"—on the site that will store all the information you enter, including your FAFSA form and any other forms. The U.S. Education Department has an online tool called FAFSA Forecaster that you can use to estimate how much aid you qualify for. You will need to reapply every year for federal aid. This is a *free* form—if you hear about services that charge a fee for completing your FAFSA, avoid them.

■ *Seek private aid.* Thoroughly investigate what you may be eligible for. Search libraries and your school's website, check scholarship search sites like www.scholarships.com and http://edu.fastweb.com, go through books that list

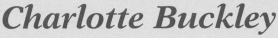

Charlotte Buckley

Hinds Community College, Jackson, Mississippi

About me:

I am 39 years old. I dropped out of high school and didn't return to school for 20 years. I wanted to finish my education, but as a single mom raising two kids, I couldn't figure out how to go back to school. My teenage daughter helped me gain the courage to get my GED through Hinds' Dropout Recovery Initiative. I discovered I had an interest in nursing and was able to find a work-study program so I could continue at Hinds, attending college classes.

Now I am applying to a nursing school in Memphis.

What I focus on:

I have a family to help support and I must balance working with going to school. First of all, the work-study program is amazing, and everyone who needs financial aid should consider work study. Though sometimes I feel very busy, I keep my goal right in front of me: a good education is a ticket to a better-paying job. Second, our family has to run on a tight budget. I did get married three years ago, so things aren't as tight as they were, but we all keep our long-term goals in view to resist spending

money on things we don't need. I've always stressed to my two kids, and now also to my two stepchildren, that a college education is a need, not a want.

What will help me in the workplace:

Living on a budget and sacrificing now for long-term goals later both involve a lot of discipline. I know from having been in the workforce that discipline enables you to make commitments to excellence even when the going gets tough. Discipline helps you weather some of the temporary storms in the working world and in life.

---

scholarships and grants, and talk with a financial aid advisor on your campus. Know details that may help you identify sources available to you (you or your family's military status, ethnic background, membership in organizations, religious affiliation, and so on). Once you have identified possibilities, apply according to the materials and guidelines provided by the organization offering aid.

■ *Consider a range of options.* Sometimes you may need to think about other options. Transferring to a less expensive school, for example, may earn you a comparable education while helping you to escape postgraduation debt. Changing your major to a field with better job prospects will potentially earn you more money to help pay off your loans. Keep an open mind.

Applying for aid

The number one rule is to apply—and apply by the deadline, or even better, early. The earlier you complete the process, the greater your chances of being considered for aid, especially when you are vying for part of a limited pool of

GET CREATIVE!

Brainstorm Day-to-Day Ways to Save Money

Think about all the ways you spend money in a month's time. Where can you trim a bit? What expense can you do without? Where can you look for savings or discounts? Can you barter a product or service for one that a friend can provide? Give yourself a day or two to brainstorm a list of ideas on a sheet of paper or computer. Write your five most workable ideas here.

1. _____
2. _____
3. _____
4. _____
5. _____

Give these a try and see how they can help you put some money toward your savings. To make the experiment tangible, put cash into a jar daily or weekly in the amounts that these changes are saving you. See what you have accumulated at the end of one month—and bank it.

funds. Here are some additional tips from financial aid experts Arlina DeNardo and Carolyn Lindley of Northwestern University:[7]

▶ *Know what applications you need to fill out.* FAFSA is required at all colleges, but some also require a form called the CSS/Financial Aid Profile (https://profileonline.collegeboard.com/prf/index.jsp).

▶ *Note the difference between merit-based and need-based aid.* Although some aid is awarded based on financial need, other assistance is merit based, meaning that it is linked to specifics such as academic performance or artistic or athletic ability.

▶ *Be aware of the total cost of attending college.* When you consider how much money you need, add books, transportation, housing, food, and other fees to tuition.

▶ *If you receive aid, pay attention to the award letter.* Know whether the aid is a grant or a loan that needs to be repaid. Follow rules such as remaining in academic good standing. Note reapplication deadlines and meet them (many require reapplication *every year*).

▶ *Spend the money you receive on your needs.* Especially if it comes in one big check, the money might look so good that you are tempted to buy a car and do some extra shopping before you get to that tuition bill. Don't let your wants distract you from your needs. Put your aid toward coursework and related food and housing expenses first.

▶ *Don't take out more money than you need.* If you max out on your total aid too early in your college career, you could run into trouble as you approach graduation. Look at your needs year by year and make sure you are only taking out what is absolutely necessary.

Finally, if you do receive aid from your college or elsewhere, follow all rules and regulations. Also, take a new look each year at what's available. You may be eligible for different grants or scholarships than when you first applied.

In part because of rising education costs that don't match increases in wages and salaries, students are borrowing ever-larger amounts of money. Consequently, the number of students *defaulting* on loans—in other words, walking away from them—is on the rise; however, even personal bankruptcy won't make student loans go away.[8] The consequences for defaulting on a loan are severe and include credit trouble, inability to apply for further aid, money taken from your salary or Social Security payment, and more. Borrow only what you can pay back later. See www.finaid.org for more helpful information about managing loans.

Student loans are one way of borrowing the money you need to live and study. Another form of borrowing—a much more expensive one—is the credit card.

What will help you use credit cards wisely?

A typical college student receives dozens of credit card offers. These offers—and the cards that go along with them—are a double-edged sword: They are a handy alternative to cash and can help build a strong credit history if used appropriately. But they also can plunge you into a hole of debt. Students are acquiring cards in droves—in fact, in 2009, only 2 percent of undergraduates had no credit history.[9]

Credit cards can be a particular danger for students. Credit companies often target students with a positive spin about credit cards, knowing that many lack knowledge about how credit works. Too much focus on what they can purchase with credit cards can lead students into trouble. Recent statistics from a survey of undergraduates illustrate the situation:[10]

► As of 2008, 50 percent of undergraduates reported having four or more credit cards.
► Students who hold credit cards carry an average outstanding balance of $3,173.
► 21 percent of undergraduates have a credit card balance between $3,000 and $7,000.
► Nine out of ten students report paying for direct education expenses, including textbooks and school supplies, with credit cards. Students who use credit cards for educational expenses estimate spending an average of $2,200 on such services alone.
► College-age consumers now have the second highest rate of bankruptcy, just after those aged 35 to 44.

Many college students charge books and tuition as well as expenses like car repair, food, and clothes. Before they know it, they are deeply in debt. It's hard to notice trouble brewing when you don't see your wallet taking a hit. Additionally, if you manage credit card accounts online, you will need to be wary of scams such as the one that took Alina by surprise, because "phishing" e-mails often impersonate credit card companies as well as banks.

How credit cards work

To charge means to create a debt that must be repaid. The credit card issuer earns money by charging interest, often 18 percent or higher, on unpaid balances. Here's an example: Say you have a $3,000 unpaid balance on your card at an annual interest rate of 18 percent. If you make the $60 minimum payment every month, it will take eight years to pay off your debt, assuming that you make no other purchases. The effect on your wallet is staggering:

Original debt	$3,000
Cost to repay credit card loan at an annual interest rate of 18 percent for 8 years	$5,760
Cost of using credit	**$2,760** ($5,760 – $3,000)

By the time you finish, you will have repaid nearly *twice* your original debt.

Keep in mind that credit card companies are in business to make money and don't have your financial best interests at heart. Focusing on what's best for your finances is *your* job, and the first step is to know as much as you can about credit cards. Start with the important concepts presented in Key 11.7, and make sure you read the fine print of any card you are considering so that you know what you are getting into.

Watch for problems

In response to recent economic changes, credit card disclaimers and policies can cause problems unless you stay alert. Here are a few you should note, both when seeking a new card and when looking at existing card statements:[11]

▶ *New fees.* In addition to annual fees becoming once again common, a card may charge fees for reward programs, paying your bill by phone, or even checking your balance.

▶ *Shrinking or disappearing grace periods.* In the past, a "grace period" of a few days may have given you a chance to pay late but avoid fees. Now, even just slightly late payments will usually result in a fee charged to your card.

▶ *Reward program changes.* Even with a reward program you've enjoyed for a while, such as airline miles or cash back, keep checking your statements. Cards may charge for reward programs or may change or remove them if you are late with a payment.

▶ *"Fee harvesting" cards.* Some cards feature low credit limits and come loaded with extra fees. After the fees are tacked onto the low credit limit, very little is left to spend and consumers often end up going over their limit—resulting in more fees.

▶ *The universal default clause.* This increasingly common policy allows creditors to increase your interest rates if you make a late payment to *any* account, not just those that you have with them. This means that if you are late on your payment for an unrelated loan, your creditors can increase your credit card APR. You can avoid this situation by paying your bills on time.

The best way to avoid mishaps is to read the fine print and to attempt to pay your bills on time as often as possible. Keep a schedule of bill due dates and check your balances regularly. Prevention is the best line of defense.

WHAT TO KNOW ABOUT	. . . AND HOW TO USE WHAT YOU KNOW
Account balance—a dollar amount that includes any unpaid balance, new purchases and cash advances, finance charges, and fees. Updated monthly.	Charge only what you can afford to pay at the end of the month. Keep track of your balance. Hold on to receipts and call customer service if you have questions.
Annual fee—the yearly cost that some companies charge for owning a card.	Look for cards without an annual fee or, if you've paid your bills on time, ask your current company to waive the fee.
Annual percentage rate (APR)—the amount of interest charged on your unpaid balance, meaning the cost of credit if you carry a balance in any given month. The higher the APR, the more you pay in finance charges.	Shop around (check www.studentcredit.com). Also, watch out for low, but temporary, introductory rates that skyrocket to over 20 percent after a few months. Look for fixed rates (guaranteed not to change).
Available credit—the unused portion of your credit line, updated monthly on your bill.	It is important to have credit available for emergencies, so avoid charging to the limit.
Cash advance—an immediate loan, in the form of cash, from the credit card company. You are charged interest immediately and may also pay a separate transaction fee.	Use a cash advance only in emergencies because the finance charges start as soon as you complete the transaction. It is a very expensive way to borrow money.
Credit limit—the debt ceiling the card company places on your account (e.g., $1,500). The total owed, including purchases, cash advances, finance charges, and fees, cannot exceed this limit.	Credit card companies generally set low credit limits for college students. Many students get around this limit by owning more than one card, which increases the credit available but most likely increases problems as well.
Delinquent account—an account that is not paid on time or for which the minimum payment has not been met.	Avoid having a delinquent account at all costs. Not only will you be charged substantial late fees, but you also risk losing your good credit rating, affecting your ability to borrow in the future. Delinquent accounts remain part of your credit record for many years.
Due date—the date your payment must be received and after which you will be charged a late fee.	Avoid late fees and finance charges by mailing your payment a week in advance.
Finance charges—the total cost of credit, including interest and service and transaction fees.	The only way to avoid finance charges is to pay your balance in full by the due date.
Minimum payment—the smallest amount you can pay by the statement due date. The amount is set by the credit card company.	Making only the minimum payment each month can result in disaster if you charge more than you can afford. When you make a purchase, think in terms of total cost.
Outstanding balance—the total amount you owe on your card.	If you carry a balance over several months, additional purchases are hit with finance charges. Pay cash instead.
Past due—your account is considered "past due" when you fail to pay the minimum required payment on schedule.	Three credit bureaus note past due accounts on your credit history: Experian, TransUnion, and Equifax. You can contact each bureau for a copy of your credit report to make sure there are no errors.

Manage credit card debt

To avoid excessive debt, ask yourself questions before charging: Would I buy it if I had to pay cash? Can I pay off the balance in full at the end of the billing cycle? If I buy this, what purchases will I have to put off or give up altogether? Even if you limit your card use to needs, you can still get into trouble. Many students put books and tuition on their cards, and if you add items like clothing, food, and car repairs, your debt can escalate quickly and can even lead to personal bankruptcy—a major blot on your credit that can last for years and should be avoided at all costs.

A few basics will help you stay in control.

▶ *Choose your card wisely.* Look for a card with a low interest rate, no annual fee, a rewards program, and a grace period (a week or two to pay your bill without having to pay interest).

▶ *Pay bills regularly and on time, and always make at least the minimum payment.* Set up a reminder system that activates a week or so before the due date. You can create an e-mail alert through your card account, make a note in your planner, or set an alarm on your electronic planner.

▶ *If you get into trouble, call the credit company and ask to set up a payment plan.* Then, going forward, try to avoid the same mistakes. If you still need help, contact organizations such as the National Foundation for Credit Counseling (www.nfcc.org) or American Financial Solutions (1-888-282-5899) for help.

▶ *Use your card for emergencies only* if you can.

▶ *Shred credit cards if and when you've closed an account* or if you feel you have too many—however, remember that even though you've destroyed the card, the debt attached to it remains until you've paid it off in full and sent a written statement to the company indicating your request to close the account.

Build a good credit score

CREDIT SCORE
A measure of credit risk calculated from a credit report using a standardized formula.

CREDITOR
A person or company to whom a debt, usually money, is owed.

Many people go through periods when they have a hard time paying bills. Falling behind on payments, however, could result in a poor **credit score** (also referred to as a *credit rating*) that can make it tough to get a loan or finance a large purchase. Your credit score is a prediction of your ability to pay back debt. If you've ever bought a car, signed up for a credit card, or purchased insurance, the deal you got was related to your credit score. If you're looking to rent an apartment, sign up for a new cell phone plan, connect utilities at your home, or even start a job where you may be required to handle money, someone will be examining your credit score.

Most credit scores are determined from a credit-scoring scale. The scale, which can run anywhere from 300 to 850, will give **creditors** an idea of how reliable you are. In general, having a higher score is related to getting better interest rates. For instance, if a person with a score of 520 and a person with a score of 720 both had a $100,000 30-year mortgage, the lower-scoring person would have a higher APR (annual percentage rate) on the loan and would ultimately pay an extra $110,325 in interest charges.[12]

If you're trying to keep your score in good shape, or if you need to get your score back on track, look at Key 11.8 to get an idea of what affects your credit.

Having an unhealthy credit rating can have several negative effects. Most notably, it means increased rates of interest, which can cost you more money in the long run. Additional effects may include the following:

To keep track of where your money goes, keep credit card receipts and include those expenses in your budget.
© Sarah Lyman Kravits

DIFFERENT FACTORS DETERMINE YOUR **CREDIT RATING**

35% How You Pay Your Bills	Remember: Always paying your bills on time is great; always paying them late is bad. Declaring bankruptcy is worse.
30% Amount of Money You Owe and the Amount of Available Credit	Statistically, people who have a lot of credit available tend to use it, which makes them a less attractive credit risk.
15% Length of Credit History	In general, the longer you've had credit, the more points you get.
10% Mix of Credit	Statistically, people with a variety of credit types usually understand how to use credit better. Thus, having different types of credit—such as credit cards, loans, and mortgages—looks better to creditors.
10% New Credit Applications	Depending on the length and overall health of your credit history, applying for new lines of credit can indicate certain behaviors signaling your reliability to lenders. Usually, multiple applications are less favorable when seen on shorter histories.

▶ An indication to a potential employer that you may be unfit to run a department or less trustworthy in security situations or when handling money

▶ Difficulty in getting a loan for a home or car

▶ Higher premiums with insurance companies, who believe that people with lower credit scores are more likely to file a claim

▶ Obstacle to renting an apartment if it appears to the landlord that you may have trouble paying your bills

▶ Extra charges from utilities such as a requirement to pay a deposit when opening a new account

Building, maintaining, and repairing credit is an ongoing challenge. The three primary credit bureaus—Experian, TransUnion, and Equifax—will provide a report to you containing your credit score and other important information about your credit history. Also, a venture called VantageScore can give you a credit score that takes the average of your scores from all three companies and may provide a more accurate and consistent view of your credit. See www.annualcreditreport.com or www.vantagescore.com for more information.

Examine Credit Card Use

Take a careful look at who you are as a credit consumer. Gather your most recent credit card statements in preparation for this exercise. Answer questions 1 through 5 separately on paper or your computer, because they contain personal information.

1. **How many credit cards do you have? List the names. For each, indicate the following:**

   ▶ **Current interest rate**

   ▶ **Current balance**

   ▶ **Amount due as late fee if you do not pay on time**

   ▶ **Approximate date card payment is due each month**

2. **Add your balances together. This total is your current credit debt.**

3. **How much did you pay last month in finance charges? Total your finance charges from the most recent statements of all cards.**

4. **Do you pay on time, do you tend to pay late, or is it variable?**

5. **Estimate how many times in a year you have to pay a late fee. Looking at how much your cards charge for late fees, estimate how much money you have spent in the last year on late fees.**

When you've gathered all your information, analyze how effectively you currently use credit. If you are satisfied with your habits, keep up the good work. If your evaluation indicates that you need to make some changes, don't waste any time. Write specific plans here and start now to change your habits.

1. _____

_____

2. _____

_____

3. _____

_____

How can you plan for a solid financial future?

Achieving long-term financial goals—buying a car or a house, having money for expenses that go beyond everyday costs, saving money for retirement and for emergencies—requires that you think critically about what you do with your money for the long term. Effective budgeting, working while in school, managing credit use, and finding financial aid contribute to your long-term goals because they help you spend wisely and maximize your savings.

Save and invest your money

Having financial security requires that you spend *less* than you earn. Then the money accumulated can go into savings accounts and investments, helping you

MULTIPLE INTELLIGENCE STRATEGIES
for Financial Management

Apply Different Intelligences to the Concept of Opportunity Cost in Economics

INTELLIGENCE	USE MI STRATEGIES TO MANAGE YOUR MONEY	APPLY MI BUDGETING STRATEGIES TO LEARN ABOUT OPPORTUNITY COST*
Verbal-Linguistic	• Talk over your financial situation with someone you trust. • Write out a detailed budget outline. If you can, store it on a computer file so you can update it regularly.	• Clarify the concept of *opportunity cost* (what you sacrifice to get something) with two personal examples: the opportunity cost of a course you are taking and of a purchase you've made or plan to make.
Logical-Mathematical	• Focus on the numbers; using a calculator and amounts as exact as possible, determine your income and spending. • Calculate how much money you'll have in 10 years if you start now to put $2,000 in a 5 percent interest-bearing IRA account each year.	• Compute the estimated opportunity cost of one year of your college education by comparing it to working full-time for the year. Consider all education-related expenses in your computation. Analyze your results.
Bodily-Kinesthetic	• Consider putting money, or a slip with a dollar amount, each month in envelopes for various budget items—rent, dining out, and so on. When the envelope is empty or the number is reduced to zero, spending stops.	• On slips of paper, write opportunity costs of a choice—for example, buying a new car—and put the slips in a pile. Then, write the benefits of the choice on more slips, and put them in a separate pile. Compare your piles—does the benefit outweigh the cost?
Visual-Spatial	• Set up a budgeting system that includes color-coded folders and colored charts. • Create color-coded folders for papers related to financial and retirement goals—investments, accounts, and so on.	• In order to see what combination of work time and school time is ideal for you, design a *production possibilities* curve that shows all of the possible combinations.
Interpersonal	• Whenever money problems come up, discuss them right away with a family member, partner, or roommate. • Brainstorm a 5-year financial plan with one of your friends.	• Meet with a friend to discuss the opportunity cost of different ways to spend your *discretionary income* (money available after you pay your monthly fixed expenses).
Intrapersonal	• Schedule quiet time to plan how to develop, follow, and update your budget. Consider financial management software, such as Quicken. • Think through where your money should go to best achieve your long-term financial goals.	• Schedule downtime to think about the opportunity cost of an extracurricular activity with which you are involved. Overall, do you benefit from this experience? If you decide that the cost is too high, change your level of involvement.
Musical	• Include a category of music-related purchases in your budget—going to concerts, buying CDs—but keep an eye on it to make sure you don't go overboard.	• Look at what you spend on music-related purchases through one term. Thinking about other ways you could use that money, calculate the opportunity cost of that expense.
Naturalistic	• Analyze your spending by using a system of categories. Your system may be based on time (when payments are due), priority (must-pay bills versus extras), or spending type (monthly bills, education, family expenses).	• Choose a category and total your spending in that category through the year. Think about something else that you would like to do with that amount of money. Is there a more favorable choice you could make in the future?

*For information on opportunity cost, see Arthur O'Sullivan, Steven M. Sheffrin, and Stephen J. Perez, *Survey of Economics: Principles, Applications, and Tools,* Upper Saddle River, NJ: Prentice Hall, 2008.

with regular expenses, long-term financial plans, and emergencies (financial advisors recommend, if at all possible, to keep enough cash in an "emergency fund" to cover three months' expenses). Savings accounts, CDs, and money market accounts are basic tools to help your money grow. If you manage them online, take a lesson from Alina and be cautious about the websites you use, e-mails you receive, and how you protect your personal information.

- **Savings accounts.** The most basic and flexible place to save money is in an account that earns **compound interest.** Most savings accounts have a variable rate of *interest*, which is a sum paid for the use of your money while it is in the bank. Here's how compound interest works: If you put $1,000 in an account that carries 5 percent interest, you will earn $50 over the course of the first year. Your account then holds $1,050. From that point on, interest is calculated on that $1,050, not just on the original $1,000. Imagine this: *If you invested that $1,000 at the age of 22 and put a mere $50 in the account each month, by the time you turned 62 you would have over $100,000.*

- **Certificates of deposit (CDs) and money market accounts.** CDs deliver a fixed rate of interest on an amount of money that you put away for a specific period of time (3 months, 6 months, one year). Money market accounts allow you to withdraw money, but they tend to require a minimum balance and restrict you to a certain number of withdrawals per month. Both kinds of accounts earn slightly more than a regular savings account and are good places to put money that you want to be able to use in the near future.

Begin saving for retirement

With so many workers switching jobs frequently and working freelance, fewer people are retiring with guaranteed retirement income other than Social Security. As more and more large and small employers are reducing or eliminating pension benefits, it is up to individual workers to put away as much money as they can for retirement. Starting early and continuing on a yearly basis gives you the benefit of growth over time.

Full-time workers whose employers offer a 401(k) retirement savings plan should sign up and contribute regularly. A 401(k) plan lets you deposit money tax-free until withdrawal, and your employer will often match your contributions. If no such plan is offered, consider looking into *individual retirement accounts* (IRAs), a retirement investing tool that accepts annual contributions up to a maximum amount. Money invested and earned through interest is not taxed until withdrawn (with a Roth IRA even withdrawn earnings are untaxed provided the withdrawal isn't early). An IRA holder can withdraw money without penalty any time after 59½ years of age.

IRAs may be your best bet for investment. Key 11.9 shows the extraordinary earning potential of an IRA. There are many different types of IRAs, and the one that is right for you will depend on your employment, your income, and the money you have available to invest. Financial institutions such as banks and investment firms offer IRAs.

COMPOUND INTEREST
Interest calculated on the principal (original investment) as well as the interest already added to the account.

USE AN IRA TO GROW YOUR RETIREMENT INVESTMENT

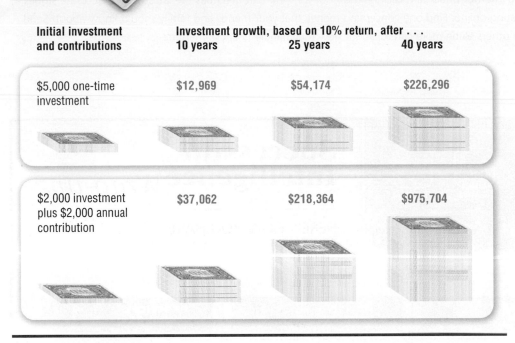

Initial investment and contributions	Investment growth, based on 10% return, after . . .		
	10 years	25 years	40 years
$5,000 one-time investment	$12,969	$54,174	$226,296
$2,000 investment plus $2,000 annual contribution	$37,062	$218,364	$975,704

Note: Calculations based on 10 percent average annual S & P Index growth from 1926 to present, as per "Investment Intelligence," Legg Mason Investor Services, 2007 (http://investorservices.leggmason.com/doc_library/1730.pdf?seq=11).

What happened to Alina? Unfortunately, Alina was unable to get any of the stolen money back. To pay for the following term's tuition costs, Alina's father asked her to be responsible for half of the missing money. Alina got a part-time child-care job that allowed her to do some homework while making money. Though she had to take out a student loan to cover the rest of her costs, Alina read the loan agreement very carefully with her past experience in mind. As a result of the difficult situation, she is feeling more skeptical of money-related communication, but also more in control of her finances and future than ever before.

Case Wrap-up

What does this mean for you? Clearly understanding financial information that comes your way is a skill that you will use again and again in your college experience and beyond. Consider the documents you will need to read thoroughly and understand throughout your life: credit card statements and other bills, bank statements, a lease for a house or apartment, health or dental insurance, or a loan agreement for tuition or a car. If you have ever misunderstood an important document, describe the situation and what happened as a result. If you have not, describe the current document you most need to understand clearly.

What effects go beyond your world? With the speed and reach of the Internet, frauds have the potential to cause harm to tens of thousands of people in very little time. Go to www.snopes.com, a website dedicated to revealing Internet fraud, and click on the "Hot 25" link that describes the latest not-so-accurate stories and scams circulating online. Find one concerning money that your friends and family should know about. Send the link and help others to be more careful about how they handle financial matters.

Successful Intelligence *Wrap-up*

HERE'S HOW YOU HAVE BUILT SKILLS IN **CHAPTER 11** :

ANALYTICAL THINKING	CREATIVE THINKING	PRACTICAL THINKING
❯ You explored the importance of watching your finances and implementing a budget.	❯ You learned about creative ways to boost income and seek financial aid.	❯ You learned strategies for managing credit cards and credit card debt.
❯ In the Get Analytical exercise, you honed your skills by considering your current credit card use, the implications of your situation, and how you might improve your use of credit.	❯ You explored how to create options for working while in school, based on information about your needs and circumstances.	❯ In the Get Practical exercise, you mapped out a reasonable budget and developed workable solutions to get your cash flow back on track.
❯ You considered the effects that financial planning can have on your future.	❯ In the Get Creative exercise, you brainstormed creative ways to save money every day.	❯ You explored practical solutions to building a healthy credit score.

Word *for* Thought

The **Indonesian** phrase *gotong-royong* (got'-ong roi'-ong) communicates that when people come together "to carry a heavy burden," the burden is lightened because it is shared. In a broader sense, the phrase says that what is good for the group is more important than what is good for one person.[13] Keep *gotong-royong* in mind as you make decisions about your money, because your actions have effects on those who share your life.

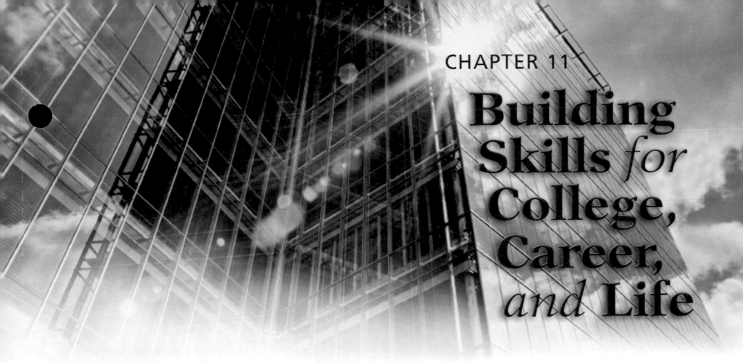

Building Skills for College, Career, and Life

Steps to Success

Your Relationship with Money

Getting a handle on money anxiety starts with an honest examination of how you relate to it.

BUILD BASIC SKILLS. Analyze yourself as a money manager. Look back to Key 11.1 on page 297 for a description of what influences how people handle money. Make notes about your personal specifics in the following areas.

I most value spending money on _____

_____

As a money manager, I would describe myself as _____

_____

My culture tends to view money as _____

_____

In handling money, my family and friends tend to _____

_____

TAKE IT TO THE NEXT LEVEL. Generate ideas about what you want to do with your money. If you had enough money for your expenses and then some, what would you do with the extra? Would you save it, spend it, or do a little of both? Imagine what you would do if you had an extra $10,000 to spend this year. Describe your plan on a separate sheet of paper.

MOVE TOWARD MASTERY. Look for practical ways to move toward the scenario you imagined. Realistically, how can you make that $10,000 a reality? You may need to change how you operate as a money manager. You may need to make some sacrifices in the short term. Come up with two specific plans here about changes and sacrifices that will move you toward your goal.

1. _____

2. _____

When you put these ideas to work, save or invest the money to reach for your goal.

Teamwork

Create Solutions Together

NEEDS AND WANTS

Goal: To share perspectives on needs, wants, and the effects of your choices.

Time on task: 10 minutes

Instructions: Gather in groups of three to five students. Have one student take notes for the group.

1. Independently, take 3 minutes to brainstorm what you consider to be *needs* that you spend money on regularly. Make a list of your needs.
2. Gather together and generate a group list of needs from your individual lists. Each group member calls out his or her items and the student taking notes puts them all into one list. Needs named by more than one student should only be listed once. Hold off on comments until the list is complete.
3. Go through each need and discuss. Is it a true need? Is it a need for some and a want for others? Could it be more of a want than a need? Be open to different perspectives. The student taking notes should create a chart with three columns: "Needs," "Wants," and "Both." As the group talks through the items on the list, this student should write each in its appropriate column.
4. Conclude by focusing on *wants*. Look at the items that found their way into your "Wants" column (if you have none, quickly generate a list of wants by having each group member volunteer one want that they spend money on). Talk together about how giving up various wants might help financially. Each group member should name a want that he or she agrees to give up in the next month to see what kind of difference it can make.

Writing

Build Intrapersonal and Communication Skills

Record your thoughts on paper, in a journal, or electronically.

EMOTIONAL INTELLIGENCE JOURNAL

You and credit. First, describe yourself as a credit user—do you pay in full or run up a balance? Pay on time or avoid the bills? Restrict use to emergences or use your card (or cards) all the time? Then describe how using credit makes you feel. Examining those feelings and their affect on how you use credit, describe a change you could make in your thinking that would help you spend more wisely.

REAL-LIFE WRITING

Apply for aid. Use Internet or library resources to find two nonfederally funded scholarships, available through your college, for which you are eligible—they can be linked to academic areas of interest, associated with particular talents that you have, or offered by a group to which you or members of your family belong. Get applications for each and fill them out. Finally, write a one-page cover letter for each, telling each committee why you should receive this scholarship. Have someone proofread your work, *send the applications,* and see what happens.

Personal Portfolio

Prepare for Career Success

BE SPECIFIC ABOUT YOUR JOB NEEDS

21st Century Learning Building Blocks

- Business Literacy
- Initiative and Self-Direction

Complete the following in your electronic portfolio or separately on paper.

As you consider specific job directions and opportunities, begin thinking about job-related factors that may affect your workplace experience and personal life, such as the following:

- Benefits, including health insurance, vacation, 401(k), and so on
- Integrity of company (its reputation)
- How the company deals with employees
- Promotion prospects/your chances for advancement
- Job stability
- Training and educational opportunities (Does the company offer in-house training or fund job-related coursework?)
- Starting salary
- Quality of employees

- Quality of management
- Nature of the work you will be doing (Will you be required to travel extensively? Will you be expected to work long hours? Will you be working in an office or in the field?)
- Your relationship with the company (Will you be a full-time or part-time employee or an independent contractor?)
- Job title
- Location of your primary workplace
- Company size
- Company's financial performance over time

Think about how important each factor is in your job choice. Then rate each on a scale of 1 to 10, with 1 being the least important and 10 the most important. As you consider each factor, keep in mind that even if you consider something very important, it may not affect you significantly until later in your career.

Finally, consider the results of a survey of college students conducted by the National Association of Colleges and Employers. When asked their top two reasons for choosing an employer, students named *integrity of organization in its dealings with employees* as number one and *job stability* as number two. How do these top choices compare to your own?[14]

Social Networking

GET RECOMMENDED

LinkedIn has a feature that can help you show recommendations from valued contacts. Users with recommendations are more likely to be picked up by employers searching LinkedIn for possible employees. Sign in to your account and proceed as follows:

- Click on "Edit My Profile."
- Under "Recommended," click on "Get Recommended."
- Follow the three steps to contact people who you think would have positive and helpful things to say about you. (Choose what you want to be recommended for, decide who you'll ask, and create your message.) Keep in mind that the more credible the sources, the more useful your recommendations will be. (A family member saying you are a great person is not as effective as a former teacher or employer talking about your skills.)
- Finally, click "send" and keep an eye out for recommendations coming in.

Careers and More

Building a Successful Future

What Would You Do?

Think about this problem as you read, and consider how you would approach it. This chapter focuses first on how to prepare for success on the job. Then it helps you analyze how you fared this term. Finally, it provides tools to help you apply the power of successful intelligence to your life now and after college.

hen Kelly Carson first stepped into her seventh-grade Spanish class, she felt a sense of potential in the idea that soon she would be able to speak to a whole new group of people. When she got home that day, she told her mother that she wanted to major in Spanish in college.

Continuing to take Spanish in high school, Kelly asked her teacher how she could practice outside the classroom. The teacher recommended her to the English as a second language (ESL) program at a local elementary school. Her first tutoring session was with a third-grade girl who spoke only a few words of English. When the girl discovered Kelly spoke Spanish, the words came pouring out, and she talked about how none of the students talked to her, she never understood the teacher, and she sat through class every day staring at a book. As Kelly worked with her, the English she learned transformed her into an active member of the class, and Kelly began to see how she could harness communication skills in order to solve problems.

Kelly entered the University of Kansas in Lawrence determined to continue teaching ESL. During her freshman year, she tutored a Mexican immigrant, Diana, a few days a week. Word spread that there was a free English teacher in Diana's building,

and more and more of her friends showed up. Kelly was amazed at the need for English teachers when hundreds of college students were learning languages a few blocks away. Overwhelmed by the demand, she wanted to figure out a way to solve this problem in a way that involved her school and its students. (To be continued . . .)

Kelly's college experience has led her to meaningful workplace goals balanced with a focus on personal life. You'll learn more about Kelly, and revisit her situation, within the chapter.

In this chapter, you'll explore answers to these questions:

> How can you prepare for career success? p. 324

> How can you conduct an effective job search? p. 332

> How can you continue to activate your successful intelligence? p. 334

> How will your learning in this course bring success? p. 338

ANALYTICAL

CREATIVE

PRACTICAL

STATUS *Check*

▶ *How prepared are you for workplace and life success?*

For each statement, circle the number that feels right to you,

from 1 for "not at all true for me" to 5 for "very true for me."

▶ I have thought about different careers that seem to suit my personality, interests, and abilities.	1 2 3 4 5
▶ I have looked into majors that match up with my career interests.	1 2 3 4 5
▶ I have, or intend to get, hands-on experience in a particular field through an internship, job, or volunteer work.	1 2 3 4 5
▶ I understand the qualities that today's employers value most.	1 2 3 4 5
▶ I save and update contact information for people I network with about career advice or job possibilities.	1 2 3 4 5
▶ I am familiar with major online job search and career planning sites.	1 2 3 4 5
▶ I know how to write an effective cover letter.	1 2 3 4 5
▶ I have a current resumé for sending out to prospective employers.	1 2 3 4 5
▶ I am prepared to give a good impression in interviews.	1 2 3 4 5
▶ Knowing how quickly the modern workplace changes, I'm ready to be flexible if a job or career choice doesn't last.	1 2 3 4 5

Each of the topics in these statements is covered in this chapter. Note those statements for which you circled a 3 or lower. Skim the chapter to see where those topics appear, and pay special attention to them as you read, learn, and apply new strategies.

REMEMBER: *No matter how prepared you are to succeed in the workplace and in life, you can improve with effort and practice.*

"Successfully intelligent people realize that the environment in which they find themselves may or may not enable them to make the most of their talents. They actively seek an environment where they can not only do competent work but also make a difference."

—Robert Sternberg

How can you prepare for career success?

Whether you have a current career, a work history of various different jobs, or no workplace experience at all, college is an ideal time to take stock of your career goals. The earlier in your college education that you consider career goals, the more you can take advantage of using college to help prepare you for work, in both job-specific and general ways.

Your career reflects your values and talents and provides the income you need to support yourself and your family in the years ahead. Choosing a career requires knowledge of yourself, your economic situation, and where you want to be in the future. Because of the personal nature of these questions, it's important to remember that the "right" career can mean something different to everyone. As you read this section, keep in mind that all of the skills you acquire in college—thinking, teamwork, writing, goal setting, and others—prepare you for workplace success, no matter what career is right for you.

Consider your personality and strengths

Because who you are as a learner relates closely to who you are as a worker, your assessment results from Chapter 3 will give you helpful clues in the search for the right career. The multiple intelligences assessment (Multiple Pathways to Learning) points to information about your natural strengths and challenges, which can lead you to careers that involve these strengths. Review Key 3.7 on page 75 to see majors and internships that tend to suit different intelligences, and look at Key 12.1 to see how those intelligences may link up with various careers.

The Personality Spectrum assessment is equally as significant, because it focuses on how you work best with others, and career success depends in large part on your ability to function in a team. Key 12.2 focuses the four dimensions of the Personality Spectrum on career ideas and strategies. Look for your strengths and decide what you may want to keep in mind as you search. Look also at areas of challenge, and try to identify ways to boost your abilities in those areas. Even the most ideal job involves some tasks that are not in your area of comfort.

Taking courses in an area of interest can help you see how well a job in this area might suit you. These students get hands-on experience in respiratory therapy as well as advice from an experienced instructor.
© Sarah Lyman Kravits

Use the information in Key 12.2 as a guide, not a label. Although you may not have all the strengths and challenges indicated by your dominant area, thinking through them will still help you clarify your abilities and interests. In addition, remember that you are capable of change, and with focus and effort you can develop your abilities. Use ideas about strengths and challenges as a starting point for your goals concerning how you would like to grow.

Finally, one other way to investigate how your personality and strengths may inform career choice is to take an inventory based on the Holland theory. Psychologist John Holland theorized that personality was related to career choice, and he came up with six different types that identify both personality and career area: Realistic, Investigative, Artistic, Social, Enterprising, and Conventional (together known as RIASEC).[1] Holland developed two interest surveys that allow people to identify their order of preference for the six types and help them link their stronger types to career areas. Ask your career center about these surveys—the Vocational Preference Inventory (VPI) and the Self-Directed Search (SDS).

Be strategic

With your knowledge about your talents and strengths, focus on making a practical, personal plan to achieve your career goals. First, create a timeline to illustrate the steps you plan to take toward a specific career goal. Working with an advisor, career office employee, or mentor, establish a time frame and write your steps by when they should happen. If your plan is 5 years long, for example, indicate what you plan to do by the fourth, third, and second years, and then the first year, including a 6-month goal and a 1-month goal for that first year. Your path may change, of course; use your timeline as a guide rather than as an inflexible plan.

After you establish your time frame, focus on details. Make specific plans for pursuing the jobs or careers that have piqued your interest. Set goals that establish whom you will talk to, what courses you will take, what skills you will work on, what jobs or internships you will investigate, and any other research you need to do. Be proactive in finding opportunities, as Kelly was.

MULTIPLE INTELLIGENCES MAY OPEN DOORS TO CAREERS

Key 12.1

MULTIPLE INTELLIGENCE	CAREERS
Bodily-Kinesthetic	• Carpenter or draftsman • Physical therapist • Mechanical engineer • Dancer or actor • Exercise physiologist
Intrapersonal	• Research scientist • Computer engineer • Psychologist • Economist • Author
Interpersonal	• Social worker • Public relations or human resources rep • Sociologist • Teacher • Nurse
Naturalistic	• Biochemical engineer • Natural scientist (geologist, ecologist, entymologist) • Paleontologist • Position with environmental group • Farmer or farm management
Musical	• Singer or voice coach • Music teacher • Record executive • Musician or conductor • Radio DJ or sound engineer
Logical-Mathematical	• Doctor or dentist • Accountant • Attorney • Chemist • Investment banker
Verbal-Linguistic	• Author or journalist • TV/radio producer • Literature or language teacher • Business executive • Copywriter or editor
Visual-Spatial	• Graphic artist or illustrator • Photographer • Architect or interior designer • Art museum curator • Art teacher • Set or retail stylist

PERSONALITY SPECTRUM DIMENSIONS INDICATE **STRENGTHS AND CHALLENGES**

DIMENSION	JOB STRENGTHS	JOB CHALLENGES	WHAT TO LOOK FOR IN JOBS/CAREERS
Thinker	• Problem solving • Development of ideas • Keen analysis of situations • Fairness to others • Efficiency in working through tasks • Innovation of plans and systems • Ability to look strategically at the future	• A need for private time to think and work • A need, at times, to move away from established rules • A dislike of sameness—systems that don't change, repetitive tasks • Not always being open to expressing thoughts and feelings to others	• Some level of solo work/think time • Problem solving • Opportunity for innovation • Freedom to think creatively and to bend the rules • Technical work • Big picture strategic planning
Organizer	• High level of responsibility • Enthusiastic support of social structures • Order and reliability • Loyalty • Ability to follow through on tasks according to requirements • Detailed planning skills with competent follow-through • Neatness and efficiency	• A need for tasks to be clearly, concretely defined • A need for structure and stability • A preference for less rapid change • A need for frequent feedback • A need for tangible appreciation • Low tolerance for people who don't conform to rules and regulations	• Clear, well-laid-out tasks and plans • Stable environment with consistent, repeated tasks • Organized supervisors • Clear structure of how employees interact and report to one another • Value of, and reward for, loyalty
Giver	• Honesty and integrity • Commitment to putting energy toward close relationships with others • Finding ways to bring out the best in self and others • Peacemaker and mediator • Ability to listen well, respect opinions, and prioritize the needs of co-workers	• Difficulty in handling conflict, either personal or between others in the work environment • Strong need for appreciation and praise • Low tolerance for perceived dishonesty or deception • Avoidance of people perceived as hostile, cold, or indifferent	• Emphasis on teamwork and relationship building • Indications of strong and open lines of communication among workers • Encouragement of personal expression in the workplace (arrangement of personal space, tolerance of personal celebrations, and so on)
Adventurer	• Skillfulness in many different areas • Willingness to try new things • Ability to take action • Hands-on problem-solving skills • Initiative and energy • Ability to negotiate • Spontaneity and creativity	• Intolerance of being kept waiting • Lack of detail focus • Impulsiveness • Dislike of sameness and authority • Need for freedom, constant change, and constant action • Tendency not to consider consequences of actions	• A spontaneous atmosphere • Less structure, more freedom • Adventuresome tasks • Situations involving change • Encouragement of hands-on problem solving • Travel and physical activity • Support of creative ideas and endeavors

Build knowledge and experience

It's hard to choose the right career path without knowledge or experience. Courses, internships, jobs, and volunteering are four great ways to build both.

■ ***Courses.*** Take a course or two in your areas of interest to determine whether you like the material and can excel. Find out what courses are required for a major in those areas and decide if you are willing to study this material during college. Check out your school's course catalogue for detailed information on the courses involved. Also, consider talking with the department chair to gain more insight into the field.

■ *Internships.* (Internships) provide supervised practical experience in different professional fields. Your career center may list summer or year-round internship opportunities. For more comprehensive guides, check out reference books like those published by Vault and Internet sources like www.internships .com and www.princetonreview.com.

■ *Jobs.* You may discover career opportunities while earning money during a part-time job. Someone who takes a legal proofreading job to make extra cash might discover an interest in law. Someone who answers phones for a newspaper company might be drawn into journalism.

■ *Volunteering.* Helping others in need can introduce you to careers and increase your experience, as Kelly discovered. Many schools establish committees to organize volunteering opportunities or sponsor their own groups. The federal government encourages volunteerism through AmeriCorps, a federal clearinghouse that awards its volunteers money to pay tuition or student loans. You may even be able to find opportunities that mesh with an area of interest. For example, if you are studying accounting, donating your time as a part-time bookkeeper in a shelter will increase your skills while you help those less fortunate than you. Many employers look favorably on volunteering.

■ *Service learning.* The goal of service learning is to provide the community with service and students with knowledge gained from hands-on experience.[2] Students in service learning programs enroll in for-credit courses in which volunteer service and related assignments are required. Service learning builds a sense of civic responsibility, helps students learn useful skills through doing, and promotes values exploration and personal change. If you are interested, talk to your advisor about whether your school offers service learning programs.

Investigate career paths

Career possibilities extend far beyond what you can imagine. Ask instructors, relatives, mentors, and fellow students about careers. Explore job listings, occupation descriptions, assessments, and other information about careers and companies at your school's career center. Check your library for books on careers or biographies of people who worked in fields that interest you. Look at Key 12.3 for the kinds of analytical questions that will aid your search. Keep the following in mind as you look.

▶ *A wide array of job possibilities exists for most career fields.* For example, the medical world consists of more than doctors and nurses. Administrators run hospitals, researchers test drugs, pharmacists prepare prescriptions, security experts ensure patient and visitor safety, and so on.

▶ *Within each job, there are a variety of tasks and skills.* For instance, you may know that an instructor teaches, but you may not realize that instructors also write, research, study, design courses, give presentations, and counsel. Take your career exploration beyond first impressions to get an accurate picture of the careers that interest you.

▶ *A variety of occupations pay well.* Rewarding jobs go beyond law, finance, and medicine. According to data from the U.S. Labor Department, careers with comfortable earnings include electricians, aircraft mechanics, and more.[3] Look up the U.S. Bureau of Labor's *Occupational Outlook Handbook* or see http://salary.com for information on average salaries in different fields.

Know what employers want

When you apply for a job, it is important to realize that prospective employers look for particular skills and qualities that mark you as

INTERNSHIP
A temporary work program in which a student can gain supervised practical experience in a particular professional field.

What can I do in this area that I like and do well?	Do I respect the company or the industry? The product or service?
What are the educational requirements (certificates or degrees, courses)?	Does this company or industry accommodate special needs (child care, sick days, flex time)?
What skills are necessary?	Do I need to belong to a union? What does union membership involve?
What wage or salary and benefits can I expect?	Are there opportunities near where I live (or want to live)?
What personality types are best suited to this kind of work?	What other expectations exist (travel, overtime, and so on)?
What are the prospects for moving up to higher-level positions?	Do I prefer the service or production end of this industry?

a promising candidate. Most employers require you to have a **skill set** that includes specific technical know-how, but in this rapidly changing workplace, general life skills and emotional intelligence may be even more crucial to your success.

> SKILL SET
> A combination of the knowledge, talent, and abilities that are needed to perform a specific job.

General skills

In the modern workplace, workers will hold an average of ten jobs through their productive working years.[4] The high rate of job and workplace change means that abilities such as successful thinking and teamwork are crucial to workplace success. Many of these general skills can also be described as *transferable* skills—general skills learned through job or life experience that you can use with (or transfer to) a new and different job or career. For example, you will need teamwork and writing skills for almost any job. Key 12.4 describes transferable skills that employers look for.

Emotional intelligence

Employers are also drawn to emotionally intelligent job candidates, as you learned in Chapter 1. Your emotional intelligence has an impact on your effectiveness. Consider this scenario: You arrive at work distracted by a personal problem and tired from studying late the night before. Your supervisor is overloaded with a major project due that day. The person you work most closely with is arriving late due to a car problem. In other words, everyone is strung out. What does an emotionally intelligent person do? Remember the three actions of emotional intelligence:

▶ *Tune in to everyone's emotions first.* You: Tired and distracted. Your co-worker: Worried about the car and about being late. Your supervisor: Agitated about the project.

▶ *Understand what the emotions are telling you.* Making the deadline that day might be more challenging than anticipated. Everyone is going to need to set aside distracted, negative thinking and maintain an extra-focused and positive state of mind to get through it.

▶ *Take action toward positive outcomes.* You come up with several ideas.

- Prioritize your task list so that you can concentrate on what is most pressing.

EMPLOYERS LOOK FOR CANDIDATES WITH THESE **IMPORTANT SKILLS**

SKILL	WHY IS IT USEFUL?
Communication	Good listening, speaking, and writing skills are keys to working with others, as is being able to adjust to different communication styles.
Analytical thinking	An employee who can analyze choices and challenges, as well as assess the value of new ideas, stands out.
Creativity	The ability to come up with new concepts, plans, and products helps companies improve and innovate.
Practical thinking	No job gets done without employees who can think through a plan for achieving a goal, put it into action, and complete it successfully.
Teamwork	All workers interact with others on the job. Working well with others is essential for achieving workplace goals.
Goal setting	Teams fail if goals are unclear or unreasonable. Employees and company benefit from setting realistic, specific goals and achieving them reliably.
Cultural competence	The workplace is increasingly diverse. An employee who can work with, adjust to, and respect people from different backgrounds and cultures is valuable.
Leadership	The ability to influence and motivate others in a positive way earns respect and career advancement.
Positive attitude	Other employees will gladly work with, and often advance, someone who completes tasks with positive, upbeat energy.
Integrity	Acting with integrity at work—communicating promptly, being truthful and honest, following rules, giving proper notice—enhances value.
Flexibility	The most valuable employees understand the constancy of change and have developed the skills to adapt to its challenge.
Continual learning	The most valuable employees take personal responsibility to stay current in their fields.

- Put a memo on your supervisor's desk saying that you are available to support her as she nails down the loose ends on her urgent project.
- Call your co-worker on his cell phone while he settles the car problem and let him know the status at work, preparing him to prioritize and to support the supervisor.
- Ask another co-worker to bring in a favorite midmorning snack to keep everyone going on what looks to be a long day.

The current emphasis on teamwork has highlighted emotional intelligence in the workplace. The more adept you are at working with others, the more likely you are to succeed.

Expect change

The working world is always in flux, responding to technological developments, global competition, and other factors. Think about the following as you prepare for your own career.

■ *Growing and declining career areas.* Rapid workplace change means that a growth area today may be declining tomorrow—witness the sudden drop in

student profile

Andrew Hillman
Queens College, Flushing, New York

About me:

I transferred to Queens College from Georgia State University because I wanted to be part of a small school environment. While at Queens College I developed a love for research and how it allows one to offer new information to the world by collecting and analyzing data in innovative ways. I am currently applying to MD-PhD schools so that I may earn a dual degree in medicine and physiology.

What I focus on:

I deliberately investigated career paths at an early stage in my under-graduate career to build my knowledge base as well as gain invaluable experience. I seek out mentors in my field of interest so that I have strong allies. I have also built experience in my areas of interest. No matter what field you choose, there are a plethora of summer-enrichment or yearlong programs and fellowships geared toward providing students with real-life experience—something graduate schools and companies value as a premium. My pre-professional advisor at Queens College has been influential in informing me about potential fellowships. The research fellowships that I have done for the past 2 years have given me the research experience mandated by MD-PhD schools all across the country. In addition they allow me to net-work with people who may offer recommendations for medical school.

What will help me in the workplace:

Doing undergraduate programs that are geared toward your field offers you the crucial head start of being able to know what's going on in your field and, just as importantly, show prospective graduate schools and businesses that you take initiative in learning your future profession.

Internet company jobs and fortunes in 2001. The U.S. Bureau of Labor keeps updated statistics on the status of various career areas. For example, for the period 2008 to 2018, of the ten fastest-growing occupations identified by the bureau, six are related to health care.[5]

■ **Workplace trends.** Companies are hiring more temporary employees (temps) and freelancers. Temporary and freelance jobs offer flexibility, few obligations, and often more take-home pay, but they have limited or no benefits. Also, in response to changing needs, companies are offering more "quality of life" benefits such as telecommuting, job sharing, and on-site child care. You can track these changes by reading hard copy or online versions of business-focused publications such as *Fortune, Business Week,* or the *Wall Street Journal.*

■ *Personal change.* Even difficult personal changes can open doors that you never imagined were there. For example, after being diagnosed with Parkinson's at only 30 years old, actor Michael J. Fox found new passions in life as a best-selling author and advocate for others suffering from the degenerative disease.

Adjusting to changes, both large (leaving an industry for a new career) and small (changing the software you use daily on the job) means putting successful intelligence to work. With the information you collect from newspapers and magazines, Internet sites, and television news, you can analyze what you are facing in the workplace. Based on your analysis, you can create options for yourself, either within your own workplace or elsewhere, and take practical action.

With what you know about general workplace success strategies, you can search effectively for a job in a career area that works for you.

How can you conduct an effective job search?

Whether you are looking for a job now or planning ahead for a search closer to graduation, you have choices about how to proceed. Maximize your success by using the resources available to you, knowing the basics about resumés and interviews, and planning strategically.

Use available resources

NETWORKING
The exchange of information or services among individuals, groups, or institutions.

Use your school's career planning and placement office, your **networking** skills, classified ads, and online services to help you explore possibilities for career areas or specific jobs.

Your school's career planning and placement office

Generally, the career planning and placement office deals with postgraduation job opportunities, whereas the student employment office, along with the financial aid office, has information about working during school. At either location you might find job listings, interview sign-up sheets, and company contact information. The career office may hold frequent informational sessions on different topics. Your school may also sponsor job or career fairs that give you a chance to explore job opportunities. Get acquainted with the career office early in your college career.

CONTACTS
People who serve as carriers or sources of information.

Networking

The most basic type of networking—talking to people about fields and jobs that interest you—is one of the most important job-hunting strategies. Networking **contacts** can answer questions regarding job hunting, occupational responsibilities and challenges, and salary expectations. You can network with friends and family members, instructors, administrators, counselors, alumni, employers, co-workers, and people you meet through extracurricular activities, as a few ideas.

Online social networking can also help you in your job search. Tools like Facebook, Twitter, and LinkedIn allow members to create personalized pages and connect with other individuals through groups, fan pages, and similar interests. During a job search, these sites can be used to meet potential employers through your contacts and showcase portfolio pieces. A word of caution: Your online presence is public. Before you post anything, remember that if you wouldn't want a potential employer (or your parents, instructor, or religious leader) to see it, don't put it online.

Online services and classified ads

Although classified ads are still helpful when looking locally, the Internet is capable of storing tons of information without any cost in paper and ink. Therefore, more employers post through online job boards, and those listings are often more detailed than the two- or three-sentence ads you'd find in a newspaper. In addition to a job description and salary information, most online postings will contain company information and a link to where you can submit an application. Use the following tips to make the most of your virtual resources:

Take advantage of career fairs sponsored by your school or town. These career fair attendees pick up useful information and applications from different employers.
© Adam Lau/AP Images

- ► Look up career-focused and job-listing websites such as CareerBuilder.com, Monster.com, America's Job Bank, BilingualCareer.com, JobBankUSA.com, or futurestep.com. Many sites offer resources on career areas, resumés, and online job searching in addition to listings of openings.
- ► Access job search databases such as the Career Placement Registry and U.S. Employment Opportunities.
- ► Check the Web pages of individual associations and companies, which may post job listings and descriptions.

If nothing happens right away, keep at it. New job postings appear, and new people sign on to look at your resume. Plus, sites change all the time. Search using the keywords "job sites" or "job search" to see what sites come up (quintcareers.com has a listing of the top fifty best job sites).

Use an organized, consistent strategy

Organize your approach according to what you need to do and when you have to do it. Do you plan to make three phone calls per day? Will you fill out one job application each week? Keep a record—on 3-by-5 cards, in a computer file or smartphone, or in a notebook—of the following:

- ► People you contact plus contact information and method of contact (e-mail, snail mail, phone)
- ► Companies to which you apply
- ► Jobs for which you apply, including any results (for example, a job that becomes unavailable)
- ► Responses to communications (phone calls to you, interviews, written communications), information about the person who contacted you (name, title), and the times and dates of contact

Keeping accurate records enables you to both chart your progress and maintain a clear picture of the process. If you don't get a job now but another opens up at the same company in a few months, well-kept records will enable you to contact key personnel quickly and efficiently.

Your resumé, cover letter, and interview

Information on resumés, cover letters, and interviews fills entire books. To get you started, here are a few basic tips on giving yourself the best possible chance.

Resumé and cover letter

Design your resumé neatly, using a current and acceptable format (books or your career office can show you some standard formats). Make sure the information is accurate and truthful. Proofread for errors and have someone else proofread it as well. Type it and print it on high-quality paper (a heavier bond paper than is used for ordinary copies). Include a brief, to-the-point cover letter that tells which job interests you and why the employer should hire you.

Prospective employers often use a computer to scan resumés, selecting those containing *keywords* relating to the job opening or industry. Resumés without enough keywords probably won't even make it to the human resources desk, so make sure to include as many keywords as you can. For example, if you are seeking a computer-related job, list computer programs you use and other specific technical proficiencies. To figure out the keywords for your field, check out occupation descriptions, job postings, and other current resumés.[6]

Change the CONVERSATION

Challenge yourself and your friends to ask—and answer—tough questions. Use the following to inspire discussion in pairs or groups.

▶ As one saying goes, "Do what you love and the money will come." Do you agree or disagree? Give examples and evidence to support your opinion.

▶ People who work freelance jobs need to be careful money managers in order to put money into savings, finance health insurance, and pay required taxes. People who are employed by companies may have less freedom but are more likely to enjoy benefits such as insurance, savings plans, and tax withholding. Which suits you better?

▶ Have you had a job application rejected, failed to get a job after an interview, or been fired from a job? How did you cope?

▶ **CONSIDER THE CASE:** Kelly saw a problem and was driven to try to solve it. Do you think that Kelly can benefit from providing English instruction to local immigrants? In what ways? How has making a difference for someone else in your life had a positive effect on you?

Interview

Be clean, neat, and appropriately dressed. Choose a nice pair of shoes—people notice. Bring an extra copy of your resumé and any other materials that you want to show the interviewer. Avoid chewing gum or smoking. Offer a confident handshake. Make eye contact. Show your integrity by speaking honestly about yourself. After the interview, no matter what the outcome, follow up right away with a formal but pleasant thank-you note.

Being on time to your interview makes a positive impression—and being late will almost certainly be held against you. If you are from a culture that does not consider being late a sign of disrespect, remember that your interviewer may not agree.

How can you continue to activate your successful intelligence?

Throughout this text you have connected analytical, creative, and practical thinking to academic and life skills. You have put them together in order to solve problems and make decisions. You have seen how these skills, used consistently and with balance, can help you succeed.

Find Useful Keywords

Name two career fields that you would consider pursuing:

1. _____

2. _____

Research resumé keywords that employers in these fields look for. On your chosen search engine, enter the words *keyword, resume,* and a word or phrase related to the field ("chemical engineering," "criminal justice," etc.). Fill in the list with ten keywords for each field. Keep them on hand to tailor your resumé for a job in either one of these fields.

Field _____

1. _____   6. _____

2. _____   7. _____

3. _____   8. _____

4. _____   9. _____

5. _____   10. _____

Field _____

1. _____   6. _____

2. _____   7. _____

3. _____   8. _____

4. _____   9. _____

5. _____   10. _____

You are only just beginning your career as a successfully intelligent learner. You will continue to discover the best ways to achieve goals that are meaningful to you. In Chapter 1, you completed a self-assessment to examine your levels of development in twenty characteristics that help successfully intelligent people stay motivated. Use the Get Analytical exercise to see how you have developed your self-motivation over the course of the term. Looking at these characteristics again as ideas that will keep you moving ahead toward your goals, you will notice that Kelly's story and many of the other profiles demonstrate most of them. According to Sternberg, successfully intelligent people apply the following techniques.[7]

1. *Motivate themselves.* They make things happen, spurred on by a desire to succeed and a love of what they are doing.
2. *Learn to control their impulses.* Instead of going with their first quick response, they sit with a question or problem. They allow time for thinking and let ideas surface before making a decision.

Evaluate Your Development

As you complete your work in the course, revisit your perceived development in Sternberg's characteristics of successfully intelligent thinkers.

1	2	3	4	5
Not at All Like Me	Somewhat Unlike Me	Not Sure	Somewhat Like Me	Definitely Like Me

Please circle the number which best represents your answer:

1. I motivate myself well.   1 2 3 4 5

2. I can control my impulses.   1 2 3 4 5

3. I know when to persevere and when to change gears.   1 2 3 4 5

4. I make the most of what I do well.   1 2 3 4 5

5. I can successfully translate my ideas into action.   1 2 3 4 5

6. I can focus effectively on my goal.   1 2 3 4 5

7. I complete tasks and have good follow-through.   1 2 3 4 5

8. I initiate action—I move people and projects ahead.   1 2 3 4 5

9. I have the courage to risk failure.   1 2 3 4 5

10. I avoid procrastination.   1 2 3 4 5

11. I accept responsibility when I make a mistake.   1 2 3 4 5

12. I don't waste time feeling sorry for myself.   1 2 3 4 5

13. I independently take responsibility for tasks.   1 2 3 4 5

14. I work hard to overcome personal difficulties.   1 2 3 4 5

15. I create an environment that helps me concentrate on my goals.   1 2 3 4 5

16. I don't take on too much work or too little.   1 2 3 4 5

17. I can delay gratification to receive the benefits.   1 2 3 4 5

18. I can see both the big picture and the details in a situation.   1 2 3 4 5

19. I am able to maintain confidence in myself.   1 2 3 4 5

20. I balance my analytical, creative, and practical thinking skills.   1 2 3 4 5

When you complete the assessment, look back at pages 22–23 for your original scores. What development do you see? List three changes that feel significant to you:

1. _____

2. _____

3. _____

As you grow, there is always room for improvement. Choose one characteristic that you feel still needs work. Analyze the specific reasons why it remains a challenge. For example, if you are still taking on too much work, is it out of a need to please others? Write a brief analysis on a separate sheet of paper or electronic file, and let this analysis guide you as you work to build your strength in this area.

3. *Know when to persevere.* When it makes sense, they push past frustration and stay on course, confident that success is in their sights. They also are able to see when they've hit a dead end—and, in those cases, to stop pushing.

4. *Know how to make the most of their abilities.* They understand what they do well and capitalize on it in school and work.

5. *Translate thought into action.* Not only do they have good ideas; they are able to turn those ideas into practical actions that bring ideas to fruition.

6. *Have a product orientation.* They want results; they focus on what they are aiming for rather than on how they are getting there.

7. *Complete tasks and follow through.* With determination, they finish what they start. They also follow through to make sure all the loose ends are tied and the goal has been achieved.

8. *Are initiators.* They commit to people, projects, and ideas. They make things happen rather than sitting back and waiting for things to happen to them.

9. *Are not afraid to risk failure.* Because they take risks and sometimes fail, they often enjoy greater success and build their intellectual capacity. Like everyone, they make mistakes—but they tend not to make the same mistake twice.

10. *Don't procrastinate.* They are aware of the negative effects of putting things off, and they avoid them. They create schedules that allow them to accomplish what's important on time.

11. *Accept fair blame.* They strike a balance between never accepting blame and taking the blame for everything. If something is their fault, they accept responsibility and don't make excuses.

12. *Reject self-pity.* When something goes wrong, they find a way to solve the problem. They don't get caught in the energy drain of feeling sorry for themselves.

13. *Are independent.* They can work on their own and think for themselves. They take responsibility for their own schedule and tasks.

14. *Seek to surmount personal difficulties.* They keep things in perspective, looking for ways to remedy personal problems and separate them from their professional lives.

15. *Focus and concentrate to achieve their goals.* They create an environment in which they can best avoid distraction to focus steadily on their work.

16. *Spread themselves neither too thin nor too thick.* They strike a balance between doing too many things, which results in little progress on any of them, and too few things, which can reduce the level of accomplishment.

17. *Have the ability to delay gratification.* Although they enjoy the smaller rewards that require less energy, they focus the bulk of their work on the goals that take more time but promise the most gratification.

18. *Have the ability to see the forest and the trees.* They are able to see the big picture and avoid getting bogged down in tiny details.

19. *Have a reasonable level of self-confidence and a belief in their ability to accomplish their goals.* They believe in themselves enough to get through the tough times, while avoiding the kind of overconfidence that stalls learning and growth.

20. *Balance analytical, creative, and practical thinking.* They sense what to use and when to use it. When problems arise, they combine all three skills to arrive at solutions.

These characteristics are your personal motivational tools. Consult them when you need a way to get moving. You may even want to post them somewhere in your home, in the front of a notebook, or as a note in your smartphone.

How will your learning in this course bring success?

You leave this course with far more than a final grade, a notebook full of work, and a credit hour or three on your transcript. You leave with a set of skills and attitudes that open the door to success in the 21st century.

Lifelong learning and the growth mindset

With knowledge in many fields doubling every 2 to 3 years and your personal interests and needs changing all the time, what you learn in college is just the beginning of what you will need to discover throughout your life to succeed. With a growth mindset—the attitude that you can always grow and learn—you are as ready to achieve the goals you set out for yourself today as you are to achieve future goals you cannot yet anticipate.

If you look back at Key 1.3 on page 7 and at the 21st Century Building Blocks in each Personal Portfolio exercise, you will see that you have built skills and knowledge in each quadrant of the 21st Century Learning grid.

The attitudes and skills you have acquired this term are your keys to success now and in the future. *As you continue in college, remind yourself that you are creating tools that will benefit you in everything you do.* See Key 12.5 for details.

Make learning a habit for life by strengthening your growth mindset in ways such as the following:

▶ *Investigate new interests.* When information and events catch your attention, take your interest one step further and find out more. Instead of dreaming about it, just do it.

▶ *Read, read, read.* Reading expert Jim Trelease says that people who don't read "base their future decisions on what they used to know. If you don't read much, you really don't know much."[8] Open a world of knowledge and perspectives through reading. Ask friends which books have changed their lives. Keep up with local, national, and world news through newspapers, magazines, and Internet sources.

▶ *Keep on top of changes in your career.* After graduation, continue your education both in your field and in the realm of general knowledge. Stay on top of ideas, developments, and new technology in your field by seeking out **continuing education** courses. Sign up for career-related seminars. Some companies offer additional on-the-job training or pay for their employees to take courses that will improve their knowledge and skills.

▶ *Spend time with interesting people.* When you meet someone new who inspires you and makes you think, keep in touch. Form a book club, get a pickup basketball game together, or join a local volunteer organization. Learn something new from everyone you meet.

▶ *Talk to people from different generations.* Younger people can learn from the broad perspective of those from older generations;

CONTINUING EDUCATION
Courses that students can take without needing to be part of a degree program.

ATTITUDES AND SKILLS ACQUIRED IN COLLEGE ARE TOOLS FOR **LIFELONG SUCCESS**

ACQUIRED SKILL	IN COLLEGE, YOU'LL USE IT TO . . .	IN CAREER AND LIFE, YOU'LL USE IT TO . . .
Investigating resources	. . . find who and what can help you have the college experience you want	. . . get acclimated at a new job or in a new town—find the people, resources, and services that can help you succeed
Knowing and using your learning styles	. . . select study strategies that make the most of your learning styles	. . . select jobs, career areas, and other pursuits that suit what you do best
Setting goals and managing stress	. . . complete assignments and achieve educational goals; reduce stress by being in control	. . . accomplish tasks and reach career and personal goals; reduce stress by being in control
Managing time	. . . get to classes on time, juggle school and work, turn in assignments when they are due, plan study time	. . . finish work tasks on time or before they are due, balance duties on the job and at home
Analytical, creative, and practical thinking	. . . think through writing assignments, solve math problems, analyze academic readings, brainstorm paper topics, work through academic issues, work effectively on team projects	. . . find ways to improve product design, increase market share, present ideas to customers; analyze life issues, come up with ideas, and take practical action
Reading	. . . read course texts and other materials	. . . read operating manuals, work guidebooks, media materials in your field; read for practical purposes, for learning, and for pleasure at home
Note taking	. . . take notes in class, in study groups, during studying, and during research	. . . take notes in work and community meetings and during important phone calls
Test taking	. . . take quizzes, tests, and final exams	. . . take tests for certification in particular work skills and for continuing education courses
Writing	. . . write essays and reports	. . . write work-related documents, including e-mails, reports, proposals, and speeches; write personal letters and journal entries
Building successful relationships	. . . get along with instructors, students, and student groups	. . . get along with supervisors, co-workers, team members, friends, and family members
Staying healthy	. . . stay physically and mentally healthy so that you can make the most of school	. . . stay physically and mentally healthy so that you can be at your best at work and at home
Managing money	. . . stay on top of school costs and make decisions that earn and save you the money you need	. . . budget the money you earn so that you can pay your bills and save for the future
Establishing and maintaining a personal mission	. . . develop a big picture idea of what you want from your education, and make choices that guide you toward those goals	. . . develop a big picture idea of what you wish to accomplish in life, and make choices that guide you toward those goals

older people can learn from the fresh perspective of youth. Communication builds mutual respect.

▶ *Delve into other cultures.* Invite a friend over who has grown up in a culture different from your own. Eat food from a country you've never visited. Initiate conversations with people of different races, religions, values, and ethnic backgrounds. Travel internationally and locally. Take a course that deals with cultural diversity. Try a term or year abroad. Learn a new language. Kelly's experience with other cultures broadened her horizons and has led her on a path toward a fulfilling career.

Think Fifty Positive Thoughts

List twenty-five things you like about yourself. You can name anything—things you can do, things you think, things you've accomplished, things you like about your physical self, and so on. (Use a separate sheet of paper or an electronic file.)

Next, list twenty-five things you would like to do in your life. These can be anything from trying Vietnamese food to traveling to the Grand Canyon to working for Teach for America. They can be things you'd like to do tomorrow or things that you plan to do in 20 years. At least five items on the list should involve your current and future education.

Finally, come up with five things you can plan for the next year that combine what you like about yourself and what you want to do. If you like your strength as a mountain biker and you want to explore a state you've never seen, plan a mountain biking trip. If you like your writing and you want to be a published author, write an essay to submit to a magazine. Be creative. Let everything be possible.

1. _____

   _____

2. _____

   _____

3. _____

   _____

4. _____

   _____

5. _____

   _____

▶ *Nurture a spiritual life.* Wherever you find spirituality—in organized religion, family, friendship, nature, music, or anywhere else—it will help you find balance and meaning.

▶ *Experience the arts.* Art is "a means of knowing the world" (Angela Carter, author); "a lie that makes us realize truth" (Pablo Picasso, painter); a revealer of "our most secret self" (Jean-Luc Godard, filmmaker). Through art you can discover new ideas and shed light on old ones. Seek out whatever moves you—music, visual arts, theater, photography, dance, performance art, film and television, poetry, prose, and more.

▶ *Be creative.* Take a class in drawing, writing, or quilting. Learn to play an instrument. Write poems for your friends or stories to read to your children. Concoct a new recipe. Design and build something for your home. Express yourself, and learn more about yourself, through art.

Lifelong learning is the master key that unlocks so many of the doors you encounter on your journey. If you keep it firmly in your hand, you will discover worlds of knowledge—and a place for yourself to continue growing within them.

Flexibility helps you adapt to change

As a citizen of the 21st century, you are likely to move in and out of school, jobs, and careers in the years ahead. You are also likely to experience important personal changes. How you react to change, especially if it is unexpected and difficult, is almost as important as the changes themselves in determining your future success. The ability to "make lemonade from lemons" is the hallmark of people who are able to hang on to hope.

Your thinking skills will help you stay flexible. As planned and unplanned changes arise, you analyze them, brainstorm solutions, and take practical action. With these skills you can adapt to the loss of a job or an exciting job offer, failing a course or winning an academic scholarship.

Although sudden changes may throw you off balance, the unpredictability of life can open new horizons. Margaret J. Wheatley and Myron Kellner-Rogers, leadership and community experts, explain: "Unpredictability gives us the freedom to experiment. It is this unpredictability that welcomes our creativity."[9] Here are some strategies for making the most of changes:

▶ *Focus on what is rather than what is supposed to be.* Planning for the future works best when you accept the reality of your situation.
▶ *Use your planning as a guide rather than a rule.* If you allow yourself to follow new paths when changes occur, you'll be able to grow from what life gives you.
▶ *Be willing to be surprised.* Great creative energies can come from the force of a surprise. Instead of turning back to familiar patterns, explore new possibilities.

With successful intelligence and a growth mindset, you will always have a new direction in which to grow. Live each day to the fullest, using your thinking skills to achieve your most valued goals. Challenge yourself to raise the bar and vault over it by seeking to improve and grow in the ways that are most meaningful to you. By being true to yourself, a respectful friend and family member, a focused student who believes in the power of learning, a productive employee, and a contributing member of society, you can change the world.

What happened to Kelly? Kelly came up with an idea for a nonprofit program, Project Bridge, that would recruit university students learning Spanish to teach ESL in-home to local residents, giving the resident a free tutor and the tutor a chance to practice Spanish and help the community. When she asked KU's Center for Community Outreach for support, the center provided her with funding, office space, people to help run the program, and access to local resources. Within a year, Project Bridge grew to more than fifty student–teacher partnerships, and it is still thriving. Wanting to further her commitment to service, Kelly joined the El Pomar Fellowship Program, a 2-year leadership development program that helps partici-pants learn how to connect nonprofit organizations with resources. She then applied to business schools, hoping to further her understanding of the problem-solving capabilities of communication so that she could make a difference for organizations. She is now working toward her MBA.

Case
Wrap-up

What does this mean for you? Doing something to improve the life of even one person in your commu-nity has ripple effects that can bring positive change to many people. You don't need to start an entire organization to be able to make a difference, of course. Use your analytical thinking skills to look carefully at what is going on around you. Think creatively to come up with ideas about what you could do. Don't rule out any idea, however small it seems. Finally, take practical action and make it happen. Involve others if you can.

What effects go beyond your world? Kelly Carson's organization, in addition to providing a service to people, also bridges a gap between cultures. You may have opportunities to make cross-cultural connections locally, if you live in a diverse area. However, even if you don't, you can look further for a chance to connect. An organization called Cross-Cultural Solutions, found at www.crossculturalsolutions.org, provides volunteering opportunities abroad all over the world in areas such as teaching, health care, and community development. Time frames are flexible, with placements from 2 to 12 weeks and even some 1-week opportunities. Explore the site. Even if you don't want to travel, it may give you ideas about other ways to make a better world.

Successful Intelligence *Wrap-up*

HERE'S HOW YOU HAVE
BUILT SKILLS IN **CHAPTER 12** :

ANALYTICAL THINKING	**CREATIVE THINKING**	**PRACTICAL THINKING**
❯ You looked carefully at which actions promote career success and impress employers.	❯ The information connecting learning styles to career may have inspired new ideas about careers to pursue.	❯ In the Get Practical exercise, you researched keywords that may be useful in building a resumé.
❯ In the Get Analytical exercise, you analyzed your progress in the twenty characteristics that help to motivate you.	❯ Reading the material about how college skills promote lifelong learning may have inspired new ideas about how you can learn.	❯ You took in the details of how to perform an effective job search.
❯ You explored how you will continue to use the skills you acquired in this course.	❯ In the Get Creative exercise, you brainstormed positive thoughts about yourself as well as plans for the near and far future.	❯ You explored specific ways to be flexible in the face of change.

Word*for*Thought

The **Navajo** translate *hozh'q* (hoe'-shk) as "the beauty of life, as seen and created by a person."[10] The word incorporates concepts such as health and well-being, balance, and happiness. The Navajo perceive that hozh'q can start with one person and extend outward indefinitely, having a unifying effect on others, the world, and the universe. Share your hozh'q with others, extending the beauty of life as far as you can.

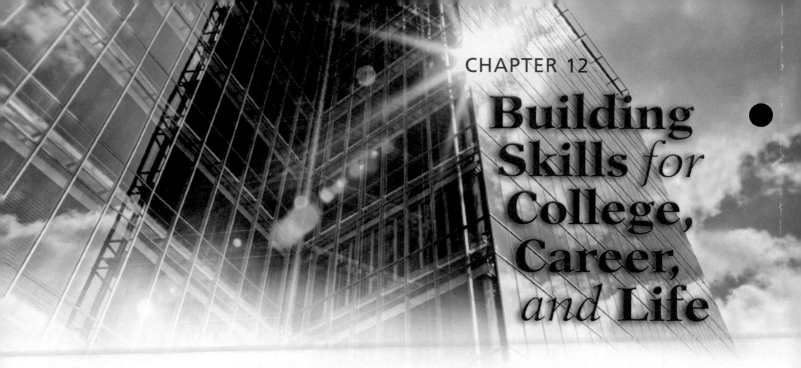

Building Skills *for* College, Career, *and* Life

Steps to Success

Become a Better Interviewee

BUILD BASIC SKILLS. Think about the questions that a job applicant would typically hear in an entry-level interview. Recall questions from job interviews you've had, look up questions using online sources such as www.quintcareers.com, or consult books on job interviews. On a separate sheet of paper or electronic file, list fifteen to twenty questions.

TAKE IT TO THE NEXT LEVEL. Imagining yourself as the interviewer, brainstorm some more creative questions to add to your list. Think about learning styles, life experiences, learning from failure, role models, and more as you ponder. Write five additional questions here:

1. _____

2. _____

3. _____

4. _____

5. _____

MOVE TOWARD MASTERY. Pair up with a student in your class and interview each other. Person A interviews Person B for 5 to 10 minutes and takes notes. Then switch roles: Person B interviews Person A and takes notes. Each person uses the set of questions developed in the first and second parts of the exercise.

When you are done, share with each other what interesting ideas stand out from the interviews. If you have suggestions, offer constructive criticism to each other about interview skills.

Write here a brief analysis and summary of your experience, including what you learned and would keep in mind for a real interview.

_____

_____

_____

Teamwork

Create Solutions Together

GIVING BACK

Goal: To research and commit to a local volunteering opportunity.

Time on task: 1 week; 30 minutes of research in between two group meetings

Instructions: In your group, come up with a list of volunteering opportunities on campus or in your local area. Each member should choose one to research independently. Create a description of your opportunity that answers questions such as the following: What is the situation or organization? What are its needs? Do any volunteer positions require an application, letters of reference, or background checks? What is the time commitment? Is any special training involved? Are there any problematic or challenging elements to this experience?

When you have the information, meet together so that each group member can describe each volunteering opportunity to the other members. As you discuss each opportunity, brainstorm how it might serve career goals, such as through building general transferable abilities, specific skills, or experience in a particular career area.

On your own following the group discussion, choose one volunteering opportunity that you feel you will have the time and ability to try next term. Contact the person or organization now to get more information and make plans.

Writing

Build Intrapersonal and Communication Skills

Record your thoughts separately on paper, in a journal, or electronically.

EMOTIONAL INTELLIGENCE JOURNAL

Revisit your personal mission. Look back in Chapter 2 at both the personal mission you wrote and the three career priorities that you felt most effectively matched up to your mission (see pp. 54–55). Thinking about how you feel now at the end of the term, and considering what has changed about the outcomes you want to make happen in your life, write an updated version of your mission. Incorporate one or more of those career priorities into your mission statement.

REAL-LIFE WRITING

Create a resumé. Start with a brainstorm using two sheets of paper or a computer file. On one electronic page or sheet of paper, list information about your education (where and when you've studied, degrees or certificates you've earned) and skills (what you know how to do, such as use various computer programs or operate certain types of equipment). On another, list job experience. For each job, record job title, the dates of employment, and the tasks you performed (if the job had no particular title, come up with one yourself). Be as detailed as possible—it's best to write down everything you remember. When you compile your resumé, you will make this material more concise. Keep this list and update it periodically as you gain experience and accomplishments.

Using the information you have gathered and Key 12.6 as your guide, draft a resumé. There are many ways to construct a resumé; consult other resources for different styles (try

Désirée Williams

237 Custer Street, San Francisco, CA 94101 • 650/555-5252 (w) or 415/555-7865 (h)
• fax: 707/555-2735 • e-mail: desiree@zzz.com

EDUCATION

2009 to present   San Francisco State University, San Francisco, CA
Pursuing a B.A. in the Spanish BCLAD (Bilingual, Cross-Cultural Language Acquisition Development)
Education and Multiple Subject Credential Program. Expected graduation: June 2012.

PROFESSIONAL EMPLOYMENT

10/10 to present   **Research Assistant, Knowledge Media Lab**
Developing ways for teachers to exhibit their inquiry into their practice of teaching in an online,
collaborative, multimedia environment.

5/09 to present   **Webmaster/Web Designer**
Work in various capacities at QuakeNet, an Internet Service Provider and Web Commerce Specialist in
San Mateo, CA. Designed several sites for the University of California, Berkeley, Graduate School of
Education, as well as private clients such as A Body of Work and Yoga Forever.

9/09 to 6/10   **Literacy Coordinator**
Coordinated, advised, and created literacy curriculum for an America Reads literacy project at
Prescott School in West Oakland. Worked with non-reader 4th graders on writing and publishing,
incorporating digital photography, Internet resources, and graphic design.

8/09   **Bilingual Educational Consultant**
Consulted for Children's Television Workshop, field-testing bilingual materials. With a research team,
designed bilingual educational materials for an ecotourism project run by an indigenous rain forest
community in Ecuador.

1/09 to 6/10   **Technology Consultant**
Worked with 24 Hours in Cyberspace, an online worldwide photojournalism event. Coordinated
participation of schools, translated documents, and facilitated public relations.

SKILLS

Languages: Fluent in Spanish.
Proficient in Italian and Shona (majority language of Zimbabwe).

Computer: Programming ability in HTML, Javascript, Pascal, and Lisp. Multimedia design expertise in Adobe
Photoshop, Netobjects Fusion, Adobe Premiere, Macromedia Flash, and many other visual design
programs.

Personal: Perform professionally in Mary Schmary, a women's a cappella quartet. I have climbed Mt. Kilimanjaro.

---

www.resume-help.org or www.howtowritearesume.net). You may want to format your resumé
according to an approach that your career counselor or instructor recommends. If you already have
a specific career focus, that field may favor a particular style of resumé (check with your career
counselor or an instructor in that area).

Keep this resumé draft in hard copy and on a computer hard drive or disk. When you need to
submit a resumé with a job application, update the draft and print it out on high-quality paper.

The list of general tips provides useful help for writing a resumé:

- Always put your name and contact information at the top. Make it stand out.
- State an objective if appropriate—when your focus is specific or you are designing this resumé for a particular interview or career area.
- List your postsecondary education, starting from the latest and working backward. This may include summer school, night school, seminars, and accreditations.
- List jobs in reverse chronological order (most recent job first). Include all types of work experience (full-time or part-time work, volunteer experiences, internships, and so on).
- When you describe your work experience, use action verbs and focus on what you have accomplished, rather than on the description of assigned tasks.
- Include keywords that are linked to jobs for which you will be applying.
- List references on a separate sheet. You may want to put "References upon request" at the bottom of your resumé.
- Use formatting (larger font sizes, different fonts, italics, bold, and so on) and indent selectively to help the important information stand out.
- Get several people to look at your resumé before you send it out. Other readers will have ideas that you haven't thought of and may find errors you have missed.

Personal Portfolio

Prepare for Career Success

REVISIT THE WHEEL OF SUCCESSFUL INTELLIGENCE

21st Century Learning Building Blocks

- Initiative and Self-Direction
- Critical Thinking and Problem Solving

Complete the following in your electronic portfolio or separately on paper. When you have finished, read through your entire career portfolio. You have gathered information to turn to again and again on your path to a fulfilling, successful career.

Without looking at these same assessments or the wheel from Chapter 1, analyze where you are after completing this course by taking the three assessments again.

ASSESS YOUR ANALYTICAL THINKING SKILLS

For each statement, circle the number that feels right to you, from 1 for "not at all true for me" to 5 for "very true for me."

1. I recognize and define problems effectively.	1 2 3 4 5
2. I see myself as a "thinker," "analytical," "studious."	1 2 3 4 5
3. When working on a problem in a group setting, I like to break down the problem into its components and evaluate them.	1 2 3 4 5
4. I need to see convincing evidence before accepting information as fact.	1 2 3 4 5
5. I weigh the pros and cons of plans and ideas before taking action.	1 2 3 4 5
6. I tend to make connections among bits of information by categorizing them.	1 2 3 4 5
7. Impulsive, spontaneous decision making worries me.	1 2 3 4 5
8. I like to analyze causes and effects when making a decision.	1 2 3 4 5
9. I monitor my progress toward goals.	1 2 3 4 5
10. Once I reach a goal, I evaluate the process to see how effective it was.	1 2 3 4 5

Total your answers here: _____

ASSESS YOUR CREATIVE THINKING SKILLS

For each statement, circle the number that feels right to you, from 1 for "not at all true for me" to 5 for "very true for me."

1. I tend to question rules and regulations. 1 2 3 4 5

2. I see myself as "unique," "full of ideas," "innovative." 1 2 3 4 5

3. When working on a problem in a group setting, I generate a lot of ideas. 1 2 3 4 5

4. I am energized when I have a brand-new experience. 1 2 3 4 5

5. If you say something is too risky, I'm ready to give it a shot. 1 2 3 4 5

6. I often wonder if there is a different way to do or see something. 1 2 3 4 5

7. Too much routine in my work or schedule drains my energy. 1 2 3 4 5

8. I tend to see connections among ideas that others do not. 1 2 3 4 5

9. I feel comfortable allowing myself to make mistakes as I test out ideas. 1 2 3 4 5

10. I'm willing to champion an idea even when others disagree with me. 1 2 3 4 5

Total your answers here: _____

ASSESS YOUR PRACTICAL THINKING SKILLS

For each statement, circle the number that feels right to you, from 1 for "not at all true for me" to 5 for "very true for me."

1. I can find a way around any obstacle. 1 2 3 4 5

2. I see myself as a "doer," the "go-to" person; I "make things happen." 1 2 3 4 5

3. When working on a problem in a group setting, I like to figure out who will do what and when it should be done. 1 2 3 4 5

4. I apply what I learn from experience to improve my response to similar situations. 1 2 3 4 5

5. I finish what I start and don't leave loose ends hanging. 1 2 3 4 5

6. I note my emotions about academic and social situations and use what they tell me to move toward a goal. 1 2 3 4 5

7. I can sense how people feel and can use that knowledge to interact with others effectively. 1 2 3 4 5

8. I manage my time effectively. 1 2 3 4 5

9. I adjust to the teaching styles of my instructors and the communication styles of my peers. 1 2 3 4 5

10. When involved in a problem-solving process, I can shift gears as needed. 1 2 3 4 5

Total your answers here: _____

After you have finished, fill in your new scores on the blank Wheel of Successful Intelligence in Key 12.7. Compare it with your previous wheel on page 27. Look at the changes: Where have you grown? How has your self-perception changed?

USE THIS NEW **WHEEL OF SUCCESSFUL INTELLIGENCE** TO EVALUATE YOUR PROGRESS

With your new scores in hand, create the most updated representation of your thinking skills. In each of the three areas of the wheel, draw a curved line approximately at the level of your number score and fill in the wedge below that line. Compare this wheel to your previous wheel and note any change and development.

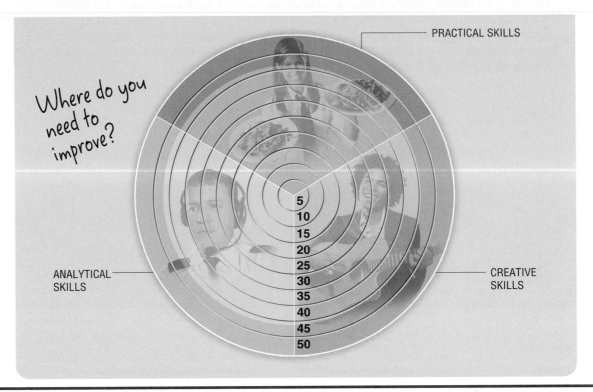

Source: Based on "The Wheel of Life" model developed by the Coaches Training Institute. © Co-Active Space 2000.

- • Note three creative ideas you came up with over the term that aided your exploration or development:

Idea 1: _____

_____

Idea 2: _____

_____

Idea 3: _____

_____

- • Note three practical actions that you took that moved you toward your goals:

Action 1: _____

_____

Action 2: _____

_____

Action 3: _____

_____

Let what you learn from this new wheel inform you about what you have accomplished and what you plan to accomplish. Continue to grow your analytical, creative, and practical skills and use them to manage the changes that await you in the future.

Social Networking

ADD YOUR RESUMÉ

Add your current resumé to the tools on LinkedIn that can help you achieve career goals. Make sure your resumé is accessible (from the hard drive or another source such as a flash drive) on the computer you are using. Sign in to your account and click on "Edit My Profile." Click on the "Import your resume" button on the right side of the screen, and follow instructions.

As you move ahead in college and life, continue to build, adjust, and use the LinkedIn profile you have built throughout this course. Make it a tool for success.

Writing a research paper or essay involves planning, drafting, revising, and editing.

Planning

The planning process involves six steps that help you think about the assignment. It now takes you from beginning practical questions, to research, to a working outline.

Pay attention to logistics

Practical questions will help you decide on a topic and depth of coverage:

1. *How much depth does my instructor expect and how long should the paper be?*
2. *How much time do I have?* Consider your other courses and responsibilities.
3. *What kind of research is needed?* Your topic and purpose may determine this.
4. *Is it a team project?* If you are working with others, determine what each person will do.

Brainstorm topic ideas

Start the process of choosing a paper topic with *brainstorming*—a creative technique to generate ideas without judging their worth (see Chapter 4):

▶ Begin by writing down anything on the assigned subject that comes to mind, in no particular order. Tap your multiple intelligences for creative ideas. To jump-start your thoughts, scan your text and notes, check library or Internet references, or meet with your instructor to discuss ideas.
▶ Next, organize that list into an outline or think link so you can see different possibilities.

Use prewriting strategies to narrow your topic

Strategies such as brainstorming, freewriting, and asking journalists' questions[1] help you decide which possible topic you would most like to pursue. Use them to narrow your topic, focusing on the specific sub-ideas and examples from your brainstorming session.

▶ *Brainstorming.* The same creative process you used to generate ideas will help you narrow your topic. Write down your thoughts about the possibilities you have chosen, do some more research, and then organize your thoughts into categories, noticing patterns that appear.
▶ *Freewriting.* When you *freewrite,* you jot down whatever comes to mind without censoring ideas or worrying about grammar, spelling, punctuation, or organization.

▶ *Asking journalists' questions.* When journalists start working on a story, they ask Who? What? Where? When? Why? How? Asking these questions will help you choose a specific topic.

Prewriting helps you develop a topic that is broad enough for investigation but narrow enough to handle. Prewriting also helps you identify what you know and what you don't know. If an assignment involves more than you already know, you need to do research.

Conduct research and take notes

Research develops in stages as you narrow and refine your ideas. In the first brainstorming-for-ideas stage, look for an overview that can lead to a working thesis statement. In the second stage, track down information that fills in gaps. Ultimately, you will have a "body" of information that you can evaluate to develop and implement your final thesis.

As you research, create source and content notes to organize your work, keep track of your sources, and avoid plagiarism.

■ *Source notes.* Source notes, written on index cards, are preliminary notes that should include the author's name; the title of the work; the edition (if any); the publisher, year, and city of publication; the issue and/or volume number when applicable (such as for a magazine); and the page numbers consulted. Notes on Internet sources should reference the website's complete name and address, including the universal resource locator (URL), which is the string of text and numbers that identifies an Internet site. Include a short summary and critical evaluation for each source.

■ *Content notes.* Content notes, written on large index cards, in a notebook, or on your computer, are taken during a thorough reading and provide an in-depth look at source material. Use them to record needed information. To supplement your content notes, make notations—marginal notes, highlighting, and underlining—directly on photocopies of sources.

Write a working thesis statement

Next, organize your research and write a *thesis statement*—the organizing principle of your paper. The thesis declares your specific subject and point of view and reflects your writing purpose (to inform or persuade) and audience (your intended readers).

Consider this to be your *working thesis,* because it may change as you continue your research and develop your draft. Be ready and willing to rework your writing—and your thesis—one or more times before handing in your paper.

Write a working outline or think link

The final planning step is to create a working outline or think link to guide your writing.

Drafting

You may write many versions of the assignment until you are satisfied. Each version moves you closer to saying exactly what you want in the way you want to say it. You face the following main challenges at the first-draft stage:

- ▶ Finalizing your thesis
- ▶ Defining an organizational structure
- ▶ Integrating source material into the body of the paper to fit your structure
- ▶ Finding additional sources to strengthen your presentation
- ▶ Choosing the right words, phrases, and general tone
- ▶ Connecting ideas with logical transitions
- ▶ Creating an effective introduction and conclusion
- ▶ Checking for plagiarism
- ▶ Producing a list of works cited

Don't aim for perfection in a first draft. Trying to get every detail right too early may shut the door on ideas before you even know they are there.

Freewriting your draft

Use everything that you developed in the planning stage as the raw material for freewriting a draft. For now, don't think about your introduction, conclusion, or organizational structure. Simply focus on what you want to say. Only after you have thoughts down should you begin to shape your work.

Writing an introduction

The introduction tells readers what the paper contains and includes a thesis statement, which is often found at the end of the introduction.

Creating the body of a paper

The body of the paper contains your central ideas and supporting evidence, which underpins your thesis with facts, statistics, examples, and expert opinions. Try to find a structure that helps you organize your ideas and evidence into a clear pattern, such as one of the several organizational options presented in Key A.1.

Writing the conclusion

A conclusion brings your paper to a natural ending by summarizing your main points, showing the significance of your thesis and how it relates to larger issues, and calling the reader to action or looking to the future. Let the ideas in the body of the paper speak for themselves as you wrap up.

Avoiding plagiarism: Crediting authors and sources

Using another writer's words, content, unique approach, or illustrations without crediting the author is called *plagiarism* and is illegal and unethical. The following techniques will help you properly credit sources and avoid plagiarism:

■ *Make source notes as you go.* Plagiarism often begins accidentally during research. You may forget to include quotation marks around a quotation, or you may intend to cite or paraphrase a source but never do. To avoid forgetting, write detailed source and content notes as you research.

■ *Learn the difference between a quotation and a paraphrase.* A *quotation* repeats a source's exact words and uses quotation marks to set them off from the rest of the text. A paraphrase, a restatement of the quotation in your own

FIND THE **BEST WAY TO ORGANIZE** THE BODY OF THE PAPER

ORGANIZATIONAL STRUCTURE	WHAT TO DO
Arrange ideas by time.	Describe events in order or in reverse order.
Arrange ideas according to importance.	Start with the idea that carries the most weight and move to less important ideas. Or move from the least to the most important ideas.
Arrange ideas by problem and solution.	Start with a problem and then discuss solutions.
Arrange ideas to present an argument.	Present one or both sides of an issue.
Arrange ideas in list form.	Group a series of items.
Arrange ideas according to cause and effect.	Show how events, situations, or ideas cause subsequent events, situations, or ideas.
Arrange ideas through the use of comparisons.	Compare and contrast the characteristics of events, people, situations, or ideas.
Arrange by process.	Go through the steps in a process: a "how-to" approach.
Arrange by category.	Divide topics into categories and analyze each in order.

words, requires that you completely rewrite the idea, not just remove or replace a few words.

■ *Use a citation even for an acceptable paraphrase.* Credit every source that you quote, paraphrase, or use as evidence (except when the material is considered common knowledge). To credit a source, write a footnote or endnote that describes it, using the format preferred by your instructor.

■ *Understand that lifting material off the Internet is plagiarism.* Words in electronic form belong to the writer just as words in print form do. If you cut and paste sections from a source document onto your draft, you are probably committing plagiarism.

Key A.2 will help you identify the types of material that instructors regard as plagiarized work.

PLAGIARISM TAKES MANY FORMS

Instructors consider the following types of work to be plagiarized:

- Submitting a paper from a website that sells or gives away research papers
- Handing in a paper written by a fellow student or family member
- Copying material in a paper directly from a source without proper quotation marks or source citation
- Paraphrasing material in a paper from a source without proper source citation
- Submitting the same paper in more than one class, even if the classes are in different terms or even different years

Students who plagiarize place their academic careers at risk, in part because cheating is easy to discover. Increasingly, instructors are using anti-plagiarism software to investigate whether strings of words in student papers match material in a database. Make a commitment to hand in your own work and uphold the highest standards of academic integrity.

Citing sources

You may be asked to submit different kinds of source lists when you hand in your paper:

▶ *References list.* Only the sources actually cited in your paper (also called a *List of Works Cited*)
▶ *Bibliography.* All the sources you consulted, whether or not they were cited in the paper
▶ *Annotated bibliography.* All the sources you consulted as well as an explanation or critique of each source

Your instructor will tell you which documentation style to use, commonly one of the following:

▶ The Modern Language Association (MLA) format is generally used in the humanities, including history, literature, the arts, and philosophy.
▶ The American Psychological Association (APA) style is the appropriate format in psychology, sociology, business, economics, nursing, criminology, and social work.

Consult a college-level writers' handbook for an overview of these documentation styles, or read about them online at www.mla.org and www.apa.org.

Get feedback

Talk with your instructor about your draft, or ask a study partner to read it and answer specific questions. Be open-minded about the comments you receive. Consider each carefully, and then make a decision about what to change.

Revising

When you *revise,* you critically evaluate the content, organization, word choice, paragraph structure, and style of your first draft. You evaluate the strength of your thesis and whether your evidence proves it, looking for logical holes. You can do anything you want at this point to change your work. You can turn things around and present information from the end of your paper up front, tweak your thesis to reflect the evidence presented, or choose a different organizational structure.

Engage your critical thinking skills to evaluate the content and form of your paper. Ask yourself these questions as you revise:

▶ Does the paper fulfill the requirements of the assignment?
▶ Do I prove my thesis?
▶ Is each idea and argument developed, explained, and supported by examples?
▶ Does the introduction prepare the reader and capture attention?
▶ Is the body of the paper organized effectively?

- Does each paragraph have a topic sentence that is supported by the rest of the paragraph?
- Are my ideas connected to one another through logical transitions?
- Do I have a clear, concise writing style?
- Does the conclusion provide a natural ending without introducing new ideas?

Check for clarity

Now check for sense, continuity, and clarity. Focus also on tightening your prose and eliminating wordy phrases. Examine once again how paragraphs flow into one another by evaluating the effectiveness of your *transitions*—the words, phrases, or sentences that connect ideas.

Editing

Editing involves correcting technical mistakes in spelling, grammar, and punctuation, as well as checking for consistency in such elements as abbreviations and capitalization. If you use a computer, start with the grammar check and spell check to find mistakes, realizing that you still need to check your work manually. Look also for *sexist language,* which characterizes people according to gender stereotypes and often involves the male pronouns *he, his,* or *him.*

Proofreading, the last editing stage, involves reading every word for accuracy. Look for technical mistakes, run-on sentences, spelling errors, and sentence fragments. Look for incorrect word usage and unclear references. A great way to check your work is to read it out loud.

Your final paper reflects all the hard work you put in during the writing process. Ideally, when you are finished, you have a piece of work that shows your researching, writing, and thinking ability.

APPENDIX B
Social Networking and Media

Social networking refers to interacting with a community of people through an online network such as Facebook, MySpace, forums (message boards), or chat rooms. *Social media* are the types of media people use to share information online (examples include Web logs or "blogs," podcasts, websites, videos, and news feeds). Social media allow participation through comments and ratings. The people who provide social media content range from experts to amateurs, which means the content will not always be accurate or trustworthy.

In general, social networking and media make three things possible:

1. Communicating information about yourself to others
2. Connecting with people who have similar interests
3. Networking with others to accomplish goals

Social networking has grown rapidly worldwide through sites like the following:

▶ **Facebook** enables users to set up personal profiles and communicate with other users through profile updates, public or private messages, games, and photos
▶ **Twitter** enables users to send or receive short text updates, or "tweets," to other users signed up on their accounts
▶ **Skype** enables users to make calls over the Internet

How they can help
you in college

Use social networking and media to:

▶ *Connect with peers to achieve academic goals.* Students might create groups that correspond to courses, study together on an Internet call, or post course-related questions and comments on a message board or chat room used by the class. (Try: Facebook, Skype)
▶ *Manage coursework and projects.* Particular sites can help you search for information, study, and ask questions. When doing a group project, social networking can help you collaborate in an online format. (Try: Evernote, Google Docs, EtherPad, Wikidot)
▶ *Network with students who have shared interests.* A student might start a blog on an academic topic and hope to attract interested readers, or look for groups or Internet forums. (Try: Facebook, MySpace, forums on specific topics)
▶ *Adjust to college.* Ask other students at your school about local issues (bus schedules, library hours), or ask students anywhere in the world about more general concerns (test anxiety). You can even use social media to stay organized. (Try: Twitter, Facebook, GradeMate, Backpack)
▶ *Focus on career development.* Put your qualifications and career goals out there for others to peruse, and build a network that may lead you to job opportunities. (Try: LinkedIn, Zumeo)
▶ *Stay connected to loved ones.* Students might tweet or blog happenings to family and old friends, post updates, or make free phone calls. A budgeting bonus: Most social networking tools cost nothing to use as long as you have Internet access. (Try: Twitter, Facebook, Skype)

▶ *Share your opinion.* Blogs allow you to communicate to an audience on a regular basis, and creating a blog is usually free. Another tool, the forum or message board, encourages individuals to come together and discuss a common knowledge or experience. (Try: Blogger, MySpace)

Ten strategies for success

Follow these guidelines to get the most from your time and energy on social networks and with social media.

1. *Control your personal information.* Read the privacy policy of any network you join. Adjust security settings, indicating what information, photos, and so on you want to be visible or invisible. Know what will always be visible to users.

2. *Control your time.* One quick check of your e-mail can lead to hours spent online that you should have spent getting something else done. To stay focused and in control:

   • Create a separate e-mail for alerts from your social networking sites.
   • Set your status to "offline" or "do not disturb" when you are studying.
   • Set up goals and rewards. Try doing a defined portion of your homework and then rewarding yourself with ten minutes on your favorite social networking site.

3. *Be an information literate critical thinker.* Evaluate what you read on social networking sites or social media with a critical eye. Use the CARS test (p. 141) to check Credibility, Accuracy, Reasonableness, and Support of any source or statement.

4. *Keep career goals in mind.* With anything you write, think: How will this look to others who may evaluate me in the future? Also, choose and post photographs carefully, because some employers use social networking sites for background checks.

5. *Use caution with forums and chat rooms.* There is no way to know who is posting on a forum or in a chat room. Consider using a name that differs from your legal name or regular e-mail address. Remember, too, that everything you write can be copied and saved.

6. *Watch your temper.* Wait, and think, before you post on emotional topics. Forums can turn into hostile environments. Snarky tweets and updates can come back to haunt you if they are viewed by potential employers, instructors, or others who may judge you by them.

7. *Separate the personal and the academic/professional.* You probably don't want an employer seeing that crass video your cousin posted on your page. Consider having two profiles on a network if you want to use one to communicate with students or advance your career.

8. *Show restraint.* Although it's easy to get carried away, keep your purpose in mind. For example, if one goal is to keep up with friends using Facebook, you are defeating your purpose if you have so many friends that you can't possibly stay up-to-date with them.

9. *Understand what a blog or website requires.* Blogs need updating at least weekly if not more often, and require time and motivation. Websites can be even more labor-intensive.

10. *Network with integrity.* Treat others with respect. Search for, and use, information legitimately. Cite sources honestly.

ENDNOTES

QUICK START

1. Alexander W. Astin, *Preventing Students from Dropping Out*, San Francisco: Jossey-Bass, 1976.

2. Robert J. Sternberg, *Successful Intelligence: How Practical and Creative Intelligence Determine Success in Life*, New York: Plume, 1997, p. 24.

CHAPTER 1

1. Adapted from "Hope in a Box," *The Oprah Winfrey Show*, October 1, 2009, www.oprah .com/world/Tererai-Trents-Inspiring-Education.

2. Thomas Friedman, *The World Is Flat*, New York: Farrar, Straus & Giroux, 2006, p. 8.

3. Daniel Pink, "Revenge of the Right Brain," *Wired Magazine*, February 2005, www.wired .com/wired/archive/13.02/brain.html?pg=1 &topic=brain&topic_set=.

4. Robert J. Sternberg, *Successful Intelligence: How Practical and Creative Intelligence Determine Success in Life*, New York: Plume, 1997, pp. 85–90; Carol S. Dweck, *Mindset: The New Psychology of Success*, New York: Random House, 2006, p. 5; and Susanne Jaeggi, Martin Buschkuehl, John Jonides, and Walter J. Perrig, "Improving Fluid Intelligence with Training on Working Memory," 2008, *Proceedings of the National Academy of Sciences USA*, 105, pp. 6829–6833.

5. Sternberg, *Successful Intelligence*, p. 11.

6. Dweck, *Mindset*, pp. 3–4.

7. The Society for Neuroscience, *Brain Facts: A Primer on the Brain and Neurosystem*, Washington, DC: The Society for Neuroscience, 2008, pp. 34–35.

8. Sternberg, *Successful Intelligence*, p. 12.

9. Ibid., p. 127.

10. Ibid., p. 11.

11. Ibid., pp. 127–128.

12. Carol Dweck, "The Mindsets," 2006, www .mindsetonline.com/whatisit/themindsets/ index.html.

13. Dweck, *Mindset*, p. 16.

14. Ibid.

15. Rick Pitino, *Success Is a Choice*, New York: Broadway Books, 1997, p. 40.

16. Dweck, *Mindset*, p. 51.

17. Center for Academic Integrity, Kenan Institute for Ethics, Duke University, "The Fundamental Values of Academic Integrity," October 1999, www.academicintegrity.org/ fundamental_values_project/pdf/FVProject .pdf.

18. Dweck, *Mindset*, p. 35.

19. Ibid., p. 33.

20. John D. Mayer, Peter Salovey, and David R. Caruso, "Emotional Intelligence: New Ability or Eclectic Traits?," September 2008, *American Psychologist*, 63, no. 6, p. 503.

21. David R. Caruso, "Zero In on Knowledge: A Practical Guide to the MSCEIT," Multi-Health Systems, 2008, p. 3.

22. Sandra Blakeslee, "Cells That Read Minds," January 10, 2006, *New York Times*, www. nytimes.com/2006/01/10/science/10mirr.html.

23. Mayer, Salovey, and Caruso, pp. 510–512.

24. Christopher J. Moore, *In Other Words: A Language Lover's Guide to the Most Intriguing Words Around the World*, New York: Walker & Company, 2004, p. 43.

25. List and descriptions based on Sternberg, *Successful Intelligence*, pp. 251–268.

CHAPTER 2

1. Stephen Covey, *The Seven Habits of Highly Effective People*, New York: Simon & Schuster, 1989, pp. 70–144, 309–318.

2. Paul Timm, *Successful Self-Management: A Psychologically Sound Approach to Personal Effectiveness*, Los Altos, CA: Crisp Publications, 1987, pp. 22–41.

3. William E. Sydnor, "Procrastination," from the California Polytechnic State University Study Skills Library, www.sas.calpoly.edu/asc/ ssl/procrastination.html. Based on *Overcoming Procrastination* by Albert Ellis. Used with permission.

4. Jane B. Burka and Lenora M. Yuen, *Procrastination: Why You Do It, What to Do About It*, Reading, MA: Perseus Books, 1983, pp. 21–22.

5. Ibid.

6. mtvU and Associated Press College Stress and Mental Health Poll Executive Summary, Spring 2008, www.halfofus.com/_media/_pr/mtvU_AP_College_Stress_and_Mental_Health_Poll_Executive_Summary.pdf.

7. Jane E. Brody, "At Every Age, Feeling the Effects of Too Little Sleep," *New York Times*, October 23, 2007, www.nytimes.com/2007/10/23/health/23brod.html.

8. Christopher J. Moore, *In Other Words: A Language Lover's Guide to the Most Intriguing Words Around the World*, New York: Walker & Company, 2004, pp. 36–37.

CHAPTER 3

1. Howard Gardner, *Multiple Intelligences: New Horizons*, New York: Basic Books, 2006, p. 180.

2. Howard Gardner, *Multiple Intelligences: The Theory in Practice*, New York: HarperCollins, 1993, pp. 5–49.

3. Gardner, *Multiple Intelligences: New Horizons*, p. 8.

4. Gardner, *Multiple Intelligences: The Theory in Practice*, p. 7.

5. C. George Boeree, "Carl Jung," 2006, http://webspace.ship.edu/cgboer/jung.html.

6. National Center for Learning Disabilities, "LD at a Glance," May 2003, www.ncld.org/LDInfoZone/InfoZone_FactSheet_LD.cfm.

7. National Center for Learning Disabilities, "Adult Learning Disabilities: A Learning Disability Isn't Something You Outgrow. It's Something You Learn to Master" (pamphlet), New York: National Center for Learning Disabilities.

8. National Center for Learning Disabilities, "LD Advocates Guide," n.d., www.ncld.org/index.php?option=content&task=view&id=291.

9. Christopher J. Moore, *In Other Words: A Language Lover's Guide to the Most Intriguing Words Around the World*, New York: Walker, 2004, p. 78.

CHAPTER 4

1. Vincent Ruggiero, *The Art of Thinking*, 2001, quoted in "Critical Thinking," http://success.oregonstate.edu/criticalthinking.html.

2. Richard Paul, "The Role of Questions in Thinking, Teaching, and Learning," 1995, www.criticalthinking.org/resources/articles/the-role-of-questions.shtml.

3. "The Best Innovations Are Those That Come from Smart Questions," *Wall Street Journal*, April 12, 2004, p. B1.

4. Sharon Begley, "Critical Thinking: Part Skill, Part Mindset and Totally Up to You," *Wall Street Journal*, October 20, 2006, p. B1.

5. Matt Thomas, "What Is Higher-Order Thinking and Critical/Creative/Constructive Thinking?" n.d., Center for Studies in Higher-Order Literacy, http://a-s.clayton.edu/tparks/What%20is%20Higher%20Order%20Thinking.doc.

6. Charles Cave, "Definitions of Creativity," August 1999, http://members.optusnet.com.au/~charles57/Creative/Basics/definitions.htm.

7. Roger von Oech, *A Kick in the Seat of the Pants*, New York: Harper & Row, 1986, pp. 5–21.

8. Dennis Coon, *Introduction to Psychology: Exploration and Application*, 6th ed., St. Paul, MN: West, 1992, p. 295.

9. Roger von Oech, *A Whack on the Side of the Head*, New York: Warner Books, 1990, pp. 11–168.

10. J. R. Hayes, *Cognitive Psychology: Thinking and Creating*, Homewood, IL: Dorsey, 1978.

11. Robert Sternberg, *Successful Intelligence*, New York: Plume, 1996, p. 219.

12. Adapted from T. Z. Tardif and R. J. Sternberg, "What Do We Know About Creativity?" in *The Nature of Creativity*, ed. R. J. Sternberg, London: Cambridge University Press, 1988.

13. Sternberg, p. 212.

14. Hayes, *Cognitive Psychology*.

15. "The Best Innovations Are Those That Come from Smart Questions," p. B1.

16. Sternberg, p. 236.

17. Robert J. Sternberg and Elena L. Grigorenko, "Practical Intelligence and the Principal," Yale University: Publication Series No. 2, 2001, p. 5.

18. Sternberg, pp. 251–269.

19. Ibid., p. 241.

20. Ibid., p. 128.

21. Christopher J. Moore, *In Other Words: A Language Lover's Guide to the Most Intriguing Words Around the World*, New York: Walker, 2004, p. 61.

CHAPTER 5

1. Francis P. Robinson, *Effective Behavior*, New York: Harper & Row, 1941.

2. John Mack Faragher, Mari Jo Buhle, Daniel Czitrom, and Susan H. Armitage, *Out of Many: A History of the American People*, 5th ed., Upper Saddle River, NJ: Prentice Hall, 2005, p. xxxvii.

3. Benjamin S. Bloom, *Taxonomy of Educational Objectives, Handbook I: The Cognitive Domain*, New York: McKay, 1956.

4. Ophelia H. Hancock, *Reading Skills for College Students*, 5th ed., Upper Saddle River, NJ: Prentice Hall, 2001, pp. 54–59.

5. Mark Bauerlein, "Online Literacy Is a Lesser Kind," *The Chronicle of Higher Education*, September 19, 2008, http://chronicle.com/article/Online-Literacy-Is-a-Lesser/28307.

6. Ibid.

7. Lori Leibovich, "Choosing Quick Hits over the Card Catalog," *New York Times*, August 10, 2001, p. 1.

8. Adam Robinson, *What Smart Students Know*, New York: Three Rivers Press, 1993, p. 82.

9. Christopher J. Moore, *In Other Words: A Language Lover's Guide to the Most Intriguing Words Around the World*, New York: Walker, 2004, p. 87.

10. John J. Macionis, *Sociology*, 6th ed., Upper Saddle River, NJ: Prentice Hall, 1997, p. 174.

CHAPTER 6

1. Alina Tugend, "Multitasking Can Make You Lose . . . Um . . . Focus," *New York Times*, October 25, 2008, p. B7.

2. System developed by Cornell professor Walter Pauk. See Walter Pauk, *How to Study in College*, 10th ed. Boston: Houghton Mifflin, 2011, pp. 236–241.

3. Information from Frank Schmalleger, *Criminal Justice Today*, 8th ed., Upper Saddle River, NJ: 2005, p. 71.

4. Christopher J. Moore, *In Other Words: A Language Lover's Guide to the Most Intriguing Words Around the World*, New York: Walker, 2004, p. 45.

CHAPTER 7

1. University of California–Irvine, "Short-Term Stress Can Affect Learning and Memory," *ScienceDaily*, March 13, 2008, www.sciencedaily.com/releases/2008/03/080311182434.htm.

2. Herman Ebbinghaus, *Memory: A Contribution to Experimental Psychology*, trans. H. A. Ruger and C. E. Bussenius, New York: Teachers College, Columbia University, 1885.

3. Bulletpoints from Kenneth C. Petress, "The Benefits of Group Study," 2004, *Education*, 124, www.questia.com/googleScholar.qst;jsessionid=L4TDXZJvQmb4whQFL7v1mjGfBgp4YGzjJyg0mL3g1SJKyjvXK4hN!-747430471!743789914?docId=5006987606.

4. Dartmouth College Academic Skills Center, "How to Avoid Cramming for Tests," 2001, www.dartmouth.edu/~acskills/handouts.html.

5. "Study Shows How Sleep Improves Memory," *Science Daily*, June 29, 2005, www.sciencedaily.com/releases/2005/06/050629070337.htm.

6. Adam Robinson, *What Smart Students Know: Maximum Grades, Optimum Learning, Minimum Time*, New York: Three Rivers Press, 1993, p. 118.

7. Christopher J. Moore, *In Other Words: A Language Lover's Guide to the Most Intriguing Words Around the World*, New York: Walker, 2004, p. 45.

CHAPTER 8

1. Ben Gose, "Notes from Academe: Living It Up on the Dead Days," *The Chronicle of Higher Education*, June 8, 2002, http://chronicle.com/article/Living-It-Up-on-the-Dead-Days/8983.

2. "Anxiety Management," Michigan Technological University, www.counseling.mtu.edu/anxiety_management.html.

3. From Paul D. Nolting, *Math Study Skills Workbook, Your Guide to Reducing Test Anxiety and Improving Study Strategies*, Boston: Houghton Mifflin, 2000. Cited in "Test Anxiety," West Virginia University at Parkersburg, www.wvup.edu/Academics/more_test_anxiety_tips.htm.

4. Christopher J. Moore, *In Other Words: A Language Lover's Guide to the Most Intriguing Words Around the World*, New York: Walker, 2004, p. 45.

CHAPTER 9

1. "For 7 Million, One Census Race Category Wasn't Enough," *New York Times*, March 13, 2001, pp. A1, A14.

2. "Conceptual Frameworks/Models, Guiding Values and Principles," National Center for Cultural Competence, 2002, http://gucchd.georgetown.edu//nccc/framework.html.

3. Information in the sections on the five stages of building competency is based on Mark A. King, Anthony Sims, and David Osher, "How Is Cultural Competence Integrated in Education?" Cultural Competence, www.air.org/cecp/cultural/Q_integrated.htm#def.

4. Martin Luther King Jr., from his sermon "A Tough Mind and a Tender Heart," *Strength in Love*, Philadelphia: Fortress Press, 1986, p. 14.

5. Betsy Israel, "The Overconnecteds," *New York Times*, November 5, 2006, Education Life, p. 20.

6. Ibid.

7. Tina Kelley, "On Campuses, Warnings About Violence in Relationships," *New York Times*, February 13, 2000, p. 40.

8. Ibid.

9. This section and chapter opener story from Highline College Honors Scholar Program Success Stories (adapted with permission from original story, online at http://flightline.highline.edu/honors/success/gaile.htm).

10. Christopher J. Moore, *In Other Words: A Language Lover's Guide to the Most Intriguing Words Around the World*, New York: Walker, 2004, p. 69.

CHAPTER 10

1. Gina Kolata, "A Surprising Secret to a Long Life: Stay in School," *New York Times*, January 3, 2007, pp. A1, A16.

2. Information in this section based on materials from Dr. Marlene Schwartz of the Rudd Center for Food Policy and Obesity at Yale University.

3. Centers for Disease Control, "Prevalence of Overweight and Obesity Among Adults: United States, 2003–2004," January 30, 2007, www.cdc.gov/nchs/products/pubs/pubd/hestats/overweight/overwght_adult_03.htm.

4. Rudd Center for Food Policy and Obesity, "Employment," 2005, www.yaleruddcenter.org/default.aspx?id=77.

5. CBS News, "Help for Sleep-Deprived Students," April 19, 2004, www.cbsnews.com/stories/2004/04/19/health/main612476.shtml.

6. "College Students' Sleep Habits Harmful to Health, Study Finds," *The Daily Orange—Feature Issue*, September 25, 2002, www.dailyorange.com/news/2002/09/25/Feature/College.Students.Sleep.Habits.Harmful.To.Health.Study.Finds-280340.shtml.

7. Herbert Benson, Eileen M. Stuart, et al., *The Wellness Book*, New York: Simon & Schuster, 1992, p. 292; and Gregg Jacobs, "Insomnia Corner," *Talk About Sleep*, 2004, www.talkaboutsleep.com/sleepdisorders/insomnia_corner.htm.

8. Mike Briddon, "Struggling with Sadness: Depression Among College Students Is on the Rise," Stressedoutnurses.com, April 22, 2008, http://www.stressedoutnurses.com/2008/04/struggling-with-sadness-depression-among-college-students-is-on-the-rise.

9. SAVE (Suicide Awareness Voices of Education), "Symptoms of Major Depression," 2010, www.save.org/index.cfm?fuseaction=home.viewPage&page_id=A806E240-95E6-44BB-C2D6C47399E9EFDB.

10. National Eating Disorders Association, "Learning Basic Terms and Information on a Variety of Eating Disorder Topics," 2010, www.nationaleatingdisorders.org/information-resources/general-information.php#facts-statistics.

11. "Alcohol Linked to 75,000 U.S. Deaths a Year," MSNBC, June 25, 2005, www.msnbc.msn.com/id/6089353.

12. Centers for Disease Control and Prevention, "Alcohol and Public Health," September 3, 2008, www.cdc.gov/alcohol/index.htm.

13. Joel Seguine, "Students Report Negative Consequences of Binge Drinking in New Survey," *The University Record*, University of Michigan, October 25, 1999, www.umich.edu/~urecord/9900/Oct25_99/7.htm.

14. Substance Abuse and Mental Health Services Administration, Office of Applied Studies, *Results from the 2007 National Survey on Drug Use and Health: National Findings* (NSDUH Series H-34, DHHS Publication No. SMA 08-4343), Rockville, MD: Author, 2008.

15. "Secondhand Smoke," October 1, 2009, American Cancer Society, www.cancer.org/docroot/PED/content/PED_10_2X_Secondhand_Smoke-Clean_Indoor_Air.asp.

16. Hilary Smith, "The High Cost of Smoking," 2007, *MSN Money*, http://moneycentral.msn.com/content/Insurance/Insureyourhealth/P100291.asp.

17. National Institutes of Health, "Clearing the Air: Quit Smoking Today," National Cancer Institute, Publication No. 08-1647, October, 2008, pp. 10–24.

18. National Survey on Drug Use and Health (NSDUH), "The NSDUH Report: College Enrollment Status and Past Year Illicit Drug Use Among Young Adults: 2002, 2003, and 2004," October 21, 2005, http://oas.samhsa.gov/2k5/College/college.htm.

19. Christopher J. Moore, *In Other Words: A Language Lover's Guide to the Most Intriguing Words Around the World*, New York: Walker & Company, 2004, p. 85.

CHAPTER 11

1. Jim Hanson, "Your Money Personality: It's All in Your Head," University Credit Union, December 25, 2006, http://hffo.cuna.org/012433/article/1440/html.

2. Ibid.

3. "Attitudes and Characteristics of Freshmen at 4-Year Colleges," *The Chronicle of Higher Education*, Fall 2007.

4. "Fast Facts," National Center for Education Statistics, 2009, http://nces.ed.gov/FastFacts/display.asp?id=31.

5. Beckie Supiano, "Many Community College Students Miss Out on Aid—Because They Don't Apply," *The Chronicle of Higher Education*, October 7, 2008, http://chronicle.com/daily/2008/10/4905n.htm.

6. Robert Tomsho, "The Best Ways to Get Loans for College Now," *The Wall Street Journal*, August 13, 2008, p. D1.

7. Beckie Supiano, "In a Rocky Economy, 10 Steady Tips About Student Aid," *The Chronicle of Higher Education*, November 7, 2008, http://chronicle.com/article/In-a-Rocky-Economy-10-Stea/1313/.

8. Anne Ryman, "Defaults on Student Loans Rising," *The Arizona Republic*, March 7, 2010, www.azcentral.com/12news/news/articles/2010/03/07/20100307student-loan-defaults-CP.html.

9. Ben Woolsey and Matt Schulz, "Credit Card Statistics, Industry Facts, Debt Statistics," CreditCards.com, January 15, 2010, www.creditcards.com/credit-card-news/credit-card-industry-facts-personal-debt-statistics-1276.php#youngadults.

10. Nellie Mae, "Undergraduate Students and Credit Cards in 2004," May 2005, www.nellie-mae.com/library/research_12.html.

11. Items in bullet list based on Michael Bowler, "Watch Out for Credit Card Traps," The Lucrative Investor, 2009, www.thelucrativeinvestor.com/watch-credit-card-traps; and Chris Arnold, "Credit Card Companies Abuse the Unwitting," November 6, 2007, NPR, www.npr.org/templates/story/story.php?storyId=16035323.

12. Pat Curry, "How Credit Scores Work, How a Score Is Calculated," Bankrate.com, November 8, 2006, www.bankrate.com/brm/news/credit-scoring/20031104a1.asp.

13. Christopher J. Moore, *In Other Words: A Language Lover's Guide to the Most Intriguing Words Around the World*, New York: Walker & Company, 2004, p. 91.

14. Eduardo Porter and Greg Winter, "'04 Graduates Learned Lesson in Practicality," *New York Times*, May 30, 2004, pp. A1, A24.

CHAPTER 12

1. Self-Directed Search, www.self-directed-search.com.

2. National Service Learning Clearinghouse, "Service Learning Is . . . ," May 2004, www.servicelearning.org/article/archive/35.

3. "The Hot Jobs with High Pay," February 2007, Career Prospects in Virginia, www.careerprospects.org/Trends/salary-high.html.

4. U.S. Department of Labor, Bureau of Labor Statistics, "Number of Jobs Held, Labor Market Activity, and Earnings Growth Among the Youngest Baby Boomers: Results from a Longitudinal Survey," August 25, 2006, www.bls.gov/news.release/pdf/nlsoy.pdf.

5. Bureau of Labor Statistics, "The 30 Fastest Growing Occupations Covered in the 2008–2009 Occupational Outlook Handbook," December 18, 2007, www.bls.gov/news.release/ooh.t01.htm.

6. Job Interview and Career Guide, "Resume: Keywords for Resumes—Keywords List," December 8, 2009, www.job-interview-site.com/resume-keywords-for-resumes-keywords-list.html.

7. List and descriptions based on Robert J. Sternberg, *Successful Intelligence*, New York: Plume, 1997, pp. 251–269.

8. Quoted in Linton Weeks, "The No-Book Report: Skim It and Weep," *Washington Post*, May 14, 2001, p. C8.

9. Margaret J. Wheatley and Myron Kellner-Rogers, "A Simpler Way," 1997, *Weight Watchers Magazine*, 30, no. 3, pp. 42–44.

10. Christopher J. Moore, *In Other Words: A Language Lover's Guide to the Most Intriguing Words Around the World*, New York: Walker & Company, 2004, p. 116.

APPENDIX A

1. Analysis based on Lynn Quitman Troyka, *Simon & Schuster Handbook for Writers*, Upper Saddle River, NJ: Prentice Hall, 1996, pp. 22–23.

Index

Note: A bold page number indicates the page on which the term is defined in the margin.

and evaluating sources, 140–142
and focus of studying, 139–140
purposes for, 139
Critical thinking, 9, 133. *See also* Analytical thinking
Criticism, offering and receiving, 251–252, 253
Cultural competence, 240–246
   activity for, 262–263
   application of, 245–246
   assessment of, 240
   definition of, 241
   development of, 241–246
   hindrances to, 243
Cultural diversity, 240–241
   adapting to, 245–246
   assessing skills in/attitudes toward, 240, 244
   and college culture, 4, 245
   and cultural competence. *See* Cultural competence
   effects of, 244–245
   and emotional intelligence, 242
   and intelligence, 62
   knowledge of, 245, 339
   prevalence of, 240
   types of, 240–241
   valuing of, 31, 241, 339
Culture. *See also* Cultural diversity
   and body language, 252, 253
   of college, 4–5

Date rape, 259
Debt, among college students, 309, 311–312
Decision making, 103–105
   activities for, 109–110, 112
   vs. problem solving, 101, 103. *See also* Problem solving
   process for, 102, 106
   strategies for, 103
Defaulting, on student loans, 309. *See also* Student loans
Delayed gratification, **270**
Depression, 277–278. *See also* Mental health issues
Dictionaries, 119, 120
Diet, and health, 270
Digital revolution, **5**
Disabilities, students with, xxxiv. *See also* Hearing loss; Learning disabilities
Discrimination, **244**–245, 246, 263. *See also* Cultural diversity
Divergent thinking, 93. *See also* Brainstorming
Diversity. *See* Cultural diversity

Drafting, of essay/research paper, 352–355. *See also* Writing process
Drug use, 283
   assessment of, 281
   effects of, 283
   and rape, 259
   and safety, 274
   treatment resources for, 284
   types of, 282–283
Dweck, Carol, 7–8, 11, 14

E-mail
   instructor communication with, xxix–xxx, xxxii, 82, 263–264
   personal communication with, xxix, 254, 276, 295, 309, 316
   registering for, xxviii
   security issues with, 276, 295, 309, 312, 316
Eating disorders, 278. *See also* Mental health issues
Ebbinghaus, Herman, 178–179
Editing
   of essay/research paper, 356. *See also* Writing process
   of essay test, 228, 229
Emotional intelligence, 15–17
   abilities of, 16–17
   activity for, 18
   application of, 16, 17, 99–100
   and career building, 329–330
   and cultural diversity, 242
   definition of, 15
   and practical thinking, 99–100
   as relationship skill, 16, 17
Employment
   and career building. *See* Career building
   changes/trends in, 330–332
   during college, 304–305
   and college education, 5, 6
Environment
   for note taking, 157
   for reading, 118
   for studying, 118, 180–183
   for test taking, 209–210, 216–217
Essay questions, in tests, 226–228, 231
Essays, writing of. *See* Writing process
Evaluation, stage of listening, 151
Evidence, for argument, 88, 89, 90–91, **140**
Exercise, and health, 271–273, 274
External vs. internal distractions, from listening, 153
Extracurricular activities, at college, xxx

Credits

Photo Credits

in Smith (1969), pp. 54–66. [18] *C*(36–60) 4th ed. 766, 771. [Joseph
Raz, "The Institutional Simon, and Sorosh, the Institutional and Intelligent
in Smith's *Concepts* appearing in 5950 Library's Shortage.